.

Memory in Medieval China: Text, Ritual, and Community

Sinica Leidensia

Edited by

Barend J. ter Haar
Maghiel van Crevel

In co-operation with

P.K. Bol, D.R. Knechtges, E.S. Rawski,
W.L. Idema, H.T. Zurndorfer

VOLUME 140

The titles published in this series are listed at *brill.com/sinl*

Memory in Medieval China:
Text, Ritual, and Community

Edited by

Wendy Swartz
Robert Ford Campany

BRILL

LEIDEN | BOSTON

The Library of Congress Cataloging-in-Publication Data is available online at http://catalog.loc.gov
LC record available at http://lccn.loc.gov/

Typeface for the Latin, Greek, and Cyrillic scripts: "Brill". See and download: brill.com/brill-typeface.

ISSN 0169-9563
ISBN 978-90-04-36862-0 (hardback)
ISBN 978-90-04-36863-7 (e-book)

In Memory of
Alan J. Berkowitz

Colleague and Friend

∵

Contents

Contributors

Sarah M. Allen
is associate professor of comparative literature at Williams College.

Robert Ashmore
is associate professor of East Asian languages and cultures at the University of California at Berkeley.

Robert Ford Campany
is professor of Asian studies and religious studies at Vanderbilt University.

Jack W. Chen
is associate professor of Chinese literature at the University of Virginia.

Alexei Ditter
is associate professor of Chinese at Reed College.

Meow Hui Goh
is associate professor of Chinese at The Ohio State University.

Christopher M.B. Nugent
is professor of Chinese at Williams College.

Wendy Swartz
is associate professor of Chinese literature at Rutgers University.

Xiaofei Tian
is professor of Chinese literature at Harvard University.

Ping Wang
is associate professor of Asian languages and literature at the University of Washington.

Introduction

Robert Ford Campany and Wendy Swartz

If recent investigations of the phenomenon of memory have emphasized anything, it is that memory—whether that of an individual or of a group—is not
adequately imagined as resembling a storage container. It is not a neutral re-
trieval or passive repetition of an inert past. It is rather a selective process, or a
cluster of processes, of recreating particular bits of the past for some purpose
in the present. Memory is "not a passive receptacle, but instead a process of
active restructuring, in which elements may be retained, reordered, or sup-
pressed."[1] In a very basic sense "the past cannot be said to be. Instead we should
say rather the past is made whenever it is reconstructed."[2]

By shaping accounts of particular aspects or moments of the past, tellers of
stories or authors of texts make claims on the present with an eye toward the
future. We might say that what they assert or imply about the past, and how
they do so, constitutes an argument to a present audience about some matter
of importance. Other tellers or authors may construct counter-memories. The
resulting body of texts about the past that survive for us to read from a society
such as that of medieval China constitutes a rich array of evidence of how as-
sertions about the past were made and for what purposes they were made. We
can also ask about the audiences for which such acts of memory were intended.
We can inquire into the ways in which readers of those texts received and appropriated them, often in the course of constructing their own, alternative portrayals of past events. Some versions of the past had relative success in winning
adoption and replication in successive generations of readers and writers,
while others fell by the wayside. Many, of course, were completely lost from the
record.

Another way to phrase the same point is to say that memory is performed.
We can then sort through the media and genres available in a culture such as
that of medieval China for the performance of memory. These included not
only several genres of writing—anecdotes, chronicles, biographical sketches,
epitaphs, personal memoirs, poems of various sorts, commentaries, critical ap-
preciations and imitations—but also ritual modes such as funerals and mourning practices. We can investigate how such media and genres were used by

---

1   James Fentress and Chris Wickham, *Social Memory* (Oxford: Blackwell, 1992), 40.
2   F. Wyatt, "The Narrative in Psychoanalysis: Psychoanalytic Notes of Storytelling, Listening, and
    Interpreting," in *Narrative Psychology: The Storied Nature of Human Conduct*, ed. Theodore R.
    Sarbin (New York: Praeger, 1986), 196.

particular agents on particular occasions. We can appreciate the craft of their performances, how they worked with or against genre conventions to get across to readers or witnesses their versions of the past. We can ask what interests these agents had in their subjects, what their arguments were and what was at stake in their representing elements of the past as they did. And we can consider how these performances were received by audiences of others.

In the case of China in classical and medieval times, recent scholarship has clustered around five aspects of memory. The most fertile topic has been how the dead or departed are remembered. In *Ancestral Memory*, Ken Brashier shows how, in Western and Eastern Han times, the ancestor cult was not a mechanical offering of food in exchange for prosperity but was rather a system of ideas and practices involving sustained mental effort by participants, supported by a network of rituals. In a companion volume, Brashier shows how the living publicly remembered deceased individuals by in effect stereotyping them, relating them to existing tropes of public memory while downplaying what made each of them distinctive.[3] Along with other funerary and memorial genres of writing,[4] entombed epitaphs (*muzhiming* 墓誌銘), particularly in the Tang period, have meanwhile been investigated recently, thanks in part to a series of conferences dedicated to them.[5] Studies of biographical and hagiographical texts have attended to the processes by which transmitted writings about the lives of individuals shaped, and at the same time were also shaped by, the social memory of those persons.[6] Both stereotyping and individuation of the remembrance of individuals have been documented in all these genres.

---

3   K.E. Brashier, *Ancestral Memory in Early China* (Cambridge, MA: Harvard University Press, 2011), and Brashier, *Public Memory in Early China* (Cambridge, MA: Harvard University Press, 2014).

4   See for example Anna M. Shields, "Words for the Dead and the Living: Innovations in the Mid-Tang 'Prayer Text' (*jiwen*)," *Tang Studies* 25 (2007): 111-45.

5   On pre-Tang periods see for example Timothy M. Davis, *Entombed Epigraphy and Commemorative Culture in Early Medieval China* (Leiden: Brill, 2016). On Tang genres and texts see for example Alexei Ditter, "The Commerce of Commemoration: Commissioned *Muzhiming* in the Mid- to Late Tang," *Tang Studies* 32 (2014): 21-46; Jessey J.C. Choo, "Shall We Profane the Service of the Dead? Burial Divinations, Untimely Burials, and Remembrance in Tang *muzhiming*," *Tang Studies* 33 (2015): 1-37; Choo and Ditter, "'On *Muzhiming*: Inaugural Workshop of New Frontiers in the Study of Medieval China, Rutgers University, May 15-16, 2015," *Tang Studies* 33 (2015): 129-34; and Choo and Ditter, "'On *Muzhiming*: Second Workshop of the New Frontiers in the Study of Medieval China, Reed College, May 23-24, 2016," *Early Medieval China* 22 (2016): 75-80.

6   See for example Robert Ford Campany, *Making Transcendents: Ascetics and Social Memory in Early Medieval China* (Honolulu: University of Hawai'i Press, 2009).

The historiography of events, dynasties, time periods, customs, regions, and places as both shaping and shaped by social memory, and social memory as shaped by standard narrative tropes and cultural patterns, have drawn increasing scholarly attention. Michael C. Rogers made an early attempt at this type of analysis in a study of documents in the *Jin shu* 晉書 (History of the Jin), while more recently two major "tropological" studies of the *Zuo zhuan* 左傳 (Zuo tradition) have appeared.[7] But medieval historiographic works—including not just the officially sponsored dynastic histories but also other, often privately composed historical works, as well as both Buddhist and Daoist histories of lineages and institutions—have yet to be treated in comparably detailed and sophisticated ways. By contrast, one written genre that has enjoyed relatively much attention, especially with regard to its varying accounts of the same events, its grounding in networks of the exchange of narratives, and its positioning close to orality, is the anecdote.[8] Provocative studies have been done on how social memory was spatially articulated by being tied to particular places on the landscape, places that were the sites of imagined historical events or of ruins or steles—places haunted and weighted by memory.[9]

Reception studies have highlighted a third aspect of memory in medieval China. We have seen detailed inquiries into how particular literary works or authors have been read, commented upon, selected, edited, and evaluated by later generations of writers even as they shaped their own readers' perceptions

---

7   Michael C. Rogers, *The Chronicle of Fu Chien: A Case of Exemplar History* (Berkeley: University of California Press, 1968); David Schaberg, *A Patterned Past: Form and Thought in Early Chinese Historiography* (Cambridge, MA: Harvard University Asia Center, 2001); Wai-yee Li, *The Readability of the Past in Early Chinese Historiography* (Cambridge, MA: Harvard University Asia Center, 2007).

8   See for example Jack W. Chen and David Schaberg, eds., *Idle Talk: Gossip and Anecdote in Traditional China* (Berkeley: University of California Press, 2014); Sarah M. Allen, *Shifting Stories: History, Gossip, and Lore in Narratives from Tang Dynasty China* (Cambridge, MA: Harvard University Asia Center, 2014); Manling Luo, *Literati Storytelling in Late Medieval China* (Seattle: University of Washington Press, 2015); and Robert Ford Campany, *Signs from the Unseen Realm: Buddhist Miracle Tales from Early Medieval China* (Honolulu: University of Hawai'i Press, 2012), 7-30.

9   See for example Stephen Owen, *Remembrances: The Experience of the Past in Classical Chinese Literature* (Cambridge, MA: Harvard University Press, 1986); Michael Nylan, "Wandering in the Ruins: The *Shuijing zhu* Reconsidered," in *Interpretation and Literature in Early Medieval China*, ed. Alan K.L. Chan and Yuet-Keung Lo (Albany: State University of New York Press, 2010), 63-102; Olivia Milburn, *Cherishing Antiquity: The Cultural Construction of an Ancient Chinese Kingdom* (Cambridge, MA: Harvard University Asia Center, 2013); and Jörg Henning Hüsemann, *Das Altertum vergegenwärtigen: Eine Studie zum "Shuijing zhu" des Li Daoyuan* (Leipzig: Leipziger Universitätsverlag, 2017).

of the textual past.[10] In addition, some studies have highlighted the ways in which readers, editors, copyists, collectors, and anthologists have changed texts in the course of attending to them in manifold ways.[11]

In contrast to the attention given to them by historians of Europe,[12] mnemonic techniques used by individuals, and the value placed on memorization of texts, are aspects of memory in medieval China that have received relatively little study to this point. A recent monograph by Christopher Nugent is a welcome exception.[13]

A final aspect of memory to be discussed here concerns the many ways in which the new was justified by grounding it in a purported, remembered old. In antiquity, the Mohists had made this a formal criterion for evaluating claims and proposals[14]; normally it operated less explicitly, but no less powerfully. This phenomenon has received little focused attention, perhaps because it was so diffuse and common in premodern China. Examples are everywhere. Buddhism's apparent relatively recent influx was justified by the claim that the originally foreign religion had actually existed in China much longer, as evidenced by supposed "Aśokan stupas" and icons[15] and by obscure references in old books to a Western sage.[16] Both Buddhist and Daoist scriptures, a great

---

10   See for example Paula Varsano, *Tracking the Banished Immortal: The Poetry of Li Bo and its Critical Reception* (Honolulu: University of Hawai'i Press, 2003), and Wendy Swartz, *Reading Tao Yuanming: Shifting Paradigms of Historical Reception (427-1900)* (Cambridge, MA: Harvard University Asia Center, 2008).

11   See for instance Xiaofei Tian, *Tao Yuanming & Manuscript Culture: The Record of a Dusty Table* (Seattle: University of Washington Press, 2005); Anna M. Shields, *Crafting a Collection: The Cultural Contexts and Poetic Practice of the Huajian ji (Collection from Among the Flowers)* (Cambridge, MA: Harvard University Asia Center, 2006); and Christopher M.B. Nugent, *Manifest in Words, Written on Paper: Producing and Circulating Poetry in Tang Dynasty China* (Cambridge, MA: Harvard University Asia Center, 2010).

12   As for example in Mary Carruthers' seminal *The Book of Memory: A Study of Memory in Medieval Culture*, 2nd ed. (Cambridge: Cambridge University Press, 2008).

13   Nugent, *Manifest in Words, Written on Paper*.

14   See A.C. Graham, *Disputers of the Tao: Philosophical Argument in Ancient China* (La Salle, IL: Open Court, 1989), 36-41, and Miranda Brown, "Mozi's Remaking of Ancient Authority," in *The "Mozi" as an Evolving Text: Different Voices in Early Chinese Thought*, ed. Carine Defoort and Nicolas Standaert (Leiden: Brill, 2013), 143-74.

15   See Erik Zürcher, *The Buddhist Conquest of China: The Spread and Adaptation of Buddhism in Early Medieval China*, 3rd ed. with foreword by Stephen F. Teiser (Leiden: Brill, 2007), 277; Robert Ford Campany, "'Buddhism Enters China' in Early Medieval China," in *Old Society, New Belief: Religious Transformation of China and Rome, ca. 1st-6th Centuries*, ed. Mu-chou Poo, H.A. Drake, and Lisa Raphals (Oxford: Oxford University Press, 2017), 23-24.

16   See Zürcher, *The Buddhist Conquest of China*, 266-76.

many of which were written or translated in the early medieval period, typically narrated their own origins in a sacred past time when their words were first spoken by a deity or a Buddha, thus arguing their own authority. New or newly burgeoning literary genres were justified by reference to their supposed precedents in exemplary ancient times.[17] Medical innovations were legitimated by tracing them back to purported ancient sages.[18] And so on.

The study of memory in early and medieval China could be justly said to be flourishing, then. The nine essays collected in this volume constitute additional new case studies in the active construction, reshaping, and uses of the past in several cultural and textual genres in medieval China. Two of these essays critically examine the careful, elaborate, and even collaborative efforts behind the construction of the memory of a dying or deceased associate and friend. In Robert Ashmore's essay, we see how Linghu Chu 令狐楚 (766-837), who exemplifies the ideal of the rhetorician minister, entrusted his protégé Li Shangyin 李商隱 (813–ca. 858) with completing, even crafting sections of, his last utterance, thereby yielding to the latter considerable power to shape his memory. Indeed, Linghu Chu, who himself had articulated the deathbed declaration of his patron Zheng Dan 鄭儋 (741-801) to great effectiveness, knew well that it would be through Li Shangyin's proxy text that his voice would be heard and his memory effectively live on. The ways in which the memory of the dead is conditioned by the particular genres used to narrate their lives are the focus of Alexei Ditter's essay, which compares two funerary compositions—an offering and an entombed epitaph written by the eminent statesman Quan Deyu 權德輿 (759-818) for his friend and colleague Zhang Jian 張薦 (744-804). Rather than treating genre as an inert frame in which information is stored, Ditter explores it as a nexus of dynamic processes that mediate literary expression and shape the transmission of memory. Genre plays a crucial role in memory construction, he argues: the choice of a particular genre signifies what kind of memory the writer intends to construct, since different genres entail different ways of emplotting information and of representing both the subject and his relation to the writer.

The (re)shaping of the memory of a larger entity—such as a fallen state—highlights issues of community and collective loss, as the essays by Xiaofei Tian and Meow Hui Goh demonstrate. Tian examines several pieces from the

---

17   On the example of the *zhiguai* 志怪 or "accounts of anomalies" genre, see Robert Ford Campany, *Strange Writing: Anomaly Accounts in Early Medieval China* (Albany: State University of New York Press, 1996), 101-59.

18   For examples see Miranda Brown, *The Art of Medicine in Early China: The Ancient and Medieval Origins of a Modern Archive* (Cambridge: Cambridge University Press, 2015).

poetic series "Singing My Cares" 詠懷 by Yu Xin 庾信 (513-581) and concludes
that the leading poet of the Liang 梁 court needed to invent a new poetic mode
in order to express adequately his experience of trauma following the collapse
of the Liang dynasty (502-557) and his dislocation to an alien zone in the north.
This new mode, which combined aulic as well as personal expression, involved
subverting or twisting established poetic conventions, playing upon readers'
expectations in novel and surprising ways. Yu Xin's creation of a new type of
aulic poetry, which Tian redefines as literature tied to the imperial family (and
not necessarily to the physical setting of the court and its formal events), was
directed toward a readership of other displaced southern courtiers who would
have been familiar with the poet's textual and experiential past. Goh's essay
similarly investigates how a subject of a fallen state remembers and reshapes
that past for future generations. Her linguistic analysis of a key work by Lu Ji 陸
機 (261-303), a two-part essay titled "A Disquisition on the Fall [of Wu]" 辯亡,
shows the ways in which Lu Ji appropriated and adapted "syntactical templates" from earlier works to shape the memory of his fallen state of Wu 吳
(222-280) and to frame the legacy of his forefathers, two famous Wu generals,
within that narrative.

Recalling and reviving a more distant past often ultimately led to a closer
scrutiny of the present. Such cases highlight how memory can serve present
needs or reflect concerns about the future. Ping Wang's essay, which focuses on
a set of eight poems by Xie Lingyun 謝靈運 (385-433), "On the Wei Crown
Prince's Ye Collection" 擬魏太子鄴中集, considers how the latter-born poet
idealizes the conviviality of Cao Pi 曹丕 (187-226) and his group through literary impersonation or imitation. Wang argues that Xie Lingyun, by speaking in
the voices of Cao Pi and his literary friends, closes the temporal gap between
them and transports himself to their bygone era or them to his own Liu-Song
劉宋 (420-479) court, where conviviality is conspicuously absent. Imitation of
past writers is one of the most complex forms of textual recall, as Wendy Swartz
discusses in her essay on literary imitation and the questions it poses for cultural memory. Her essay explores the implications of how Jiang Yan 江淹 (444-
505), a writer who has positioned himself as the guardian and transmitter of
the whole of a literary past, survives for us in what would turn out to be lost or
nearly lost writers in his imitation series, "Thirty Poems in Various Forms" 雜體
詩三十首. Swartz addresses such thorny questions as: In the production of imitations, what sorts of negotiations occur between a writer's views of the past
and the cultural forces at play in the present? What are the potential gains and
risks involved when writers recall and re-present the past through imitation?

Two essays in this volume examine the anecdote genre and the issues it
raises as a scarcely verifiable and easily transmissible form of memory. Sarah

Allen's close reading of a ninth-century account of events that allegedly took place during the reign of Tang Emperor Xuanzong 玄宗 (r. 712-756), "Xu Yunfeng" 許雲封, shows both the appeal and the unreliability of the anecdote for understanding the past. Anecdotes can animate past events and vivify actors in past times. As embodied forms of living social memory they can also supplement the picture of the past, filling in gaps in history. Anecdotes stake a powerful claim to believability by interweaving new details into known historical truths, thereby giving the details a firmer foothold in collective memory. But they are not verifiable and may even contradict other sources. This complicates their reliability as a basis for historical knowledge. Nonetheless, their suspect credibility did not prevent later readers from appropriating and excising aspects useful for representing the past in ways they desired. Jack Chen's essay explores how anecdotes function as an encoded form of memory that reflects a community's values. In an examination of select passages on mourning and sincerity in the *Liji* 禮記 (Record of ritual) and *Shishuo xinyu* 世說新語 (Talk of the ages and new anecdotes), he observes a similarity between anecdote and ritual, which likewise preserves an institutional memory of normative responses that is transmissible.

Whereas most of the essays in this volume treat the active construction of the past and its implications, Christopher Nugent's essay examines a different kind of mnemonic performance. Nugent demonstrates how a popular primer, the *Qianzi wen* 千字文 (Thousand character text), became a mnemonic tool for learning and remembering a surprisingly wide body of literary and historical knowledge. The lines from this primer functioned as compact, easily memorized pegs, which, along with other mnemonic cues provided by paratextual devices such as annotations, enabled students to recall parts of their cultural heritage on demand.

The nine essays collected here were first presented at the 11th Annual Meeting of the Chinese Medieval Studies Workshop at Rutgers University. The workshop's theme that year, memory, was chosen to honor our friend Alan Berkowitz, who passed away in 2015. Members of this group met regularly over a decade to discuss ideas and read texts in a convivial atmosphere, an atmosphere Alan had no small part in creating and enriching. It is to the cherished and fond memory of our friend that we dedicate this volume.

Bibliography

Allen, Sarah M. *Shifting Stories: History, Gossip, and Lore in Narratives from Tang Dynasty China.* Cambridge, MA: Harvard University Asia Center, 2014.

Brashier, K.E. *Ancestral Memory in Early China*. Cambridge, MA: Harvard University Press, 2011.

Brashier, K.E. *Public Memory in Early China*. Cambridge, MA: Harvard University Press, 2014.

Brown, Miranda. *The Art of Medicine in Early China: The Ancient and Medieval Origins of a Modern Archive*. Cambridge: Cambridge University Press, 2015.

Brown, Miranda. "Mozi's Remaking of Ancient Authority." In *The "Mozi" as an Evolving Text: Different Voices in Early Chinese Thought*, edited by Carine Defoort and Nicolas Standaert, 143-74. Leiden: Brill, 2013.

Campany, Robert Ford. "'Buddhism Enters China' in Early Medieval China." In *Old Society, New Belief: Religious Transformation of China and Rome, ca. 1st-6th Centuries*, edited by Mu-chou Poo, Harold A. Drake, and Lisa Raphals, 13-34. Oxford: Oxford University Press, 2017.

Campany, Robert Ford. *Making Transcendents: Ascetics and Social Memory in Early Medieval China*. Honolulu: University of Hawai'i Press, 2009.

Campany, Robert Ford. *Signs from the Unseen Realm: Buddhist Miracle Tales from Early Medieval China*. Honolulu: University of Hawai'i Press, 2012.

Campany, Robert Ford. *Strange Writing: Anomaly Accounts in Early Medieval China*. Albany: State University of New York Press, 1996.

Carruthers, Mary. *The Book of Memory: A Study of Memory in Medieval Culture*. 2nd edition. Cambridge: Cambridge University Press, 2008.

Chen, Jack W., and David Schaberg, eds. *Idle Talk: Gossip and Anecdote in Traditional China*. Berkeley: University of California Press, 2014.

Choo, Jessey J.C. "Shall We Profane the Service of the Dead? Burial Divinations, Untimely Burials, and Remembrance in Tang *muzhiming*." *Tang Studies* 33 (2015): 1-37.

Choo, Jessey J.C., and Alexei Ditter. "'On *Muzhiming*: Inaugural Workshop of New Frontiers in the Study of Medieval China, Rutgers University, May 15-16, 2015." *Tang Studies* 33 (2015): 129-34.

Choo, Jessey J.C., and Alexei Ditter. "'On *Muzhiming*: Second Workshop of the New Frontiers in the Study of Medieval China, Reed College, May 23-24, 2016." *Early Medieval China* 22 (2016): 75-80.

Davis, Timothy M. *Entombed Epigraphy and Commemorative Culture in Early Medieval China*. Leiden: Brill, 2016.

Ditter, Alexei. "The Commerce of Commemoration: Commissioned *Muzhiming* in the Mid- to Late Tang." *Tang Studies* 32 (2014): 21-46.

Fentress, James, and Chris Wickham. *Social Memory*. Oxford: Blackwell, 1992.

Graham, A.C. *Disputers of the Tao: Philosophical Argument in Ancient China*. La Salle, IL: Open Court, 1989.

Hüsemann, Jörg Henning. *Das Altertum vergegenwärtigen: Eine Studie zum "Shuijing zhu" des Li Daoyuan*. Leipzig: Leipziger Universitätsverlag, 2017.

Li, Wai-yee. *The Readability of the Past in Early Chinese Historiography.* Cambridge, MA: Harvard University Asia Center, 2007.

Luo, Manling. *Literati Storytelling in Late Medieval China.* Seattle: University of Washington Press, 2015.

Milburn, Olivia. *Cherishing Antiquity: The Cultural Construction of an Ancient Chinese Kingdom.* Cambridge, MA: Harvard University Asia Center, 2013.

Nugent, Christopher M.B. *Manifest in Words, Written on Paper: Producing and Circulating Poetry in Tang Dynasty China.* Cambridge, MA: Harvard University Asia Center, 2010.

Nylan, Michael. "Wandering in the Ruins: The *Shuijing zhu* Reconsidered." In *Interpretation and Literature in Early Medieval China,* edited by Alan K.L. Chan and Yuet-Keung Lo, 63-102. Albany: State University of New York Press, 2010.

Owen, Stephen. *Remembrances: The Experience of the Past in Classical Chinese Literature.* Cambridge, MA: Harvard University Press, 1986.

Rogers, Michael C. *The Chronicle of Fu Chien: A Case of Exemplar History.* Berkeley: University of California Press, 1968.

Schaberg, David. *A Patterned Past: Form and Thought in Early Chinese Historiography.* Cambridge, MA: Harvard University Asia Center, 2001.

Shields, Anna M. *Crafting a Collection: The Cultural Contexts and Poetic Practice of the Huajian ji (Collection from Among the Flowers).* Cambridge, MA: Harvard University Asia Center, 2006.

Shields, Anna M. "Words for the Dead and the Living: Innovations in the Mid-Tang 'Prayer Text' (*jiwen*)." *Tang Studies* 25 (2007): 111-45.

Swartz, Wendy. *Reading Tao Yuanming: Shifting Paradigms of Historical Reception (427-1900).* Cambridge, MA: Harvard University Asia Center, 2008.

Tian, Xiaofei. *Tao Yuanming & Manuscript Culture: The Record of a Dusty Table.* Seattle: University of Washington Press, 2005.

Varsano, Paula. *Tracking the Banished Immortal: The Poetry of Li Bo and its Critical Reception.* Honolulu: University of Hawai'i Press, 2003.

Wyatt, F. "The Narrative in Psychoanalysis: Psychoanalytic Notes of Storytelling, Listening, and Interpreting." In *Narrative Psychology: The Storied Nature of Human Conduct,* edited by Theodore R. Sarbin, 193-210. New York: Praeger, 1986.

Zürcher, Erik. *The Buddhist Conquest of China: The Spread and Adaptation of Buddhism in Early Medieval China.* 3rd edition with foreword by Stephen F. Teiser. Leiden: Brill, 2007.

CHAPTER 1

Artful Remembrance: Reading, Writing, and Reconstructing the Fallen State in Lu Ji's "Bian wang"

Meow Hui Goh

In 280 Sun Hao 孫皓 (242-284), the last ruler of the State of Wu 吳 (222-280), surrendered to the invading Jin 晉 army, bringing an end to Wu as well as the "Three States" era. Though physically lost, Wu lived on in the communication of the people of post-Wu time; in conversations, debates, letters, poems, prose writings, and more, "why was Wu lost?" was a hot-button topic. Amidst verbal jabs from the winners (i.e. the Jin) and critical comments from historians, voices from "the subjects of the fallen state" (*wangguo zhi chen* 亡國之臣) competed to be heard. One of the strongest of these came from Lu Ji 陸機 (261-303), a proud Wu man whose grandfather and father were meritorious generals of that state. According to his biography in *Jin shu* 晉書 (History of Jin), when Wu fell, Lu Ji, at twenty years of age, "retired to his hometown and closed his door to study conscientiously, lasting a total of ten years."[1] It was also at this time that he wrote some of his works on Wu. Turning to literary learning and writing in the face of political rupture, Lu Ji seemed to have found not merely solace, meaning, and renewal, but also the means to assert his voice as "a subject of the fallen state."

Not all of Lu Ji's works on Wu have survived. But one that did survive—a two-part essay titled "Bian wang" 辯亡 (A disquisition on the fall [of Wu])—presents a new, unique voice of remembrance.[2] To *bian* 辯 is to "argue out

---

1   *Jin shu* (Beijing: Zhonghua shuju, 2010), 54.1467.

2   For the text of "Bian wang," see *Sanguo zhi* (Beijing: Zhonghua shuju, 1985), 48.1179-82 n. 1; Xiao Tong, ed., *Wen xuan* (hereafter cited as *WX*) (Shanghai: Shanghai guji chubanshe, 1997), 53.2310-29; and *Jin shu*, 54.1467-72. From here on, references to my citation of the work are to the version in *Wen xuan*. For translations of the work, see David R. Knechtges, "Han and Six Dynasties Parallel Prose," *Renditions* 33 & 34 (1990): 78-94; Emile Gaspardone, "Le Discours de la perte du Wou par Lou Ki," *Sinologica* 4 (1958): 189-225. The date of Lu Ji's "Bian wang" is not completely certain: his biography in *Jin shu* (54.1467) seems to suggest that it was written not long after Wu's defeat by Jin in 280, when he retired to his family estate to study and write, but there are also indications that it might have been written after Chen Shou had completed his *Wu shu* 吳書 (History of Wu), that is, probably around 291, when Lu Ji moved to Luoyang to

alternatives, dispute; debate, controvert."[3] But Lu Ji's "Bian wang" is as commemorative as it is argumentative. Essentially, he attempted not only to explicate the reasons for the fall of Wu but also to celebrate its past legacy and his own forefathers' achievements as statesmen. At times coolly analytical, at times mournfully regretful, often unabashedly celebratory, his voice as a prideful "subject of the fallen state" was one not heard before in earlier works. However, as a "readerly" writer who always looked to past works for inspiration, Lu Ji brought the literary resources at his disposal to bear on his remembrance. Working with and against his models, he constructed a textual space between imitation and innovation. By charting his technical moves—how he made use of "template lines" found in earlier works, revised and transformed them, and eventually abandoned them—throughout the essay, I will present Lu Ji as a remembering subject who was both traditional and inventive.

Reading and Writing

How does remembering take form? What is the process of remembrance? In a literary culture, these questions often concern not only writing practices, but also reading practices. In his study of "public memory" in early China, K.E. Brashier sheds important light on the practice of reciting or chanting canonical texts repeatedly, suggesting that it played a crucial role in commemorative and other memorial practices during the time.[4] He brings into focus reading practices described as *song* 誦, *du* 讀, *yong* 詠, *feng* 諷, and the like, all of which were oral-performative.[5] His study helps us understand how recitative forms of textual learning shaped remembrance in early China, raising, at the same time, the question of how textual learning might play a similar role in later time. Focusing on Lu Ji's "Bian wang," I will argue that reading, writing, and remembrance are connected in very specific ways in this third century example.

By lucky chance, we have some surviving letters that Lu Ji's brother Lu Yun 陸雲 (262-303) wrote to him, which give us a glimpse into their reading and writing practices. Interestingly, when speaking of "reading a work," Lu Yun uses

---

accept an appointment (see *Lu Shiheng wenji jiaozhu*, annot. Liu Yunhao, 2 vols. [Nanjing: Fenghuang chuanmei chuban jituan, 2007], 10.979, 10.1025 n. 10).

3   Paul W. Kroll, *A Student's Dictionary of Classical and Medieval Chinese* (Leiden: Brill, 2015), 22.

4   K.E. Brashier, *Public Memory in Early China* (Cambridge, MA: Harvard University Asia Center, 2014), 9-57.

5   Ibid.

the word *du* 讀, "to read aloud," only occasionally; more often, he uses the words *shi* 視, "to view," or *sheng* 省, "to review," such as in these examples:

> Before, I was reviewing Huangfu Shian's (Huangfu Mi 皇甫謐; 215-282) *Biographies of Lofty Gentlemen*...[6] 前省皇甫士安《高士傳》…

> Viewing "Nine Passages," I see that it often has fine phrases...[7] 視《九章》時有善語…

> Having viewed "Nine Songs," I felt as if I have returned to my own, completely cut off [from others]...[8] 視《九歌》便自歸謝絕…

> I have reviewed "An Account on Ascending to the High-Above"...[9] 省《登遐傳》…

In contrast to the prevalent use of words that indicate oral-performative practices in early Han accounts about textual learning, Lu Yun's use of *shi* and *sheng*, both of which have a radical associated with sight—*jian* 見 ("to see") in the case of *shi* and *mu* 目 ("eye") in the case of *sheng*—seemed to indicate a shift to the "visual." There is no doubt that recitation and chanting continued to be practiced in textual learning and reading in the early medieval period, and, as Lu Yun's letters suggest, listening to the recitation of a text, reading it aloud, and what he called "viewing" or "reviewing" it were not completely separate activities.[10] However, I will argue that Lu Yun's prevalent use of the words

---

6   *Lu Shilong wenji jiaozhu*, 8.1044.

7   Ibid., 8.1063.

8   Ibid.

9   Ibid., 8.1071.

10   In one of his letters, Lu Yun writes: "I once heard Tangzhong recite 'Nine Songs' by sighing it out. In the past when I read *Songs of the South*, I did not quite like it. In recent days when I viewed it, I found that it was in fact extremely pure, flowing on like a river" (*Lu Shilong wenji jiaozhu*, 8.1063). Here, he juxtaposes *wen* ("listen to"), *du* ("to read aloud"), and *shi* ("to view"), suggesting that listening to a text or reading it aloud and "viewing" it are not completely distinct activities. A study that supports such a description of early medieval reading practices is Antje Richter's *Letters & Epistolary Culture in Early Medieval China* (Seattle: University of Washington Press, 2013), where she points out that both reading aloud and silent reading occurred in the early medieval practice of reading letters (88). For more on medieval reading practices, see Chapters 2, 3, and 4 of Christopher M.B. Nugent, *Manifest in Words, Written on Paper: Producing and Circulating Poetry in Tang Dynasty China* (Cambridge, MA: Harvard University Asia Center, 2011), and Jack W. Chen, "On the Act and Representation of Reading in Medieval China," *Journal of the American Oriental Society* 129.1 (2009): 57-71.

shi and *sheng* is significant: they suggest a shift to examining a work more closely, often by observing how its language is used or crafted. In his letters written to Lu Ji, Lu Yun often focuses on specific lines and even specific words when discussing a work, as in the following example:

> Among the lines there are "thenceforth" and "thereupon"—these are good for making transitions, but if they can be left out the pace will be faster, so one might as well not have them. Also, these [transitional words] certainly cannot be used in the middle of a line, so even if there are few of them it is not unusual. As for using tetrasyllabic lines to make transitions, it is best that they come in four lines. In the past I have opined that the line "As the fast-striking hand turns back, [the sound] becomes heavy and mournful"[11] in your "Qi xian" becomes isolated when linked with the two lines before...[12]

> 文中有「於是」、「爾乃」，於轉句誠佳，然得不用之益快，有故不如無。又於文句中自可不用之，便少亦常。云四言轉句，以四句為佳。往曾以兄《七羨》「回煩手而沉哀」結上兩句為孤…

He comments on how the function words *yushi* 於是 and *naier* 爾乃 are used, how the transition from one section to the next should be made, how many parallel lines to put together, and other such "technical" matters. Even though we have lost Lu Ji's letters, his most famous work, "Wen fu" 文賦 (A *fu* on literature), also reflects a similar attention to the "techniques" of writing. In his preface to "Wen fu," he writes: "Whenever I view [here he uses *guan* 觀, which also has a *jian* radical] the compositions of talented literati, I secretly grasp how they applied their effort. Even though there are many changes in the ways they dispel words and employ diction, the beauty and ugliness or the good and bad within them can be obtained and spoken about."[13] His comment about being

---

11   *Fan shou* ("fast-striking hand") is a description of exceptionally complex ways of playing a musical instrument; it appears to be a general description applicable to string instruments as well as wind and percussion instruments. Given that Lu Ji's "Qi xian" is no longer extant, it is difficult to know what the term specifically describes in this work. An extant fragment of Lu Ji's "Gu chui fu" 鼓吹賦 (Drums and pipes *fu*) contains these lines: 騁逸氣而憤壯，繞煩手乎曲折.

12   *Lu Shilong wenji jiaozhu*, 8.1060.

13   The original reads: 余每觀才士之所作，竊有以得其用心。夫放言遣辭，良多變矣，妍蚩好惡，可得而言. wx, 17.761-62. For a complete translation and discussion of "Wen fu," see Stephen Owen, *Readings in Chinese Literary Thought* (Cambridge, MA: Council on East Asian Studies, Harvard University, 1992), 73-181.

able to observe how writers "dispel words and employ diction" by "viewing" (*guan*) their works calls to mind Lu Yun's way of "viewing" or "reviewing" a work.

Another aspect of the Lu brothers' reading practice that is noteworthy is how closely they associated "viewing" a work with composing their own work. Lu Yun mentions this many times in his letters, such as in these instances:

> Before I was reviewing Huangfu Shian's *Biographies of Lofty Gentlemen* and hence wrote "*Fu* on Uninhibited Folks"…[14] 前省皇甫士安《高士傳》，復作《逸民賦》

> I have reviewed "An Account on Ascending to High-Above," thereupon I wrote "An Eulogy on Ascending to the High-Above," completing it within a short time.[15] 省《登遐傳》，因作《登遐頌》，須臾便成

> In the meantime, I have viewed "An Account of the Great Waste Land" and wished to write "*Fu* on the Great Waste Land."[16] 間視《大荒傳》，欲作《大荒賦》

As we can see, *sheng* or *shi*, that is, "viewing" or "reviewing," a work often leads Lu Yun to *zuo*, that is, composing his own work. In fact, it appears as if Lu Yun is actively seeking inspiration in earlier works for his own writing. In his "Wen fu" proper, Lu Ji also connects the act of reading with the act of writing:

佇中區以玄覽	He stands in the very center, observes in the darkness,
頤情志於典墳	Nourishes feeling and intent in the ancient canons.
…	…
游文章之林府	Roams in the groves and treasure houses of literary works,
嘉麗藻之彬彬	Admires the perfect balance of their intricate and lovely craft.
慨投篇而援筆	With strong feeling he puts aside the book and takes his writing brush
聊宣之乎斯文	To make it manifest in literature.[17]

Here, it seems, earlier works can serve as inspiration at two levels: "nourishing" the mind and heart in preparation for writing, and offering models for the craft of writing. While the former might involve calling earlier works to mind in a sort of meditation, the latter clearly involves placing the works before one's

---

14   *Lu Shilong wenji jiaozhu*, 8.1044.

15   Ibid., 8.1071.

16   Ibid., 8.1090.

17   This translation is by Stephen Owen, *Readings in Chinese Literary Thought*, 87, 92, 94.

eyes. Were the Lu brothers imitating earlier works? Lu Yun used the following words to describe the relationship between a work and an earlier work or between a writer and an earlier one: *fang* 倣 ("to model after"), *dui* 對 ("to be paired with"), *bi* 比 ("to be compared with"), *yue* 越 ("to surpass"), and *guo* 過 ("to outdo").[18] What these words reveal is a critical approach to imitation, in that as one models after a work, he is at the same time fixing its flaws or improving upon it. As such, imitation is criticism. While much has been written about Lu Ji's "imitation" (*moni* 模擬) in the area of poetry, less attention has been given to his prose works.[19] But even as I describe how he imitated earlier works in his "Bian wang" essay in this essay, my purpose is not to study his prose imitation per se, but rather to examine how it shaped his remembrance. I argue that the Lu brothers' way of reading, which involves examining the language of a work critically, foregrounds the specific way by which Lu Ji uses earlier works to construct his remembrance in "Bian wang." If, as James Wertsch writes, "human action, including thinking, remembering, and other mental processes," always "involves an irreducible tension between active agent and cultural tool,"[20] Lu Ji's essay is a paramount example of how this tension played out in third-century China. Arguing that collective memory is a form of "instrumental distribution," Wertsch points to the importance of recognizing the role of "cultural tools such as calendars, written records, computers, and narratives" in the process of remembrance.[21] In this case, expository prose, as a "cultural tool" of which there has already been many earlier examples, clearly guides Lu Ji's remembrance; at the same time, it is also that which he manipulated to construct his remembrance of Wu. While he clearly looked to earlier

---

18   See, for example, *Lu Shilong wenji jiaozhu*, 8.1089, 1095, 1117, 1136.

19   For an article that discusses imitation in Lu Ji's "Bian wang," see Yang Zhaolei, "*Cong Bianwang lun kan Lu Ji nigu zhong de chuangxin qingxiang*," *Wuhan keji daxue xuebao* 13.3 (2011): 362-66. For discussions of Lu Ji's "imitation poetry," see Chiu-Mi Lai, "The Craft of Original Imitation: Lu Ji's Imitations of Han Old Poems," in *Studies in Early Medieval Chinese Literature and Cultural History in Honor of Richard B. Mather and Donald Holzman*, ed. Paul W. Kroll and David R. Knechtges (Provo, Utah: T'ang Studies Society, 2003), 17-48; Lin Wenyue, "Lu Ji de nigushi," in *Zhonggu wenxue lun cong* (Taipei: Da'an, 1989), 123-58. For discussions of early medieval "imitation poetry" in general, see Kinugawa Kenji, "Rikuchō mogishi shōkō," *Chūgoku bungaku hō* 31 (1980): 29-63; Brigitta A. Lee, "Imitation, Remembrance and the Formation of the Poetic Past in Early Medieval China," Ph.D. diss., Princeton University, 2007.

20   James V. Wertsch, "Collective Memory," in *Memory in Mind and Culture*, ed. Pascal Boyer and James V. Wertsch (Cambridge: Cambridge University Press, 2009), 119. See also his *Mind as Action* (New York: Oxford University Press, 1998), 23-30.

21   Wertsch, "Collective Memory," 119.

models of expository prose to construct his own remembrance of the fallen state, these models proved insufficient when it came to deep, personal memory. While guided by his "cultural tool," Lu Ji was therefore also attempting to reinvent it at the same time. As a result, his "Bian wang" is nothing short of a new, unique collage of shared and personal memories.

"Bian wang": An Overview

Lu Ji's "Bian wang" was not the only voice coming from "the subjects of the fallen state." In fact, following the demise of Wu, there was great interest among individual Wu men in compiling a history of their now-lost state. This is evident from the various titles that are recorded, such as *Wu shu* 吳書 (A history of Wu) attributed to Zhou Chu 周處 (236-297), a Wu native who went on to serve the Jin court;[22] another work by the same title attributed to another Wu native, Wei Zhao 韋昭 (204-273);[23] as well as *Wu shi* 吳事 (Affairs of Wu) attributed to Gu Yanxian 顧彥先 (d. 312), also a Wu native.[24] Lu Yun's surviving letters show that compiling their own version of Wu history was a matter of great importance to the Lu brothers, in spite of their access to and familiarity with similar works by others, including Chen Shou's 陳壽 (233-297) *Wu shu*.[25] In Lu Yun's words, their *Wu shu* project is "a matter that does not decay" (*buxiu shi* 不朽事), without which "the affairs of this one state will be lost" 此一國事 遂亦失.[26] He discussed with Lu Ji issues ranging from who to include with a biography (*zhuan* 傳), where to place someone's biography, whom to consult for more information. In one letter, he mentions that Chen Shou's *Wu shu* includes the two works "Wei ci Jiuxi wen" 魏賜九錫文 and "Fen tianxia wen" 分天下文 but that their *Wu shu* does not include these.[27] He also writes with much regret that their biographies of their grandfather and father, Lu Xun 陸遜 (183-245) and Lu Kang 陸抗 (226-274), respectively, have not yet been completed, while opining that those composed by others "mostly do not exhaust the reasoning" 多不盡理.[28] These snippets of the two Lu brothers' conversation suggest that

---

22 *Lu Shiheng wenji jiaozhu* 10.1082.

23 *Sui shu* (Beijing: Zhonghua shuju, 2014), 33.955.

24 *Lu Shilong wenji jiaozhu*, 8.1121.

25 Ibid., 8.1117-18.

26 Ibid., 8.1117, 1122.

27 Ibid., 8.1117. "Wei ci Jiuxi wen" 魏賜九錫文 could be Pan Xu's 潘勗 (d. 215?) "Ce Wei gong Jiuxi wen" 冊魏公九錫文 and "Fen tianxia wen" could be Hu Zong's 胡綜 (185-243) "Zhongfen tianxia mengwen" 中分天下盟文.

28 Ibid.

their version of the history of Wu was meant to be an improvement or even a revision or correction of what was already in circulation at the time; it was, in that sense, a kind of counter-history or counter-memory to existing accounts, including Chen Shou's court-sanctioned work. It is also in the context of discussing the compilation of a Wu history that Lu Yun mentions Lu Ji's "Bian wang" essay, comparing it to Jia Yi's 賈誼 (200-168 BCE) work of a similar nature, "Guo Qin" 過秦 ("Faulting Qin").[29] This shows that Lu Ji likely composed his essay as part of his and his brother's larger attempt to remember Wu's history. At one point in a letter, Lu Yun commented that unlike others, Lu Ji could "depict both the official and the personal" 公私並敘 when compiling their forefathers' biographies. Indeed, his comment would be appropriate for Lu Ji's "Bian wang" essay too, since, unlike Jia Yi's "Guo Qin," it is a work about a fallen state written not from the vantage point of a distant and impartial commentator, but from that of a deeply involved subject-cum-descendent.

In "Bian wang," Lu Ji presents his argument on Wu's demise by considering three factors—timeliness (*tianshi* 天時), geographical advantage (*dili* 地利), and human coordination (*renhe* 人和)—and he leaves no doubt that he considers *renhe* the most crucial factor in a state's growth and survival. To arrive at the conclusion that Wu's demise was due to the later loss of human coordination, he uses the larger part of his essay to recall the earlier history of Wu, highlighting the achievements of its rulers and officials. In the essay, he weaves together the names of forty-nine individuals in total, constructing a remembrance of decisive founders, worthy rulers, courageous generals, resourceful strategists, loyal ministers, skillful diplomats, and wise advisers. His remembrance evokes a sense of heroism and victory rather than one of destruction and loss. Lu Ji's refusal to name the "anti-heroes"—so to speak—is on clear display when he deals with the difficult years toward the end of Wu. He alludes to the problems under Sun Xiu's 孫休 (r. 258-264) reign only in one phrase— "those who were wicked and vicious let loose their brutality" 姦回肆虐;[30] and he hints at Sun Hao's misrule only with the phrase, "Even though the head of the state was flawed..." 元首雖病.[31] In his narrative, the "anti-heroes"— those who shall not be named—are unfortunate accidents in Wu's history. Between

---

29   Ibid. In *Wen xuan*, Jia Yi's "Guo Qin" appears only in one piece entitled "Guo Qin lun" (see 51.2233-40). A fuller version of "Guo Qin" is given, without title, in *Shi ji* (Beijing: Zhonghua shuju, 2002), 6.276-84; a truncated version titled "Guo Qin" is cited in *Han shu* (Taipei: Hongye shuju youxiangongsi, 1996), 31.1821-26; the *Wen xuan* version is the same as that in *Han shu* but now named "Guo Qin lun." Hereafter my references are to the *Shi ji* version.

30   *WX*, 53.2317.

31   Ibid., 53.2318.

the named and the unnamed, there were clear judgments on who the true Wu men were and what the true Wu state was. If only those great rulers and officials were still alive, Lu Ji seems to suggest, the state of Wu would still be thriving. He even fantasizes about the longevity of Wu, pointing out that all that is needed is for the latecomers to follow the path that had been laid down by earlier generations. By Lu Ji's account, Wu was not a state destined for failure, but one whose aspirations and potential were unexpectedly—and unjustifiably—derailed. But how exactly did he pull off this argument? This question will have to be answered by closely examining how Lu Ji deployed linguistic elements to construct his essay—indeed, by the Lu brothers' own way of viewing a work.

Composing an Argument

Lu Ji clearly looked at earlier discourses on "the rise and fall of a state" (*xing wang* 興亡) for inspiration. One earlier work that is particularly worthy of mention is Jia Yi's "Guo Qin," which, as previously noted, was cited by Lu Yun for comparison with Lu Ji's "Bian wang."[32] This passage from "Guo Qin" serves well to demonstrate how it might have influenced Lu Ji's work:

> Chen She's (d. 208 BCE) station was not prestigious like those of the gentlemen of Qi, Chu, Yan, Zhao, Hann, Wei, Song, Wei, and Zhongshan; his hoes, harrows, and guisarmes were not as sharp as their curved halberds and long spears; his masses of convict-guards could not withstand the armies of the nine states; his ability to plan deeply and think far, maneuver armies and dispatch troops, cannot be compared with that of men of the past. However, victory and defeat were swapped, their accomplishments were the opposite of what they should be...Why so? It was [because] benevolence and righteousness were not practiced, causing a shift in the momentum of the offensive and the defensive.[33]

> 陳涉之位，非尊於齊、楚、燕、趙、韓、魏、宋、衞、中山之君；鉏櫌棘矜，非銚於句戟長鎩也；適戍之眾，非抗於九國之師；深謀遠慮，行軍用兵之道，非及鄉時之士也。**然而**成敗異變，功業相反也...**何也**？仁義不施而攻守之勢異**也**。

---

32   *Lu Shilong wenji jiaozhu*, 8.1117.

33   *Shi ji*, 6.282.

This is a major passage. It constitutes Jia Yi's overall argument that Qin's expeditious fall after the First Emperor's death was caused by his and his heir's failure to practice "benevolence and righteousness" (*ren yi*). Here and elsewhere in his essay, Jia Yi presents Qin's collapse in the hands of Chen She and his rebel armies as ironic, pointing out they were inferior compared to Qin's much more formidable opponents in the nine states during the pre-unification period. The rhetorical force of Jia Yi's argument is rooted in his linguistic deployment: he first contrasts Chen She and his armies with those of the nine states by repeating the "A *fei* B" (i.e. A is not B) line structure four times; then, he points out the ironical outcomes of history using the conjunction *raner* ("however"); finally, he arrives at the conclusion about practicing *ren yi* by way of the automatism in *ziwen zida* 自問自答 ("raising a question for oneself to answer"), that is, via the "*he ye/...ye*" ("Why so? It was [because]...") construction.

Interestingly, Lu Ji has discerned Jia Yi's linguistic structuring, imitating it while he presents the fall of Wu similarly as an irony, as this passage from "Bian wang" shows:

> The generals of Cao [Cao] (155-220) and Liu [Bei] (161-223) were not those that [Jin] could have elected in one generation; the troops of the former days could not match those of the past in number;[34] the paths for battles and defense were not constrained by former strategies; the advantage gained from the natural terrain did not change suddenly; yet, victory and defeat went against reasoning, past and present were incongruous. Why so? It was [because] between then and now there had been changes: the ability to assign and appoint [the right people] had shifted.

> 夫曹、劉之將**非**一世所選，向時之師**無曩**日之眾，戰守之道**抑**有前符，險阻之利俄然**未**改，**而**成敗貿理，古今詭趣，**何哉**？彼此之化殊，授任之才異**也** 。

Resonating with Jia Yi's argument about Qin, Lu Ji points out that Wu, too, had more powerful enemies, that is, the Cao Cao and Liu Bei regimes, in the past and equally abundant resources in more recent years, and yet the state ironically perished. This leads to his conclusion about the shift in "the ability to assign and appoint [the right people]." Lu Ji not only appropriates Jia Yi's argumentative logic, he also uses Jia Yi's syntactical structuring. Notice that his passage also begins with four lines that use negation, which are followed by the

---

34   "The troops of the former days" refers to the Jin army that invaded the Wu in 280, when Sun Hao surrendered without putting up a fight.

similar conjunction *er* ("yet/however") and the question-and-answer structure *"he zai/...ye."* Below is a side-by-side comparison of the linguistic patterns of Jia Yi and Lu Ji's passages:

Jia Yi: 非… 非… 非… 非… 然而成敗異變，功業相反也。… 何也？… 也。

Lu Ji: 非… 無… 抑 (有)… 未… 而成敗貿理，古今詭趣，何哉？… 也。

In this imitation, we detect Lu Ji's critical "reviewing" of Jia Yi's language: as he models after Jia Yi's syntactical structures, he also modifies them by using a variation of negatives—*fei, wu, yi, wei*—to replace Jia Yi's repetitive use of *fei*.

Lu Ji's dynamic imitation of Jia Yi's prose produces more than new variations in syntactical structuring. By appropriating Jia Yi's argumentative logic, Lu Ji achieves a sort of double-edged judgment aimed not only at the failings of Sun Hao and his supporters, but also at the "victory" of Jin, the conqueror of his state. When he points out that Wu had resisted much more formidable enemies in Cao Cao's and Liu Bei's armies in the past and that the Jin army was no comparison to those, he is insinuating that Jin's victory over Wu was incidental, the result of Wu's own internal problems rather than of Jin's strength. Much thought and emotion can be read into Lu Ji's statement: his regrets about Sun Hao's surrender, his romanticized memory of the Three States period and the "heroes" of that era, and his dignified resistance as a "subject of the fallen state" against his conqueror.[35] Though modeled after Jia Yi's work, Lu Ji's essay, the first example of an expository prose written by "a subject of the fallen state" about the fall of his own state, reveals a complexity—both argumentative and emotional—rarely seen in earlier or contemporaneous works. Comparing Lu Ji's essay to Jia Yi's, Lu Yun comments that "'A Disquisition on the Fall [of Wu]' is already a good match for 'Faulting Qin' and has accomplished what it should" 《辯亡》則已是《過秦》對事，求當可得耳.[36] We can only speculate on what it was that Lu Yun saw in "Bian wang" that was a "match" for "Guo Qin," but it is clear that Lu Ji's task was more difficult than Jia Yi's: while providing a sound analysis of why Wu fell, he also could not avoid the issues and emotions that came with being "a subject of the fallen state." As he shifts into the commemorative mode, he continues to use the strategy of dynamic and critical imitation, but, as we shall see, that strategy eventually gives way as he deals with the most personal part of his remembrance.

---

35   As mentioned, Sun Hao surrendered to the Jin army without a fight, a turn of events that appeared to have caused Lu Ji deep regret.

36   *Lu Shilong wenji jiaozhu*, 8.1117.

Shaping a Community of Loyal Ministers and Mighty Generals

Centered on human actors, Lu Ji's essay places a strong emphasis on Wu's talents. In depicting the loyal ministers and mighty generals of Wu, he seemed to have also surveyed earlier works for syntactical templates. In this regard, he appears to have drawn broadly from earlier discourse on "the rise and fall of a state," such as those represented by not only Jia Yi's "Guo Qin" or the like, but also the historian's "appraisal" (*zan* 贊) or "evaluation" (*ping* 評) attached to the end of a historical biography. Below is the core passage in his essay in which he lists thirty-five Wu officials in a continuous sequence.

於是張昭為師傅；

Thereupon, Zhang Zhao was made the Grand Mentor;

周瑜、陸公、魯肅、呂蒙之疇
入為腹心，出作股肱；

Those in the company of Zhou Yu, Master Lu [Xun], Lu Su, and Lü Meng were taken in like entrails and hearts, dispatched like arms and thighs;

甘寧、凌統、程普、賀齊、
朱桓、朱然之徒奮其威；

The likes of Gan Ning, Ling Tong, Cheng Pu, He Qi, Zhu Huan, and Zhu Ran whipped up their might;

韓當、潘璋、黃蓋、蔣欽、周泰
之屬宣其力；

Those belonging to the kind of Han Dang, Pan Zhang, Huang Gai, Jiang Qin, and Zhou Tai propagated their efforts.

風雅則諸葛瑾、張承、步騭，
以名聲光國；

For moral suasion and elegance, there were Zhuge Jin, Zhang Cheng, and Bu Zhi, who honored the state with their name and fame;

政事則顧雍、潘濬、呂範、呂岱，
以器任幹職；

In matters of governance, there were Gu Yong, Pan Jun, Lü Fan, and Lü Dai, who carried out their duties with great competence;

奇偉則虞翻、陸績、張溫、張惇，
以諷議舉正；

Exceptionally magnificent were Yu Fan, Lu Ji, Zhang Wen, and Zhang Dun, who rectified the court by admonition and reasoning;

奉使則趙咨、沈珩，以敏達延譽；

Among the emissaries were Zhao Zi and Shen Heng, who spread the good name [of the state] by conveying messages adeptly;

術數則吳範、趙達，以機祥協德；

For prognostication and arithmetic, there were Wu Fan and Zhao Da, who promoted virtuousness by prophetizing omens;

董襲、陳武殺身以衛主；

> As for Dong Xi and Chen Wu, they sacrificed their
> lives to protect the Sovereign,

駱統、劉基強諫以補過。

> While Luo Tong and Liu Ji corrected his mistakes
> through strong admonition.[37]

Two syntactical structures stand out in the passage given above. The first is the grouping of people's names using *zhi chou* 之疇, *zhi tu* 之徒, and *zhi shu* 之屬. Lu Ji used this syntactical structure to create three parallel lines that take the following forms:

> 周瑜、陸公、魯肅、呂蒙之疇入為腹心，出作股肱；
> Person, Person, Person, Person 之疇+verb phrase
>
> 甘寧、凌統、程普、賀齊、朱桓、朱然之徒奮其威；
> Person, Person, Person, Person, Person, Person 之徒+verb phrase
>
> 韓當、潘璋、黃蓋、蔣欽、周泰之屬宣其力；
> Person, Person, Person, Person, Person 之屬+verb phrase

Jia Yi's "Guo Qin" contains lines that are similarly structured:

> … 甯越、徐尚、蘇秦、杜赫之屬為之謀，
> Person, Person, Person, Person 之屬+verb phrase
>
> 齊明、周最、陳軫、召滑、樓緩、翟景、蘇厲、樂毅之徒通其意，
> Person, Person, Person, Person, Person, Person, Person, Person 之徒+verb
> phrase
>
> 吳起、孫臏、帶佗、倪良、王廖、田忌、廉頗、趙奢之屬制其兵。[38]
> Person, Person, Person, Person, Person, Person, Person, Person 之屬+verb
> phrase

Again, it appeared as if Lu Ji had avoided the repetition of *zhi shu* 之屬 in "Guo Qin" by alternating *zhi chou* 之疇, *zhi tu* 之徒, and *zhi shu* 之屬.

The second major syntactical structure in Lu Ji's passage is one that organizes people into different categories. For example:

---

37   *WX*, 53.2312-14.

38   *Shi ji*, 6.279.

風雅則諸葛瑾、張承、步騭，以名聲光國；
Category, 則 Person, Person, Person+ 以-verb phrase

奇偉則虞翻、陸績、張溫、張惇，以諷議舉正；
Category, 則 Person, Person, Person, Person+ 以-verb phrase

術數則吳範、趙達，以機祥協德；
Category, 則 Person, Person+ 以-verb phrase

A simpler version of the syntactical structure used in these lines can be found in the following "appraisal" in the *Han shu* 漢書, where fourteen categories of talents are listed in one sequence:

漢之得人，於茲為盛	Han's recruitment of talents prospered from this time on:
儒雅則公孫弘、董仲舒、兒寬	For Confucian elegance, there were Gongsun Hong, Dong Zhongshu, and Ni Kuan;
篤行則石建、石慶	For honest conduct, there were Shi Jian and Shi Qing;
質直則汲黯、卜式	For substance and forthrightness, there were Ji An and Bu Shi;
推賢則韓安國、鄭當時	For promoting the worthy, there were Han Guoan and Zheng Dangshi;
定令則趙禹、張湯，	For fixing ordinances, there were Zhao Yu and Zhang Tang;
文章則司馬遷、相如，	For literary composition, there were Sima Qian and [Sima] Xiangru;
滑稽則東方朔、枚皋，	For comic wittiness, there were Dongfang Shuo and Mei Gao;
應對則嚴助、朱買臣，	For response and reply, there were Yan Zhu and Zhu Maichen;
曆數則唐都、洛下閎，	For calendar and arithmetic, there were Tang Du and Luoxia Hong;
協律則李延年，	For harmonizing the pitch-pipe, there was Li Yannian;
運籌則桑弘羊，	For strategizing, there was Sang Hongyang;
奉使則張騫、蘇武，	For emissaries, there were Zhang Qian and Su Wu;
將率則衛青、霍去病，	For generals and leaders, there were Wei Qing and Huo Qubing;
受遺則霍光、金日磾…	For receiving testamentary, there were Huo Guang and Jin Ridi…[39]

---

39   *Han shu*, 8.2634; this text is also appended to *Shi ji*, 112.2964-65.

Here we notice that, on the one hand, Lu Ji's categories are not so different from those in this *Han shu* "appraisal": while the latter includes "Confucian elegance" 儒雅, "calendar and arithmetic" 曆數, and "emissaries" 奉使, Lu Ji has "windy elegance" 風雅, "prognostication and arithmetic" 術數, and the exact same category "emissaries" 奉使. On the other hand, his use of the syntactical templates found in earlier works was a dynamic one, as revealed by his more complex syntactical patterning (i.e. "category, 則 Person, Person, Person" combined with " 以-verb phrase") when compared to what is found in *Han shu* (i.e. simply "category, 則 Person, Person, Person"). It is also worth adding that the syntactical patterning of the last two lines of Lu Ji's passage, though a simple one, is also commonly used for depicting multiple people in earlier works. Compare the two lines by Lu Ji with two similar lines found in the above-mentioned appraisal from *Han shu*:

Lu Ji:
董襲、陳武殺身以衛主；
Person, Person+ 以-verb phrase

駱統、劉基強諫以補過。[40]
Person, Person+ 以-verb phrase

Han shu:
而蕭望之、梁丘賀、夏侯勝、韋玄成、嚴彭祖、尹更始以儒術進，
Person, Person, Person, Person, Person, Person+ 以-verb phrase

劉向、王褎以文章顯…[41]
Person, Person+ 以-verb phrase

The three syntactical patterns discussed above are common ones used in earlier works such as "Guo Qin" and *Han shu* for the specific purpose of placing people in groups or categories. As a result, people are not remembered as individuals per se but by their association with one another and their utility in the grand scheme of things, such as in the function of the state. Often used in building parallel lines (*paiju* 排句), as in Lu Ji's and his predecessors' examples, these syntactical patterns allow for extensive listing of names and deeds, giving the impression of a complete recall. Weaving together his remembrance of the talented people of Wu by diversifying and complicating these syntactical

---

40   *WX*, 53.2314.
41   *Han shu*, 8.2634; also in *Shi ji* 112.2965.

templates, Lu Ji presents them as a particularly close-knit and complementary matrix of loyal ministers and mighty generals that functioned to keep Wu in flawless operation. Underlying this impression of completeness and perfection, as will become clear in the later part of this essay, is nevertheless a more selective and contentious remembrance.

Imaging the Wise and Benevolent Ruler

In depicting Sun Quan 孫權 (182-252), the founding emperor of Wu, Lu Ji again made use of "syntactical templates" found in earlier works. A particularly telling comparison is with Ban Biao's 班彪 (3-54) portrayal of Liu Bang 劉邦 (256-195 BCE), the Han dynasty founder, in his essay "Wang ming lun" 王命論.[42] There are a number of similar line patterns in Ban Biao's passage on Liu Bang and Lu Ji's on Sun Quan, seen in the following examples:

Example (1)
Ban Biao:
In addition, he was trustworthy, sincere, good at strategizing, and open to receiving advice. He could not wait to acknowledge the good in others. He employed others as if they were himself, complied with admonition as if following the river's flow, and corresponded with the time as if hastening toward it.[43]

加之以信誠好謀，達於聽受，見善如不及，用人如由己，從諫如順流，趣時如嚮赴
[Person] 加之以V.P., V.P., V.P.+ 如+V.P., V.P.+ 如+V.P., V.P.+ 如+V.P., V.P.+ 如+V.P. (Key: V.P. = verb phrase)

Lu Ji:
Taizu, completing the establishment of Wu with virtue, was bright and sagacious, capacious and magnanimous. He sought out the worthy as if lagging behind, cared for the people as if they were young children, treated learned men with resplendent virtue, and endeared the benevolent by baring his heart.[44]

---

42   Ban Biao's "Wang ming lun" is included in *Han shu*, 100a.4208-12, and *WX*, 52.2263-68.

43   *WX*, 52.2267.

44   Ibid., 53.2321.

太祖成之以德，聰明叡達，懿度弘遠矣。其求賢如不及，恤民如稚子，接
士盡盛德之容，親仁馨丹府之愛。
Person 成之以 N., V.P., V.P., V.P.+ 如+V.P., V.P.+ 如+V.P., V.P.+ 之, V.P.+ 之
(Key: N. = noun; V.P. = verb phrase)

Example (2)
Ban Biao:
當食吐哺，   Spitting out his food while eating,
納子房之策   he accepted Zifang's recommendation.[45]
V.P., 納 Person 之策   (Key: V.P. = verb phrase)

Lu Ji:
披懷虛己   Opening up and humbling himself,
以納謀士之算   he accepted the strategists' plans.[46]
V.P., 以納 Person 之算   (Key: V.P. = verb phrase)

Example (3)
Ban Biao:
寤戍卒之言   Enlightened by the words of a border guard,
斷懷土之情   he cut off his attachment to the land.[47]
寤 Person 之言, 斷 V.O. 之情   (Key: V.O. = verb-object)

Lu Ji:
賢諸葛之言   Taking Zhuge [Jin]'s words to be worthy,
而割情欲之歡   he severed the pleasures of passion and
                                        desire.[48]
賢 Person 之言, 而割 N. 之歡   (Key: N. = noun)

Example (4)
Ban Biao:
高四皓之名   Holding the Four Hoary Heads in high
                                        regard,
割肌膚之愛   he severed his love for physical intimacy.[49]
高 Person 之名, 割 N. 之愛   (Key: N. = noun)

---

45   Ibid., 52.2267.
46   Ibid., 53.2322.
47   Ibid., 52.2267.
48   Ibid., 53.2322.
49   Ibid., 52.2267.

Lu Ji:

高張公之德　　　　Holding Master Zhang in high regard for
　　　　　　　　　　his virtue,

而省游田之娛　　　he held back the enjoyment of outing and
　　　　　　　　　　hunting.[50]

高Person 之德, 而省 V.O. 之娛　(Key: V.O. = verb-object)

By mapping Sun Quan onto these "syntactical templates" for depicting a ruler, what Lu Ji produced was essentially a generic remembrance of the Wu emperor: like Liu Bang, he was eager to recruit and promote talented people, willing to listen to admonition, and showed respect and care for his advisers. However, as we would expect from Lu Ji, his mapping was not an exact one. By diversifying and expanding on these line patterns, and raising the register of his diction, he was able to construct a particularly vivid and lively image of Sun Quan. His construction seems to suggest that to remember someone is to not only see his semblance in earlier models but also to parse out his distinctiveness. Only by mapping Sun Quan onto and against the image of the good rulers of the past can one remember him as one of them and yet distinct in his own way.

　　Lu Ji uses associative remembrance both in his creation of Sun Quan's image as a ruler and in his depiction of the ministers and generals of Wu. This way of remembering people is manifested linguistically through pairing or grouping, either by placing names side-by-side or by mapping a person onto someone else's image. Associative remembrance is so strong in early historical discourse on people that an individual is rarely portrayed simply on his own: Jia Yi's "Guo Qin," Ban Biao's "Wangming lun," and the *Han shu* appraisal cited above are all good examples of this. While Lu Ji's use of associative remembrance through syntactical templates was active, even critical, it occasionally revealed the pressure of earlier models. A good example is the following two lines that he wrote of Sun Quan:

拔呂蒙於戎行　He plucked Lü Meng from the military ranks
識潘濬於係虜　And spotted Pan Jun among the captives.[51]

This first line is a reference to Lü Meng's promotion from his low rank as a young soldier in the army of his uncle Deng Dang 鄧當. What is revealing here is the fact that the one who actually discovered and plucked Lü Meng out of his

---

50　Ibid., 53.2322.

51　Ibid., 53.2321.

low rank was Sun Ce 孫策 (175-200), Sun Quan's older brother, and not Sun Quan himself.[52] I would surmise that it was his template lines, such as these lines by Ban Biao about Liu Bang—"He lifted Han Xin from the rank and file/ And took in Chen Ping from his exile" 舉韓信於行陳，收陳平於亡命—that pressured Lu Ji into stretching his reference here. His references are otherwise all quite truthful in the sense that they can be corroborated by other accounts such as those found in *Sanguo zhi* 三國志 (The records of the Three States).

Imprinting the Forefathers

There is no doubt that part of Lu Ji's aim in writing this essay was to commemorate his grandfather Lu Xun and his father Lu Kang as Wu generals. To achieve this, he appears to have gone to some length to manipulate the technique of pairing and grouping individuals. This passage from Chen Shou's *Sanguo zhi* biography of Sun Quan can serve as a context for analyzing Lu Ji's portrayal of Lu Xun:

> He treated Zhang Zhao with the respect shown to a Grand Mentor, while Zhou Yu, Chen Pu, Lü Fan, and others were made generals and leaders. As he recruited outstanding talents and sought out reputable men, Lu Su, Zhuge Jin, and others became his retainers.[53]

> 待張昭以師傅之禮，而周瑜、程普、呂範等為將率。招延俊秀，聘求名士，魯肅、諸葛瑾等始為賓客。

Here, Chen Shou lists six major aides to Sun Quan, obviously excluding Lu Xun. By comparison, Lu Ji would not only include Lu Xun, but also place him toward the top of his list:

於是張昭為師傅;　　　　　　　Thereupon, Zhang Zhao was made the Grand Mentor;
周瑜、陸公、魯肅、呂蒙之疇　Those in the company of Zhou Yu, Master Lu [Xun], Lu Su, and Lü Meng

入為腹心　　　　　　　　　　　were taken in like entrails and hearts,
出作股肱...　　　　　　　　　　and dispatched like arms and thighs...[54]

52　See Li Shan's notes in *WX*, 53.2321 and Knechtges, "Han and Six Dynasties Parallel Prose," 88 n. 55.

53　*Sanguo zhi*, 47.1116

54　*WX*, 53.2312.

He lists Lu Xun immediately after Zhou Yu in this passage, and he would pair Lu Xun with Zhou Yu again in two other parts of his essay:

> Yet Zhou Yu pressed ahead with a single force, expelled them (i.e. Cao Cao and his troops) from Red Cliff, causing them to lose their banners and confuse the tracks, barely able to stay alive as they retreated into the distance... Yet Master Lu likewise defeated them (i.e. Liu Bei and his troops) at Xiling, crushing their armies and sending them into dispersal, causing Liu Bei to be trapped before he could be rescued, only to lose his life at Yong'an.[55]

> 而周瑜驅我偏師，黜之赤壁，喪旗亂轍，僅而獲免，收跡遠遁... 而陸公亦挫之西陵，覆師敗績，困而後濟，絕命永安。

執鞭鞠躬，	He held his horse whip and bended his body
以重陸公之威；	to show his respect for Master Lu (Xun);
悉委武衛，	He dispatched all his military guards
以濟周瑜之師。	to support Zhou Yu's troops.[56]

In the popular memory of later times, including our own, Zhou Yu is by far the more remembered figure, mostly due to romanticized characterizations of him and his victory over Cao Cao in the battle at Red Cliff in works like Su Shi's 蘇軾 (1037-1101) "Nian nu jiao" 念奴嬌 and Luo Guanzhong's 羅貫中 (ca.1280-1360) *Sanguo yanyi* 三國演義. The *Sanguo zhi* passage cited above, though obviously not intended to be an extensive listing of Sun Quan's aides, might inadvertently hint at Zhou Yu's higher standing in popular memory even as early as the third century. Seen in this light, Lu Ji's repeated matching of Lu Xun with Zhou Yu can be seen as a purposeful manipulation of the technique of pairing, aimed at upholding his grandfather's status.

It is indisputable that Lu Xun, Sun Quan's Chancellor, and Lu Kang, a Grand Marshal under Sun Hao, were important, influential, and highly respected members of the Wu court. However, Lu Yun's letters clearly reveal that the Lu brothers were very concerned about how their two forefathers were portrayed. While it may appear natural for a son or grandson to be biased toward his own forefathers and wish for them to be remembered in positive light, I would argue that in this case Lu Ji actually felt the need to defend his grandfather's and father's legacies. Doing so toward the end of his essay, he no longer relies on

---

55   Ibid., 53.2315.
56   Ibid., 53.2322.

associative remembrance, which has guided his depiction of Wu officials all along, choosing instead to emphasize the singularity of Lu Xun and Lu Kang. To show the full picture, I will begin with a peculiar statement that Lu Ji cites in his argument. In the last part of his essay, Lu Ji singles out one specific opinion for rebuttal. He attributes it to only an unspecified interlocutor:

> Someone said: "Wu and Shu were two states that were bounded together like lips and teeth. As Shu was annihilated, Wu was destroyed; the reasoning for this was unmistakable."[57]

> 或曰：「吳、蜀脣齒之國，蜀滅則吳亡，理則然矣。」

Why is this opinion so significant that Lu Ji feels the need to raise and then refute it? Lu Xun and Lu Kang were no doubt deeply involved in Wu's dealings with Shu throughout their entire official careers. As Lu Ji reminds us in his essay, it was Lu Xun who led a successful campaign against Liu Bei's advance in 222,[58] not only destroying Liu Bei's encampment in the Yiling 夷陵 area (considered the western region from the Wu perspective; Sun Quan would change its name to Xiling 西陵),[59] but also inflicting tens of thousands of deaths on his armies, completely defeating them.[60] As this was Liu Bei's last battle before his death the following year, the defeat can be said to have contributed to his death, and this is exactly how Lu Ji viewed it. Later on, as the Wu-Shu relationship stabilized and improved under the stewardship of Zhuge Liang 諸葛亮 (181-234) on the Shu side, Lu Xun continued to play a major role on the Wu side. In this period, Wu-Shu relations peaked with the signing of a treaty of alliance, in which the two states vowed to back each other in the case of an attack by Wei and not to encroach upon each other's land.[61] However, a revealing moment for the nature of the Wu-Shu relationship came in 263, when Wei launched a major attack on Shu, defeating Zhuge Zhan 諸葛瞻 (227-263) and forcing Liu Chan's surrender.[62] The most detailed account of Wu's immediate

---

57   Ibid., 53.2324.

58   This was the second year of the Zhangwu 章武 reign period and the first year of the Huangwu 黃武 reign period.

59   Sun Quan changed its name to Xiling in 222; see *Sanguo zhi*, 47.1126.

60   Ibid., 58.1346-47, 32.890 (here Lu Xun is referred to by his original name Lu Yi 議). Liu Bei was forced to ascend the Ma'an Mountain 馬鞍山, where he came under Lu Xun's attack from all four directions.

61   *Sanguo zhi*, 47.1135.

62   Ibid., 33.900.

response is found in *Xiangyang ji* 襄陽記.[63] According to this account, when the news of Shu's defeat reached Wu, Emperor Jing 景, that is, Sun Xiu, dispatched an army to the west. As *Xiangyang ji* has it, "outwardly, [Wu was acting] on the pretext of rescuing and aiding [Shu]; inwardly, they wanted to attack Luo Xian 羅憲 (218-270),"[64] the Shu governor of Badong 巴東, which bordered Wu on the west.[65] When Luo Xian put up a strong resistance,[66] Lu Kang was the one who led an army to increase the encirclement of Luo Xian, which lasted for six months. It was not until a Wei army came to Luo Xian's rescue that Lu Kang retreated.[67] Wu's "intent to absorb Shu" 兼蜀之志, as *Xiangyang ji* puts it, was fully revealed in this episode. This brief sketch sums up what may be called Wu's "westward strategy." As a study by Chen Jinfeng 陳金鳳 suggests, the reason Lu Xun and other members of the Lu clan were stationed in Jingzhou 荊州 for prolonged periods was not only for "defending against the north," but also for "guarding against the west."[68] Lu Xun and Lu Kang were evidently involved in shaping this westward strategy of Wu, which was directly tied to Wu's handling of its relationship with Shu.

The reception of Wu's westward strategy was not unanimous. Luo Xian was, unsurprisingly, highly critical. He reportedly said this when he came under Wu's attack: "Our dynasty has been toppled, but even though Wu is bounded to us like lips and teeth, they do not rescue us from our troubles. Instead, they seek to benefit from them, abandoning our alliance and defying our treaty. Now that Han [that is, Shu] has been lost, how can Wu survive for long? How, then, can I allow myself to be turned into a surrendered captive of Wu!"[69] 本朝傾覆，吳為唇齒，不恤我難而徼其利，背盟違約。且漢已亡，吳何得久，寧能為吳降虜乎！ In these words attributed to Luo Xian, we hear the same opinion that Lu Ji refers to in his essay. But the charges made against Wu through Luo Xian—that is, that Wu had committed a strategic as well as a moral mistake—were somewhat muted by Lu Ji, since he only used *huo yue* ("someone said")—as opposed to a more specific source—to set up the interlocution about these charges. Even within the Wu court, there were different feelings and opinions about its westward strategy and, in particular, its attack

---

63   *Xiangyang ji*, also known as *Xiangyang qiujiu ji* 襄陽耆舊記, was attributed to Xi Zhaochi 習鑿齒 (d. 383).

64   *Sanguo zhi*, 41.1008 n. 1; *Jin shu*, 57.155.

65   Luo Xian was guarding Yong'an City 永安城 during the Wei attack.

66   Luo Xian put up a strong resistance against the Shu general Bu Xie 步協, who could not contain him.

67   *Sanguo zhi*, 41.1008 n. 1; *Jin shu*, 57.1552.

68   Chen Jinfeng, "Yizhou zhanlue yu Wu Shu guanxi," *Jiang Han luntan* 2 (2008): 117.

69   *Sanguo zhi*, 41.1008 n. 1; *Jin shu*, 57.1551.

on Luo Xian. The *Sanguo zhi* recounts that Hua He 華覈 (d. ca. 275), an Aide-to-the-Secretariat (*Zhongshu cheng* 中書丞), had submitted a memorial to express his dissent upon hearing Shu's defeat. In it, he subtly makes the point that Wu should not have "lost and abandoned" Shu; mentioning Lu Kang's name, he was possibly directing his criticism at the Wu general as well.[70]

Seen in the ensuing context following the demise of Shu and, later Wu, the argument that Wu's destruction was inevitably tied to Shu's could be interpreted as a veiled criticism of Wu's action against Shu following the latter's defeat by Wei and of its westward strategy in general. And this certainly had ramifications for how Lu Xun and Lu Kang's legacies were judged. As mentioned before, Lu Yun had complained that others' accounts of their forefathers "mostly did not exhaust the reasoning."[71] By singling out the Shu argument for rebuttal, Lu Ji is attempting to "exhaust the reasoning" on his forefathers' behalf. Where it concerns Wu, Lu Ji insists that human factor is the most crucial in a state's survival; but in analyzing Shu's defeat, he nonetheless attributes it to the difficult terrain in the west, that is, to the lack of *di li*, "geographical advantage." To make this point, he inserts the voice of his grandfather Lu Xun, quoting his description of Liu Bei's offensive, undertaken in Shu's difficult terrain, as a "long snake" (*changshe* 長蛇), adding that "the course [of its eventual demise] was clear."[72] As pointed out by David Knechtges, "there is no other mention of Lu Xun's metaphor of comparing the Shu army to a long snake" in available sources.[73] This detail suggests that what Lu Ji is recounting here is based on his family lore, that is, narrative about his grandfather that he had heard growing up. Furthermore, Lu Ji also channels his father Lu Kang's voice, writing that following Shu's defeat, "the Son of Heaven, having gathered various opinions, consulted Grand Marshal Master Lu [Kang]"; and then he cites Lu Kang's advice to the emperor in full. He follows this with a description of how Lu Kang, "with a *single* force of thirty thousand," defeated the rebel Bu Chan 步闡 (d. 272) in Xiling and later, "*separately* commanded five thousand crack troops to repulse the water battalion in the west." In this final part of his narrative, Lu Ji no longer relies on pairing or grouping; instead, he highlights

---

70   *Sanguo zhi*, 65.1464.

71   *Lu Shilong wenji jiaozhu*, 8.1117-18.

72   Ibid., 10.1020-21.

73   Knechtges, "Han and Six Dynasties Parallel Prose," 91 n. 70. By the metaphor, Lu Xun meant that the front and back of the Shu army were so far apart that it was vulnerable to attack. *Changshe*, "long snake," was often used as a derogatory term to refer to one's enemy in the early medieval period (see, for example, Du Tao's 杜弢 [d. 315] letter in *Jin shu* 70.2622); Lu Xun's usage was obviously different here.

his two forefathers as a singular force and presence in Wu history. In the end, he goes further, using his father's death to mark the startling decline of Wu.[74]

It is also worth mentioning that Hua He, who was critical of Wu's decision to abandon Shu, would later be memorialized in the *Sanguo zhi* for his admonitions of the emperor.[75] Chen Shou gave him this high praise: "I have observed that Hua He had presented sound advice several times while expecting his own demise—he was nothing short of a loyal minister" 予觀覈數獻良規，期於自盡，庶幾忠臣矣.[76] But in listing the good officials of Wu in his essay, Lu Ji did not include Hua He's name. In this omission, one detects a much more selective and contentious remembrance beneath the surface of Lu Ji's "complete" recall; through his manipulation of pairing and his later shift to singularity in depicting his forefathers, we also see how he was not held up by his cultural tool, but rather, used it fully to his advantage.

Conclusion

Lu Ji was not a passive reader, nor was he a passive writer. His attitude of examining the works of earlier writers, observing the "many changes in how they dispel words and employ diction" and grasping "the beauty and ugliness or the good and bad" in them, is revealed in his dynamic and critical imitation of earlier works, after which he not only modeled his syntactical structuring and even argumentative logic, but also transforming what he borrowed as well. The result, as far as remembrance is concerned, was an active play between Lu Ji, the one who was remembering, and the cultural tool he relied on for his remembrance. In the end, the textual space for remembrance that was gained through the specific reading practice of examining techniques and the specific writing practice of critical imitation was not a completely delimiting one. In the hand of a skillful writer, syntax and diction, naming and pairing, and argument and narrative were maneuvered, consciously and actively, into an artful remembrance that is both personal and collective, traditional and inventive. While earlier expository prose about a bygone state was written from the perspective of a distant and objective observer, Lu Ji appropriated that perspective to invent the voice of the subject of a fallen state. Doing so, he was engaging with more than remembrance: he was engaging with the literary history of remembrance as well.

---

74   *Lu Shiheng wenji jiaozhu*, 10.1021.
75   *Sanguo zhi*, 65.1469.
76   Ibid., 65.1470.

Bibliography

Brashier, K.E. *Public Memory in Early China*. Cambridge, MA: Harvard University Asia Center, 2014.

Chen Jinfeng 陳金鳳. "Yizhou zhanlue yu Wu Shu guanxi" 益州戰略與吳蜀關係. *Jiang Han luntan* 2 (2008): 111-18.

Chen, Jack W. "On the Act and Representation of Reading in Medieval China." *Journal of the American Oriental Society* 129.1 (2009): 57-71.

Gaspardone, Emile. "Le Discours de la perte du Wou par Lou Ki." *Sinologica* 4 (1958): 189-225.

Han shu 漢書. Compiled by Ban Gu 班固. Taipei: Hongye shuju youxiangongsi, 1996.

Jin shu 晉書. Compiled by Fang Xuanling 房玄齡. 10 vols. Reprint, Beijing: Zhonghua shuju, 2010.

Kinugawa Kenji 依川賢次. "Rikuchō mogishi shōkō" 六朝模擬詩小考. *Chūgoku bungaku hō* 中國文學報 31 (1980): 29-63.

Knechtges, David R. "Han and Six Dynasties Parallel Prose." *Renditions* 33 & 34 (1990): 78-94.

Kroll, Paul W. *A Student's Dictionary of Classical and Medieval Chinese*. Leiden: Brill, 2015.

Lai, Chiu-Mi. "The Craft of Original Imitation: Lu Ji's Imitations of Han Old Poems." In *Studies in Early Medieval Chinese Literature and Cultural History in Honor of Richard B. Mather and Donald Holzman*, edited by Paul W. Kroll and David R. Knechtges, 17-48. Provo, Utah: T'ang Studies Society, 2003.

Lee, Brigitta A. "Imitation, Remembrance and the Formation of the Poetic Past in Early Medieval China." Ph.D. diss., Princeton University, 2007.

Lin Wenyue 林文月. "Lu Ji di nigushi" 陸機的擬古詩. In *Zhonggu wenxue lun cong* 中古文學論叢. Taipei: Da'an, 1989.

Lu Shiheng wenji jiaozhu 陸士衡文集校注. Annotated by Liu Yunhao 劉運好. 2 vols. Nanjing: Fenghuang chuanmei chuban jituan, 2007.

Lu Shilong wenji jiaozhu 陸士龍文集校注. Annotated by Liu Yunhao 劉運好. 2 vols. Nanjing: Fenghuang chuban chuanmei chuban jituan, 2010.

Nugent, Christopher M.B. *Manifest in Words, Written on Paper: Producing and Circulating Poetry in Tang Dynasty China*. Cambridge, MA: Harvard University Asia Center, 2011.

Owen, Stephen. *Readings in Chinese Literary Thought*. Cambridge, MA: Council on East Asian Studies, Harvard University, 1992.

Richter, Antje. *Letters & Epistolary Culture in Early Medieval China*. Seattle: University of Washington Press, 2013.

Sanguo zhi 三國志. Compiled by Chen Shou 陳壽. 5 vols. Reprint, Beijing: Zhonghua shuju, 1985.

Shi ji 史記. Compiled by Sima Qian 司馬遷. 10 vols. Reprint, Beijing: Zhonghua shuju, 2002.

Sui shu 隋書. Compiled by Wei Zheng 魏徵. 6 vols. Reprint, Beijing: Zhonghua shuju, 2014.

Wertsch, James V. "Collective Memory." In *Memory in Mind and Culture*, edited by Pascal Boyer and James V. Wertsch, 117-37. Cambridge: Cambridge University Press, 2009.

Wertsch, James V. *Mind as Action*. New York: Oxford University Press, 1998.

Xiao Tong 蕭統, ed. *Wen xuan* 文選. 6 vols. Reprint, Shanghai: Shanghai guji chubanshe, 1997.

Yang Zhaolei 楊朝蕾. "Cong 'Bianwang lun' kan Lu Ji nigu zhong de chuangxin qingxiang" 從辯亡論看陸機擬古中的創新傾向. *Wuhan keji daxue xuebao* 13.3 (2011): 362-66.

CHAPTER 2

Intertextuality and Cultural Memory in Early Medieval China: Jiang Yan's Imitations of Nearly Lost and Lost Writers

Wendy Swartz

Early medieval poets bore witness to and participated in one of the most re-markable expansions of cultural wealth in Chinese history. This boom included the addition of new literary genres and discursive forms, as well as the produc-tion and preservation of numerous examples of these various genres and forms. New areas of learning were also developed in the forms of an imported philosophy and religion (e.g. Buddhism) and of the indigenous, metaphysical *xuan* 玄 learning that probed into the mystery of the Dao through a syncretic use of various scholastic traditions and intellectual currents. Furthermore, the period from the third to the sixth century was marked by the rapid accumula-tion of commentaries on classical texts and translations of foreign works. The impact of contemporary intellectual trends on poetry in this formative period was profound. Key material conditions supported this cultural and intellectual growth. The increasing availability and affordability of paper during this pe-riod substantially facilitated the preservation, duplication, and circulation of texts. Scholars could write out texts, either word for word or for their essential points, during their course of study, so as not to forget the information. This learning and mnemonic practice yielded additional copies of texts. Book own-ers could hire scribes to make copies of their books and readers could travel to private libraries or otherwise borrow from individuals to transcribe duplicate copies of books. Even poorer households could boast some sort of library col-lection.[1] The avenues and means for readers and writers to access books in-creased exponentially during this period.

For their creative acts, early medieval writers had at their disposal a diverse range of textual sources and cultural signs that extended beyond the canonical literary heritage. Many capitalized on the growing web of literary and cultural materials, whose textual strands could be woven into new patterns and

---

1   For more on book circulation in the early medieval period, see Li Duanliang, *Zhongguo gudai tushu liutong shi* 中國古代圖書流通史 (Shanghai: Shanghai renmin wenxue chubanshe, 2000), 118-70.

configurations. To read and write well demanded fluency in the growing, shared textual tradition. In early medieval China, cultural literacy was very much determined by competence in *xuan* discourse and the ability to mobilize its continually expanding set of allusions, arguments, notions, and values for diverse purposes and audiences. This cultural currency underwrote a fluidity in composing poetic texts that freely wove together materials from different sets of sources (*rujia* 儒家 texts and *daojia* 道家 texts), different brands of thought (Lao-Zhuang, Classicist, and Buddhist), and different branches of learning (poetry, classics, philosophy, and religion). Writers' use of a heterogeneous assemblage of resources illustrates the fluid, intertextual configuration of early medieval poetry and thought.

How early medieval writers understood and manipulated the textual and cultural signs of a common lexicon to produce meaning is the concern of intertextual study. Intertextuality is "the general discursive space that makes a text intelligible," as Jonathan Culler writes.[2] A pioneer in the theory of intertextuality, Julia Kristeva argued for the "literary word" to be approached as "an *intersection of textual surfaces* rather than a *point* (fixed meaning), as a dialogue among several writings: that of the writer, the addressee... and the contemporary or earlier cultural contexts."[3] This argument is adapted from the Russian philosopher and literary critic Mikhail Bakhtin. In this view, meaning is produced by an intertextual constellation of signs and is layered or multifaceted rather than fixed or singular. Each instance of quotation, allusion, adaptation, or rewriting creates a semantic saturation that potentially enriches both the manifest and source texts.

Mastery of texts—as demonstrated by recognition, quotation, allusion, continuation or revision—enabled a writer to participate in the preservation, transmission, and revitalization of that very culture. On the framework for communication within a culture across time, Aleida Assmann writes with particular insight:

> Through culture, humans create a temporal framework that transcends the individual life span relating past, present, and future. Cultures create a contract between the living, the dead, and the not yet living. In recalling, iterating, reading, commenting, criticizing, discussing what was

---

2   Culler, *The Pursuit of Signs: Semiotics, Literature, Deconstruction* (Ithaca: Cornell University Press, 1981), 106.

3   Kristeva, *Desire in Language: A Semiotic Approach to Literature and Art*, trans. Thomas Gora, Alice Jardine, and Leon S. Roudiez (New York: Columbia University Press, 1980), 65.

deposited in the remote or recent past, humans participate in extended horizons of meaning-production.[4]

From this vantage point, the past, especially for strong written cultures, becomes an inherited and continually replenished store of textual and cultural signs and patterns with which writers maintain an organic, constantly evolving relationship of give and take. Cultures are continually coming into being, their capital continually being used, expanded, even squandered or lost. Literature stores and manifests the memory of this continuous process. In her powerful analysis of the relation between intertextuality and cultural memory in Russian Formalist literature, Renate Lachmann argued that "the memory of a text is its intertextuality. Literature supplies the memory for a culture and records such a memory. Intertextuality demonstrates the process by which a culture continually rewrites and retranscribes itself."[5] Intertextuality is a form of participation in a textual tradition. And literature is the compendium of a society's cultural memory, which is stored, encoded, objectified, and embodied in symbolic forms such as texts. As a store of shared knowledge, experiences, and signs, cultural memory as manifested in literature can be accessed, interpreted, and reshaped in new commemorative acts by any one of its participating members. Each resultant text becomes a confluence of interpretation and invention, remembrance and revision.

Questions for Cultural Memory: Jiang Yan's Imitations Project

One of the most complex forms of textual recall is imitation.[6] Like quotation and allusion, *imitatio*, the imitation of models, constitutes an act of homage to past works and writers. On a more functional level, these forms of remembrance can help preserve the past. Ralph Waldo Emerson once mused about how through quotation and imitation, Dante "absorbed" and "survives for us" the works of Albert, St. Buonaventura, and Thomas Aquinas.[7] Yet through this very absorption, which always transforms the foreign matter, these acts of commemoration reshape the past as they summon it to the present. Imitation

---

4 Assmann, "Canon and Archive," in *A Companion to Cultural Memory Studies*, ed. Astrid Erll and Ansgar Nünning (Berlin: De Gruyter, 2010), 97.

5 Lachmann, *Memory and Literature: Intertextuality in Russian Literature*, trans. Roy Sellars and Anthony Wall (Minneapolis: University of Minnesota Press, 1997), 15.

6 On literary imitation, see also pp. 101ff. in this volume.

7 Emerson, "Quotation and Originality," in *Letters and Social Aims* (Boston: Houghton, Mifflin, 1904), 179.

not only serves to preserve, but can also revitalize, the past. On this point, Lachmann writes:

> *Imitatio* becomes an act of memory: it draws up cultural summae, establishes new paths toward continuity, and stores up cultural information. Indeed, *imitatio* emerges as the very textual practice that reveals that the work of forging new signs is a process of resuscitation. This is the reanimation of dead meaning and dead form that offsets any cultural loss, that builds up semantic tension, and that places the older text inside a new one and thereby recharges it.[8]

From this vantage point, imitation performs a monumental service for a culture's memory: it saves information for a culture, it counterbalances cultural loss in its revitalization of past works and forms, and it links together the past, present, and future. However, the act of resuscitating the dead is neither a simple nor innocuous procedure, as Lachmann's choice of metaphor already implies. The "dead" that is brought back to life is never the same as its previous incarnation. The reanimated dead writer is reshaped or disfigured, depending on the perspective, and always managed by the new text. While an imitation may offset the cultural loss of a forgotten or obscure writer, or even simply of a well-known past writer in cases where aspects of that writer's output have gotten lost in the temporal distance, and may thus represent a gain in the overall assessment of a culture's heritage, how is the restoration made, and at what cost? How has the new text recast the old one in an effort to sustain and save it? The stakes are even higher for a culture's memory when old texts that were the objects of imitation have become limited, fragmentary, or lost.

Examples from Jiang Yan's 江淹 (444-505) magisterial series of imitations, "Thirty Poems in Various Forms" 雜體詩三十首, make a strong case in point. The ambition and scope of Jiang Yan's imitations project are unparalleled in early medieval China. Jiang wrote imitations of thirty well-known poets spanning from the Han period to the author's own time, with each poem characterizing the earlier or contemporaneous poet with a perceived main theme or subgenre (e.g. "singing my cares" for Ruan Ji, "telling my grief" for Pan Yue, "farmstead dwelling" for Tao Yuanming). As suggested by the pastiche quality of his imitations, Jiang Yan seems to have drawn from each subject's larger corpus of texts when possible, rather than merely a single piece. Through quotation, adaptation, reminiscence, amplification, and/or trimming, these imitations are represented as essential summaries of the imitated poets. The models selected by Jiang Yan would soon find their place in the first or second rank of Zhong Rong's 鍾嶸 (ca. 469-518) *Shipin* 詩品 (Grades of the poets) and the

---

8 Lachmann, *Memory and Literature*, 198-99.

imitations they inspired in Jiang Yan would later be canonized in the *Wen xuan* 文選 (Selections of refined literature). His imitations project can be said to be successful in at least the following respects: it not only elevated Jiang Yan to be the most represented Qi-Liang poet in the *Wen xuan*, but also many of his imitations were praised by later critics as faithfully resembling his models, with one imitation even fooling some Song editors who included the piece as the sixth poem in Tao Yuanming's "Returning to the Farm to Dwell" (Five poems) series as well as the usually astute reader, Su Shi 蘇軾 (1037-1101), who wrote a poem to match what he believed to have been Tao's work.

Furthermore, after the completion of this imitations project, Jiang Yan's poetic output dramatically declined according to available evidence, as if there was little left to write after his summary of the various achievements in the development of pentasyllabic verse. Jiang Yan's alleged lack of productivity late in life not surprisingly invited sneering speculation and critical judgment from other writers. His official biography in the *Nan shi* 南史 (History of the Southern Dynasties) records a story about how Zhang Xie 張協 (ca. 255-ca. 310) once appeared in Jiang Yan's dream to demand the return of a bolt of brocade he had lent to Jiang and how Guo Pu 郭璞 (276-324) appeared in another dream to take back the multicolored brush he had loaned Jiang.[9] Mockery and bemusement color the speculation that without the writing instruments borrowed from other poets, Jiang could no longer produce beautiful works on his own. The condemnation is clear: his talent was exhausted only because it was merely on loan. This anecdote surely implies an indictment of the perils of making the imitation of others the whole basis of one's creative talent. But does it not also suggest the notion that composition is the utilization of available sources, and when those sources have been exhausted, there remains nothing with which to write? And if writing is a form of remembrance, then the completion of a summary of the whole range of voices in pentasyllabic verse, past and present, could signify in a figural reading that the writer has remembered all that he cares to remember through his writing.

Several arguments in Jiang Yan's preface to this imitations series suggest that the author viewed this project as an effort to draw up a summa of pentasyllabic poetry. At the outset, he maintains that examples of poetry from different eras and various writers each can be distinct from one another yet all can be admirable. He then goes on to denounce other readers for embracing a single bias toward the one and only model each fancies:

> The songs of Chu and the airs of Han are not of a single structure; the compositions of Wei and the creations of Jin are also of two distinct

---

9   See *Nan shi* 南史 (Beijing: Zhonghua shuju, 1975), 59.1451; the *Shipin* includes only Jiang Yan's dream of Guo Pu in a nearly identical anecdote.

forms. Just as when indigo and crimson form a multicolor pattern, their mixed and motley transformations are inexhaustible; or when the *gong* and *shang* modes produce sounds, their pliant, delicate manner is without end. Therefore, moth-like eyebrows might not have the same appearance, though they all move the soul; and fragrant plants might not share the same scent, but they all gladden the spirit. Is it not so? As for the various worthies in our world, each is stuck in his own infatuations. All who discuss the sweet must despise the bitter; and all who like vermilion must reject the plain. How can this be called a thorough understanding or tolerant view, or fondness for the distant and universal love?[10]

夫楚謠漢風，既非一骨。 魏制晉造，固亦二體。譬猶藍朱成彩，雜錯之變無窮。宮商為音，靡曼之態不極。故娥眉詎同貌而俱動於魄，芳草寧共氣而皆悅於魂。不其然歟？至於世之諸賢，各滯所迷，莫不論甘而忌辛，好丹而非素。豈所謂通方廣恕，好遠兼愛者哉？

Jiang moreover notes that the development of pentasyllabic verse from the Han through the Jin produced such diverse styles that evaluating the superiority of one over another would be as meaningless as trying to "discriminate between black and brown or warp and weft, or differentiate between gold and jade or falling and rising." Rather than to make judgmental discriminations between things that are simply different, he advocates a universal appreciation of the various writers and styles: "This lowly writer humbly submits that all can share in the beautiful and the good" 僕以為亦合其美並善而已. The selection of thirty particular styles to imitate so as to exemplify "the beautiful and the good" implies a summa of pentasyllabic verse at its best. In this essay I am not interested in reading Jiang Yan's imitations against the bodies of original works for the sake of evaluating which is superior or what is new. Rather, I will explore the implications of how a writer who has positioned himself as the guardian and transmitter of the whole of a literary past remembers that past, and in cases where he preserved for us what would turn out to be lost or nearly lost writers, what questions his imitations pose for cultural memory.[11] His imitations of Sun Chuo 孫綽 (314-371), Xie Hun 謝混 (381?-412), and Xu Xun 許詢 (ca. 326-after 347) furnish the examples used in this study.

---

10   Lu Qinli 逯欽立, ed., *Xian Qin Han Wei Jin Nanbeichao shi* 先秦漢魏晉南北朝詩 (hereafter cited as *XS*) (Beijing: Zhonghua shuju, 1983), 2:1569. I thank Zeb Raft for his comments on my reading of Jiang Yan's preface and poems.

11   For a book-length study that examines Jiang Yan's imitations vis-à-vis their models and the early medieval culture surrounding imitation writing, see Nicholas Morrow Williams, *Imitations of the Self: Jiang Yan and Chinese Poetics* (Leiden/Boston: Brill, 2015).

Heterogeneity and Containment: The Case of Sun Chuo

Sun Chuo is relatively little known today when measured against his stature in his own time. The early medieval historian Tan Daoluan 檀道鸞 (fl. 459) described the poet as being, along with Xu Xun, "the literary patriarch of his time" (*yi shi wen zong* 一時文宗).[12] Sun also distinguished himself as one of the most colorful and flamboyant figures in the impressive cast of characters that starred in stories recorded in the early medieval cultural compendium *Shishuo xinyu* 世說新語 (Talk of the ages and new anecdotes). These anecdotes feature not only his talent as a poet but also his brazen penchant for self-promotion, which can be seen in several comical episodes in which the poet attempted to elevate his stature by claiming intimacy with deceased personages in elegies he was tasked to write. Most of Sun Chuo's works have not survived, a fate shared by many other examples of *xuanyan* 玄言 poetry, which used concepts, symbols, and lexica from the *Laozi* 老子, *Zhuangzi* 莊子, and *Classic of Changes* 易經, to discourse on the Dao (whose marker is *xuan*, translated variously as "mysterious," "abstruse" or "dark"). For much of its reception, this type of poetry was maligned and disregarded, and it is now mostly lost. The scathing reviews by late Six Dynasties critics surely had something to do with its later neglect. Tan Daoluan decried the damage that Sun Chuo and Xu Xun allegedly inflicted upon the classical tradition by incorporating materials from the alternative repertoires of Daoist and Buddhist texts.[13] Zhong Rong added the charge of the supposed ruination of the "affective force of Jian'an 建安 poetry" with bland, insipid discourse on philosophical principles.[14] Were it not, then, for the fortuitous discovery of fragments of the seventh-century anthology *Wenguan cilin* 文館詞林 (Lodge of literature and forest of lyrics) during the nineteenth and early twentieth century in Japan, the work and legacy of Sun Chuo would have been mostly a matter of anecdote, for only a mere handful of poems and Jiang Yan's imitation piece had been transmitted. The recovery of three long exchange poems by Sun Chuo in these fragments has yielded a fuller picture of the range and complexity of his poetry.[15]

---

12   Excerpt from Tan's *Xu Jin yangqiu* 續晉陽秋, cited in *Shishuo xinyu* (hereafter cited as *SSXY*), 4/85.

13   See *SSXY*, 4/85

14   *Shipin jizhu* 詩品集注, ed. Cao Xu 曹旭 (Shanghai: Shanghai guji chubanshe, 1994), 24.

15   A fourth exchange poem has been attributed to Sun Chuo, one written to Wen Jiao 溫嶠, who became a national hero after aiding the suppression of both Wang Dun 王敦 (266-324) and Su Jun 蘇峻 (d. 328) in the early years of the Eastern Jin. However, Cao Daoheng 曹道衡 has convincingly cast doubt on the attribution of this work to Sun Chuo. Given

For most of Chinese literary history, Jiang Yan's imitation of Sun Chuo's style could boast an outsized influence on the readers' imagination. It, along with a few of Sun's own works that circulated independently in anthologies, purported to represent the poet at his finest or most defining.[16]

孫廷尉綽雜述 "Chamberlain Sun Chuo: Miscellaneous Accounts"

太素既已分	The Primordial Purity, once divided,[17]
吹萬著形兆	Blew on the myriad things, manifesting all phenomena.
寂動苟有源	Should stillness and action each have a source,
因謂殤子夭	Then it would be calling premature a child's death.[18]

4

---

that Wen Jiao died in 329, Sun Chuo would have been merely 15 or so (calculating from a birth year of 314) when he supposedly presented this poem to the great general, an unlikely event. See Cao, *Zhonggu wenxueshi lunwen ji* 中古文學史論文集 (Beijing: Zhonghua shuju, 2002), 311. David Zebulon Raft, while acknowledging that the poem's attribution is uncertain, nonetheless makes an argument for reading this work as a patronage poem plausibly written by the precociously talented Sun Chuo to the famous general. See Raft, "Four-syllable Verse in Medieval China" (Ph.D. diss., Harvard University, 2007), 334-36.

16   For example, Sun Chuo's "Rhapsody on Roaming the Celestial Terrace Mountains" 遊天 台山賦 was included in the *Wen xuan* and his two Lanting 蘭亭 poems circulated independently of his other works.

17   In the opening of *Zhuangzi* 2, "Qi wu lun," Nanguo Ziqi "leaned against an armrest" with a look of profound detachment and tranquility. He then describes contemplating the piping of Heaven, which blows on the myriad things in different ways so that each may be self-so, and compared it against the lesser kinds of piping of earth and men. See *Zhuangzi jishi* 莊子集釋 (hereafter cited as *ZZJS*), ed. Guo Qingfan 郭慶藩 (Beijing: Zhonghua shuju, 1961), 1:43-50.

18   A reference to one of the famous paradoxes from "Qi wu lun," where Zhuangzi levels the extreme old age of Ancestor Peng and the premature death of a child: "no one has lived longer than a dead child, and Ancestor Peng died young." The commentary by Guo Xiang 郭象 on the correlative Mount Tai and Ancestor Peng paradoxes is relevant to this discussion and instructive of how early medieval readers might have construed this passage: "If each one is in accord with its own nature and function, and is in tacit harmony with its ultimate capacity, then a form that is large is not excessive, nor a small one insufficient... As there is nothing small or large, and there is neither longevity nor brevity, the chrysalis does not envy the old tree trunk." *ZZJS*, 1:81. My translation is based on Wing-Tsit Chan's in *A Source Book in Chinese Philosophy* (Princeton: Princeton University Press, 1963), 329-30. In other words, if one's life is measured not in terms of countable time but fulfillment of one's natural course and ultimate capacity, then there is no brevity (or longevity) with which to be concerned. Following Zhuangzian logic, then, there is no discrimination between stillness and action, hence neither has a source. If one were to suppose that they

道喪涉千載	The Way has been lost for a thousand years—
津梁誰能了	Who knows the ford and bridge?[19]
思乘扶搖翰	I wish to mount feathered wings carried by the whirlwind—
8 卓然淩風矯	Riding the wind to rise high above.
靜觀尺棰義	I calmly contemplate the meaning of the foot-long rod:
理足未嘗少	There is reason enough that it does not diminish.[20]
冏冏秋月明	Bright, bright shines the autumn moon,
12 憑軒詠堯老	Leaning against the balcony, I sing of Yao and Laozi.
浪迹無蚩妍	Cast away physical traces, and neither ugliness nor beauty remains,[21]
然後君子道	Only then does the way of the gentleman appear.
領略歸一致	Comprehension returns to a single unity;
16 南山有綺皓	On Southern Mountain, there was Whitepate Qi.[22]
交臂久變化	Though they were linked arm in arm, what is enduring was transformation;[23]
傳火迺薪草	To pass on the fire, there are indeed tinder and grass.[24]

---

do have a source, then it would like calling a child's death premature, which runs counter to Zhuangzian paradoxical truth.

19 That is to say, the way to save the world.

20 A reference to one of the rejoinders used by rhetoricians in debating the logician Hui Shi: "Take a foot-long rod and cut it in half each day, and after ten thousand generations, it still will not be used up." zzjs, 3:1106. The basic reasoning is that any whole can be split in half indefinitely. The *Wen xuan* commentator Lü Yanji 呂延濟 suggested that the splitting of the rod indefinitely signifies the splitting of time indefinitely, without an end point. Each day can be split to morning and night, or by extension, life and death, where day follows night, or life follows death, ad infinitum.

21 When asked about the man of virtue, Chun Mang replied that, "The man of virtue rests without thinking, moves without deliberating, and harbors neither right nor wrong, beauty nor ugliness." See *Zhuangzi* 12, "Tian di," in zzjs, 2:441.

22 Qili Ji 綺里季, along with Master Huang of Xia 夏黃公, Master Dongyuan 東園公, and Mister Luli 甪里先生, withdrew to Mount Shang in protest of the harsh policies of the Qin government and would later collectively be known as the Four Whitepates (*sihao* 四皓). See *Shiji* (Beijing: Zhonghua shuju, 1982), 55.2044-47, and *Han shu* (Beijing: Zhonghua shuju, 1962), 40.2033-36. For a discussion of the various versions of the "Four Whitepates" lore, see Alan Berkowitz, *Patterns of Disengagement: The Practice and Portrayal of Reclusion in Early Medieval China* (Stanford: Stanford University Press, 2000), 64-80.

23 In the *Zhuangzi*, Confucius teaches Yan Hui about the unstoppable workings of transformation. Although he and Yan Hui have gone through life side by side, they are unable to stop change and, by ultimate extension, death. See *Zhuangzi* 21, "Tian Zifang," in zzjs, 2:709.

24 When Laozi died, his friend Qin Shi went to mourn him and left after emitting three cries. Laozi's disciples questioned him about the casual brevity of his expression of mourning,

矗矗玄思清	With steady effort, thoughts on the mystery become clear,
20 胸中去機巧	I remove from my breast all contrivance and craft.[25]
物我俱忘懷	When one has forgotten all things and oneself,[26]
可以狎鷗鳥	Then he can cozy up to the seagulls.[27]

Although the poem's title promises a theme of diversity or heterogeneity, the text itself is contrarily singular in orientation and composition. Nearly all of the lines in this story of Sun Chuo's quest for understanding the mysterious Dao and for transcendence allude to the *Zhuangzi*. The arc of the narrative is charted by major themes drawn from that text: the disintegration of the primordial state of purity into myriad phenomena and the unity of all comprehension into a single whole (ll. 1-2, 15); the leveling and, ultimately, transcendence of arbitrary distinctions between apparent opposites such as stillness and action, longevity and brevity, beauty and ugliness (ll. 3-4, 13); accepting transformation as an uncontainable force and its ultimate phase, death, as simply part of the natural cycle of things (ll. 17-18); and, finally, embracing the virtue of

---

to which Qin Shi replied, "Your master came since it was his time to come, and left since he followed the way it is. If one is at peace with time and accepts following along with things, then neither sorrow or happiness can enter. This is what the ancients called being freed from the binds of God. This refers to when the fire burns out, one adds more tinder; then the fire passes on, and no one knows where it would end." Both quotations from the *Zhuangzi* speak to the idea that death is as natural as life and underscore the insignificance of death, which is merely that of the body. See *Zhuangzi* 3, "Yangsheng zhu," in *zzjs*, 1:128-29.

25 In *Zhuangzi* 12, "Tian di," the man of complete virtue is described as having "forgotten all about achievement, profit, contrivance, and craft." *zzjs*, 2:436.

26 Guo Xiang's commentary on the passage in which Nanguo Ziqi in "Qi wu lun" said that he lost himself is relevant: "I lost myself means I forgot myself. Since have I forgotten myself, then how could anything in this world be worth recognizing?" *zzjs*, 1:45. In other words, forgetting self and other, as well as any distinction between the two, leads to a transcendent, all-encompassing understanding.

27 The *Wen xuan* commentator Li Shan 李善 cites a story in the *Zhuangzi* about how a man played with seagulls at the shore every day and how the seagulls came to him a hundred times. However, one day when his father asked him to catch one so he can also play with it, the seagulls did not descend to the shore that day. This anecdote does not appear in the extant *Zhuangzi*, though it is preserved in the *Liezi*. See *Liezi jishi* 列子集釋, ed. Yang Bojun 楊伯峻 (Beijing: Zhonghua shuju, 1979), 2.67-68. For the Chinese text of Jiang Yan's poem, see Xiao Tong 蕭統, ed., *Wen xuan* (hereafter *wx*) (Shanghai: Shanghai guji chubanshe, 1986), 31.1467-69. I have emended the surname given in the *Wen xuan* from Zhang 張 to Sun 孫.

forgetting artificial constructs (contrivance and craft) and boundaries (between self and other) to return to an originary simplicity and wholeness (ll. 19-22).

This imitation poem is fabricated of mostly quotations and allusions to the *Zhuangzi*, thereby indicating Jiang Yan's recognition of the intertextual nature of Sun Chuo's works. Although we cannot ascertain exactly how much and which lines are taken from Sun Chuo's mostly lost corpus, for a number of other imitations in the series there is evidence that Jiang Yan liberally borrows or adapts phrases and elements from the original body of works.[28] The act of composing a piece from existing textual strands that are themselves composed of foreign textual strands would add yet another layer of interpretation and signification to the text at hand. Whether Jiang Yan quoted Sun Chuo quoting the *Zhuangzi* or whether he quoted the *Zhuangzi* while writing on behalf of Sun Chuo may be beyond the reach of research, but the saturation of this imitation poem with *Zhuangzi* allusions reveals two significant points: first, the fluid, composite, and intertextual constitution of early medieval poetry and thought; and second, an apparent effort on Jiang's part to circumscribe and contain Sun Chuo's heterogeneous assemblage of literary and cultural resources that is attested by his extant works and descriptions of his corpus by Six Dynasties historians and critics.

Sun Chuo's "Poem to Yu Bing" 與庾冰詩 in one hundred and four lines, for example, demonstrates a pragmatic use of diverse, sometimes incongruous repertoires of literary and cultural meanings. Although the poem is too long to cite in full here, the range of its appropriation of available sources can nonetheless be appreciated in the following outline.[29] This poem casts a portrait of the great statesman Yu Bing (296-344), the younger brother of Yu Liang 庾亮 (289-340), within a larger picture of the decline of Western Jin and the founding of Eastern Jin. It draws mostly from the *Yijing* and *Shijing* 詩經 (Classic of poetry) to explain matters of cosmology and politics but relies substantially on Lao-Zhuang ideas in recasting old cosmological paradigms. The cataclysmic disaster story of a dynastic collapse that led to the abandonment of the old

---

28   For example, in Jiang Yan's imitation of Tao Yuanming, he mixes and matches phrases from the earlier poet's farmstead works, especially "Returning to the Farm to Dwell" 歸園田居 and "The Return" 歸去來兮辭. Jiang creates a dense collage of imagistic phrases taken from Tao's works, such as "planting sprouts," "eastern hill," "carrying a hoe," "unstrained wine," "a young son waiting," "growth of mulberry and hemp," and "a pure heart."

29   For a detailed discussion of this poem and others by Sun Chuo, see Swartz, *Reading Philosophy, Writing Poetry: Intertextual Modes of Making Meaning in Early Medieval China* (Cambridge, MA: Harvard University Asia Center, 2018).

heartland of Chinese civilization in the north to foreign invaders and the subsequent mass migration to the south seems best told in *Yijing* language. An allusion to Adversity 否 (hexagram 12) and Peace 泰 (hexagram 11) in the first stanza signifies how any rise eventually leads to decline, just as any concentration in a situation leads first to excess then depletion, according to the pattern laid out in the *Yijing*. Sun Chuo thus depicts the fall of the dynasty as a matter of course, part of a naturalized cycle of events. The *Shijing* serves as another rich repertoire of cultural and literary signs for discussing matters of state and governance. In one passage, the poet links the decline of Western Jin to the momentous fall of Western Zhou through an allusion to *Shijing* 65, "Drooping Millet" 黍離, which traditionally has been read as the lament of an official traveling through the former capital of Western Zhou now laid to waste. Or Sun describes the founding of Eastern Jin with a line adapted from *Shijing* 241, "August" 皇矣, which asserts Heaven's bestowal of the mandate. Replacing "west" (where the Zhou settlement was located) in the original line with "east" (i.e., south of the Yangzi, where the Eastern Jin was founded), Sun Chuo writes, "[Heaven] looked and turned its gaze to the east" 乃眷東顧 (l. 18), to claim that the rise of Eastern Jin was sanctioned by Heaven's will.

To address the issues of the causes behind the decline of Western Jin and the founding of Eastern Jin as well as the role of Heaven in those events, Sun Chuo borrows from the *Laozi* to articulate a view of the universe that is consonant with early medieval intellectual values. The first four stanzas of the poem grapple with locating the historical causes of turmoil: did the Western Jin collapse because "the virtue [of Emperors Hui and Huai] was not sufficient" (l. 9)? What were the greater challenges in the founding of Eastern Jin: the external threats in the form of Jie 羯 troops led by Shi Le 石勒 (d. 333) or internal ones in the form of rebel troops led by Su Jun 蘇峻 (d. 328) (ll. 27-32)? How does Heaven's will fit into this narrative? These questions are addressed in the fifth stanza of the poem:

遠惟自天	From afar it was something that came from Heaven,
抑亦由人	But it was also something caused by men.
道苟無虧	If the Way was not deficient,
釁故曷因	Then what caused the disaster?
遑遑遺黎	Frantic were the displaced folk—
死痛生勤	The dying were in agony, the living in misery.
撫運懷□	Abiding by destiny's course [one-character lacuna],
天地不仁	"Heaven and Earth are not humane."[30]

---

30   *XS*, 2:898.

Is it Heaven at work or humans at fault? Did the fall of Western Jin and rise of Eastern Jin, or the formation of a new state and its obstructions, enact a naturalized, preordained cycle of events? Or is Heaven humane insofar as it wants what is good for humankind and punishes or rewards those who rule or not according to its Way (or Will), a venerable strain of thought that dates to ancient Zhou texts (e.g. *Shijing*) and powerfully re-articulated by the Han classicist official Dong Zhongshu 董仲舒 (ca. 179-ca. 104)?[31] These implicit questions are answered by a single line at the end of the stanza, quoted verbatim from *Laozi* 5: "Heaven and Earth are not humane."[32] Sun Chuo's reading of this line is surely informed by the commentary of Wang Bi 王弼 (226-249 CE), with which *xuanxue* 玄學 adepts were certainly familiar. According to Wang Bi, this line means that "Heaven and Earth follow naturalness, without acting consciously or starting anything, letting the myriad things govern themselves. Thus, they 'are not humane.'"[33] Questions of divine intervention or human agency are ultimately decided by a view of the human course vis-à-vis cosmic order that is championed in *xuan* learning. Heaven and Earth are neither partial nor activist: as such, they allow all things (including dynastic rule) to fulfill their natural course rather than impose upon them some contrived, artificial scheme. The *Laozi*, as interpreted by Wang Bi, is judiciously appropriated by Sun Chuo to reconcile the historically various views of divine and human agency and to re-cast the issue as each thing simply following its own natural course.

In one of Sun Chuo's best-known works, "Rhapsody on Roaming the Celestial Terrace Mountains" 遊天台山賦, the poet in similar fashion draws from various materials, ranging from Lao-Zhuang concepts to Buddhist ideas, to express his spiritual ascent toward enlightenment. Sun Chuo references key terms from both teachings before merging all into one in the end: for example, Existence (or Being) 有 and Non-existence (or Non-being) 無, which appear in the first chapter of the *Laozi* as references to *xuan*, or the Dao, and whose relationship figured centrally in Wei-Jin *xuan* thought; or Form (*se* 色) and Emptiness (*kong* 空), whose distinction some Mahāyāna texts erase by, for example, positing Form as Emptiness. The last section of the rhapsody, which

---

31   For Dong Zhongshu's development of a heaven-man correlative cosmology, see his major work *Chunqiu fanlu* 春秋繁露 (Strings of pearls from the *Spring and Autumn Annals*), now available in a translation by Sarah A. Queen and John S. Major, *Luxuriant Gems of the Spring and Autumn* (New York: Columbia University Press, 2016).

32   The entire passage from *Laozi* 5 reads: "Heaven and Earth are not humane and treat the myriad things as straw dogs."

33   *Wang Bi ji jiaoshi* 王弼集校釋 (hereafter cited as *WBJJS*), ed. Lou Yulie 樓宇烈 (Beijing: Zhonghua shuju, 1999), 1:13.

describes the end of the poet's spiritual journey that culminates at the summit of this sacred mountain, offers a dazzling mélange of Lao-Zhuang and Buddhist thought.[34]

散以象外之說	Inspired by the doctrine of "beyond images,"[35]
暢以無生之篇	Illumined by the texts on "non-origination,"[36]
悟遣有之不盡	I become aware that I have not completely dismissed Existence,
覺涉無之有間	And realize that there are interruptions in the passage to Non-existence.
泯色空以合跡	I destroy Form and Emptiness, blending them into one;
忽即有而得玄	Suddenly I proceed to Existence where I attain the Mystery.
釋二名之同出	I release the two names that come from a common source,
消一無於三幡	Dissolve a single Non-existence into the Three Banners.[37]
恣語樂以終日	All day long giving oneself to conversation's delights,
等寂默於不言	Is the same as the still silence of not speaking.
渾萬象以冥觀	I merge the myriad phenomena in mystic contemplation,
兀同體於自然	Unconsciously join my body with the Naturally-so.

The cross-pollination between Mahayana Buddhist and Lao-Zhuang thought through translation, interpretation, and intertextual work during the Wei-Jin period fostered this type of hybridization of Eastern Jin *xuan* discourse and lent support to the idea that the Ultimate could be discussed in various, interchangeable terms. In his "Rhapsody," Sun Chuo uses the various terms available to him from *xuan* discourse and Buddhist learning to convey the Ultimate

---

34   Sun Chuo, "You Tiantai shan fu," in *WX*, 11.493-501. I have followed with slight modification David Knechtges' translation of the rhapsody in *Wen xuan or Selections of Refined Literature, Volume Two: Rhapsodies on Sacrifices, Hunting, Travel, Sightseeing, Palaces and Halls, Rivers and Seas* (Princeton: Princeton University Press, 1987), 243-53.

35   A reference to Daoist teachings which paradoxically state that the Dao cannot be represented in words or images.

36   A designation for Buddhist sutras which teach that dharmas have neither birth nor extinction.

37   Here I depart from Knechtges' rendering ("Dissolve the Three Banners into a single Non-existence") and follow the original grammar of the line. It seems to me that Sun Chuo's point is the connectedness or lack of distinction between apparent opposites: the shared source between existence (*you*) and non-existence (*wu*); and the indistinction among the Three Banners, which according to Li Shan, refer to form (*se*), emptiness (*kong*), and contemplation (*guan* 觀). Hence, the distinction between part and whole is rejected: two names come from a single source, and a single non-existence dissolves into three banners.

Way or Truth, such as *wu* (non-existence), *xuan* (mystery), and the non-duality between *kong* (emptiness) and *se* (form).

The two examples above, among others in Sun Chuo's corpus, provide a window into the ways in which the poet used quotation and allusion to appropriate from a heterogeneous repertoire of cultural and literary meanings, contributing to the growing web of emergent textual relationships in this formative period for literary, cultural, and intellectual history. While writers from this period bore witness to a rapidly expanding repertoire of literary and cultural resources, the cultural workings at play in this period of growth were protean and not easy to contain. Sun Chuo is credited with (or castigated for, depending on the perspective) substantially incorporating Lao-Zhuang terms as well as introducing Buddhist language into poetry. At stake for writers like Sun Chuo was not merely the expansion of an existing container (i.e. received tradition) but also engaging and negotiating with new kinds of organisms (new sources or languages). Jiang Yan's imitation, which is almost entirely composed of quotations from one source—the *Zhuangzi*—gives little indication of the heterogeneity and complexity of Sun Chuo's poetics. It too neatly encapsulates Sun Chuo's intertextual relations with various texts and continually morphing materials into a singular focus on one such text. Jiang Yan, like his contemporary Tan Daoluan, may have deemed that Buddhist terms did not properly belong in classical poetry and chose to excise that element in his rewriting of Sun Chuo. And, as with both Tan and Zhong Rong who ignored Sun Chuo's extensive use of *Shijing* in their denunciation of his departure from tradition, Jiang excluded that source in his representation of Sun Chuo's style to showcase the one source which Jiang apparently decided best epitomized the poet's style.

The Resilience of Convention: The Case of Xie Hun

Composing an imitation piece involves as much definition as selection, representation as fabrication. Jiang Yan's imitation of Sun Chuo distorts the fuller picture of his predecessor's intertextual poetics but distinctly reflects the single aspect by which he would have future readers remember his predecessor. Whereas an aim to contain and fit Sun Chuo into a particular place in literary history may well have steered Jiang Yan's trimmed version of that poet, it would seem that poetic conventions and habits governed Jiang Yan's rewriting of another nearly lost poet, Xie Hun.

謝僕射混遊覽　"Supervisor Xie Hun: Excursion and Sightseeing"

信矣勞物化	Truly I fret over the transformation of things:
憂襟未能整	With this worry in my breast, I cannot set my collar straight.
薄言遵郊衢	So I'll follow along the outskirts thoroughfare,
4　挖彎出臺省	Gather the reins and leave the Palace Pavilion.
凄凄節序高	Chill, chill—the season has progressed to its peak;
寥寥心悟永	Vast, vast—my heart understands the eternal.
時菊耀巖阿	Season's chrysanthemums cast their glow on grottoed hills,
8　雲霞冠秋嶺	While rosy clouds cap autumnal summits.
眷然惜良辰	Fondly I cherish this fine day,
徘徊踐落景	Treading back and forth upon the falling sunrays,
卷舒雖萬緒	Furling and unfurling—the threads are myriad;
12　動復歸有靜	Action always returns to stillness.
曾是迫桑榆	So as I press toward the mulberry and elm,
歲暮從所秉	In the twilight of my years, I shall follow what my heart holds true.
舟壑不可攀	Since a boat in the ravine cannot be held in place,[38]
16　忘懷寄匠郢	I shall forget my cares, entrusting them to the carpenter and man from Ying.[39]

This poem begins with a reference to a major theme in the *Zhuangzi*—the transformation of things—in which it is cast as the determinative force of all life. "The human body has ten thousand transformations that never come to an end," while death merely constitutes one such transformation, according to Zhuangzian philosophy.[40] Contemplation of transformation and, by extension,

---

38　An allusion to a story in *Zhuangzi* 6, "Da zong shi": when someone hides his boat in the ravine, he believes that it will be secure. However, in the middle of the night, a strongman comes to shoulder it and takes it away. In ignorance, he does not know how it happened. See *ZZJS*, 1:243. The strongman is likened to transformation (and, its ultimate iteration, death). Guo Xiang's commentary to this passage states: "The transformations of life and death cannot be escaped... Of the forces that have no force, there is none that is greater than transformation... Therefore, without stopping even momentarily, it suddenly already has brought on something new. For this reason, there is no moment in which the myriad things between heaven and earth are not changing."

39　A reference to a story in *Zhuangzi* 24, "Xu Wugui," about sympathetic understanding between friends. There once was a plasterer from Ying 郢, who so trusted his friend Carpenter Shi 石 that he would ask the carpenter to slice off specks of mud that got on his nose. The carpenter would wield and move his axe like the wind, while his friend stood without losing his calm countenance the whole time. See *ZZJS*, 3:843. For the Chinese text of Jiang Yan's poem, see *WX*, 31.1471-72. On Carpenter Shi, see also pp. 77-78 in this volume.

40　See *Zhuangzi* 6 and *Zhuangzi* 15, in *ZZJS*, 1:244 and 2:539, respectively.

its ultimate iteration, death, seems to lead the poetic subject to an outing in nature where further meditations arise. The poetic subject's investigation of this philosophical theme then leads to an appreciation of the workings of both continual change and a return to the beginning, articulated through two other textual references. The "furling" and "unfurling" of the myriad things allude to *Huainanzi* 2: "The ultimate way does not act. Now a dragon, now a snake: expanding and contracting, furling and unfurling, they change and transform along with the times."[41] The statement "Action always returns to stillness" summarizes the lesson in *Laozi* 16: "As such, I observe their return. Things proliferate, yet each returns to its root. Returning to one's root is called stillness, which means returning to one's destiny." Wang Bi's commentary, which both Jiang Yan and Xie Hun would have known, further explains, "All that exists arises from emptiness (虛 *xu*), and action arises from stillness (靜 *jing*). Therefore, although the myriad things act together, in the end they return to empty stillness. This is the ultimate truth of things. Each returns to its beginning, and when it has returned to its root, it becomes still."[42] The natural course for all things is constant transformation, the ultimate manifestation of which is death. Just as each thing returns to its beginning, all action returns to stillness or, correlatively, all living beings return to death, as Zhuangzi suggests in "Qi wu lun" 齊物論 (Discussion on leveling things). These reflections on death expressed through choice allusions to the *Huainanzi* and *Laozi* adumbrate the philosophical acceptance of it in the final passage of the poem, which is, in turn, conveyed by two allusions to the *Zhuangzi*. The parable of the boat hidden in the ravine teaches about the precariousness of the boat (life) and how a strongman (death) comes unexpectedly to take it away.[43] Following this implicit acknowledgment of the inevitability of death, the poetic subject impassively declares that he shall "forget cares" and entrust his feelings to the likes of the plasterer from Ying who stood calmly while his friend Carpenter Shi sliced off specks of mud from his nose in the "Xu Wugui" 徐无鬼 chapter of the *Zhuangzi*.[44] The mood of equanimity at the poem's end not only represents a complete reversal of the one of apprehension at the beginning, but also underscores the philosophical tenor sustaining the entire poem.

For a poem purportedly about sightseeing, there is very little description of sights. Instead of natural imagery, philosophical allusions and reflections dominate this poem. Even the rare instance of a scenic description of season's

---

41   *Huainanzi jishi* 淮南子集釋, ed. He Ning 何寧 (Beijing: Zhonghua shuju, 1998), 1:113.

42   *WBJJS*, 1:36.

43   See *Zhuangzi* 6, in *ZZJS*, 1:243.

44   See *Zhuangzi* 24, in *ZZJS*, 3:843.

chrysanthemums and autumnal peaks serves to set into relief the philosophical theme of transformation. This imitation poem, composed significantly by
allusions to the *Zhuangzi* and *Laozi*, no more squares with the descriptions of
Xie Hun's poetry by Six Dynasties historians and critics than it does with its title. In his denunciation of Sun Chuo and Xu Xun's use of Daoist and Buddhist
language in their poetry, Tan Daoluan hailed Xie Hun as the turning point in
what seemed to him a disastrous trend instigated by Sun and Xu.

> Henceforth Guo Pu's pentasyllabic verse was the first to combine Daoist
> phrases and set them into rhyme. Xu Xun and Sun Chuo of Taiyuan each
> emulated them and moreover added the [Buddhist] language of the
> three worlds [past, present and future], and the normative style of the
> *Odes* and *Elegies* came to an end. Xun and Chuo together were literary
> patriarchs of their era; from then on, writers all imitated them. During
> the Yixi reign (405-419), Xie Hun was the first to change [the prevailing
> style].[45]

> 故郭璞五言始會合道家之言而韻之。詢及太原孫綽轉相祖尚，又加以
> 三世之辭，而《詩》、《騷》之體盡矣。詢、綽並為一時文宗，自此
> 作者悉體之。至義熙中，謝混始改。

Shen Yue 沈約 (441-513) similarly credited Xie Hun with "completely reform-
ing" the sweeping trend of the time.[46] Zhong Rong chimed in as well to cast Xie
Hun as one of the saviors of the classical poetic tradition who managed to alter
its declining course set into motion by Sun and Xu's "bland" (*dan* 淡) and "flat"
(*ping* 平) philosophical verse. In the *Shipin*, Zhong Rong praised Xie Hun for
"gloriously continuing the work" of a few Western Jin predecessors who first
sought to change the rampant practice by introducing a new style.[47] This assessment by Six Dynasties historians and critics of Xie Hun as a revitalizing
new voice diametrically opposes Jiang Yan's imitation piece, which continues
the dominant mode of using Lao-Zhuang language and themes.

Even more curiously, Jiang's imitation bears only superficial resemblance to
the sightseeing poem that apparently served as a model. Xie Hun's "Touring
West Pond" 遊西池詩, later included in the *Wen xuan*, is one of the few remaining pieces from his corpus. Its survival challenges Jiang Yan's representation of
the poet and grants Xie Hun participation in how history remembers him.

---

45   Cited in *SSXY*, 4/85.

46   See *Song shu* 宋書 (Beijing: Zhonghua shuju, 1974), 67.1778.

47   *Shipin jizhu*, 24-28.

悟彼蟋蟀唱	I understand the singing of those crickets:[48]
信此勞者歌	Truly this is the song of ones who have toiled.[49]
有來豈不疾	Time comes and goes—is it not in a rush?
4　良遊常蹉跎	Fine outings have too often been missed.
逍遙越城肆	Carefree we could be striding through the city marketplace,
願言屢經過	How I wish we might frequent there.
迴阡被陵闕	A curving path extends past mounds and towers,
8　高臺眺飛霞	From the tall terrace, we could see rosy clouds in flight.
惠風蕩繁囿	A gentle breeze sweeps over the blooming park,
白雲屯曾阿	While white clouds gather on layered peaks.
景昃鳴禽集	As the sun descends, singing birds flock to their perch;
12　水木湛清華	Trees stand clear and glorious in the water, pellucid.
褰裳順蘭沚	I lift my robe to follow along the thoroughwort islet,
徙倚引芳柯	And linger, drawing close the fragrant boughs.
美人愆歲月	The time has passed for the fair one;
16　遲暮獨如何	In the year's twilight, what shall I do?
無為牽所思	Do not let these thoughts fetter you,
南榮戒其多	Nanrong was warned against their excess.[50]

Like the imitation poem, this one begins with a reference to the swift passage of time, continues to an account of an excursion, and concludes with an allusion to the *Zhuangzi* about transcending cares. The similarities end there. The main theme of this poem, given the premise of a year drawing to its end as signaled by the "singing of the crickets" borrowed from *Shijing* 114, is not fretting over imminent death, but rather missing opportunities to enjoy excursions with friends. With only one allusion to the *Zhuangzi*, the poem represents a marked departure from *xuanyan* poetry, which borrowed significantly from the Lao-Zhuang corpus. Instead, the focal point of this poem is an extended description of scenes in nature that the poet would have liked to experience together with a friend. Nature's activity manifests in the rosy clouds in flight, a gentle breeze sweeping over a blooming park, as well as the setting sun and

---

48　This alludes to the opening lines of *Shijing* 114, "Crickets" 蟋蟀: "Crickets in the hall, the year is near its end. If I do not make merry today, months and years will pass me by."

49　This alludes to *Shijing* 165, "Hewing the Trees" 伐木, a poem about the natural need for companionship. Those who hew trees sound to one another, just as birds cry out in search of mates.

50　*WX*, 22.1034-35. In *Zhuangzi* 23, "Gengsang Chu," the title character advises Nanrong Chu to "keep the body whole, cling to life, and not busy oneself with thoughts and deliberations." *ZZJS*, 3:777.

homing birds. Nature's stillness can be observed in the luminously clear image of trees in the placid water. Such imagistic descriptions of nature's workings are transfigured into an abstract statement about activity and stillness in Jiang Yan's hands.

If Xie Hun was widely considered to have reformed the established mode represented by *xuanyan* poetry, a point his sole surviving excursion poem would support, why did Jiang Yan represent Xie Hun in such a way that renders the imitation work hardly distinguishable from *xuanyan* poems? The simplest answer would be that, for Jiang Yan, change is relative: Xie Hun borrowed less from Lao-Zhuang than did Sun Chuo or Xu Xun, an assessment quantifiably demonstrable by Jiang's imitation pieces, and he therefore may still be considered to have been a reformer of the prevailing trend. A more nuanced answer concerns the influence of convention and existing language upon all writing, including self-consciously reflective forms such as imitation and revision. Even if Jiang Yan meant to cast Xie Hun as the new voice his contemporaries heard and hailed, we must consider the likelihood that the poetic language (broadly defined as rhetorical tools, semantic associations and established patterns) to which *xuanyan* poets contributed for two centuries was as much in command of the writer as the writer was in command of the language he used. In re-writing the poetry of Xie Hun, however new that style may have been, Jiang Yan still worked within the sphere of established—albeit changing—poetic conventions.

Semblance of a Lost Poet Preserved: The Case of Xu Xun

Not a single poem has survived intact from the corpus of the other "literary patriarch of his time" named along with Sun Chuo in Tan Daoluan's account—Xu Xun. Fragments from three poems totaling eight lines reveal very little about this alleged master poet.[51] In addition to his reputed literary talent, Xu Xun was also famed for his resolute eschewal of office and lofty air of detachment, according to anecdotes in the *Shishuo xinyu*.[52] The style and content of

---

51   For these fragments, see XS, 2:894.

52   When asked by the famous monk Zhi Dun 支遁 to compare himself to Xu Xun, Sun replied that "as far as exalted feelings and remoteness are concerned, your disciple has long since inwardly conceded Xu's superiority. But in the matter of a single humming or a single intoning of poetry, Xu will need to sit facing north [as a student before a teacher]." SSXY, 9/54; trans. Richard Mather, *Shih-shuo Hsin-yü: A New Account of the Tales of the World*, 2nd ed. (Ann Arbor: Center for Chinese Studies, The University of Michigan, 2002), 283.

his poetry must, then, mostly be surmised from secondary sources. A response poem from Sun Chuo to Xu Xun is an especially crucial source, for its eighth stanza purports to summarize his friend's original poem to him:

貽我新詩	You presented me with a new poem,
韻靈旨清	Spiritual in resonance, pure in meaning.
粲如揮錦	Brilliant as a fluttering brocade,
琅若叩瓊	Sonorous as carnelian when struck.
既欣夢解	You are glad since you have understood the dream,[53]
獨愧未冥	But still ashamed for not yet reaching the depths.
慍在有身	Resentment lies in "having a body,"[54]
樂在忘生	Joy lies in "forgetting life."[55]
余則異矣	I am different from this:
無往不平	There is no going that is not leveled for me.
理苟皆是	If Truth were like this in every case,
何累於情	Why should we become entangled by feelings?[56]

Sun Chuo affirms that he has appreciated both the sound and sense of his friend's communication, before proceeding to summarize a key point of Xu's address: Xu had expressed joy in having understood the meaning of "the dream"

---

53   *Zhuangzi* 18, "Zhi le," tells a story about the dream of the skull; see my discussion in this section. I thank Liu Yuanju of Academia Sinica for her insight on this allusion.

54   An allusion to *Laozi* 13: "What is meant by self-importance being 'a great calamity that can cost one his person?' The reason I suffer such a great calamity is that I am bound by my own person [*you shen* 有身, i.e. bodily existence]. When I am no longer bound by my own person, what calamity could befall me?" *WBJJS*, 1:29; trans. Richard John Lynn, *The Classic of the Way and Virtue* (New York: Columbia University Press, 1999), 71.

55   This phrase conjures up two passages in the *Zhuangzi* about forgetting one's person (*wang qi shen* 忘其身): seeing life and death as equal in value ("the reason I find it good to live is the same as why I find it good to die"); accepting the state of things (*shi zhi qing* 事之情 or *wu zhi qing* 物之情) and the fact that man cannot intervene with it. See *Zhuangzi* 4, "Ren jian shi," and *Zhuangzi* 6, "Da zong shi," in *ZZJS*, 1:155, 241-44.

56   This refers to the famous debate between He Yan and Wang Bi on whether sages possessed emotions. He Yan opined that the sages were free from feelings of pleasure, anger, sadness or joy, whereas Wang Bi argued that sages, like others, have common emotions. However, unlike others, the sages possess an uncommon, numinous intelligence that enables them to identify with nothingness. Thus, according to Wang Bi, their emotions are such that "they respond to things, but without becoming attached to things" 應物而無累於物. See Wang Bi's biography by He Shao 何劭, as appended to Zhong Hui's biography in the *Sanguo zhi* 三國志 (Beijing: Zhonghua shuju, 1982), 28.795. For the Chinese text of Sun Chuo's poem, see *XS*, 2:900.

but is ashamed for not having attained a more profound level of understanding, that is to say, complete enlightenment; he still views his bodily existence as a source of resentment and being able to forget life as cause for joy. The dream refers not to the famous Zhuangzi-butterfly episode about accessing reality and epistemology in Chapter 2, "Discussion on Leveling Things," but likely alludes to the dream of the skull in Chapter 18, "Ultimate Happiness" 至樂, whose theme of death's value vis-à-vis life seems more consonant with the rest of the stanza. In that story Zhuangzi went to Chu and found an old, dried up skull, which he asked, "Were you greedy for life and lost your reason" and thus came to this? That night the skull appeared in Zhuangzi's dream and revealed to him the perfect happiness to be found in death, cast as a realm of absolute freedom that transcends all constraints of time and duty. The skull concluded that he would not trade death for life, which is characterized as "troubles" (*lao* 勞).[57] Although Xu may have grasped the signification of this dream, he still feels the demands placed on one's existence (e.g. honor, favor, station) and the burden of valuing life over death, according to Sun's summary of Xu's poem.

Although we cannot know whether Sun Chuo made a fair reading of Xu Xun's poem, at play here seems less an implicit critique of Xu's alleged spiritual deficiency than an unabashed exhibit of Sun's supposed superior understanding. He tells Xu that he is different from his friend ("I am different from this"), since he suffers neither the resentment nor joy of life or death ("There is no going that is not leveled for me"). Given the way things are in the world, Sun knows better than to become entangled by his emotions ("Why should we become entangled by feelings?"). Moreover, to distinguish himself from Xu Xun, Sun Chuo draws from Wang Bi's famous response to He Yan 何晏 (189?-249) about whether the sages had feelings: "the feelings of sages are such that the sages respond to things, but without becoming entangled by them." Sun has cast himself in the role of the sage and, by extension, his younger friend and rival, to whom others have often compared him, as the student. Why should engagement with worldly affairs matter so long as one is free of the emotional weight of it? The message of Sun Chuo, a known careerist, to his friend, a renowned recluse, is clear: true enlightenment for him hinges upon the mind, not matter.

If one were to judge by Sun Chuo's digest and revision of Xu Xun's poem alone, Xu's reputation for lofty transcendence would hardly seem justified. Although it is said that Sun Chuo himself once acknowledged his friendly rival's superiority in terms of "exalted feelings" and "remoteness," at least in this

---

poetic account Xu appears to be mired in the mundane.[58] Jiang Yan's imitation of Xu Xun presents an alternative picture, one that is congruous with available historical and anecdotal accounts which portray an untrammeled and enlightened recluse.

許徵君詢自序 Summoned Gentleman Xu Xun: Self-Account

張子闇內機	Master Zhang was oblivious to inner workings,
單生蔽外象	Whereas Sir Shan was unaware of outer phenomena.[59]
一時排冥筌	If for a time you cast away the dimming fish trap,[60]
4 泠然空中賞	Then you'll have the pleasure of soaring lightly through the void.[61]
遣此弱喪情	Leave behind this feeling of losing your childhood home;[62]
資神任獨往	Rely instead on your spirit, entrusting yourself to journey alone.[63]
採藥白雲隈	I pluck herbs by the bend of white clouds,
8 聊以肆所養	And shall abandon myself to self-cultivation.
丹葩曜芳蕤	Crimson flowers shine in their fragrant bloom;
綠竹陰閑敞	Green bamboos shade a placid expanse.
苕苕寄意勝	Far, far away, I lodge my feelings beyond,
12 不覺陵虛上	Unaware I ascend into the void above.
曲櫺激鮮飇	The window's curved lattices are stirred by fresh gales—

---

58   See note 52.

59   Following the Wuchen 五臣 edition of the *Wen xuan*, which reads 象 for 像. The story of Zhang Yi and Shan Bao appears in *Zhuangzi* 19, "Da sheng": Zhang Yi worked tirelessly to advance his material situation by currying favor with the rich and powerful. When he was merely forty, he fell ill to an internal fever and died as a result. By contrast, Shan Bao shunned an activist, profit-seeking life and secluded himself among the cliffs, drinking only water. When he was seventy, he still looked as a child. He met his death by a hungry tiger, who devoured him. See *ZZJS*, 2:646.

60   In a parable about language and meaning from Chapter 26, "Wai wu," Zhuangzi argues that "the reason the fish trap exists is for the fish; once you've gotten the fish, then you can forget the trap. The reason the rabbit snare exists is for the rabbit; once you've gotten the rabbit, then you can forget the snare. The reason why words exist is for their meaning; once you've gotten the meaning, then you can forget the words." *ZZJS*, 3:944.

61   In "Qi wu lun," Liezi is described as "riding the wind and soaring lightly with skill."

62   A reference to an argument in "Qi wu lun" that challenges the conventional hatred of death: "How do I know that in hating death that I am not like a man, who having lost his childhood home, has forgotten the way back?" *ZZJS*, 1:103.

63   The phrase *du wang* (journeying alone) does not appear in the text of the *Zhuangzi*, but in Guo Xiang's commentary. For example, Guo associates "embracing the uncarved block and journeying alone" with following the Way. *ZZJS*, 2:322. The concept of *du* (solitariness, independence), however, is well developed in the *Zhuangzi*.

石室有幽響	In the stone chamber are sounds of seclusion.
去矣從所欲	Away I have gone to follow my wish,
16 得失非外獎	Loss and gain are not to be determined by external forces.
至哉操斤客	How perfect, the sojourner wielding his axe![64]
重明固已朗	His clear discernment was due to mutual understanding.
五難既灑落	Now that the "Five Obstacles" have been shed,[65]
20 超迹絕塵網	I transcend these tracks and cut through the dusty net.[66]

This poem presents a radically different figure than the insecure apprentice from Sun Chuo's representation. In Jiang Yan's imitation of Xu Xun, the adept masterfully delineates the path to transcendence. Neither Zhang Yi, a successful careerist who succumbed to an internal issue in the form of a deadly fever, nor Shan Bao, an exemplary recluse who perished with an external threat in the form of a hungry tiger, illustrates in the *Zhuangzi* story the perfect way since one only minded the outer, whereas the other only minded the inner. Instead, true transcendence requires casting away conceptual containers such as language, symbolized by the Zhuangzian parable of the fish trap, and forgetting conventional fears and biases such as the abhorence of death. In the *Zhuangzi*, death is compared to one's childhood home, and so dying is merely a returning that should be accepted as part of the natural process. The highest level of attainment also entails the cultivation of one's body through the ingestion of medicinal herbs. In following the Way, the adept sheds remaining obstacles, such as joy and anger or concern for reputation and profit, and ultimately achieves transcendence of the world.

The facts that Jiang Yan titled his imitation of Xu Xun as "Self-Narration" and that this account consists of lessons for transcendence amalgamated from the *Zhuangzi* and the writings of an earlier adept, Xi Kang 嵇康 (ca. 223-ca. 262), suggest that an account of *his transcendence* constituted a major aspect of Xu's poetry. Jiang Yan's imitation of Xu Xun is thus invaluable in giving the lost poet a voice, however mediated. It is a voice which fruitfully complicates, even challenges, the version by Sun Chuo.

---

64 See note 39.

65 According to Xi Kang's "Answer to [Xiang Xiu's] Refutation of My 'Essay on Nurturing Life'" 答難養生論, the "Five Obstacles" to nurturing life are: 1) that reputation and profit are not exterminated; 2) that joy and anger are not eliminated; 3) that sound and form are not cast away; 4) that taste and flavor are not renounced; and 5) that spiritual meditations are dispersed and scattered. See *Xi Kang ji jiaozhu* 嵇康集校注, ed. Dai Mingyang 戴明揚 (Beijing: Renmin wenxue chubanshe, 1962), 4.191-92.

66 *WX*, 31.1469-70.

Conclusion

Jiang Yan's imitations of nearly and completely lost writers poses thorny questions for cultural memory. These texts represent bodies of works that have mostly disappeared and their value lies precisely in offering a memory of what is no longer present. Unless Xu Xun's works are somehow recovered in the future, Jiang Yan's imitation of Xu Xun uniquely offers readers one intact picture and compact summary of the lost poet's works. The costs to a culture's memory, however, are equally considerable. His imitations of Sun Chuo and Xie Hun yield partial, even distorted, pictures when seen alongside those poets' extant corpus and considered in light of the assessments by other contemporary readers.

Representation and selection in the work of imitation writing are to a great extent memory construction—both willfully remembering and forgetting and willing others to forget as well. One might point out that in order for memory to function, one needs to forget. Indeed, the tragic consequence of remembering everything and forgetting nothing is memorably impressed upon the readers of Jorge Luis Borges' "Funes, the Memorious," a short story about a boy cursed with this strange ability after he was thrown from a horse and became crippled. Unsurprisingly, he dies in the end. "The truth is that we all live by leaving behind," explains the narrator.[67] Similarly, literary history can only be written by excluding some aspects. Yet that which the self-appointed guardian of a literature's past chooses to preserve or to discard, to add or modify, reveals as much about his view of the past as about the cultural forces at play as outlined below.

In a period that bore witness to massive gains in cultural wealth in the forms of new literary genres and a proliferation of examples, early medieval literary critics and historians sought to manage the multiplication and spread of literary texts by composing cohesive or systematic accounts using the tools of definition, selection, and/or ranking. Critical readers attempted to address the need to arbitrate not only what was good literature but what literariness even was. Jiang Yan's imitations project may lay claim to such an ambition: in drawing up a summa of pentasyllabic poetry, it establishes a canon of poets ordered by a specific theme identified with each, and judges what should be considered their "fine" and "excellent" aspects. The choices Jiang Yan made in the case of Sun Chuo—what to include and what to exclude in representing the poet's intertextual mode of writing—suggest an effort to simplify a heterogeneous

---

67   Borges, "Funes, The Memorious," trans. Anthony Kerrigan, in *Ficciones* (New York: Grove Press, 1962), 113.

and amalgamate poetry that blurred the very boundaries by which literary historians and critics at the time sought to demarcate it.

Cultural workings in the form of poetic language and conventions can be discerned in Jiang Yan's imitation of Xie Hun. This work "absorbed" and "survived for us" less the new style of the reformer than deep-rooted and pervasive poetic habits that held sway over writers for several centuries. As surely as his chosen model, conventional thematic associations (the passage of time—transformation—death—transcendence), common repertoire of sources (e.g., the *Zhuangzi* and *Laozi*), and established modes of writing (allusive and intertextual) guided the imitator's hand.

Bibliography

Assmann, Aleida. "Canon and Archive." In *A Companion to Cultural Memory Studies*, edited by Astrid Erll and Ansgar Nünning, 97-107. Berlin: De Gruyter, 2010.

Berkowitz, Alan. *Patterns of Disengagement: The Practice and Portrayal of Reclusion in Early Medieval China*. Stanford: Stanford University Press, 2000.

Borges, Jorge Luis. "Funes, The Memorious." Translated by Anthony Kerrigan. In *Ficciones*, edited by Anthony Kerrigan. New York: Grove Press, 1962.

Cao Daoheng 曹道衡. *Zhonggu wenxueshi lunwen ji* 中古文學史論文集. Beijing: Zhonghua shuju, 2002.

Culler, Jonathan. *The Pursuit of Signs: Semiotics, Literature, Deconstruction*. New York: Cornell University Press, 2001.

Emerson, Ralph Waldo. "Quotation and Originality." In *Letters and Social Aims*. Boston: Houghton, Mifflin and Company, 1904.

Han shu 漢書. Compiled by Ban Gu 班固. Beijing: Zhonghua shuju, 1962.

Huainanzi jishi 淮南子集釋. Edited by He Ning 何寧. Beijing: Zhonghua shuju, 1998.

Knechtges, David, trans. *Wen xuan or Selections of Refined Literature, Volume Two: Rhapsodies on Sacrifices, Hunting, Travel, Sightseeing, Palaces and Halls, Rivers and Seas*. Princeton: Princeton University Press, 1987.

Kristeva, Julia. *Desire in Language: A Semiotic Approach to Literature and Art*. Translated by Thomas Gora, Alice Jardine, and Leon S. Roudiez. New York: Columbia University Press, 1980.

Lachmann, Renate. *Memory and Literature: Intertextuality in Russian Literature*. Translated by Roy Sellars and Anthony Wall. Minneapolis: University of Minnesota Press, 1997.

Li Ruiliang 李瑞良. *Zhongguo gudai tushu liutongshi* 中國古代圖書流通史. Shanghai: Shanghai renmin wenxue chubanshe, 2000.

Liezi jishi 列子集釋. Edited by Yang Bojun 楊伯峻. Beijing: Zhonghua shuju, 1979.

Lu Qinli 逯欽立, ed. *Xian Qin Han Wei Jin Nanbeichao shi* 先秦漢魏晉南北朝詩. Beijing: Zhonghua shuju, 1983.

Lynn, Richard John, trans. *The Classic of the Way and Virtue: A New Translation of the Tao-te Ching of Laozi as Interpreted by Wang Bi.* New York: Columbia University Press, 1999.

Mather, Richard B., trans. *Shih-shuo Hsin-yü: A New Account of Tales of the World.* 2nd ed. Ann Arbor: Center for Chinese Studies, The University of Michigan, 2002.

Nan shi 南史. Compiled by Li Yanshou 李延壽. Beijing: Zhonghua shuju, 1975.

Nicholas Morrow Williams. *Imitations of the Self: Jiang Yan and Chinese Poetics.* Leiden/Boston: Brill, 2015.

Queen, Sarah A., and John S. Major, trans. *Luxuriant Gems of the Spring and Autumn.* New York: Columbia University Press, 2016.

Raft, David Zebulon. "Four-syllable Verse in Medieval China." Ph.D. diss., Harvard University, 2007.

Shiji 史記. Compiled by Sima Qian 司馬遷. Beijing: Zhonghua shuju, 1982.

Shipin jizhu 詩品集注. Edited by Cao Xu 曹旭. Shanghai: Shanghai guji chubanshe, 1994.

Swartz, Wendy. *Reading Philosophy, Writing Poetry: Intertextual Modes of Making Meaning in Early Medieval China.* Cambridge, MA: Harvard University Asia Center, 2018.

Sanguo zhi 三國志. Compiled by Chen Shou 陳壽. Beijing: Zhonghua shuju, 1982.

Song shu 宋書. Compiled by Shen Yue 沈約. Beijing: Zhonghua shuju, 1974.

Wang Bi ji jiaoshi 王弼集校釋. Edited by Lou Yulie 樓宇烈. Beijing: Zhonghua shuju, 1999.

Xi Kang ji jiaozhu 嵇康集校注. Annotated by Dai Mingyang 戴明揚. Beijing: Renmin wenxue chubanshe, 1962.

Xiao Tong 蕭統, ed. *Wen xuan* 文選. With commentary by Li Shan 李善. Shanghai: Shanghai guji chubanshe, 1986.

Zhuangzi jishi 莊子集釋. Edited by Guo Qingfan 郭慶藩. Beijing: Zhonghua shuju, 1961.

CHAPTER 3

On Mourning and Sincerity in the *Li ji* and the *Shishuo xinyu*

Jack W. Chen

When we mourn, we are caught within a state of psychological impasse in which we fruitlessly seek to keep alive our dead in memory despite knowing that this is impossible.[1] The experience of such grief demands rationalization even when reason is inadequate, and if we cannot make sense of our grief, then we need ways in which it can be structured so that we can find our way back to the ordinary world from memory's prison. At least this is how Michael J. Puett, in a recent essay, understands the role of mourning ritual, arguing that:

> ... in the case of the mourning rituals, the goal is not to inculcate a particular view of the ancestors. The goal of the rituals is to break us from our tendency to fall into dangerous patterns at the death of a loved one and to help us channel these dispositions more productively. Out of the disjunction between these two will hopefully come a more refined way of responding to the world.[2]

Puett argues against the notion that the primary function of ritual is to encode our subjectivity with determinate ways of thinking and acting, to shape us in a way that conforms to prevailing societal belief systems. What he offers instead is a view of ritual that might be thought of as regulatory (both in the sense of normativizing and as managerial practice), allowing us to negotiate experiential traumas in an idealized, imaginary space. This is what he calls elsewhere

---

1   The relationship between mourning and memory is set forth by Sigmund Freud in his essay, "Mourning and Melancholia." See *On the History of the Psycho-Analytic Movement, Papers on Metapsychology and Other Works*, vol. 14 of *The Standard Edition of the Complete Psychological Works of Sigmund Freud*, edited by James Strachey and translated by Strachey in collaboration with Anna Freud and with the assistance of Alix Strachey and Alan Tyson (London: The Hogarth Press and the Institute of Psycho-Analysis, 1953), 243-58.

2   Puett, "Ritual and Ritual Obligations: Perspectives on Normativity from Classical China," *Journal of Value Inquiry* 49 (2015): 549.

the world of "as if," or the subjunctive world.[3] In his view, ritual creates a realm in which we act out idealized versions of ourselves, how we *should* behave, and then releases us back to the ordinary world to reside in this disjunctive experience of being between who we might be and who we are.

The *Li ji* and the Regulation of Mourning

A major source for Puett's reading of ritual is the "Tan Gong" 檀弓 chapter of the *Li ji* 禮記 (Record of ritual).[4] Of particular importance is this passage: "Mourning ritual is the utmost [realization] of sorrow and grief; it restrains sorrow by following the changes [of feeling], and it is how the superior person keeps in mind those who bore him" 喪禮，哀戚之至也；節哀，順變也；君子念始之者也。[5] This is not the most transparent statement, and one might ask what is meant by the terms "utmost" (*zhi* 至), "restrain" (*jie* 節), "follow" (*shun* 順), and "change" (*bian* 變). Puett translates the passage a little differently than I have: "The rites of mourning are the extreme [expression] of grief and sadness. In modulating grief, one [learns to] accord with the changes [of life and death]. This is how the refined person remembers from where he came."[6] The key difference is in how one understands the phrase *shunbian* 順變, which seems to mean "to follow in accord with changes." The question is, what are the "changes" in question? Puett's reading points to changes on the scale of a person's entire life, turning the mourning rite into a structure that will shape appropriate response to extremities of emotion over the human *durée*. In the

---

3   This is elaborated in greater detail in Adam B. Seligman, Robert P. Weller, Michael J. Puett, and Bennett Simon, eds. *Ritual and Its Consequences: An Essay on the Limits of Sincerity* (New York: Oxford University Press, 2008). A similar argument about the function of mourning ritual is made by the Italian anthropologist Ernesto de Martino in his *Morte e painto rituale nel mondo antico: dal lamento pagano al pianto di Maria* (Torino: Boringhieri, 1975). De Martino's work is discussed in James S. Amelang, "Mourning Becomes Eclectic: Ritual Lament and the Problem of Continuity," *Past & Present* 187 (2005): 3-31.

4   The chapter is titled after an otherwise unknown character named Tan Gong, who is mentioned in its opening lines.

5   *Li ji xunzuan* 禮記訓纂, annotated by Zhu Bin 朱彬 (1753-1834), edited by Rao Qinnong 饒欽農 (Beijing: Zhonghua shuju, 1996), 4.127. I have consulted both the translations in James Legge, trans., *Li Chi: Book of Rites. An Encyclopedia of Ancient Ceremonial Usages, Religious Creeds, and Social Institutions*, edited by Ch'u Chai and Winberg Chai, 2 vols. (New York: University Books, 1967), 167; and *Li ji jinzhu jinyi* 禮記今註今譯, annotated and translated by Wang Meng'ou 王夢鷗, 2nd rev. ed. (Taipei: Taiwan Shangwu yinshuguan, 1984), 162.

6   Puett, "Ritual and Ritual Obligations," 544.

absence of other evidence, I would read this on a more local scale, understanding the changes as referring to the moderation of emotions over the course of mourning. To be sure, a less expansive reading does not deny the possibility of Puett's interpretation: how one emerges from the trauma of loss, guided by the norming structures of ritual, can (and probably does) affect the entirety of one's sense of identity. This said, I agree with Puett that ritual gives structure to memory, providing a modulated way to remember whence a person comes, though I would add that ritual form might itself be considered a structure of memory. As I discuss in the following paragraph, what ritual provides is a form through which the painful repetitions of memory may be managed, one that thereafter becomes inextricable from memory.[7]

Here, it is worth consulting the explanation of this passage found in Kong Yingda's 孔穎達 (574-648) subcommentary to the *Liji*, which was one of the *zhengyi* 正義 ("correct meaning") commentaries compiled by order of Tang Emperor Taizong 唐太宗 (r. 626-49). The subcommentary reads:

> This speaks of how a person may perhaps encounter disaster. Although he may be stricken with despondency and sorrow, this is still not the extremity of sorrow. It is only when he experiences the mourning ritual for his parents that it is the utmost extreme of sorrow and grief. Since this is the utmost extreme, if there is no form of restraint, one fears that he will harm his nature.... As for the reason he restrains his sorrow, it is because he desires to accord with the despondency and sorrow of the filial son and to be allowed to gradually change [that is, move on from his grief]. As for the reason why he must follow these changes [of feeling], it is because the superior person thinks on how his parents gave birth to him, and yet fears that this will harm his nature, thus he follows these changes.

> 言人或有禍災，雖或悲哀，未是哀之至極。唯居父母喪禮，是哀戚之至極也。既為至極，若無節文，恐其傷性 ... 。所以節哀者，欲順孝子悲哀，使之漸變也... 。所以必此順變者，君子思念父母之生已，恐其傷性，故順變也.[8]

The subcommentary explains that the mourner "restrains his sorrow" so that he may "accord with the despondency and sorrow of the filial son" and so "be

---

7   For a discussion of managing the trauma of loss in examples of poetry, see Tian Xiaofei's essay in this volume.

8   Quoted in *Li ji xunzuan*, 4.128.

allowed to gradually change." The term *bian* thus initially refers to the course of mourning rather than to the entire life of the mourner. The second part of the explanation, however, addresses a broader context for the changes dictated by ritual, stating that the mourner "must follow these changes" because he "keeps in mind how his parents gave birth to him" but also "fears that this will harm his nature." The mourner uses the graduated changes prescribed by ritual to balance his feelings of grief for his parents against the necessity of finding a way through the grief. Here, it is the more expansive context of the mourner's life that is at stake, since a modulated response to death is what preserves the grieving son's nature and keeps him from following his parents into the grave. Or, to put it another way, the memory of the parent is what endangers the child: the child remembers the parent but should not remain within the memory if he is to survive. Ritual is what restructures memory, and what is more, becomes the very structure of memory that allows one to pass through its trauma and live.

Although Puett grounds his argument in the *Li ji*, he is actually not making a specific argument about ritual in early China, but about the nature of ritual as a broader cultural modality. This is why, in part, Puett seeks to find evidence for a more expansive claim for ritual's role in regulating the trauma of extreme emotion. Puett's larger argument has to do with a posited contrast between two different modes of self-understanding, which he refers to as ritual and sincerity. If we understand the mode of ritual as an imaginary normative world (the world of "as if") that is separate from this world but nevertheless shapes us and guides our responses in this world, then the mode of sincerity argues for an interior cohesion of selfhood that will inform this world (what Puett calls the world of "as is"). Sincerity is "characterized by a search for motives and for purity of motives"; it "privileges intent over action."[9] To the adherent of sincerity, ritual is mere convention; it does not possess inherent value insofar as it is empty form. Puett points out that the ritual and sincerity modes are co-existent in each of us, as alternative frames of understanding, although it is clear where his sympathies lie. Moreover, Puett argues that sincerity is a worldview identified with modernity and with modernity's peculiar emphasis on the self as the locus of valuation, thus situating ritual as a traditional or premodern mode of thinking. This binarism, depicted by Puett as a historical metanarrative, is debatable, particularly because the concept of sincerity lies at the heart of much discussion of mourning ritual in early and medieval China.

---

9   See Seligman et al., *Ritual and Its Consequences*, 105.

Affective Sincerity in the *Li ji*

Let me return, then, to the early Chinese context, and reconsider the question of ritual and sincerity in regard to the question of mourning. Here, we do find statements such as the one Puett offers from the *Li ji* as evidence for a ritual understanding that proceeds from mourning and may help to guide and shape one's social conception of selfhood. The need for limitations on the expression of mourning is clear in passages such as this one: "Beating [one's breast] and flailing [in grief] are the utmost [expressions] of sorrow. Yet they have set counts that serve as limiting procedures" 辟踊，哀之至也。有筭，為之節文也.[10] These "set counts" (*suan* 筭) and "limiting procedures" (*jiewen* 節文) regulate the extremes of emotional response, preserving the mourner from injury to self since the "utmost" (*zhi* 至) expression of grief would take the mourner into potentially dangerous emotional territory.

However, potential self-injury is not always the reason given for regulating grief through ritual procedures. Another take on this problem can be seen in the following passage, which is concerned with excess of feeling and the transmitability of ritual form:

> Among the people of Bian there was one whose mother died and who wept like a child. Master Kong said, "As for sorrow, this is indeed sorrow, but it would be difficult to continue this. As for ritual, it is what can be transmitted, and thus crying and flailing have their limits."

> 弁人有其母死而孺子泣者。孔子曰：「哀則哀矣，而難為繼也。夫禮，為可傳也，故哭踊有節。[11]

Kong Yingda's subcommentary on this passage reads: "The sages instituted rituals, allowing later people to be able to transmit and to continue them; thus, they instituted limits for crying and flailing, and in this way took moderation as the proper measure—how could one exceed this to such an extent?" 夫聖人

---

10 *Li ji xunzuan*, 4.129. See also Legge, *Li Chi*, 169; and Wang Meng'ou, *Li ji jinzhu jinyi*, 4.160. The term *jiewen* 節文 literally means "writs of restrictions" but in this context, it is the *suan* 算 that serves as the source of the restriction, and not a separate text, thus I have translated this as "limiting procedures."

11 *Li ji xunzuan*, 3.104. See also Legge, *Li Chi*, 145-46; and Wang Meng'ou, *Li ji jinzhu jinyi*, 3.122. For a different translation and reading of this passage, see Michael David Kaulana Ing, *The Dysfunction of Ritual in Early Confucianism* (New York: Oxford University Press, 2012), 118-19.

制禮，使後人可傳可繼，故制為哭踊之節，以中為度耳，豈可過甚。[12]   The continuation (*ji* 繼 and *chuan* 傳) of ritual form is what is at stake in how Confucius here understands the problem of excessive grief. He acknowledges the mourner's sincerity, but his main concern is with how the affective sincerity of the man's grief cannot be passed down in a normative ritual procedure. To put it in Weberian terms, while the excessive grief of the mourner may represent a charismatic display of grief, such mourning cannot be routinized and thus normalized as a regular institution within society.[13] The limitations (*jie*) of mourning thus refer here not simply to how one provides a stable, standard measure for the expression of filial mourning, but more importantly, to a reproducible and universalizable form for mourning in the community. As opposed to the regulation of private memory through ritual form, what this represents is the institutional function of ritual, the way in which ritual serves as the basis for encoding cultural memory.

In the above example, we see a rather formalistic and conventional understanding of ritual in the *Li ji*, where ritual form is understood as a means of encoding cultural norms and transmitting them over time—that is, embodying a technology of cultural mnemonics. However, the *Li ji* also contains statements that speak to the importance of emotional sincerity and indeed privilege sincere emotional response over the proper observance of ritual form. The following passage is one example:

> Zilu said, "I have heard this from the Master: In terms of mourning ritual, to be deficient in sorrow and to have a surfeit of ritual is not as good as being deficient in ritual and having a surfeit of sorrow; and as for sacrifices, to be deficient in reverence and to have a surfeit of ritual is not as good as being deficient in ritual and having a surfeit of reverence."

> 子路曰：「吾聞諸夫子：喪禮，與其哀不足而禮有餘也，不若禮不足而哀有餘也。祭禮，與其敬不足而禮有餘也，不若禮不足而敬有餘也.」[14]

This passage prioritizes the internal responses of grief and reverence over outward displays of ritual devotion, arguing that it would be better to have a

---

12   Quoted in *Li ji xunzuan*, 3.104.

13   On the routinization of charisma, see Max Weber, *Economics and Society: An Outline of Interpretive Sociology*, ed. Guenther Roth and Claus Wittich (Berkeley: University of California Press, 1968), 1121-23.

14   *Li ji xunzuan*, 3.99. See also Legge, *Li Chi*, 141; and Wang Meng'ou, *Li ji jinzhu jinyi*, 3.113.

deficiency in ritual and a surfeit of sorrow than a surfeit of ritual and a deficiency in sorrow. There is, however, a question of what a "surfeit of ritual" (*li you yu* 禮有餘) or "being deficient in ritual" (*li buzu* 禮不足) means. Kong Yingda's subcommentary defines the former as an excess of "mourning paraphernalia and clothing" 明器衣衾之屬, suggesting that the passage is criticizing those who put on an extravagant performance of ritual obligation through the sheer number of objects used. While the *Li ji* clearly makes arguments for the ritual moderation of emotion (and how emotion might be regulated through ritual), here one finds an argument for what might be called affective sincerity, an interior cohesion of feeling that trumps the exterior performance of ritual. This passage thus provides a counterexample to the main thrust of Puett's argument, but more importantly, it brings to the fore the way in which the *Li ji* is concerned with the question of balance between the two poles of ritual and sincerity. Ritual may provide an imaginary structure for regulating unbearable emotional excess, but it is emotional response that informs the rite, giving it reason and purpose. How one strikes the right balance between ritual form and affective sincerity is the problem that this last example takes up, even as other parts of the *Li ji* articulate a greater emphasis on emotional moderation or on routinization of ritual practice.

Elsewhere in the *Li ji*, we find an even greater emphasis on the mourner's affective response, which, when expressed fully, *should* bring injury to the mourner's body. Yet, even in such passages, this toll that grief takes on the body is mediated through ritual, making it difficult to distinguish between the effects of emotional sincerity and the effects of the mourner's subordination to ritual strictures. We see this in the following passage, which comes from the "Wen sang" 問喪 (Asking about mourning) chapter:

> When the parent has just died, [the son] pins and wraps his hair[15] and goes barefoot; he folds in his shirtfront[16] and crosses his arms, crying. With a distressed and grieving heart and with painful and worried thoughts, his kidneys suffer injury, his liver becomes dessicated, and his lungs become charred. Neither water nor brew should enter his mouth

---

15   This phrase *jisi* 雞斯 is glossed by the Zheng Xuan 鄭玄 (127-200) commentary as meaning *jixi* 笄纚, "to pin and wrap [one's hair]." Cited in *Li ji xunzuan*, 35.825.

16   This phrase *cha shangren* 扱上衽 occurs as *cha ren* 扱衽 in a few other passages in the *Li ji*, and it seems to refer to how mourning garb is worn, with the shirt front or lapels folded or tucked under the sash. It is unclear whether the *shang* 上 should be understood as modifying *ren* 衽 or as a verb meaning "to pull up." See the annotation in Wang Meng'ou, *Li ji jinzhu jinyi*, 56.

for three days, and he should not light fires. Thus, those in the neighborhood should prepare gruel and porridge for him and feed him. Now, as grief and sorrow are within, therefore his appearance without will change. As pain and worry are within, therefore his mouth finds nothing sweet, and his body finds no ease in sensuous pleasures.

親始死，雞斯徒跣，扱上衽，交手哭。惻怛之心，痛疾之意，傷腎，乾肝，焦肺。水漿不入口三日，不舉火。故鄰里為之糜粥以飲食之。夫悲哀在中，故形變於外也。痛疾在心，故口不甘味，身不安美也.[17]

The first sentence describes the initial steps in the ritual actions of mourning, which are how the mourner demonstrates that he is entering into a conventional role. However, the second sentence shifts the perspective to describe how the mourner's feelings lead to physiological dysfunction, how grief causes serious injury to the mourner inside. We then move back to ritual, which imposes a term of privation upon the body and indeed may be as much the cause of the internal organs' failure as grief is. Finally, in the last sentence, we move from inside to outside, from the grief within to the resulting corporeal changes without. Grief deprives the mourner of joy, and so he finds nothing sweet and takes no ease in bodily pleasure.

If one vision of early Chinese mourning ritual advocated measured forms of grief, here we find the dangerous possibility of grief that brings lasting harm to the body. This passage is prescriptive, telling the mourner how he should behave and feel, and thus it can be read as a conventional process that takes the bereaved through defined (and thus controlled) stages of grief. What is interesting is the way in which the perspective shifts between ritual form and affective sincerity, without clear resolution of how the balance is to be struck. To be sure, the mourner cannot remain in the perilous state of mourning, though the account of the physical changes caused by grief speak to the corporeal reality of traumatic memory and emotional injury, which cannot be addressed through ritual and yet also cannot be separated from it.

Exemplary Mourning in *Shishuo xinyu*

The *Li ji* is a heterogeneous text, and its statements about ritual draw upon different ideas from within early China. This heterogeneity was in turn reflected

---

17   *Li ji xunzuan*, 35.825. For translations, see Legge, *Li Chi*, 2:375; and Wang Meng'ou, *Li ji jinzhu jinyi*, 901-2.

in later discussions of ritual mourning, which responded to the various strands of the *Li ji* and to other early texts, inheriting questions of ritual observance and affective sincerity while situating them within contemporary debates. The *Shishuo xinyu* 世說新語 (Recent anecdotes from the talk of the ages), compiled in the name of the Liu-Song prince Liu Yiqing 劉義慶 (403-444), is perhaps not the first text that would come to mind for discussions of mourning practice, as it is usually treated as a repository for early medieval metaphysical conversations, historical gossip, and literary anecdotes. Nevertheless, the problem of mourning is central to the *Shishuo xinyu*, which not only devotes all of Chapter 17, "Mourning the Departed" ("Shang shi" 傷逝), to this topic but also returns to scenes of mourning throughout the entire collection.

In fact, the first chapter, "Virtuous Conduct" ("De xing" 德行), takes up the theme of mourning in a number of anecdotes, such as the following:

> Wang Rong and He Qiao met with the "great bereavement" [the death of a parent] at the same time, and both were praised for their filiality. Wang was reduced to "chicken-bone"-like thinness and kept to his bed; He wept and cried, but completed the ritual observances. Emperor Wu [Sima Yan 司馬炎 (236-290)] said to Liu Yi, "Have you been observing the behavior of Wang and He?[18] I have heard that the sorrow and suffering of He exceeds ritual observance, causing people to worry about him." Yi said, "He Qiao, although he has completed all ritual observances, has suffered no injury to spirit or health. As for Wang Rong, although he did not complete the observances, his sorrow has brought such devastation that his bones stick out. I consider He Qiao to exemplify filiality while alive, but Wang Rong to exemplify filiality unto death. Your Majesty should not worry himself over Qiao, but instead, over Rong."

王戎、和嶠同時遭大喪，俱以孝稱。王雞骨支牀，和哭泣備禮。武帝謂劉仲雄曰：「卿數省王、和不？聞和哀苦過禮，使人憂之。」仲雄曰：「和嶠雖備禮，神氣不損；王戎雖不備禮，而哀毀骨立。臣以和嶠生孝，王戎死孝。陛下不應憂嶠，而應憂戎.」[19]

---

18 For the reign and biography of Jin Emperor Wu 晉武帝 (r. 265-290), see *Jin shu* 晉書, edited by Fang Xuanling 房玄齡 (579-648) (Beijing: Zhonghua shuju, 1974), 3.49-88.

19 *Shishuo xinyu jiaojian* 世說新語校箋, compiled by Liu Yiqing 劉義慶 (403-444) and annotated by Yang Yong 楊勇 (Beijing: Zhonghua shuju, 2006), 1.17.18. For all of my translations, I have consulted Liu I-Ch'ing, *Shih-shuo hsin-yü: A New Account of Tales of the World*, translated and annotated by Richard B. Mather, 2nd ed. (Ann Arbor: Center for Chinese Studies, The University of Michigan, 2002); and *Xinyi Shishuo xinyu* 新譯世說新語, annotated and translated by Liu Zhenghao 劉正浩, Qiu Xieyou 邱燮友, Chen

This anecdote compares the respective responses to the loss of a parent by Wang Rong 王戎 (234-305), one of the Seven Worthies of the Bamboo Grove, and He Qiao 和嶠 (d. 292), who would rise to the position of Director of the Secretariat in the early Jin court. He Qiao wept and displayed the regular expressions of grief, but he was nonetheless able to complete the proper ritual observances. Wang Rong, by contrast, was unable to complete the observances, and indeed wasted away until he was close to death. The Han imperial descendant Liu Yi 劉毅 (ca. 210-85), who appears nowhere else in the *Shishuo xinyu*, thus characterizes He Qiao as "filiality while alive" (*shengxiao* 生孝) and Wang Rong as "filiality unto death" (*sixiao* 死孝). While there is no explicit value judgment as to which form of mourning is more filial, it is Wang Rong's overwhelming grief, his inability to complete the rites, and his self-starvation that make him worthy of concern in the conversation between Jin Emperor Wu 晉武帝 (r. 265-90) and Liu Yi. In this way, "filiality unto death" is more noteworthy, given that "filiality while alive" is the expected standard of behavior for the bereft.

In many ways, this anecdote dramatizes the comment made by Zilu in the *Li ji* regarding the superiority of sincere feeling over ritual formalism. Wang Rong is so committed to his grief that he wills himself almost to death, following his parent (in this case, his mother) into the grave. It is not exactly that He Qiao is lacking sincerity of feeling, but he performs the mourning observances in a conventional manner and would not be worth commenting on if it were not for Wang Rong's simultaneous, more extravagant performance. Indeed, Wang Rong's mourning is so noteworthy that it is represented a few anecdotes later in the same chapter of the *Shishuo xinyu*:

> In meeting with the distress [of his mother's death], Wang [Rong] of Anfeng, with his exemplary nature, surpassed all others [in the grief that arose from the filiality]. Director Pei [Kai] went to offer his condolences and said, "If such lamentation could indeed injure a person, then Junchong [Wang Rong's style-name] will not be able to avoid the criticism that he has destroyed his nature."

> 王安豐遭艱，至性過人。裴令往弔之，曰：「若使一慟果能傷人，濬沖必不免滅性之譏.」[20]

Manming 陳滿銘, Xu Tanhui 許錟輝, and Huang Junlang 黃俊郎 (Taipei: Sanmin shuju, 2003).

20   *Shishuo xinyu jiaojian*, 1.20.21.

Here, the characterization of Wang Rong's grief, which surpasses all others, is presented as arising from his "exemplary nature" (*zhixing* 至性). While this "exemplary nature" is not defined in the anecdote itself, it would seem to refer to the absolute sincerity of his filiality, a claim of interior dedication and cohesion of character that manifests itself in a noteworthy display of grief. This time the comment on Wang Rong comes from Pei Kai 裴楷 (237-291), a prominent Jin court official famed for his fine appearance and manners (indeed, known by contemporaries as the "Man of Jade," *yuren* 玉人). Pei Kai calls into question the wisdom of Wang Rong's excessive grief, noting that his nature is precisely what others will say is destroyed in the course of his mourning.

Mourning as Performance

In both of these anecdotes, the act of mourning is the subject of commentary from a member of the social community. This complicates the *Li ji*'s concern with the rightful balance between ritual and emotion, adding the wrinkle of contemporary opinion or judgment. In the *Shishuo xinyu*, the mourner is as if on a stage: his actions are scrutinized by his peers. This textually represented scrutiny calls attention to the performative nature of ritual observance and emphasizes the external reception of the act over the interior pain of memory. In other words, *Shishuo xinyu* places value on the extravagance of mourning insofar as it is this excessiveness that becomes the focus of social talk and commentary. Indeed, for the community represented in this early medieval world it is the capacity to attract gossip, to be talked about in a kind of social focalization, that stands as the currency of value, rather than whether one follows or disregards proper ritual procedure. Excessive mourning is behavior that is worth talking about, and the representations of such mourning in *Shishuo xinyu* always come with an evaluative comment, a judgment of the community. But the question of ritual and sincerity remains: In any given instance, is the performance of noteworthy behavior a sincere manifestation of inward character and thus necessitated by an interior coherence, or is it a performance designed to attract attention from the community and thus realize the subject within a social network of talk and evaluation?

For the world of the *Shishuo xinyu*, the answer may be both. Much of this collection of anecdotes is dedicated to the evaluation of character and action, with the assumption of coherence between the exterior manner or appearance and the interior qualities of a person. At the same time, these evaluations of character take place within the public space of talk and gossip, as virtuoso performances in which the evaluator seeks to demonstrate his (or, less commonly, her) command of social knowledge and linguistic skill. Such acts of evaluation are informed by older practices of political recommendation based on defined character traits (most prominently, filiality) from the Han dynasty, but within the world of *Shishuo xinyu*, these speech acts are often ends in themselves.[21] Indeed, the successful performance of an evaluation is often more noteworthy than whoever or whatever occasioned the evaluation in the first place, and arguably demonstrates an even more significant talent in the eyes of this textually represented community.

If the act of evaluation places mourning observance upon a public stage, then the mourner cannot avoid the consciousness that his ritual actions are being read as evidence for interior character, which in turns affects his performance of the ritual. This self-awareness highlights the relationship between ritual performance and audience in a way that differs from the world of the *Record of Ritual*, which does not seem to conceive of the potential distortions of intention created by the observing audience. Here we see again the lingering influence of the old recommendation procedures, particularly given the central importance of filiality within medieval political institutions. The consciousness of social judgment and political recommendation on the part of the mourners cannot but have changed how their mourning was enacted, and this can be seen in the following story:

> The brothers Wu Daozhu [Tanzhi] and Wu Fuzi [Yinzhi] were residing in Danyang Commandery. Later, they met with the distress of the passing of their mother, Madame Tong, and wept together day and night. Whenever thoughts [of her] arose, or when guests came to pay condolences, they would howl and flail in extremities of sorrow. Passers-by shed tears on their behalf. Han Kang[bo] at the time was magistrate of Danyang and his mother, surnamed Yin, was in the commandery. Every time she heard

---

21   On Han practices of character evaluation and political recommendation, see Yao Wei 姚
      維, *Cai xing zhi bian: renge zhuti yu Wei Jin xuanxue* 才性之辨— 人格主題與魏晉玄學
      (Beijing: Renmin chubanshe, 2007), 20-28; Yan Buke 閻步克, *Chaju zhidu bianqian shigao*
      察舉制度變遷史稿 (Beijing: Zhongguo renmin daxue chubanshe, 2009), 16-99; and
      Dingxin Zhao, "The Han Bureaucracy: Its Origin, Nature, and Development," in *State
      Power in Ancient China and Rome*, ed. Walter Scheidel (Oxford: Oxford University Press,
      2015), 68-71, 82-83. Related to this, I have translated sections from the *Renwu zhi* 人物志
      (Treatise on personality) by Liu Shao 劉劭 (fl. 3rd c.), which deals with political character
      evaluation, alongside selections from the *Shishuo xinyu* in "Classifications of People and
      Conduct: Liu Shao's *Treatise on Personality* and Liu Yiqing's *Recent Anecdotes from the Talk
      of the Ages*," in *Early Medieval China: A Sourcebook*, ed. Wendy Swartz, Robert Ford Cam-
      pany, Yang Lu, and Jessey J.C. Choo (New York: Columbia University Press, 2014), 350-69.

the weeping of the two Wu brothers, she would be filled with sorrow. She told Kangbo, "If you ever serve as selector of officials, you should look after them well." Kangbo himself understood the two men well. As it turned out, Han Kangbo later indeed became Minister of Personnel. The elder Wu did not outlast the observance of mourning, though the younger Wu thereupon attained great honors.

吳道助、附子兄弟，居在丹陽郡。後遭母童夫人艱，朝夕哭臨。及思至，賓客弔省，號踊哀絕，路人為之落淚。韓康伯時為丹陽尹，母殷在郡，每聞二吳之哭，輒為悽惻。語康伯曰：「汝若為選官，當好料理此人。」康伯亦甚相知。韓後果為吏部尚書。大吳不免哀制，小吳遂大貴達.[22]

Wu Tanzhi 吳坦之 and Wu Yinzhi 吳隱之 (both fl. late 4th century and identified here by their childhood names) appear in the *Shishuo xinyu* only in this anecdote. As the anecdote relates, Wu Tanzhi did not survive his grief. The younger brother Yinzhi, who managed to survive his grief, is featured in the *Jin shu* "Collected Biographies of Good Officials" ("Liangli liezhuan" 良吏列傳), where the text records how he went on to serve in a number of prestigious positions in the court and elsewhere.[23] We may understand the brothers as respectively representing "filiality unto death" and "filiality while alive," though both enact performances of absolute filial sincerity that wins them the notice of the community. Moreover, the community that witnesses their filiality is not content to simply play the role of audience but actively intervenes in their lives, weeping in sympathy with them and eventually ensuring that the surviving brother is recommended to high office.

Still, whereas the earlier tales about Wang Rong suggest that he is unable to do anything but mourn, even at the cost of completing the proper ritual, the brothers Wu exhibit their grief under two specific situations: whenever they think of their mother, and whenever guests come to pay respects. To be said to have wept uncontrollably at the memory of their departed mother describes their affective sincerity, but to perform the same acts in the presence of guests speaks to an awareness of public opinion and what is conventionally expected for filial sons mourning a parent. I would not go so far as to argue that the Wu brothers were behaving in this way in order to secure public praise, given that the elder brother dies (again, evidence of sincerity), but this detail complicates how we might understand the effect upon mourning ritual of an audience that

---

22   *Shishuo xinyu jiaojian*, 1.47.45
23   See *Jin shu*, 90.2340-43.

is not content simply to observe from afar. This is the anecdote that stands at the end of the first chapter of the *Shishuo xinyu*, and it captures many of the themes found in the first chapter, most notably the tension between sincerity of character, conventional expectations, and public opinion. In fact, if we see in *Shishuo xinyu* a special interest in the sincerity of mourning at the expense of conventional norms, it is a representation of sincerity that is almost always complicated by self-consciousness of the community's judgments, turning the exhibition of sincerity into a performance of sincerity.

In many of the scenes of mourning found in Chapter 1, the mourner is the object of talk by the community, with little or no opportunity to explain himself or his actions. Still, as with the other figures who exemplify moral behavior in this chapter, it is the community that often provides the necessary evaluation, providing interpretive guidance for the reader. In anecdotes in other chapters, however, the central figure is called upon to explain himself. Wang Rong, who figures in two anecdotes from this first chapter, appears also in the chapter of the *Shishuo xinyu* dedicated to mourning (Chapter 17), this time in conversation with Shan Jian 山簡 (253-312), the son of his fellow member of the Seven Worthies, Shan Tao 山濤 (205-83). The anecdote reads:

> When Wang Rong lost his son Wanzi [Sui 綏, ca. 257-275], Shan Jian went to see him. Wang's grief was such that he could not control himself. Jian said, "For a child that was just a 'critter at the bosom', why should you come to this?" Wang said, "A sage may forget his feelings, and the basest people cannot attain feelings. Where feelings are most concentrated is precisely among our kind." Jian was persuaded by his words and grieved all the more on his behalf.

> 王戎喪兒萬子，山簡往省之，王悲不自勝。簡曰：「孩抱中物，何至於此？」王曰：「聖人忘情，最下不及情；情之所鍾，正在我輩。」簡服其言，更為之慟.[24]

Here, Wang Rong has lost his son, identified by his child-name as Wang Sui, although the nineteen-year-old Sui could hardly be called a "critter at the bosom" (*baozhong wu* 抱中物). The commentary by Liu Xiaobiao 劉孝標 (462-521) suggests that Wang Rong should be emended to his cousin Wang Yan 王衍 (256-311), who did indeed lose his child in infancy. Whichever Wang it was, the main point of the anecdote turns on the defense of the mourner's uncontrollable grief at the death of a child rather than of a parent, for which filiality

---

24   *Shishuo xinyu jiaojian*, 17.4.583.

provided license. Shan Jian questions Wang Rong's inability to master himself, particularly for a child who was still in infancy and thus nothing more than a *wu* 物, a "critter" or "thing." (This is, of course, an outrageous question, but in the anecdote it is presented as a question that may be entertained.) Wang's response is not an argument about or against ritual convention, but instead an argument about the innate feelings of human beings. He divides humans into three classes: sages (*sheng* 聖), the "most base" (*zui xia* 最下), and "those of our kind" (*wobei* 我輩). The sages may forget feeling and the base may not even have feelings, but for those who belong to Wang's class of person, feeling is what is most concentrated (*zhong* 鍾), and thus it is only natural for Wang to mourn unreservedly for his child. However, to whom does "our kind" refer? Does he mean the *mingshi* 名士, the "gentlemen of repute" who comprise the social network represented in *Shishuo xinyu*? Or does he mean his immediate circle of friends and family, the Seven Worthies and their scions? Whatever Wang Rong's intent may be, by positing a class of people who might be called "our kind" Wang forces Shan Jian to either agree with him, thus confirming Shan's own status as "our kind," or to disagree, making Shan not "our kind." Shan, of course, is persuaded by this argument, though one might also say that he has no real choice, given the coercive nature of Wang's rhetorical tactic.

Friendship and Anecdotal Commemoration

The performance of affective sincerity thus becomes a new behavioral norm for a particular group of individuals, superseding, in many ways, the older ritual discourse on mourning. In place of the theater of ritual we find a theater of affect, one that privileges a "natural" response to the experience of death without the moderating procedures found in classical ritual theory. Moreover, it is not only the death of one's parent that might fill one with a life-threatening grief; the death a close friend might also be sufficient justification. This can be seen in the following story about the prominent monk Zhi Dun 支遁 (314-366) and his friend Faqian 法虔:

> After Zhi Daolin [Dun] mourned for Faqian, his spirits were depleted and spent, and his manner increasingly diminished. He often said to others, "In the past, Carpenter Shi abandoned his hatchet after the man from Ying [died], Master [Bo]ya halted his strings after Zhongzi [Qi died].[25] If

---

25   The story of Carpenter Shi is recorded in *Zhuangzi* 24 ("Xu Wugui" 徐无鬼); see *Zhuangzi jishi* 莊子集釋, ed. Guo Qingfan 郭慶藩 (1844-96?) (Beijing: Zhonghua shuju, 1961),

I surmise from my own example and examine others, indeed this is not empty talk! Ever since the one who wordlessly matched me departed, when I speak no one appreciates it. My heart is stuffed up and knotted—I will perhaps perish!" And indeed, after a year Zhi died.

支道林喪法虔之後，精神霣喪，風味轉墜。常謂人曰：「昔匠石廢斤
於郢人，牙生輟絃於鍾子，推己外求，良不虛也！冥契既逝，發言莫
賞，中心蘊結，余其亡矣！」卻後一年，支遂殞.[26]

Zhi Dun is known in *Shishuo xinyu* for his skill at "pure conversation" (*qingtan* 清談) and his scholarship on the *Zhuangzi* 莊子. While he has a number of famous conversation partners, it would seem that Faqian was the one who really understood him, despite the fact that Faqian appears only in this anecdote. In his lament over Faqian's death, Zhi Dun makes mention of two earlier stories of exemplary friendship: that of Carpenter Shi 匠石 in the *Zhuangzi*, who could slice a dab of plaster from the nose of his friend (the man from Ying) using a hatchet, and that of the master musician Boya 伯牙 and his perfect auditor Zhongzi Qi 鍾子期. In both of these stories, the death of the friend means an end to the talented person's ability (or reason) to perform, illustrating the integral relationship between talent and appreciation. This relationship is, moreover, typical of themes central to the *Shishuo xinyu*, insofar as the virtuosic performance of talent (in whatever form) always requires a public audience that will comment on it and evaluate it. Zhi Dun goes one further than either Carpenter Shi and Boya, himself dying a year after his friend has died, for no other reason, it would seem, than a lack of being appreciated.

And yet Zhi Dun's death does not mark the end of his presence in *Shishuo xinyu*: after all, the world of talk continues well after death. In a brief vignette, we see Dai Kui 戴逵 (d. 396), a recluse known for his musical and painterly abilities, make one last comment on Zhi Dun's life:[27]

Dai Kui saw Zhi Dun's grave and said, "His virtuous tones are not yet distant, but the arching trees are already clustered. I hope that his rarefied

---

24.843. On Carpenter Shi, see also pp. 51-52 in this volume. The story of Bo Ya and Zhongzi Qi is found in a variety of different early sources, including *Liezi* 列子 5 ("Tang wen" 湯問); see *Liezi jishi* 列子集釋, ed. Yang Bojun 楊伯峻 (Beijing: Zhonghua shuju, 1978), 5.178.

26   *Shishuo xinyu jiaojian*, 17.11.586.

27   On Dai Kui, see *Jin shu*, 94.2457-59. His biography preserves his essay, "Fangda wei fei dao lun" 放達為非道論 (On anti-libertinism).

arguments will go on and on, and not end together with his allotment of *qi*."

戴公見林法師墓，曰：「德音未遠，而拱木已積。冀神理綿綿，不與氣運俱盡耳.」[28]

Dai Kui's words declare a hope (*ji* 冀) that Zhi Dun's discursive brilliance will be remembered even when the man himself is gone. This is not an act of mourning so much as it is a valediction, but this comment recalls the memorial work of mourning, which defines simultaneously the space in which the dead may be remembered and the means by which the living may be preserved. After all, the fixing of the dead in their proper place is one of the main functions of mourning ritual, the means by which the living are able to go on with their lives.

What the Dai Kui anecdote foregrounds, however, is how the pain of memory that might pin the bereaved to the moment of loss is transformed into commemoration, a shared experience of loss that marks the bereaved as a community who will remember the dead together. This happens on both the diegetic level of the anecdotal narrative and through the very form of the anecdote itself. Thus, we may first note that Dai Kui's wish is performative, and by speaking the words, he makes it real, at least, for the members of the community who will remember Zhi Dun. At the same time, what transmits the words beyond Dai Kui's time is the anecdote that inscribes and records a particular moment, perhaps not always faithfully or precisely but almost always in a *memorable* manner, so that the moment is shared from one generation to the next.

It is here that I will conclude, with the point that anecdotes are communal forms that encode memory, allowing the transmission and preservation of a shared moment through time. After all, the very existence of the anecdote is evidence of a social community that remembers an occasion and seeks to preserve it through its retelling across a network of interested parties. In this way, the form of anecdote recalls that of ritual, which, as noted above, encodes the institutional memory of proper response to what might seem an overwhelmingly private trauma. Ritual universalizes experience, teaching us how others have managed grief so that in the end we feel less alone in our experiences. Similarly, we may share in the commemoration of anecdote, a sharing of experience that is not lessened by the fact that we may not quite fully experience the affect that is represented. For the *Shishuo xinyu*, the repeated scenes of

---

28   *Shishuo xinyu jiaojian,* 17.13.588.

mourning not only address the ritual history of grief, thematizing the question of how one should properly respond, but also return us to again and again to the ways in which mourning makes public a private moment, inviting commentary from the social world beyond and even, at times, providing the possibility of a shared, communal experience.

Bibliography

Amelang, James S. "Mourning Becomes Eclectic: Ritual Lament and the Problem of Continuity." *Past & Present* 187 (2005): 3-31.

De Martino, Ernesto. *Morte e painto rituale nel mondo antico: dal lamento pagano al pianto di Maria*. Torino: Boringhieri, 1975.

Freud, Sigmund. *On the History of the Psycho-Analytic Movement, Papers on Metapsychology and Other Works*. Vol. 14 of *The Standard Edition of the Complete Psychological Works of Sigmund Freud*. Edited by James Strachey and translated by Strachey et al. London: The Hogarth Press and the Institute of Psycho-Analysis, 1953.

Ing, Michael David Kaulana. *The Dysfunction of Ritual in Early Confucianism*. New York: Oxford University Press, 2012.

Jin shu 晉書. Compiled by Fang Xuanling 房玄齡. Beijing: Zhonghua shuju, 1974.

Legge, James, trans. *Li Chi: Book of Rites. An Encyclopedia of Ancient Ceremonial Usages, Religious Creeds, and Social Institutions*. Edited by Ch'u Chai and Winberg Chai. 2 vols. New York: University Books, 1967.

Li ji jinzhu jinyi 禮記今註今譯. Annotated and translated by Wang Meng'ou 王夢鷗. 2nd ed. Taipei: Taiwan Shangwu yinshuguan, 1984.

Li ji xunzuan 禮記訓纂. Annotated by Zhu Bin 朱彬 and edited by Rao Qinnong 饒欽農. Beijing: Zhonghua shuju, 1996.

Liezi jishi 列子集釋. Edited by Yang Bojun 楊伯峻. Beijing: Zhonghua shuju, 1978.

Liu I-Ch'ing. *Shih-shuo hsin-yü: A New Account of Tales of the World*. Translated and annotated by Richard B. Mather. 2nd ed. Ann Arbor: Center for Chinese Studies, The University of Michigan, 2002.

Puett, Michael J. "Ritual and Ritual Obligations: Perspectives on Normativity from Classical China." *Journal of Value Inquiry* 49 (2015): 543-50.

Seligman, Adam B., Robert P. Weller, Michael J. Puett, and Bennett Simon. *Ritual and Its Consequences: An Essay on the Limits of Sincerity*. New York: Oxford University Press, 2008.

Shishuo xinyu jiaojian 世說新語校箋. Compiled by Liu Yiqing 劉義慶 and annotated by Yang Yong 楊勇. Beijing: Zhonghua shuju, 2006.

Swartz, Wendy, Robert Ford Campany, Yang Lu, and Jessey J.C. Choo, eds. *Early Medieval China: A Sourcebook*. New York: Columbia University Press, 2014.

Weber, Max. *Economics and Society: An Outline of Interpretive Sociology.* Edited by Guenther Roth and Claus Wittich. Berkeley: University of California Press, 1968.

Xinyi Shishuo xinyu 新譯世說新語. Annotated and translated by Liu Zhenghao 劉正浩, Qiu Xieyou 邱燮友, Chen Manming 陳滿銘, Xu Tanhui 許錟輝, and Huang Junlang 黃俊郎. Taipei: Sanmin shuju, 2003.

Yan Buke 閻步克. *Chaju zhidu bianqian shigao* 察舉制度變遷史稿. Beijing: Zhongguo renmin daxue chubanshe, 2009.

Yao Wei 姚維. *Cai xing zhi bian—renge zhuti yu Wei Jin xuanxue* 才性之辨--- 人格主題與魏晉玄學. Beijing: Renmin chubanshe, 2007.

Zhao, Dingxin. "The Han Bureaucracy: Its Origin, Nature, and Development." In *State Power in Ancient China and Rome*, edited by Walter Scheidel, 56-89. Oxford: Oxford University Press, 2015.

Zhuangzi jishi 莊子集釋. Edited by Guo Qingfan 郭慶藩. Beijing: Zhonghua shuju, 1961.

CHAPTER 4

"Making Friends with the Men of the Past": Literati Identity and Literary Remembering in Early Medieval China

Ping Wang

The place and identity of the literati-scholar (*shi* 士) in premodern Chinese society and his relationship to the ruler constituted a perennial literary theme. According to the most widely accepted cultural-historical narratives, the triumph of Confucianism and the institutionalization of the scholar's position under the Han Emperor Wu in the second century BCE had the ironic effect of frustrating the literati-scholar even more due to his dependency on the state and court. Major changes in the social identity and intellectual activity of the *shi* class would have to wait until after the fall of the Han Empire.[1] Leading thinkers of the twentieth century, such as Lu Xun 魯迅 (1881-1936) and Qian Mu 錢穆 (1895-1990), regarded the third century as a period that witnessed "the rise of individualism," "the awakening of literature," and "the liberation of the scholar."[2] This essay calls attention to the importance of the "group" and "social" dimensions of literati identity, however constructed, in early medieval China when the making of an individual literati-scholar was largely determined by whom he associated with rather than whom he served. In other words, this essay argues that the other side of the coin to "individualism" is group identity socially performed.

---

1   See Wilhelm, "The Scholar's Frustration: Notes on a Type of Fu," in *Chinese Thought and Institutions*, ed. John K. Fairbank (Chicago: Chicago University Press, 1973), 315; Hsu Cho-yun, *Ancient China in Transition: An Analysis of Social Mobility, 722-222 B.C.* (Stanford: Stanford University Press, 1965), 53-77. Hsu pointed out, in times of turmoil toward the end of the Spring and Autumn period, the *shi* performed military tasks, and by the Warring States period, the duties of the *shi* class became more and more involved in areas of civil services; also refer to Yu Ying-shih, *Shi yu Zhongguo wenhua* 士與中國文化 (Shanghai: Shanghai renmin chubanshe, 1987), 4-10.

2   Qian Mu 錢穆, "Du *Wen xuan* 讀文選," in *Zhongguo xueshu sixiangshi luncong* 中國學術思想史論叢 (Taipei: Dongda tushu, 1976-80), 3:97-133. Lu Xun 魯迅, "Wei Jin fengdu ji wenzhang yu yao ji jiu zhi guanxi" 魏晉風度及文章與藥及酒之關係, in *Lu Xun quanji* 魯迅全集 (Beijing: Renmin wenxue chubanshe, 1981), 3:501-19.

In her essay "Confucian Piety and Individualism in Han China," Michael Nylan brought into question the appropriateness of using "individualism" merely as a concept to describe Wei-Jin (220-420) life and the perceived "dramatic liberation from the most restrictive aspects of Confucian hierarchy and ritual prevailing in the Han."[3] One of the important points she formulated is as follows:

> It is clear by late Eastern Han times that the *shi*, in response to the "Proscribed Factions" legislation, had come to define their own identity largely by their pronounced opposition to other powerful groups (mainly the *waiqi* 外戚, eunuchs, and military men above, as well as the despised commoners below, called the "cold people"). The need by the *shi* to maintain their separate group identity, and also to celebrate it, led to the writing of "exemplary lives" and to the coining of those in-group witticisms called *qingyi* 清議 ("pure critiques"). Hence, the greater emphasis on character evaluation found in the late Han and Wei-Jin periods, far from being a sign of rampant individualism, may well have portended a strong desire for greater group cohesion.[4]

What Nylan characterizes here as a conscious endeavor for group identity may have been covert and secondary to the primarily centrifugal crumbling of the scholastic class in the second century. Eventually, the loss of the court as a platform left scholars feeling abandoned and isolated. The fear and frustration as epitomized in the figure of Qu Yuan 屈原 (ca. 340-278 BCE) suddenly became a personal reality to the *shi*. Ironically, it was due to this newly found although initially undesirable freedom that the sense of the self gained expression in intellectual as well as political life. The self-absorbed tone of Qu Yuan and his peculiar vision of seeing everything around him as an alienating and negating force emerged to be familiar, natural, relatable, and even endearing. This principle of the self, around which the *shi* class centered their communications, would become the defining feature of their class. It would replace the ruler as the sole audience and change the platform to be one of at least seeming equality. In other words, Qu Yuan's voice was proliferated to produce social groups of the *shi* class.

---

3   Michael Nylan, "Confucian Piety and Individualism in Han China," *Journal of the American Oriental Society* 116.1 (1996): 1-27. Here, as elsewhere in this essay, I have silently emended other Romanization systems to Hanyu Pinyin.

4   Ibid., 24.

From the "Seven Masters of Jian'an" (*Jian'an qizi* 建安七子) to the "Eight Associates of Jingling" (*Jingling bayou* 竟陵八友), early medieval China was dotted with groups of eminent writers. The freedom that the Jian'an masters had in choosing whom to support among the contending regional powers was not unlike the Spring and Autumn or the Warring States periods. However, this freedom could, by no means, be quickly translated into political status or social capital for the *shi* class. If anything, a greater sense of crisis was acutely felt, which inevitably drove the scholars to each other, seeking understanding and sharing the burden of a volatile reality and an unpredictable future. In their search for political employment and ideological affiliation, they found attractive the "Jiupin zhongzheng" 九品中正 selection system that was implemented by Cao Cao (155-220) 曹操. Unlike the hierarchical court system of the Han, the apparent equalitarian patron-client relation was the first real attempt at a social order based on meritocracy. Cao Cao recognized the intellectual and moral leadership of the men of letters or masters of the text.[5] He hosted scholars whose service was instrumented around the "principle of the self," which institutionalized the singular identity of the author.

The Singular Identity of the Author

Singularity is, first and foremost, an extreme case of identity in which others are completely excluded.[6] The first known Chinese poet Qu Yuan famously lamented: "In the entire state, there is no one; no one understands me" 國無人莫我知.[7] It is in such a moment of complete exclusion that Qu Yuan's identity as a poet is cast. Only those who have been treated unfairly or driven to the edge of the society would become writers: "......they withdrew and put their deliberations into writing in order to give full expression to their outrage, intending to reveal themselves purely through writing that would last into the future," as Qu Yuan's biographer Sima Qian 司馬遷 (145-ca. 86 BCE) famously opined in

---

5   See Tang Zhangru 唐長孺, "Jiupin zhongzheng zhidu shishi" 九品中正制度試釋, in *Tang Zhangru wencun* 唐長孺文存 (Shanghai: Shanghai guji chubanshe, 2006), 92-123. For "masters of the text," see Martin Kern, "Ritual, Text, and the Formation of the Canon: Historical Transitions of Wen in Early China," *T'oung Pao* 87.1-3 (2001): 43-91, especially 83-86.

6   See Owen, "Singularity and Possession," in *The End of Chinese Middle Ages* (Stanford: Stanford University Press, 1996), 12-33.

7   *Chu ci buzhu* 楚辭補註, ed. Hong Xingzu 洪興祖 (1090-1155) (Taipei: Da'an chubanshe, 1995), 1.67.

his letter to Ren An.[8] For the historian who had endured unspeakable humiliation, authorship is born of inhuman exclusion. The singularly personal existence yields a value that transcends what is commonly human and bears on the singularity of the author. It is with this conviction that Sima Qian not only rescued authors from the ruins of history, but also became an author himself. His list of authors goes beyond the obvious Qu Yuan-Jia Yi 賈誼 (ca. 200-168 BCE) pair.[9] Bo Yi 伯夷 (ca. 11th c. BCE) and Shu Qi 叔齊 (ca. 11th c. BCE) also were turned into poets.[10]

> When King Wu had settled the lawlessness of the Shang, all the world gave their allegiance to the Zhou; yet Bo Yi and Shu Qi thought that to be something shameful, and out of their sense of right they refused to eat the grain of Zhou. They lived as hermits on Shou-yang mountain and picked bracken ferns to eat. As they were dying of hunger, they composed a song, whose words go: "We climbed West Hill, / we picked its bracken. / Brute force for brute force— / he knew not it was wrong. / Shen-nong, Yu and Xia / gone in a flash, / where can we turn? /Ah, let us depart now, /our lifespans are done." And then they died of hunger on Shou-yang Mountain.[11]

In a similar fashion, a song was performed when Jing Ke 荊軻 (d. 227 BCE), the fearless assassin, was embarking on a mission without hope to return. Bursting into a song or the mode of singing is employed in Sima Qian's history as the default for expressions of personal and authentic emotions.[12]

> Then he set out. The crown prince and all his associates who knew what was happening put on white robes and caps of mourning to see the party off, accompanying them as far as the Yi River. After they had sacrificed to the god of the road and chosen their route, Gao Jianli struck up his lute and Jing Ke joined in with a song in the mournful *bianzhi* mode. Tears streamed from the eyes of the company. Jing Ke came forward and sang

---

8   For the Chinese text, see *Han shu* 漢書, comp. Ban Gu 班固 (32-92), (Beijing: Zhonghua shuju, 1962), 62.2735 and *Wen xuan* 文選 (Shanghai: Shanghai guji chubanshe, 1986), 41.64-65. The translation is by Stephen Owen, *An Anthology of Chinese Literature* (New York: W.W. Norton, 1996), 141.

9   *Shi ji*, 84.2481-504.

10   Ibid., 61.2121-29.

11   For the Chinese text, see *Shi ji*, 61.2123; translation by Owen, *An Anthology of Chinese Literature*, 143.

12   On ending in music-making, see also p. 131 in this volume.

this song: "Winds cry *xiao xiao*, / Yi waters are cold. / Brave men, once gone, / Never come back again." Shifting to the *yu* mode with its martial air, Jing Ke sang once more; this time the eyes of the men flashed with anger and their hair bristled beneath their caps. Then he mounted his carriage and set off, never once looking back.[13]

Xiang Yu 項羽 (233-202 BCE) is yet another warrior whose life was reduced to a song before his last battle. He lost the all-under-heaven to his rival Liu Bang 劉邦 (256-195 BCE), the founding emperor of the Han. The pair makes the most intriguing rivalry in Chinese cultural history. Its memory is passed down in a condensed form on the Chinese chessboard where the battle line is marked as Han versus Chu. The winner Liu Bang, dubbed the King of Han, received an empire that would last for four centuries. The image of the opponent Xiang Yu, also known as the Hegemon King of Chu, is made indelible through a Peking Opera titled "Farewell My Concubine," which depicts the poignant sight of parting and death, as the invincible Xiang Yu helplessly burst into a song: "My strength is such to move mountains and my vehemence covers the world. / Now that fate is not on my side, my dappled steed can run no more. / My dappled steed can run no more, so what can I do? / My beauty, Yu, what do I do with you?"

As is famously known, Lady Yu, moved by the song, drew the king's sword and committed suicide. Suicide was also Xiang Yu's resolution when confronted by inescapable fate. His final battle culminated in the severing of the hegemon king's head with his own sword to be used as a claim for ransom by an old friend who had emerged on the enemy's side. Xiang Yu's body would be cut up and divided into pieces, each of which was worthy of a noble title and a fiefdom. Hence his body became part of the Han empire.[14] Xiang Yu's story is moving because it is a salient case of the power of "fate" or *shi* 時. *Shi* means "fate" in the sense of a "fatal moment." Xiang Yu's feeling of exclusion was shared by his vanquisher Liu Bang to whom was attributed the "Song of the Great Wind": "A great wind rises, clouds swiftly scatter about; / my might dominates the world, and I have come home; / where may I find brave men to guard my borders."[15] This was a song performed at a banquet hosted by Liu Bang upon returning to his hometown in Pei, where he had launched his quest to

---

13   For the Chinese text, see *Shi ji*, 86.2533-34; translation by Burton Watson, *Records of the Grand Historian: Qin Dynasty* (New York: Columbia University Press, 1993), 174.

14   *Shi ji*, 7.336; Watson, *Records of the Grand Historian: Qin Dynasty*, 47.

15   For the Chinese text, see *Shi ji*, 8.389; translation by Watson, *Records of the Grand Historian: Qin Dynasty*, 82.

conquer China. A hundred and twenty children sang in chorus while the Han founding emperor reportedly danced to it. In this song, the sense of loneliness is palpable, as if mourning the loss of Xiang Yu. As one might recall, Liu Bang and Xiang Yu both had hailed from Chu, and they were fated to clash with each other on their destined courses to supremacy. Their "meeting," fated and fatal, was rare.

"Meeting" (*yu* 遇), in both the sense of "meeting one's time" and to meet a "like-minded friend" (*zhiyin* 知音), is a perennial theme in the Chinese cultural tradition. Yet writings predominantly were about the failure to "meet," whose remedy was found in the idea of seeking "friends in antiquity" (*shangyou* 尚友).[16] Sima Qian's construction of Qu Yuan's life is clearly a case of *shangyou*. Their frustration, both real and imagined,[17] was pervasive and, as I have argued above, came to be the very seed of literati expression. The Ruist virtue of "filial piety" was applied to "service to one's ruler," and by extension to "loyalty to the local administrator responsible for bureaucratic selection."[18] The result of this was that "members of the elite *shi* class could not be entirely certain whether they owed ultimate loyalty [both *zhong* 忠 and *xiao* 孝] to the central government, to local administrators, or to parents."[19] Such conditions in the Eastern Han aggravated the already lamentable collective fate of the scholar, especially when serving the state was the one and only option for a scholar. Men were left without recourse if that perilous path proved unviable, because "not to serve" would incur a different kind of accusation or calamity.[20] The need to write and justify a life outside the court—such a life choice would be interpreted as opposing the court or open dissent—brought about new discursive patterns whose communicative functions may take on the guise of gratuitous entertainment and aesthetic delight. It is exactly due to the conceptually slippery and subjective nature of entertainment and delight that dead serious attempts to "avert threatening, sometimes perhaps life-threatening, charges of

---

16   *Mengzi* 孟子, *Shisanjing zhushu*, 10B.17; see also D.C. Lau, *Mencius*, 158.

17   On the exasperating problems faced by the *shi* class in the Eastern Han, see Nylan, "Confucian Piety and Individualism in Han China," 16.

18   Ibid.

19   Ibid.

20   Whereas Wilhelm argues in "The Scholar's Frustrations" essay that the one central question that the *fu* writers explored was "the position of the scholar in government and his relations to the ruler, on whom, in turn, his position depends," Dominik Declercq in *Writing Against the State* argues in light of a study of the *shelun* 設論 (hypothetical discourse) that this type of writing serves as a real defense when an educated man chose not to serve.

disloyalty and political dissidence" could be read otherwise.[21] Like the writings of "not meeting" (*buyu*), both the language and purport of "hypothetical discourses" speaking about the dilemma of the *shi* may strike the reader as ambiguous.

However, what may be ambiguous to the reader removed from the intellectual and political context was evident to a member of the *shi* class. That the man of service was stuck between a rock and a hard place is something that could be best understood by his fellow men. In the turmoil toward the end of the Han, some unintended consequences transpired to the advantage of the man of service. With the dissolution of the central court and emergence of regional powers, educated elites suddenly had more freedom to choose whom to serve. This new dynamic, interpreted as the cause for a beginning of "pure literature" and a newfound independence of literary men as Lu Xun hypothesized, are better understood in light of the salon culture, which constituted a different stage than the court where the *shi* class could only write suggestively about their "experience of exclusion." On this new stage, writing takes on a new function, that is to say, to promote and protect their class, and to "ward off the claims that the state was making on their lives."[22] This is an important way in which the relation between the educated elite and the state changed.

Scholars at the Wei court were less protected, but also less controlled by the de facto ruler Cao Cao, against whom they constituted an opposition based on moral superiority. The "famed gentlemen" (*mingshi* 名士), who in the final decades of the rapidly deteriorating Eastern Han dynasty resided outside the court, "came to attract a following of hundreds, sometimes thousands, of private students and retainers for their independent stand against the dynasty."[23] As the tables were turned, no other writing speaks more directly than Cao Cao's poetry about the changed dynamics between the scholars and the state and how poetry emerged as a means of social interaction and personal validation.

---

21   Martin Kern, "A Review of *Writing Against the State: Political Rhetorics in Third and Fourth Century China*," *Chinese Literature: Essays, Articles, Reviews* 23 (2001): 141-52.

22   Ibid., 143.

23   Declercq, *Writing Against the State*, 138.

Cao Cao: The Regent-Ruler Singing as the New Poet

At the end of the Han, Cao Cao quickly rose to power to become the regent of the Han.[24] A man of political acumen, he was an avid reader and poet. His *Wei shu* biography contains the following oft-cited passage about the man's cultured trait:

> In establishing the great enterprise, he practiced both military might and cultural elegance. In his more than thirty years of leading the army, he was never without a book in his hands. During the day he discussed military strategy, and at night he pondered the classics and their commentaries. When climbing heights, he would always compose a poem. In creating a new-style poem, he would set it to pipes and strings. These all became song lyrics.

> 是以剏造大業，文武並施，御軍三十餘年，手不捨書，晝則講武策，夜則思經傳，登高必賦，及造新詩，被之管絃，皆成樂章.[25]

Cao Cao's extant poetic works consist of fewer than two dozen poems that are almost evenly divided between the tetrasyllabic and the pentasyllabic form. The forms, structures, and themes of these pieces are evident through the table below.

	Title	No. of characters in each line	Lines/Words/ Stanzas	Theme	Musical tune
1	Driving the Six Dragons 駕六龍	mixed 3, 4, 5, 6, or 7	89/378/3	Escape—roaming to the immortal land	The Pneuma Emerges 氣出倡
2	Since Initial Life 厥初生	5 - 1st & last L	20/93/1	Lament over the brief cycle of life/ yearning for the immortal land	The Germinal Breach 精列

---

24 For Cao Cao's biography, see *Wei shu* 魏書 (Beijing: Zhonghua shuju, 1974), 1.1-55. For modern critical biographies of Cao Cao, see Wang Zhongluo 王仲犖, *Cao Cao* 曹操 (Shanghai: Renmin chubanshe, 1956); Kroll, "Portraits of Ts'ao Ts'ao: Literary Studies on the Man and the Myth" (Ph.D. Diss., University of Michigan, 1976); and Rafe de Crespigny, *Imperial Warlord: A Biography of Cao Cao 155-220 AD.* (Leiden: Brill, 2010).

25 *Wei shu*, 1.54.

	Title	No. of characters in each line	Lines/Words/ Stanzas	Theme	Musical tune
3	Amid Heaven and Earth 天地間	4 - 1st C	32/126/1	Praise of or propaganda for ideal government	Crossing the Passes and Mountains 度關山
4	Twenty-Two Reigns of the Han 惟漢廿二世	5	16/80/1	Lament over the fall of the Han	Dew on the Shallot 薤露
5	East of the Pass There Were Dutiful Men 關東有義士	5	16/80/1	Lament over the death of rebel soldiers and commoners	Wormwood Village 蒿里行
6	Over Ale, Praising a Time of Supreme Peace 對酒歌太平時	mixed 3, 4, 5, 6, 7, or 8	24/122/1	Praise of time of peace and plenty; good government	Over Ale 對酒
7	Driving Rainbow and Sunbow 駕虹蜺	mixed 3-3-7	19/78/1	Escape—roaming to the immortal land	Mulberries by the Path 陌上桑
8	Zhou in the West 周西	4	40/178/6	Praise of sage rulers of the past: King Wen of Zhou, Duke Huan of Qi, and Duke Wen of Jin	Short Song #1 短歌行 #1
9	Over Ale, Let's Sing 對酒當歌	4	24/96/6	Lament over brevity of life, unfinished course, yearning for able and sympathetic supporters.	Short Song #2 短歌行 #2
10	At Dawn I Ascend Mount Sanguan 晨上散關山	4 & 5 alternate	48/222/4 First couplet in each stanza repeats.	Lament over hardships of travel; encounter and roaming with immortals	Qiuhu's Song #1 秋胡行 #1

	Title	No. of characters in each line	Lines/Words/ Stanzas	Theme	Musical tune
11	Going North I Ascend Mount Taihang 北上太行山	5	24/120	Soldier's lament	Bitter Cold 苦寒行
12	Ascending Mount Taihua 願登泰華山	4 & 5 alternate	50/215/5	Lament and perplexity over life's purpose; roaming with immortals	Qiuhu's Song #2 秋胡行 #2
13	Ancient Duke Danfu 古公亶甫	4	28/196/7	Praise of ancient worthies	Excellent Indeed! #1 善哉行 #1
14	Pitying Myself 自惜	5	24/120/6	Lament over the loss of one's father, possibly Cao Cao's own	Excellent Indeed! #2 善哉行 #2
15	On the Day of Grave Misfortune 來日大難	4	24/96/6	Lament and roaming with immortals	Excellent Indeed! #3 善哉行 #3
16	Facing Stele Rock on the East 東臨碣石	4	63/261/5	Grandiose lament over the self and universe	Strolling Out the Broad Gate 步出夏門行
17	Great Goose Goes Out to the Northern Frontier 鴻雁出塞北	5	20/100/5	Soldier's lament	Variation on the East and West Gates 卻東西門行

The above table indicates that a majority of Cao Cao's poems were laments about life's woes, such as aging, death, displacement, loss, and separation.[26] These topics reflect also an obsession with escaping from these human condi-

---

26   The number of characters in the poetic lines is indicated. For example, 4 means tetrasyllabic and 5 means pentasyllabic pieces. The minus "-" sign denotes exceptions. "L" means "line(s)" and "C" "couplet(s)."

tions through feasting and roaming to fabled mountains and legendary lands of immortality. Modern scholarship has long explained such pessimism and hedonism in light of historical realities of warfare, famine, and plagues in the aftermath of the collapse of the Han empire. From the perspective of genre development, these poems were a continuation of the old Han *yuefu* tradition.[27] Cao Cao, in his poetic re-creations, tended to insert a distinct persona that evinces authenticity and (com)passion. The persona generates an identity that is at the same time revealing of his private feelings and emblematic of his political ambition. Cao Cao wrote two "Short Song" (*Duange xing* 短歌行) poems: the less famous one of the two praises three exemplary kings in early history, to each of whom two stanzas are devoted, following a pattern of recounting the meritorious deeds first and then listing rewards bestowed, some of which are verbal ones as meted out by Confucius or even Cao Cao himself.[28] Cao Cao performs a complex multilayered role in this highly patterned construction. Cao's self-comparison to Confucius as the moral judge is as evident as his aspiration to be equal to, if not superior to, the three sagacious kings. The double role, as both the judge of historical personalities and the judged one, is made possible through a persona that meditates on, mediates, and imitates history. The result of such doubling and layering is that Cao Cao as the speaker comes off as more than the aggregate of the moral paragons. The portrayal of King Wen of Zhou 周文王 "holding two parts of the world divided into three" is an analogue to Cao's initial and modest ambition; Qi Duke Huan's 齊桓公 unification of the nine feudal states mirrors Cao's grand vision; and Jin Duke Wen's 晉文公 humble and loyal service to the nominal Zhou King which earned him universal acclaim and a far-reaching reputation sounds almost like a promise by Cao Cao to remain loyal to Han. The tripartite structure paints the picture of an ideal regent whose cultured elegance and moral power win over the entire world, which would bow at the very mention of his name. The last line reads: "His name proliferates profusely like the budding fragrant flowers" 其名紛葩.[29] The self-depicted image of a sage-king looming large between the lines throughout the poem detracts from its poetic subtlety. The poem is a recounting of Cao Cao's political blueprint and ambition. His audience was imaginably

---

27   Qian Zhixi 錢志熙, *Wei Jin Nanbeichao shige shi shu* 魏晉南北朝詩歌史述 (Beijing: Beijing daxue chubanshe, 2005), 30-32.

28   For the Chinese texts, see *Song shu* 宋書 (Beijing: Zhonghua shuju, 1974), 21.610; *Wen xuan*, 27.1281-82; and Xia Chuancai 夏傳才, *Cao Cao ji zhu* 曹操集註 (Zhengzhou: Zhongzhou guji, 1986), 24-26. For translations of them, see Kroll, "Portraits of Ts'ao Ts'ao," 87-93, 114-15; Jean-Pierre Diény, *Les Poèmes de Cao Cao* (Paris: Collège de France, Institut des hautes études chinoises, 2000), 108-17.

29   *Song shu*, 2.610.

somewhat put off and perhaps repulsed by his overbearing and over-confident tone. However, in the more famous "Short Song," any distance or discomfort between the poetic persona and the audience would be dissolved by the Dukang 杜康 ale,[30] which is offered to the audience at the poem's opening:

	對酒當歌	The ale is poured; now allow me to sing for you:[31]
	人生幾何	How brief is human life!
	譬如朝露	It is like the morning dew.
4	去日苦多	How sad even more that much of it is gone!
	慨當以慷	Swelling and surging inside me
	憂思難忘	Is a woeful thought, hard to lay aside.
	何以解憂	How can I dissolve my woes?
8	唯有杜康	It is only through Dukang's brew.
	青青子衿	"Blue is the lapel of your gown,
	悠悠我心	Longing is my heart."[32]
	但為君故	It is for you
12	沉吟至今	That I have been doleful to this day.
	呦呦鹿鳴	"Yo-yo cries the deer,
	食野之苹	Eating clover on the meadow."[33]
	我有嘉賓	For my worthy guests,
16	鼓瑟吹笙	The zither and the panpipes are played.
	明明如月	Prominent as the moon,
	何時可掇	My yearning never ceases to be.
	憂從中來	As it swells from within,
20	不可斷絕	It cannot be severed nor does it end.
	越陌度阡	You have traveled the paths and crossed the lanes;
	枉用相存	You have condescended to visit me.
	契闊談讌	Let's feast and talk—
24	心念舊恩	Forever, my heart harbors such deep beneficence.

---

30   Li Shan cites a lost work by Wang Zhu 王著, claiming that Du Kang was a steward in the time of the Yellow Emperor (Huangdi 黃帝) and held the title "governor of Jiuquan (Wine Spring)" 酒泉太守. Dukang is thus a metonymy for ale. See *Wen xuan*, 27.1281.

31   For the reading of *dangge* 當歌 as *changge* 唱歌, see Wang Yunlu 王雲路, *Liuchao shige yuci yanjiu* 六朝詩歌語詞研究 (Harbin: Heilongjiang jiaoyu chubanshe, 1999), 145. For an interpretation of *dang* as a synonym of *dui* 對 (in the presence of), see Xu Xunxing 許巽行, *Wen xuan biji* 文選筆記 (Taipei: Guangwen shuju, 1966), 5.24b.

32   These lines allude to Mao #91 and this allusion indicates Cao Cao's longing for men of talent.

33   These lines are taken from Mao #161, the most famous banquet poem in the *Shi jing*. The scientific name for *ping* 苹 is *Anaphalis margaritacea*.

月明星稀	Bright is the moon, sparse are the stars;
烏鵲南飛	Ravens and sparrows fly south,
繞樹三匝	Circle the tree thrice—
28 何枝可依	On what branch to roost?
山不厭高	The mountain does not refrain from piling high;
海不厭深	The ocean does not refrain from sinking deeper.
周公吐哺	The Duke of Zhou paused during his meal,
32 天下歸心	And so the world turned to him in their hearts.[34]

In a foregrounded mode of singing, the persona performs his emotions, which begin with a lament over the brevity of life, a trite pathetic trope but nevertheless effective, since "buried beneath every cliché is some shared human concern."[35] What breathes life into this commonplace saying about a commoner's feeling is that the speaker is all but a commoner. The mildly drunk regent of all-under-heaven who sheds his golden armor to address his subjects as equals is nothing but a cliché. Cao Cao's persona reduces the historical person to a kind of sentiment readily shared. Driven by this essential condition of singularity, human quests, whatever form and scale they take, are often searches for reciprocity or *yu*, that is, to meet one's match and/or worth.

The motives of someone exposed to the public eye are subject to constant speculation. Such exposure is both a disadvantage and an advantage. The public eye projects a virtual stage on which every action and utterance prompts assessment. To win over the audience is to have them see eye to eye with you. Counterintuitively, this would actually entail revealing rather than concealing, that is to say, baring more than one expects to see and know so as to give a false sense of empowerment, which then encourages confident and voluntary decision-making. Cao Cao, on more than one occasion, had to bare his heart in public announcements.[36] The "Short Song" is just another example. Cao Cao's poetic presentation is different from the early war speeches in the *Book of Documents* where we find coercion, although they share a similar goal: Cao performed his song to persuade his army to fight for him in what he hoped to be a decisive victory leading to the unification of the state. As history would

---

34   The Duke of Zhou was so intent on meeting worthy men he would spit out his unchewed food to greet a visitor.

35   Stephen Owen, *Remembrances: The Experience of the Past in Classical Chinese Literature* (Cambridge, MA: Harvard University Press, 1986), 16.

36   In 210, the fifteenth year of the Jian'an reign, Cao Cao issued an edict titled "An Edict on Yielding Counties to Show My True Intention" (*Rang xian zi ming ben zhi ling* 讓縣自明本志令). See *Wei shu*, 1.32.

bear witness, the battle at the Red Cliff the following day turned out to be a disastrous failure. But Cao Cao would not have known this. He was performing the song to win over the support of the *shi* class. To do so, one must first relinquish his true condition (*qing* 情), that is to say, the true heart and mind. Due to the reasonable gap between the unknowable motive of a private self and the pronounced agenda of a public voice, official documents such as edicts and pronouncements are not the best media for this. With poetry, one can claim to play (perform) one's true self.

One particular feature seen in Cao Cao's works is the convincing projection of a persona vacillating between a comrade and a leader. This is achieved through a delicate balance between the use of allusions and a more direct expression in the singing mode. The juxtaposition of *Odes* quotations with the more colloquial and popular song style outcry is a key technique found in the new pentasyllabic poetry. In the "Short Song," the frequent reference to *qing* 情, or one's innermost condition and true feelings, seen in various phrases skillfully strewn across the poem without crowding it, is remarkable. So is the use of the first person pronoun *wo* 我, a favored poetic choice of Cao. Much of the poem is filled with words such as "inner thoughts," "brooding," "reflections," "pondering," and "emotions," denoting his repeated emphasis on unrequited yearning. The poem, however, makes a turn in the final stanza by introducing a rather bizarre image of ravens and sparrows hesitantly circling about to find a bough on which to roost. One might read this image as goading the overly cautious and suspecting literati who cannot be easily persuaded, especially in their heart. The poem concludes with an allusion from the *Odes*. The Duke of Zhou, the venerated regent of Zhou, was said to have broken off his meal many times in an eagerness to receive visitors. It is clear that here at the end of the poem and the banquet possibly, Cao Cao resumes his role of leader from the previous confessional and commiserating mode and makes what could be an unabashed self-comparison to the virtuous Duke. However, readers are more likely to tolerate this final unconcealed gesture of pride after being granted the gratification of seeing the sobbing hero. Similar self-alignment with the Duke of Zhou is found at the end of poem #11, a campaign song that ends with a revelatory naming of Mao #156 "Eastern Mountain," traditionally attributed to the Duke of Zhou who "sings" of his most arduous yet significant campaign to the East.

Lamenting the lack of like-minded friends to undertake a grand enterprise with him in front of a roomful of guests is a tactful demand of loyalty. A bit of thinly veiled propaganda, it is nonetheless a moving piece "expressing admiration for itinerant intellectuals of the period."[37] The power of this piece derives

---

37   Owen, *Anthology*, 280.

to a large extent from the believable persona of a leader whose authenticity comes from the singing and drinking mode. Never before had there been an occasion where a poem was performed *by* a ruler to address his subordinates as equals; the ruler was to be performed *to* in earlier traditions. Never before was the line between the poetic persona and the person performing the song so blurred. Professional performers often spoke in the role of other persons. What Cao Cao did was unprecedented; he not only broke the poetic conventions but also social barriers. The old *Shijing* type of poetry had been a form for indirect admonition. Cao Cao's poetry was a form of direct appeal. The key to this new form is an authentic and direct personal voice. In other words, Cao Cao's performance of a *yuefu* song is a singular event in which the form of poetry was transformed.

I use the word "singular" in the sense of "literary singularity" as defined by Derek Attridge in his *The Singularity of Literature*.[38] The singularity of Cao Cao's performance of the "Short Song" in front of his court resulted from the "grafting" of the true personal voice onto that of performer. In other words, he speaks directly to his audience using a hybrid form to obfuscate the line between the public and the personal, and to disguise the political in the social context. Hence his war speech assumes the form of a banquet song urging his guests to drink, sing, and become emotionally aligned with him. It is in this singular social moment that the differences among those present are set aside as Cao Cao's performance moves the audience. Qian Mu calls this kind of writing by Cao Cao "literature by men of letters" or *wenren zhi wen* 文人之文, a creation to be used in place of the utilitarian genres.[39] The conspicuous utility of social writings that Cao Cao and members of his court engaged verges on intentional role-playing. Neither a true member of the elite *shi* class nor a "scholar of the text" in the Han sense of the word *wenren*, Cao Cao, an anomaly and an unlikely hero, nevertheless emerged to be a champion of *wen*. He was well positioned to initiate and allow for a new social structure in which he would rule without the constraints of the old Han system, in which his family background had rendered him unworthy. In other words, both Cao Cao, the *de facto* ruler, and members of the *shi* class needed a new socio-political stage

---

38   Derek Attridge, *The Singularity of Literature* (London: Routledge, 2004), 63: "The singularity of a cultural object consists in its difference from all other such objects, not simply as a particular manifestation of general rules but as a peculiar nexus within the culture that is perceived as resisting or exceeding all pre-existing general determinations.... Singularity is not pure: it is constitutively impure, always open to contamination, grafting, accidents, reinterpretation, and recontextualization. Nor is it inimitable: on the contrary, it is eminently imitable, and may give rise to a host of imitations."

39   Qian Mu, "Du *Wen xuan*," 101.

that would allow a different way of interaction. The new personal voice invented by Cao Cao fit this new social arena perfectly.[40]

Socializing Through Writing: The Cao Brothers and Literary Criticism

Cao Cao's policy of using talent, not family background, as the determinant of employment and his meritocratic system made social groups matter as much as family background. In other words, the weight of personal fulfillment tilted toward social standing and recognition. The ruler's centrality was replaced by sociability with one's peers. To be part of a social network was essential to one's success. The official and social paths of a *shi* merged into one. This new system was not at all less complicated; it was simply different since one's place in the network could depend on just as unpredictable factors as when one's fate depended on a single person, namely the emperor. Social communications through poems created a bond sustaining a group and giving its members an identity that in turn anchored the group identity.

Ronald Miao, in his study of the Jian'an writers, rightly points out that the members of the group were "immortalized" by Cao Pi's letter.[41] Their official obligation was to write for Cao Cao and serve as his secretaries, but their association with each other created an interesting social dynamic that was at the same time competitive and convivial.

[They went] on pleasure excursions and attended court festivities. A regular feature of these social activities was the writing of poetry. This was the first time that such a large homogeneous group of literati had gathered around a ruling house noted for its literary interest and accomplishments... Under the circumstances, it is natural that Cao Pi and Cao Zhi should find occasion to reflect on the writings of their associates, and from these personal evaluations proceed to larger questions of genre, talent, and the purpose of literature itself.[42]

---

40   For a study of the Jian'an banquet poems, see Robert Joe Cutter, "Cao Zhi's (192-232) Symposium Poems," *Chinese Literature: Essays, Articles, Reviews* 6.1-2 (1984): 1-32.

41   Miao, "Literary Criticism at the End of the Eastern Han," *Literature East and West* 11.3 (1972): 1013-34. On creating the posthumous image of a literary figure, see also pp. 203ff. and 255ff. in this volume.

42   Ibid., 1015. See also Robert Joe Cutter, "To the Manner Born? Nature and Nurture in early Medieval Chinese Literary Thought," in *Culture and Power in the Reconstitution of the*

The Jian'an writers composed for each other. Among the genres practiced, poetry was the most viable for social gatherings, due to its short and compressed
form. The writing, exchanging, and circulating of poems not only shaped leisure activities of the Jian'an era, but also formed the group's identity as *wenren*.
As Miao points out, there was a "greater degree of creative freedom," and he
attributes this freedom to the "gradual sterility of classical studies," the "growing appeal of Daoist and other philosophies," and the "demand for men of
practical talent."[43] What Miao does not point out is that the political needs for
Cao Pi 曹丕 (187-226), Cao Cao's son, to assume the role as a patron. In order to
establish their authority, Cao Zhi 曹植 (192-232) and Cao Pi both relied on literary communications as a means to gather talented men around themselves.
These writings, such as Cao Zhi's "Letter to Yang Dezu" (composed in 216),[44]
Cao Pi's "Lun wen" (Essay on literature),[45] and "Letter to Wu Zhi" (composed
after 217),[46] inaugurated a new front in literary criticism as well as poetic
composition.[47]

Chinese Realm, 200-600, ed. Scott Pearce, Audrey Spiro, and Patricia Ebrey (Cambridge,
MA: Harvard University Asia Center, 2001), 53-71, 261-73.

43   Miao, "Literary Criticism at the End of the Eastern Han," 1017. Cf. Knechtges, "Letters in the
      Wen xuan," in *A History of Chinese Letters and Epistolary Culture*, ed. Antje Richter (Leiden:
      Brill, 2015), 189-238.

44   *Quan Sanguo wen* 全三國文, in *Quan shanggu Sandai Qin Han Sanguo Liuchao wen* 全上
      古三代秦漢三國六朝文, comp. Yan Kejun 嚴可均 (1762-1843) (Beijing: Zhonghua
      shuju, 1991), 3:16.5a-6b.

45   For the Chinese text, see *Wen xuan*, 52.2270-72. Miao dates this piece to before 217, the
      year when an epidemic claimed the lives of Xu Gan, Chen Lin, Ying Yang, and Liu Zhen.
      See Miao, "Literary Criticism," 1015. By contrast, Owen dates this piece to after the death of
      all seven men: "Cao Pi's main concern, however, is those writers of generation older than
      himself, the 'Seven Masters of the Jian-an.' All had been friends of Cao Pi, and all were
      dead. Cao Pi tries to assume the role of critic and even-handed judge, beginning by
      addressing the question of vanity and envy." Owen, *Anthology*, 359. See also Okamura
      Shigeru 岡村繁, "Sō Hi no Tenron Rombun ni tsuite" 曹丕の《典論論文》について,
      Shinagaku kenkyū 24/25 (1960): 75-85; Wang Yunxi 王運熙, "Cao Pi 'Dian lun Lun wen' de
      shidai jingshen" 曹丕《典論·論文》的時代精神, in *Zhongguo gudai wenlun guankui*
      中國古代文論管窺 (zengbu ben 增補本) (Shanghai: Shanghai guji, 2006), 100-7; Cai
      Zhongxiang 蔡鍾翔, "'Dian lun Lun wen' yu wenxue de zijue" 《典論·論文》與文學
      的自覺, *Wenxue pinglun* (1983:5): 19-25, 56; Owen, *Readings in Chinese Literary Thought*
      (Cambridge, MA: Harvard University Press, 1992), 57-72.

46   See *Wen xuan*, 42.1896-98.

47   Holzman, "Literary Criticism in China in the Early Third Century A.D.," *Asiatische Studien*
      28.2 (1974): 114.

In the space of some five years, between A.D. 216 and 220, there appeared three works of critical importance which modified, if not drastically changed, the Confucian view of literature. For the first time, the intrinsic value of literature was discussed, and this in turn led to an examination of the nature of authorship and the distinctive properties of literary forms... Cao Pi was writing about literature from a new perspective. Writers, he seems to affirm, must be judged in terms of their success in particular literary forms, and that this success relates ultimately to native talent.[48]

However, while considering these letters and essays by the Cao brothers as demonstrating "unprecedented interest in literary criticism" and citing this as proof for the "new orientation" and "new autonomy" of literature and poetry, Donald Holzman also notes their political orientation and makes the following important evaluation:

Cao Zhi's letter is remarkable because it discusses literature, because it is the first purely 'literary' letter in Chinese history, but the general judgments it passes on literature are almost all backward-looking, 'antique', and politically oriented. Cao Zhi's whole life and work can be said to have been politically oriented, resolutely turned toward the antique values that were rapidly undergoing change during his lifetime... Cao Zhi seems to feel himself on the eve of some great event, and by sending off his youthful works, he seems to take stock of his past experience and, incidentally, strike out at some enemies and flatter some friends.[49]

The purpose of the letter was a cover for the set of writings that Cao Zhi was sending to Yang Xiu 楊修 (175-219), with the hope of receiving the senior scholar's endorsement. The twenty-four-year old son of Cao Cao, known for his talent in writing, bluntly compares the talented writers gathered around his warlord father with birds caught in a net. He plays the condescending critic, calling them inferior to himself. His criticism seems marred by his political and social alliances. Confident of his own talent, Cao Zhi seeks recognition from Yang Xiu. Clearly Cao Zhi's true ambition lies in politics, hoping to become the heir to the Wei kingdom. Relegating poetry and rhapsody to the status of minor arts, Cao Zhi speaks of his hope to assist the state and benefit the people, and accomplish something that will last forever. Yang Xiu, in his response, takes Cao Zhi to task: "Now, if you do not forget your great work of governing

---

48   Miao, "Literary Criticism at the End of the Eastern Han," 1014, 1028.

49   Holzman, "Literary Criticism in China in the Early Third Century A.D.," 113, 115.

the land and leave behind a brilliant reputation that will last a thousand years, if your merits are engraved on a bell like that of Duke Jing and your name written on bamboo or silk, you will do so naturally, because of the excellence of your inherent qualities. How could literature (*wenzhang*) interfere with this?"[50] Holzman calls this statement a "declaration of independence" for literature, a "refusal to see it as something absolutely inferior to canonical studies or to an active political life."[51]

Responding to this exchange between Cao Zhi and Yang Xiu were Cao Pi's "Letter to Wu Zhi" and "Essay on Literature." Cao Pi's evaluation of the scholars is much more objective and respectful than the dismissive tone of his younger brother. Speaking as a patron instead of someone seeking patronage, Cao Pi's voice comes off as seeming more compassionate, especially in the "Letter to Wu Zhi." An oft-quoted passage presents a harmonious scene in which the scholars and the young ruler partied as equals and exchanged writings as peers:

> In days gone by, when we amused ourselves together, we would ride out in our chariots one after another, and sit together with our mats touching: not for an instant could we be separated. We would fill our wine cups and pass them on to another and then, when the strings and winds played together and our ears were hot from the wine, we would raise our heads and chant poetry. How unconscious we were then, not knowing our own happiness! We thought that we would each live for a hundred years, and stay together forever! Who would have thought that within a few years we would be almost completely destroyed? It pains me to talk of it.[52]

The social scene described left an indelible mark on the psyche of the *wenren* or "men of letters," because this represents the ideal of their collective identity, which is to be treated with respect by the ruling class as associates and equals. This vision, nevertheless, is a retrospectively sentimental recollection of those days gone by. Through this letter, Cao Pi turned the Jian'an era into a legend, something that would be evoked repeatedly for the convivial social circle. The group cohesion does not necessarily erase the individual identity, as Cao Pi, in his letter, also emphasizes the "singular identity" of the writer:

---

50   For Cao Zhi's "Yu Yang Dezu shu," see *Wen xuan*, 42.1901-4. For an English translation, see Holzman, "Literary Criticism," 121; Knechtges, "Letters in the *Wen xuan*," 205-6.

51   Holzman, "Literary Criticism in China in the Early Third Century A.D.," 121.

52   Ibid., 123. Translation by Holzman.

Literature is ruled by temperament (*qi*) and if a writer's temperament is clear or turbid, his style (*ti*) will be so too: this is not something that can be achieved by force. To take an example from music: if you asked two musicians to play exactly the same melodic line and to follow exactly the same rhythm, they would not be able to do so. Not even a father or an elderly brother would be able to explain the way of playing in exactly the same way to his son or younger brother, because each one has his own way of controlling his breath, and each one has his own technique that is innate within him.[53]

Such is the appeal of the Jian'an memory. It lives on in the admiration and as-piration of later writers, and it is evoked especially in times when a *wenren* is abandoned by the world and the presence of a sympathizing patron and a sup-porting group is sorely missed.

Remembering the Jian'an Court: Xie Lingyun's "On the Wei Crown Prince's Ye Collection" 擬魏太子鄴中集

When Xie Lingyun, the demoted Duke and the lone scion of the Chen Com-mandery Xie clan, lay sick in the remote Southeastern coast in exile, it was natural for him to find comfort in the memory of Jian'an.[54] We have, in Xie Lingyun's collection, a set of poems entitled "On the Wei Crown Prince's Ye Collection" (hereafter "On the Wei Crown Prince") which he had written to re-stage the Jian'an social scene. Each of the eight pentasyllabic poems is attributed to a member of the Jian'an group.[55] This type of writing, dubbed "prosopopoeia" or "literary impersonation," is not unusual in the early medi-

---

53   *Wen xuan*, 52.2271; translation by Holzman, "Literary Criticism in China in the Early Third Century A.D.," 130-31.

54   See Frodsham, *The Murmuring Stream: The Life and Works of the Chinese Nature Poet Hsieh Ling-yün (385-433), Duke of K'ang-Lo* (Kuala Lumpur: University of Malaya Press, 1967), 2:79n117.

55   For the Chinese text, see *Wen xuan*, 30.1432-9. For studies of these poems, see for example Brigitta Lee, "The Rhetoric of Poetic Style: Imitation as a Form of Literary Criticism," in "Imitation, Remembrance and the Formation of the Poetic Past in Early Medieval China" (Ph.D. diss., Princeton University, 2007), 156-230; Nicolas Williams, "Community and Indi-vidual at the Jian'an Court," in "The Brocade of Words: Imitation Poetry and Poetics in the Six Dynasties" (Ph.D. diss., University of Washington, 2010), 210-226; and Rebecca Doran, "Perspective and Appreciation in Xie Lingyun's 'Imitations of the Crown Prince of Wei's Gatherings in Ye,'" *Early Medieval China* 17 (2011): 51-73.

eval literary tradition.[56] Xie Lingyun, by restaging the Jian'an court, gives a literary performance on what is sorely missed in his time. With the dwindling of
his own group, Xie's own identity cannot but be threatened. It is in this sense of
imminent loss that he relates closely with Cao Pi.[57] Heading the set is a longer
preface written in the voice of Cao Pi:

> At the end of Jian'an era, I was dwelling in the Ye palace. In the morning,
> we went on excursions, and in the evening we held banquets. We dedi-
> cated ourselves to pleasure and joy to the utmost. In general, a fine hour,
> a beautiful sight, an appreciative mind, and a joyful event—these four
> things are hard to have at the same time. Now with my younger brother,
> my friends, and a few scholars, we can have them all. Since antiquity,
> such revelry is not found in books or documents. Why so? In the times
> of King Xiang of Chu, there were Song Yu, Tang Le, and Jing Cuo;[58] at
> the court of King Xiao of Liang, there were Zou Yang, Mei Sheng, Yan Ji,
> and Sima Xiangru.[59] The associates were refined, yet their patron was not
> cultivated. In Emperor Wu of Han's court, Xu Yue and others were fully
> equipped to engage in conversations and furnish responses, yet there was
> suspicion and jealousy among the various power groups.[60] How could
> they obtain appropriately candid meetings? I do not wish to slander

56   On literary imitation, see also Wendy Swartz's essay in this volume.

57   Xie Lingyun's list of writers excludes Kong Rong 孔融 (153-208) from Cao Pi's list of the
      Seven Masters, but adds Cao Zhi to the group. For studies of the "Seven Masters of Jian'an,"
      see for example Zhang Keli 張可禮, *Jian'an wenxue lungao* 建安文學論稿 (Jinan: Shan-
      dong jiaoyu chubanshe, 1986); Han Geping 韓格平, *Jian'an qizi zonglun* 建安七子綜論
      (Dongbei shifan daxue chubanshe, 1998); Itō Masafumi 伊藤正文, *Kenan shijin to sono
      dentō* 建安詩人とその伝統 (Tokyo: Sōbunsha, 2002); Wang Pengting 王鵬廷, *Jian'an
      qizi yanjiu* 建安七子研究 (Beijing: Beijing daxue chubanshe, 2004); Wang Mei 王玫,
      Jian'an wenxue jieshou shi lun 建安文學接受史論 (Shanghai: Shanghai guji chubanshe,
      2005).

58   Song Yu 宋玉 (3rd c. BCE), Tang Le 唐勒 and Jing Cuo 景差 are names mentioned at the
      end of Qu Yuan's biography in the *Shi ji* as disciples of Qu Yuan and as talented writers at
      the Chu court. See *Shi ji*, 84.2491.

59   Zou Yang 鄒陽 (ca. 206-129 BCE), Mei Sheng 枚乘 (?-140 BCE), [Yan] Zhuang Ji 莊忌 (ca.
      188-105 BCE), and Sima Xiangru (179-117 BCE) served at the court of the Prince of Liang, Liu
      Wu 劉武, brother of the Han Emperor Jing 漢景帝 (r. 157-141 BCE). See Knechtges and
      Chang, *Ancient and Early Medieval Chinese Literature: A Reference Guide* (Leiden: Brill,
      2012-14), 1:663-67, 4:2310-12, and 4:2361-63. See also Michael Loewe, *A Biographical Diction-
      ary of the Qin, Former Han and Xin Periods, 221 BC-AD 24* (Leiden: Brill, 2000), 753-54.

60   Xu Yue 徐樂, Zhuang An 莊安, and Zhufu Yan 主父偃 were all Gentlemen of the Palace
      (*Langzhong* 郎中) at the Han Emperor Wu's court. See *Shi ji*, 112.2953-65; Knechtges and

our contemporaries and they sure will be regarded as worthy by future generations. Years and months pass on like flowing currents. Almost completely withered and fallen are my friends. With this composition, I wish to remember them. Thinking of past events, my heart becomes heavy.

建安末，余時在鄴宮，朝游夕燕，究歡愉之極。天下良辰美景，賞心樂事，四者難並。今昆弟友朋，二三諸彥，共盡之矣。古來此娛，書籍未見，何者？楚襄王時有宋玉、唐景，梁孝王時有鄒、枚、嚴、馬，游者美矣，而其主不文；漢武帝徐樂諸才，備應對之能，而雄猜多忌，豈獲晤言之適？不誣方將，庶必賢于今日爾。歲月如流，零落將盡，撰文懷人，感往增愴.[61]

Adopting Cao Pi's voice, this preface is filled with effusive praise of the Jian'an court at Ye 鄴 (modern Linzhang, southern Hebei), the place where Cao Cao governed as the Lord of Wei 魏公. The pleasures shared at the gathering among the Cao princes, their friends, and scholars are described as "ultimate" and "unprecedented" (ji 極). Yet the tone of the preface is in general not joyful, but pensive in the speaker's lament on the loss of the time and the personalities of that era. The scholars are compared to plants and their death is called "wilting and withering" (lingluo 零落), borrowing the term Cao Pi had used in his "Letter to Wu Zhi."[62] Xie Lingyun's literary impersonation of Cao Pi is not only seen in verbal affinity but also spiritual closeness. Since his interest lies in the social cohesion of wenren, Xie's preface lists also the groups that existed before the Jian'an era. However, the mutual appreciation was not always readily present. While lauding the conviviality of Cao Pi and his associates, he faults the Chu King Xiang 楚襄王 (r. 297-262 BCE) and the Liang King Xiao 梁孝王 (185-144 BCE), both patrons of writers, for being "uncultivated" (buwen 不文) and for lacking an "appreciative mind" (shangxin 賞心). He accuses the writers at the court of the Han Emperor Wu 漢武帝 (157-87 BCE, r. 141-87 BCE) of harboring jealousy that interfered with honest communication. When it comes to his own time, Xie Lingyun wryly comments that he refrains from slandering (wu 誣) them. Writing in Cao Pi's voice, Xie Lingyun accentuates a social ideal missing at the Liu-Song court. What is expressed in Cao Cao's "Short Song" and Cao Pi's "Letter to Wu Zhi" constitutes the basis for Xie Lingyun's idealization.

Chang, A Reference Guide, 3:1727-28, 4:2309, 4:2324-26; and Loewe, A Biographical Dictionary, 624.

61   Wen xuan, 31.1432.

62   Ibid., 42.1896.

Arguing that the convivial gatherings exist only in the illusory memory of Cao Pi,[63] Zhu Xiaohai has written the following about Cao Pi's recollection of the time he spent with his associates: "Excursions to Nanpi were nothing more than snippets of the life of a bunch of privileged men, together with their drinking buddies, indulging themselves in cock fighting, dog racing, and other sensual pleasures. Its glamor derives from the aura of memory."[64] Such a view, however, fails to take into consideration the power of remembering in forging a collective identity, in this case, that of the *shi* class. As Jan Assmann writes:

> The elements of collective identity are underpinned by factors that are purely symbolic, and the social body is simply a metaphor—an imaginary construct. As such, however, it has its own position in reality. The collective or "we" identity is the image that a group has of itself and with which its members associate themselves.[65]

The excursions, the parties, and the poetry are elements of the collective identity of the Jian'an writers. They were associates and equals of their patron who reciprocated the writers' loyalty with their appreciation of the *wen*. They were "one for all and all for one." The glue for the cohesion was *wen*. Cao Pi famously claimed *wenzhang* 文章 as "the great endeavor by which to govern the state, a splendid activity that does not decay."[66] As the newly named heir of Cao Cao, Cao Pi saw the utility in establishing *wen* as the moral principal around which to unify his supporters. This was not at all surprising, given what his father Cao Cao had done before him.

Cao Pi's representation of the past powerfully reaffirmed the social and cultural identity of the *shi* class. Xie Lingyun, in his repetition and re-interpretation of that past, threw into sharp relief the "connective structure" of the Jian'an group. There was a need to celebrate that structure, precisely when his friends were being killed off at court and his own life was endangered in exile. Similarly, death and doom were reasons why Cao Pi commemorated a happier

---

63   See Cao Pi's fond recollection of excursions to Nanpi in his letter to Wu Zhi written in 215, "Letter to Magistrate Wu Zhi" 與朝歌令吳質書, in *Wen xuan*, 42.1894-96. See also Knechtges, "Letters in the *Wen xuan*," 203-4.

64   Zhu Xiaohai 朱曉海, "Du *Wenxuan* zhi 'Yu Zhaoge ling Wu Zhu shi' deng san pian shu hou" 讀《文選》之「與朝歌令吳質書」等三篇書後, *Guangxi shifan daxue xuebao* (Zhexue shehui kexue ban) 40.1 (2004): 70-5.

65   Assmann, *Cultural Memory and Early Civilization: Writing, Remembrance, and Political Imagination* (Cambridge: Cambridge University Press, 2011), 113-14.

66   *Wen xuan*, 52.2271.

time in the past. Of Cao Pi's group, Ruan Yu 阮瑀 (170?-212) passed away in 212.[67] A few years later, a plague wiped out many members of Cao Pi's close circle: Ying Yang 應瑒 (170?-217), Liu Zhen 劉楨 (170?-217), Xu Gan 徐幹 (170-217/18), and Chen Lin 陳琳 (160?-217).[68] At the time when the letter was written in 217, all seven masters named by Cao Pi in his "Lun wen" were dead. Cao Pi himself must have also felt the weight of time and change. He was no longer an invincible young man in his twenties when he was conferred the title of "leader of court gentlemen for miscellaneous uses" 五官中郎將 in 211, the occasion prompting his excursions to Nanpi.[69] In the span of merely six years, things had changed drastically. Losing close associates probably heightened his sense of mortality. Cao Pi wrote to Wu Zhi, discussing "writing" as a way of "establishing oneself eternally," a point he also brought up in his "Lun wen." Readers are often struck by Cao Pi's salient criticism that writers often "despise each other." But might he be lamenting the brevity of life and the urgency of establishing literary immortality? He himself was certainly productive, as the "Basic Annals" from the *Wei shu* 魏書 indicates: "When Emperor Wen resided in the Eastern Palace, his compositions reached over a hundred pieces" 帝初在東宮，蓋百餘篇.[70]

In Xie Lingyun's reconstruction of Cao Pi's literary gathering, he fantasizes a kind of constancy and reifies an ideal. Through prosopopoeia, Xie partakes vicariously in a moment and an ideal immortalized. The following translations and reading of the poems attempt to shed light on how Xie Lingyun, through these compositions, writes himself into the Jian'an group and constructs an identity missing or disappearing from his own time.

The first poem of the set is titled "Crown Prince of Wei" 魏太子. To name the pieces after members of the Cao court draws attention to the peculiar nature of Xie's poetry set: they are at the same time eulogy for and commemoration of the Jian'an writers, and the latter-born poet's homage to them through writing in their voice. In the poetic space, the persona, the subject matter, and the poet himself seem to merge seamlessly, especially in the following poem on or in the persona of Cao Pi.[71]

---

67   Ibid., 42.1895.
68   Ibid., 42.1897.
69   *Wei shu*, 1.26, 1.53.
70   Ibid., 2.88.
71   *Wen xuan*, 30.1433.

百川赴巨海	A hundred streams pour into the vast ocean;
眾星環北辰	Myriad stars circle around the northern polar star.[72]
照灼爛霄漢	Gleaming and shining, they light up the heavenly river;
4　逖裔起長津	Far and distant, they rise from the long ford.[73]
天地中橫潰	Between Heaven and Earth, there is a time of turmoil;
家王拯生民	A king of the Cao clan saved the common folk [from disaster].[74]
區宇既滌蕩	Within the realm, all has been scoured clean,
8　羣英必來臻	As outstanding talents certainly flock to join the king.
忝此欽賢性	Though unworthy of this post, I respect men of worthy character;
由來常懷仁	All along have I constantly cherished the humane.
況值眾君子	More so is this the case, having met all these gentlemen,
12　傾心隆日新	Who whole-heartedly honor daily renewing [their virtue].[75]
論物靡浮說	We discuss physical things instead of superficial discourses;
析理實敷陳	We analyze principles by displaying the concrete matters.
羅縷豈闕辭	Our detailed expositions are not lacking for words;
16　窈窕究天人	Into the subtle and profound, we investigate heaven and humankind.
澄觴滿金罍	Clear ale fills our bronze vessels to the brim;
連榻設華茵	Joined couches are placed on the luscious grass.
急弦動飛听	Agitated strings stir up high-flying sounds,
20　清歌拂梁塵	As piercing singing brushes the dust on the beams.[76]
莫言相遇易	Don't think that meeting is all too easy—
此歡信可珍	Such joy is precious indeed.

The first section of the poem, couplets 1-4, focuses not on Cao Pi, but on his father Cao Cao who is praised here as a savior of the world and a worthy ruler

---

72   This line can be paraphrased as: the followers of the benevolent ruler surround him respectfully. Cf. *Analects*, 2/1: "He who conducts government by means of virtue is just like the northern pole star, which stays in its place and yet all the stars surround it" 為政以德，譬如北辰，居其所而眾星共之.

73   Both *xiaohan* 霄漢 and *changjin* 長津 refer to the Milky Way.

74   Both *hengliu* 橫流 and *hengkui* 橫潰 are metaphors for disorder using the image of floods. Here the metaphor refers to the chaos at the end of the Han.

75   *Rixin* 日新 alludes to the *Tuanzhuan* 彖傳 commentary of Hexagram 26 in the *Yijing* 易經: "Everyday the virtue is renewed" 日新其德. See Richard Wilhelm (1873-1930), *The I Ching; or, Book of Changes*, trans. Cary F. Baynes (Princeton: Princeton University Press, 1967), 104.

76   For the allusion to "dust on the beams," see *Wen xuan*, 30.1427.

who attracts talents with his virtue. Couplets 5-8 portray Cao Pi as a humble and caring patron, eager to serve the scholars whom he regards as his teachers. The last section, couplets 9-11, describes a banquet scene and admonishes the reader to cherish its rarity. Stylistically, the first two sections do not display imitative efforts of Jian'an poetry. Instead it bears similarity to Xie's poem praising his own grandfather and great grand-uncle who saved the Jin from falling.[77] Like Cao Pi, Xie was a scion of a powerful family. Despite their aspirations and striving, they seemed to fall short in the shadow of their forebears. Feelings of inadequacy may be something with which they both struggled. Xie Lingyun, at this point of his life, was particularly lonely. As a result, his lament that the convivial gathering at the court should be treasured is equally poignant as Cao Pi's sentimental expressions in the "Letter to Wu Zhi." I would argue that by merging his voice with that of Cao Pi, Xie re-imagined and re-constructed proper social bonds. Even from the remote Yongjia, Xie Lingyun could reach the capital audience through his much admired poetry. It was for that community that Xie praised the Cao father and son, reminding them of what is sorely missed in the Liu-Song court.

Wang Can, another noble offspring meeting a time of chaos, is both the subject and "author" of the second piece in Xie's group of poems.[78] Xie prefaces the poem with emotions of sorrow: "He hailed from Qinchuan (modern Xi'an area) and was an offspring of a noble family. Having encountered disorder, he roamed and drifted. He lamented to himself in effusive sentiments" 家本秦川，貴公子孫，遭亂流寓，自傷情多.[79]

幽厲昔崩亂	Kings You and Li of old experienced collapse and turmoil;
桓靈今板蕩	Emperors Huan and Ling of Han were shaken and overthrown.[80]
伊洛既燎煙	Between the rivers Yi and Luo there was smoke from conflagrations;

---

77 For "Shu zude shi" 述祖德詩, see *Wen xuan*, 19.912-14.

78 For more information on Wang Can as a writer, see Knechtges and Chang, *A Reference Guide*, 2:1144-49.

79 *Wen xuan*, 30.1433-34.

80 These two lines use references to the fall of the Western Zhou and its final rulers King You (d. 771 BCE) and King Li (d. 828 BCE) to establish a parallel to the fall of the Han. During Emperor Huan's (132-167) and Emperor Ling's (156-189) reigns, the Han court was plagued with power struggles between the consort families and the eunuchs. Note that the phrase *bandang* 板蕩 contains the titles of two Mao poems, #254 and #255, dealing respectively with Kings You and Li.

4	函崤沒無像	Over Hangu Pass and Mount Yao, all were sunken into the sightless.[81]
	整裝辭秦川	Putting together my travel gear, I took leave of Qinchuan;[82]
	秣馬赴楚壤	Foddering my horse, I departed for the land of Chu.[83]
	沮漳自可美	The land of Rivers Ju and Zhang were truly beautiful;
8	客心非外獎	Yet to the heart of a sojourner, it had no external appeal.[84]
	常嘆詩人言	Often, I reflected on the words by the *Odes* poet:
	式微何由往	"In times of decline, where can I go?"[85]
	上宰奉皇靈	The supreme chancellor, reverently serving the August Divine One[86]
12	侯伯咸宗長	Was widely honored by lords and noblemen.
	雲騎亂漢南	Cavalry thick as clouds disrupted the area south of the Han River;
	紀郢皆掃蕩	The land of Ji and Ying was swept clean.
	排霧屬盛明	Pushing aside the fog, I beheld the Splendorous Luminescence;
16	披雲對清朗	Separating clouds, I faced the Lucid Brilliance.[87]
	慶泰欲重疊	Felicity and peace were about to multiply;
	公子特先賞	The young lord was particularly appreciative of talented men.[88]
	不謂息肩願	It was not that I wished to take refuge,[89]
20	一旦值明兩	But that I encountered Light Paired.[90]
	並載游鄴京	Sharing a chariot, we roamed the capital in Ye;

---

81 The area between Rivers Yi and Luo designates the Eastern Capital Luoyang, which was sacked by Dong Zhuo 董卓 (d. 192). Hangu Pass and Mount Yao 函崤 are landmarks east of Chang'an, the Western Capital, which was also ransacked. Cf. Cao Zhi's "Two Poems to Ying Yang" 送應氏詩, in *Wen xuan*, 20.974-75; Wang Can's "Seven Sorrows I," in *Wen xuan*, 23.1087. It is noteworthy that Xie Lingyun adopts Wang Can's famous phrase, *luan wu xiang* 亂無象, with a minor modification.

82 Xie assumes Wang Can's voice, narrating his departure from the heartland. Cf. the third line of Wang Can's "Seven Sorrows I," in *Wen xuan*, 23.1087.

83 Cf. the fourth line of Wang Can's "Seven Sorrows I," *Wen xuan*, 23.1087.

84 Cf. Wang Can's "*Fu* on Ascending the Tower" (*Denglou fu* 登樓賦), especially lines 5-6 and 13-14. In this famous *fu* piece, Wang Can gives a moving account of his emotions while surveying the land of Chu, a place Wang Can regarded as barbaric even after a decade of residence there. See *Wen xuan*, 11.489-90.

85 "Shi wei" 式微 is the title of Mao #36.

86 August Divinity refers to the Han Emperor Xian 獻帝 (181-234).

87 Lines 11-18 recount Cao Cao's military campaign against Jingzhou and Wang Can's new affiliation with Cao Cao and Cao Pi. Both "Splendorous Luminescence" and "Lucid Brilliance" are effusive honorific references to the regents of Han.

88 Lines 19-20 praise Cao Pi, the heir-designate, as a benevolent patron of men of letters.

89 *Xijian* 息肩, literally, "resting shoulders." See Knechtges, *Wen xuan*, 1:245, lines 48-49.

90 *Mingliang* 明兩 is a kenning for crown prince.

方舟泛河廣	In linked boats, we sailed across the Yangzi.
綢繆清燕娛	Intimately, we enjoyed the pleasures of the lord's feast;
24 寂寥梁棟響	On quiet nights, there were clear sounds circling the beams.
既作長夜飲	Having had our night long drinking,
豈顧乘日養	How could we fret over the daily sustenance?[91]

The first five couplets of this poem recall the theme and semantics of Wang Can's famous poems entitled "Seven Sorrows" as well as his *Fu on Ascending the Tower.*" The next five couplets reflect Xie Lingyun's own verbal penchant for the rich and gorgeous, appropriate for narrating significant historical events. The final three couplets, echoing Cao Pi's writings, focus on the topic of the entire set, that is, the patronage of the Cao court. In this piece, Xie weaves together the fate of Jian'an writers and that of his own. Both groups witnessed historical upheavals and were personally affected by them. Banquets and excursions represented poetically hope and solace.

The third poem of this set is titled "Chen Lin." In the poem's preface, Xie Lingyun speaks of Chen Lin in his position as a secretary to Yuan Shao 袁紹 (d. 202) and that, as a result, Chen Lin could recount much of the disorder and chaos he had witnessed.[92]

皇漢逢屯邅	August Han encountered adversity and difficulty;
天下遭氛慝	All under heaven experienced malicious miasmas.[93]
董氏淪關西	Dong Zhuo ransacked the area west of the Pass;
4 袁家擁河北	Yuan Shao held the area north of the River.[94]
單民易周章	People were exhausted from being subject to turbulent transferences;[95]
窘身就羈勒	In straightened conditions, I allowed myself to be tethered.[96]
豈意事乖己	Who could have predicted that affairs would go awry?
8 永懷戀故國	In constant yearning, I longed for the old state.
相公實勤王	The Prime Minister toiled earnestly on behalf of the Emperor;[97]
信能定蜇賊	For certain, he would be capable of disposing pests and thieves.

91　Lines 21-26 recall the excursions and banquets at Yecheng.

92　The original reads: 袁本初書記之士，故述喪亂事多. *Wen xuan*, 30.1434. For an account of Chen Lin as a writer, see Knechtges and Chang, 1:109-12.

93　For *fen* 氛 or miasmas, see *Liji zhengyi* 禮記正義, *Shisanjing zhushu*, "Yueling" 月令, 17.1383.

94　Yuan Shao 袁紹 (153-202) raised an army and occupied the region north of the Yellow River.

95　*Dan* 單 could also be read as *dan* 癉 or "exhausted." See the following relevant line in Mao #254: "The people below are completely exhausted" 下民卒癉.

96　This refers to Chen Lin's service under Yuan Shao.

97　*Xianggong* 相公 refers to Cao Cao.

復覩東都輝	Once again, we would be able to see the glory of the Eastern Palace,
12 重見漢朝則	And time again to witness the precepts of the Han court.
余生幸已多	Looking on my life, I was abundantly fortunate;
矧乃值明德	How much more so that I encountered His Luminous Virtue.[98]
愛客不告疲	Favoring guests, he never complained of weariness;[99]
16 飲燕遺景刻	Drinking and feasting, we lost track of the water clock's notches.
夜听極星闌	The evening concerts extended till the morning star shone;
朝游窮曛黑	Our morning excursions ended only when it became pitch dark.
哀哇動梁埃	Sorrowful singing stirred the dust on the beams;
20 急觴蕩幽默	Urged to raise our cups, drinking shook the secluded and reticent.[100]
且盡一日娛	We briefly exhausted the pleasures of a single day,
莫知古來惑	And were unaware of the age-old delusion.

This poem devotes the final five couplets to praise the patronage of the Cao court and to describe the social gatherings held under its auspices, whereas the first four couplets comment on Chen Lin's service under Yuan Shao before Cao Cao brought order to north China, as briefly mentioned in couplets 5-6. The three parts of the poem can be summarized as the historical chaos, the personal fate, and the restoration of group identity.

Xie Lingyun's fourth poem is titled after Xu Gan, likely the most learned scholar in the Jian'an group. Cao Pi ranked him above all other writers in his court, praising Xu Gan for writing the philosophical work *Zhong lun* 中論.[101] Around the year 207, Cao Cao invited Xu Gan to join his staff and appointed him as a consultant to the Army of the Minister of Works.[102] In 208, he accompanied Cao Cao on a southern expedition and participated in the battle at the Red Cliff. Around this time Xu Gan wrote "Xu zheng fu" 序征賦 (*Fu recounting the expedition*).[103] In 211, Cao Pi was appointed Leader of Court Gentlemen for Miscellaneous Uses, and Xu Gan served as his secretary. He participated in outings and banquets with Cao Pi and Cao Zhi. Around 214, he became an instructor to Cao Zhi, who now held the position of Marquis of Linzi (modern Shandong, Zibo 淄博). Around 216, Xu Gan was ill and retired to a remote

98   His Luminous Virtue refers to Cao Pi.

99   Similar lines are found in "Lord's Feast" poems by Cao Zhi and Ying Yang. See *Wen xuan*, 20.943 and 20.947.

100   *Youmo* means "quiet silence." See *Chuci buzhu*, "Huaisha" 懷沙.

101   For an account of Xu Gan as a writer, see Knechtges and Chang, *A Reference Guide*, 3:1684-89.

102   See Yu Shaochu 俞紹初, "Jian'an qizi nianpu" 建安七子年譜, in *Jian'an qizi ji* 建安七子集 (Beijing: Zhonghua shuju, 2005), 406.

103   See *Quan Sanguo wen*, 55.1360b.

village. For the rest of his life, Xu Gan devoted his time exclusively to writing the *Zhong lun*.

In Xie Lingyun's short preface to the poem "Xu Gan," he notes: "Xu Gan was without aspiration for officialdom since his youth, and he harbored thoughts of Mount Ji and River Ying. Because of the troubles of the world, he served. His writings are often unadorned" 少無宦情，有箕潁之心事。故仕世多素辭.[104]

	伊昔家臨淄	Previously I had lived in Linzi,
	提攜弄齊瑟	Where, clasping a friend's hands, I played the Qi zither.[105]
	置酒飲膠東	Setting out wine, we drank in Jiaodong;[106]
4	淹留憩高密	For a long sojourn, I rested at Gaomi.[107]
	此歡謂可終	In pleasure [like this], I would say I could end my years;
	外物始難畢	External things, after all, could not remain intact.
	搖蕩箕濮情	Shaken and stirred, I aspired for Ji and Pu;[108]
8	窮年迫憂慄	In old age, I was pressed by worries and fear.
	末塗幸休明	In dire circumstances, fortune led me to blessed illumination,[109]
	棲集建薄質	[Allowing me to] rest and establish my meager talents.
	已免負薪苦	Already exempted from the work of bearing firewood,
12	仍遊椒蘭室	I rambled in chambers scented with fagara and thoroughwort.
	清論事究萬	In our pure conversations, we investigated myriad matters;
	美話信非一	Of refined dialogues, there was truly not just one.
	行觴奏悲歌	Passing the cup, a sorrowful song was performed;
16	永夜繫白日	[Merry-making] at night was extended to the daytime.
	華屋非蓬居	Gorgeous rooms were not my thatched dwelling;
	時髦豈余匹	The luminaries of the time were not my peers.
	中飲顧昔心	Deep in my cups, I reflected on my previous intention—
20	悵焉若有失	Rueful, I was at a loss.

---

104 *Wen xuan*, 30.1435. Mount Ji and River Ying were places where the recluses Xu You 許由 and Chao Fu 巢父 had dwelled. See Huangfu Mi 皇甫謐 (215-282), *Gao shi zhuan* 高士傳, *SBBY* (Taipei: Taiwan zhonghua, 1965), 1.2a-3a. "Unadorned writings" refers to Xu Gan's non-poetic works, of which *Zhong lun* is the prime example.

105 *Tixie* 提攜 means "to hold someone by the hand." See *Liji zhengyi*, "Qu li shang" 曲禮上, 15.1234.

106 Jiaodong in the Later Han was part of the coastal kingdom of Beihai 北海, east of modern Pingdu 平度, Shandong. See Tan Qixiang 譚其驤, *Zhongguo lishi dituji* (Shanghai: Ditu chubanshe, 1982), 2:45.

107 Gaomi 高密 was also located in Beihai.

108 Ji here refers to Xu You and Pu refers to Zhuang. Both are places associated with recluses, hence with sentiments of disengagement.

109 *Xiuming* 休明, or blessed illumination, refers to just and orderly rule, a compliment to Cao Cao.

The poem on "Xu Gan" saliently departs from the previous three poems in theme. The first part, composed of four couplets, describes Xu Gan's life before he served the Cao court. Although he enjoyed the companionship of friends, Xu Gan was troubled by poverty and ill health and yearned for life in reclusion. In the remaining six couplets, in Xu Gan's voice, the poem praises the Cao court and its patronage. However, the thread of yearning for quietude continued in this part, which gives an overall tone of ruefulness rather than celebration.

The fifth poem is on Liu Zhen (d. 217), whose style name was *zi* Gonggan 公幹. Liu Zhen was the most accomplished in five-syllable line poems. In the preface, Xie Lingyun describes Liu Zhen as "eccentric," "yet claiming the most vigorous style in writing," and that "his [literary] attainments were classical and extraordinary" 卓犖偏人而文最有氣所得頗經奇.[110] In Zhong Rong's 鍾嶸 (466-518) *Shi pin* 詩品, Liu Zhen is placed in the top rank and praised for the *qi* or "vigor" of his poetry: "His style originates in the *Odes*. Relying on his vigor, he was fond of the unusual.... However, the vigor of his poetry exceeds embellishment, which is regrettably lacking" 其源出於古詩，仗氣愛奇。。。但氣過其文，雕潤恨少.[111] Xie Lingyun and Zhong Rong's comments echo the value Cao Pi placed on *qi* in his remark of "*qi* is the key element of writing" 文以氣為主 in the "Lun wen."[112] Starting with Liu Zhen's origin, the poem gives a full account of Liu Zhen's life.[113]

貧居晏里閈　In poverty, I lived in the "low gate" village of Yanzi,[114]
少小長東平　Having grown up in Dongping.[115]
河袞當衝要　Yanzhou, near the Yellow River, stood as a strategic thoroughfare;

110　*Wen xuan*, 30.1436.

111　*Shi pin jian zhu*, 63-4.

112　*Wen xuan*, 52.2271.

113　For an account of Liu Zhen as a writer, see Knechtges and Chang, *A Reference Guide*, 1:595-97. For fuller accounts of Liu Zhen's life, see Wang Yunxi, "Liu Zhen pingzhuan" 劉楨評傳, in *Han Wei Liuchao Tang dai wenxue luncong* (zengbu ben) 漢魏六朝唐代文學論叢增補本 (Shanghai: Fudan daxue chubanshe, 2002), 308-17; and Itō, "Ryū Tei den ron," in *Kenan shijin to sono dentō*, 115-37.

114　*Yanli* 晏里 refers to the hometown of Yanzi 晏子 (ca. 578-500 BCE), a native of Yiwei 夷維 (modern Gaomi, Shandong), who served as a minister of Qi. He wittily defended himself and Qi when the King of Chu attempted to insult him on account of his short stature. For Yanzi's biography, see *Shiji*, 62.2134-37.

115　Liu Zhen's native place was Ningyang 寧陽 in Dongping 東平 (modern Ningyang county, Shandong). See *Wei shu*, 21.599.

4	淪飄薄許京	Drifting and fleeing, I came upon the capital Xu.[116]
	廣川無逆流	In the broad stream, there are no opposing currents;[117]
	招納廁群英	Summoned, I was placed side by side with the many prodigies.
	北渡黎陽津	Northward we crossed the Liyang ford;[118]
8	南登紀郢城	Southward we ascended the walls of Jiying.[119]
	既覽古今事	Having surveyed matters of ancient and present times,
	頗識治亂情	I knew well the true circumstances of rule and misrule.
	歡友相解達	Dear friends understood and promoted each other;[120]
12	敷奏究平生	In presenting petitions, we investigated matters in life.
	矧荷明哲顧	Even more so, with the intelligent one looking upon us,
	知深覺命輕	His acknowledgement profound, I felt my life's inconsequence.
	朝遊牛羊下	In the morning, we roamed until the cows and sheep came down;
16	暮坐括揭鳴	At dusk, we sat around till the roosters crowed.[121]
	終歲非一日	At the year's end, many days went by,
	傳卮弄清聲	Fine wine was passed along, echoing clear tones.
	辰事既難諧	Time and event hardly converged in harmony,
20	歡願如今并	Yet the wish for joy is today fulfilled.
	唯羨肅肅翰	Only I do envy those birds, swooshing by;
	繽紛戾高冥	Fluttering, they reach beyond the lofty heaven.

---

116   Xu is Xuchang 許昌 (modern day Henan), which was made capital after Emperor Xian was taken in by Cao Cao for protection.

117   The broad stream stands metaphorically for Cao Cao who takes in talented men like the tributaries flowing in to join a major river.

118   Liyang (in modern Henan), a garrison for Cao Cao's troops on the northern bank of the Yellow River, was the site of a major battle against the southbound army of Yuan Shao.

119   Jiying (modern Yingxian, Hubei) was located on the Yangzi River, near Jiangling 江陵. This was where Cao Cao stationed his troops on his campaign against Liu Biao who had controlled the territory of Jingzhou 荊州.

120   The meaning of this line is not clear. I am opting for a literal understanding. The term *huanyou* 歡友 basically means "dear/good friends." Cf. Lu Ji's 陸機 "Ni jinri liang yanhui" 擬今日良宴會: "On a leisurely evening, I called my dear friends and set out drinks in the wind-facing gallery" 閑夜命歡友，置酒迎風館 (*Wen xuan*, 30.1426). Li Shan explains the term *jieda* 解達 as "conversing together and promoting each other" 言相談說而進達也 and cites the gloss in *Fangyan* 方言 for *jie* 解 as *shuo* 說 (speak/converse). See *Wen xuan*, 30.1436.

121   These two lines are a reference to Mao #66, "Gentlemen at Service" 君子于役, which contains these lines: "The roosters perch in their coup; / The sun is setting. / The goats and cows come down back; / The gentleman is away on service; / How could I not think of him" 雞棲于塒，日之夕矣，羊牛下來，君子于役，如之何勿思.

This poem, like the others, covers three areas: a description of the era, the consolation of friendship, and a personal touch. The last is not only seen in the poem, but also at a meta level, that is to say, a poetic style through which the style of the named person is approximated. Specifically in this piece, besides making overt references to one of Liu Zhen's "Miscellaneous Poems,"[122] Xie's piece also mimics the *qi*—embodied in the personal style of one's writing—of Liu Zhen. The way in which the *Odes* references appear in Liu Zhen's poetic composition often evokes a sense of *gu* or antiquarianism, a much recognized and appreciated trademark in medieval criticism. The enthusiasm and ambition expressed in the final couplet of "Liu Zhen" is a far cry from the yearning for quietude in the Xu Gan piece. The poetic tone here is uplifting rather than depressing.

The sixth poem in Xie Lingyun's set is on Ying Yang, whose style name was Delian 德璉.[123] Ying Yang was initially appointed to serve under Cao Zhi and only later did he become part of the literary salon under Cao Pi. Ying Yang, as Xie Lingyun would say in the poem's preface, "hailed from regions in the vicinity of Ru and Ying, where the two rivers flow through the Han Commandery of Runan 汝南 (modern Henan) into the Huai River. He encountered dispersal and separation due to the events of his day and his writings were filled with laments on his drifting and floating in life" 汝潁之士，流離世故，頗有飄薄之歎.[124] Whereas Xie concludes the Liu Zhen poem with a bird image, which is a common trope in Jian'an poetry that denotes freedom and sometimes career success, the Ying Yang poem begins with crying geese amidst the clouds.

嗷嗷雲中鴈	Caw, caw cried the geese in the clouds,[125]
舉翮自委羽	Raising their pinions, they took leave from Mount Tucked Wings.[126]

---

122   See Williams, *The Brocade of Words*, 197.

123   For an account of Ying Yang as a writer, see Knechtges and Chang, *A Reference Guide*, 3:1941-43.

124   *Wen xuan*, 30.1437.

125   "Geese in the Clouds" alludes to Mao #181, "Great Geese," which contains these lines: "The great geese are in flight; / Sorrowful is their cawing and crying" 鴻雁于飛，哀鳴嗷嗷. The Mao preface explains that the piece was a praise of King Xuan 宣王 who provided a home to those people who had been scattered about.

126   *Weiyu* 委羽, literally meaning "tucked wings," is the name of a mountain north of Yanmen 雁門 where the mythical Torch Dragon 燭龍 lay in hiding. See *Huainanzi* 淮南子 (Beijing: Zhonghua shuju, 1989), 2.150.

	求涼弱水湄	Seeking coolness on the banks of the Weak Water,[127]
4	違寒長沙渚	They eschewed the chill on the sandbars of Changsha.
	顧我梁川時	Thinking back on my days in Liangchuan,[128]
	緩步集潁許	I paced leisurely, as I had come to rest in Ying and Xu.[129]
	一旦逢世難	On one day, I encountered the catastrophe of our age;
8	淪薄恒羈旅	Tossed about, my journeys on the road were constant.
	天下昔未定	Previously, the all-under-heaven had yet to be settled,
	託身早得所	Entrusting myself in the early days, I secured a place in the world.
	官渡厠一卒	At Guandu, I was a mere soldier in the troops;[130]
12	烏林預艱阻	At Wulin, we predicted hardship and setbacks.[131]
	晚節值眾賢	In my late age, I met this group of worthies—
	會同庇天宇	Together, we were protected under the heavenly canopy.[132]
	列坐廕華榱	Arrayed in seating, we were sheltered under the floriated pillar;
16	金樽盈清醑	Bronze goblets were filled with pure spirits.
	始奏延露曲	We began with a performance of the "Receiving Dew"[133]
	繼以闌夕語	And continued with conversations extending into the night.
	調笑輙酬答	Jesting and joking, we responded to each other;
20	嘲謔無慙沮	Teased and laughed at, there were no feelings hurt.
	傾軀無遺慮	Bending down, I harbor no qualms or worries—
	在心良已敘	In my heart, these good things have already been noted.

Following the bird allegory in the opening of this poem is a description of a serviceman who encounters hardship in times of turmoil. The second part of the poem, consisting of five couplets, is an account of how the Cao court rescued and protected the poet, who now finds contentment and vows to repay the favor with his life.

---

127 Weak Water is the name of a river lying to the east of Mount Kunlun. The name was given to denote that the water was not enough to bear the weight of a feather. See Knechtges, *Wen xuan*, 2:32.

128 Liangchuan 梁川 was another name for Daliang 大梁 (modern Kaifeng).

129 Ying and Xu refer respectively to Yingchuan 潁川 and Xuchang 許昌, where Cao Cao had his government seat.

130 Guandu 官渡 (modern Henan) was the site where Cao Cao defeated Yuan Shao.

131 Wulin 烏林 (modern Hebei) was where Cao Cao was defeated by Zhou Yu 周瑜 (175-210).

132 This refers to Cao Cao.

133 *Yanlu* 延露 also reads *Yanlu* 延路 or "Endless Road." It is the title of a low-register, vulgar song. "Receiving Dew" is likely the embellished version. See *Huainanzi*, 18.619; *Wen xuan*, 5.231, 13.602.

The penultimate piece in Xie Lingyun's "On the Wei Crown Prince's Ye Collection" is "Ruan Yu."[134] An older member of the group, Ruan Yu, having studied with the eminent scholar Cai Yong 蔡邕 (133-192), came to serve Cao Cao as a secretary. The preface Xie Lingyun provides is short: "[Ruan Yu] was in charge of records and writing, and therefore his writings were filled with words of elegant grace" 管書記之任，故有優渥之言.[135]

	河洲多沙塵	On the river islets, there was much sandy dust;
	風悲黃雲起	The wind howls and yellow clouds arose.
	金羈相馳逐	Golden-bridled horses galloped side by side,
4	連翩何窮巳	Together in close succession, their race went on and on.
	慶雲惠優渥	Felicitous clouds sent down abundant moisture and rain;
	微薄攀多士	A humble man, I rose to the rank of the "multiple gentlemen."[136]
	念昔渤海時	Thinking back on those years in Bohai,[137]
8	南皮戲清沚	Where in Nanpi we frolicked in the limpid streams.[138]
	今復河曲遊	Now we roamed along the bend of the Yellow River;[139]
	鳴葭汎蘭氾	Sounding the reed pipes, we bobbled along the banks of thoroughwort.
	躍步陵丹梯	Walking leisurely, we climbed the vermilion steps;
12	並坐侍君子	Side by side, we served our lord,
	妍談既愉心	We engaged in conversations that delighted our hearts;
	哀音信睦耳	Mournful tones indeed were pleasant to hear,
	傾酤係芳醳	Pouring ale followed by fine liquors—
16	酌言豈終始	In drinking, who would know when to end?
	自從食萍來	Since the time that I "fed on duckweed,"[140]

134   For an account of Ruan Yu as a writer, see Knechtges and Chang, *A Reference Guide*, 1:775-777.

135   *Wen xuan*, 30.1438.

136   *Duoshi* 多士 or "multiple gentlemen" alludes to the *Shijing* (Mao 235) phrase 濟濟多士, which appears in "Wen wang" 文王 and "Qingmiao" 清廟 to describe the support King Wen enjoyed among his officers and the protection they received.

137   Bohai 渤海 was modern Hebei.

138   Nanpi 南皮 was a county in Bohai Commandery. See Cao Pi's "Letter to Magistrate of Zhaoge Wu Zhi," which contains the line: "Every so often I would look back on our excursions in Nanpi, which were unforgettable" 每念昔日南皮之游，誠不可忘. See *Wen xuan*, 42.1895.

139   Cao Pi's letter includes similar lines: "Then we yoked our chariots and went on excursions. Heading north we followed the bend of the Yellow River" 時駕而遊，北遵河曲. See *Wen xuan*, 42.1896.

140   "Eating duckweed" or "feeding on duckweed" alludes to Mao #161. It refers here to the time when Ruan Yu was receiving the patronage of Cao Cao.

唯見今日美　I only recognized the joy of this day.

This poem gives a full elaboration of the Cao court's support of the scholars during a chaotic time. The entire poem can be read as a general account without particular references to Ruan Yu himself. Given Ruan Yu's position as a recorder, it is apt that Xie Lingyun's poem presents an account that speaks on behalf of those who have benefited from their host.

The last piece of this set is devoted to Cao Zhi, or "Marquis of Pingyuan" 平原侯.[141] The preface of the piece reads: "The prince did not take to worldly matters, and only took delight in roaming with associates. In his writings, there were evident laments about mortality."[142]

朝遊登鳳閣	Roaming in the morning, we ascended the phoenix tower;
日暮集華沼	At dusk, we gathered by the floriated pond.
傾柯引弱枝	From drooping boughs, tender twigs hung down;
4　攀條摘蕙草	Pulling the branches, we plucked patchouli.
徒倚窮騁望	Pacing to and fro, we gazed far into the distance—
目極盡所討	What our eyes could see were all that had been conquered.
西顧太行山	Looking westward, it was Taihang Mountain;
8　北眺邯鄲道	Northward, we saw the thoroughfare to Handan.
平衢修且直	Smooth roads were long and straight;
白楊信裊裊	White poplars waved in the wind.
副君命飲宴	The Heir Apparent ordered a drinking feast;[143]
12　歡娛寫懷抱	In happiness and joy, we poured out what had been on our mind.
良遊匪晝夜	With good friends we roamed, forgetting day or night—
豈云晚與早	Who cared whether it was morning or evening?
眾賓悉精妙	All guests were outstanding and wondrous,
16　清辭灑蘭藻	Their pure words sprinkled forth like fragrant ornaments.
哀音下迴鵠	Mournful sounds brought down circling geese;
餘哇徹清昊	Lingering echoes pierced into the pure heaven.
中山不知醉	On ale from Zhongshan, we did not get drunk;
20　飲德方覺飽	Only by virtue of drinking could we feel sated.
願以黃髮期	We wish we could grow old like this,
養生念將老	Nourishing our lives as we approached old age.

141　For an account of Cao Zhi as a writer, see Knechtges and Chang, *A Reference Guide*, 1:90-106.

142　*Wen xuan*, 30.1438. The original reads: 公子不及世事但美遨遊然頗有憂生之嗟.

143　The Heir Apparent is Cao Pi.

This poem, written in the voice of Cao Zhi, begins with two couplets of scenic description that invites allegorical reading. The images of "ascending phoenix" and "gathering blossoms" in the first couplet are metaphors for the talented men of service hosted by the Cao family. This image of patronage continues into the second couplet in which drooping boughs join with tender twigs and fragrant herbs are collected. After having presented his father's court as thronged with men of talent, Cao Zhi moves onto a journey scene, which reminds one of Cao Cao's own poems on military campaigns. Couplets five to ten offer an account of the banquet scene. Cao Zhi's piece serves well as the final piece, as it summarizes the overall experience at the Cao court. His personal voice of loss is fitting, as the "roaming immortal" theme was one of Cao Zhi's favorite topics.

Xie Lingyun, in constructing each poem in the set, incorporates certain biographical aspects and poetic features known of the Jian'an writer. Each poem displays a distinctive personal tone. The shared component of the set, constituting an overarching theme throughout the eight poems, is the description of the gathering and banquet held under the auspices of the court. Xie Lingyun's reconstruction of the Jian'an court and their writings is an act of preserving as well as creating the Jian'an memory. Such a memory is important for Xie Lingyun's own identity as well as the collective identity of the literati men of early medieval China.

The self is constructed through social interaction rather than having an existence separate from it.[144] Remembering the past, or a certain kind of past remembered in a certain way, has the social function of articulating and strengthening a particular kind of identity that is either missing or weakened. In the 420s, with the waning of the power of noble families, the social status of someone like Xie Lingyun was very much in question. His re-construction of an imagined group setting and group composition, in addition to the salient purpose of memorializing, constitutes also a cohesive force between him and the group from which he had drifted apart in time and space. The Jian'an group, in Xie Lingyun's memory and commemoration, came to stand for the ideal of patronage and the scholar's position in society.

---

144   George Mead, *Mind, Self & Society from the Standpoint of a Social Behaviorist* (Chicago: University of Chicago Press, 1934).

Bibliography

Assmann, Jan. *Cultural Memory and Early Civilization: Writing, Remembrance, and Political Imagination*. Cambridge: Cambridge University Press, 2011.

Attridge, Derek. *The Singularity of Literature*. London: Routledge, 2004.

Cai Zhongxiang 蔡鍾翔. "'Dian lun Lun wen' yu wenxue de zijue" 《典論·論文》與文學的自覺. *Wenxue pinglun* (1983.5): 19-25, 56.

Cheng Yu-yu 鄭毓瑜. *Liuchao qingjing meixue zonglun* 六朝情境美學總論. Taipei: Xuesheng shuju, 1996.

Chu ci buzhu 楚辭補註. Edited by Hong Xingzu 洪興祖 (1090-1155). Taipei: Da'an chubanshe, 1995.

Connery, Christopher Leigh. "Jian'an Poetic Discourse." Ph.D. diss., Princeton University, 1991.

Cutter, Robert Joe. "Cao Zhi's (192-232) Symposium Poems." *Chinese Literature: Essays, Articles, Reviews* 6.1 & 2 (1984): 1-32.

Cutter, Robert Joe. "To the Manner Born? Nature and Nurture in Early Medieval Chinese Literary Thought." In *Culture and Power in the Reconstitution of the Chinese Realm, 200-600*, edited by Scott Pearce, Audrey Spiro, and Patricia Ebrey, 53-71. Cambridge, MA: Harvard University Asia Center, 2001.

Declercq, Dominik. *Writing Against the State: Political Rhetorics in Third and Fourth Century China*. Leiden: Brill, 1998.

De Crespigny, Rafe. *Imperial Warlord: A Biography of Cao Cao 155-220 AD*. Leiden: Brill, 2010.

Diény, Jean-Pierre. *Les Poèmes de Cao Cao (155-220)*. Paris: Collège de France, Institut des hautes études chinoises, 2000.

Doran, Rebecca. "Perspective and Appreciation in Xie Lingyun's 'Imitations of the Crown Prince of Wei's Gatherings in Ye.'" *Early Medieval China* 17 (2011): 51-73.

Frodsham, J.D. *The Murmuring Stream: The Life and Works of the Chinese Nature Poet Hsieh Ling-yün (385-433), Duke of K'ang-Lo*. Kuala Lumpur: University of Malaya Press, 1967.

Gu Nong 顧農. *Jian'an wenxue shi* 建安文學史. Changsha: Hunan jiaoyu, 2000.

Han Geping 韓格平. *Jian'an qizi zonglun* 建安七子綜論. Changchun: Dongbei shifan daxue chubanshe, 1998.

Han shu 漢書. Compiled by Ban Gu 班固 (32-92). Beijing: Zhonghua shuju, 1962.

Holzman, Donald. "Literary Criticism in China in the Early Third Century A.D." *Asiatische Studien* 28.2 (1974): 113-49.

Hsu Cho-yun 許倬雲. *Ancient China in Transition: An Analysis of Social Mobility, 722-222 B.C.* Stanford: Stanford University Press, 1965.

Huainanzi 淮南子. *Xinbian zhuzi jicheng* 新編諸子集成. Beijing: Zhonghua shuju, 1989.

Huang Yazhuo 黃亞卓. *Han Wei Liuchao gongyan shi yanjiu* 漢魏六朝公宴詩研究. Shanghai: Huadong shifan daxue chubanshe, 2007.

Itō Masafumi 伊藤正文. *Kenan shijin to sono dentō* 建安詩人とその伝統. Tokyo: Sōbunsha, 2002.

Itō Masafumi 伊藤正文. "Ryū Tei den ron" 劉楨傳論. In *Yoshikawa hakushi taikyū kinen Chūgoku bungaku ronshū* 吉川博士退休紀念中國文學論集. Tokyo: Chikuma shobō, 1968. Reprinted in *Ken'an shijin to sono dentō* 建安詩人とその伝統. Tokyo: Sōbunsha, 2002.

Kern, Martin. "Ritual, Text, and the Formation of the Canon: Historical Transitions of Wen in Early China." *T'oung Pao* 87.1-3 (2001): 43-91.

Knechtges, David R. "Letters in the *Wen xuan*." In *A History of Chinese Letters and Epistolary Culture*, edited by Antje Richter. Leiden: Brill, 2015.

Knechtges, David R. "Group Literary Composition at the Court of Ye in the Later Eastern Han." Unpublished manuscript.

Knechtges, David R., trans. *Wen xuan or Selections of Refined Literature*. Vol. 1: *Rhapsodies on Metropolises and Capitals*. Princeton: Princeton University Press, 1982.

Knechtges, David R., trans. *Wen xuan or Selections of Refined Literature*. Vol. 2: *Rhapsodies on Sacrifices, Hunting, Travel, Sightseeing, Palaces and Halls, Rivers and Seas*. Princeton: Princeton University Press, 1987.

Knechtges, David R., trans. *Wen xuan or Selections of Refined Literature*. Vol. 3: *Rhapsodies on Natural Phenomena, Birds, Animals, Aspirations and Feelings, Sorrowful Laments, Literature, Music, and Passions*. Princeton: Princeton University Press, 1996.

Knechtges, David R. and Taiping Chang, eds. *Ancient and Early Medieval Chinese Literature: A Reference Guide*. Leiden: Brill, 2012-14.

Kroll, Paul W. "Portraits of Ts'ao Ts'ao: Literary Studies on the Man and the Myth." Ph.D. diss., University of Michigan, 1976.

Lau, D.C., trans. *Mencius*. Harmondsworth: Penguin, 1970.

Lee, Brigitta. "The Rhetoric of Poetic Style: Imitation As a Form of Literary Criticism." In "Imitation, Remembrance and the Formation of the Poetic Past in Early Medieval China." Ph.D. diss., Princeton University, 2007.

Li Wenlu 李文祿. *Jian'an qizi pingzhuan* 建安七子評傳. Shenyang: Shenyang chubanshe, 2001.

Liji zhengyi 禮記正義. *Shisanjing zhushu.*

Liu Zeming 劉則鳴. "Xie Lingyun 'Ni Yezhong ji bashou' kao lun" 謝靈運《擬鄴中集八首》考論. *Shanghai shifan daxue xuebao* (Shehui kexue ban) 29.1 (2000): 66-73.

Loewe, Michael. *A Biographical Dictionary of the Qin, Former Han and Xin Periods, 221 BC-AD 24*. Leiden: Brill, 2000.

Lu Xun 魯迅. "Wei Jin fengdu ji wenzhang yu yao ji jiu zhi guanxi" 魏晉風度及文章與藥及酒之關係. In *Lu Xun quanji* 魯迅全集. Beijing: Renmin wenxue chubanshe, 1981.

Mao shi zhushu 毛詩註疏. *Shisanjing zhushu.*

Mengzi 孟子. *Shisan jing zhushu.*

Miao, Ronald. "Literary Criticism at the End of the Eastern Han." *Literature East and West* 11.3 (1972): 1013-34.

Nylan, Michael. "Confucian Piety and Individualism in Han China." *Journal of the American Oriental Society* 116.1 (1996): 1-27.

Okamura Shigeru 岡村繁. "Sō Hi no Tenron Rombun ni tsuite" 曹丕の《典論論文》について. *Shinagaku kenkyū* 24/25 (1960): 75-85.

Owen, Stephen. *An Anthology of Chinese Literature: Beginnings to 1911* New York: W.W. Norton, 1996.

Owen, Stephen. *Readings in Chinese Literary Thought.* Cambridge, MA: Harvard University Press, 1992.

Owen, Stephen. *Remembrances: The Experience of the Past in Classical Chinese Literature.* Cambridge, MA: Harvard University Press, 1986.

Owen, Stephen. "Singularity and Possession." In *The End of Chinese Middle Ages.* Stanford: Stanford University Press, 1996.

Owen, Stephen. *The Late Tang: Chinese Poetry of the Mid-Ninth Century (827-860).* Cambridge, MA: Harvard University Asia Center, 2006.

Qian Mu 錢穆 (1895-1990). "Du *Wen xuan*" 讀文選. In *Zhongguo xueshu sixiangshi luncong* 中國學術思想史論叢. Taipei: Dongda tushu, 1976-80.

Qian Zhixi 錢志熙. *Wei Jin Nanbeichao shige shishu* 魏晉南北朝詩歌史述. Beijing: Beijing daxue chubanshe, 2005.

Quan Sanguo wen 全三國文. See Yan Kejun.

Quan Tang shi 全唐詩. Beijing: Zhonghua shuju, 1960.

Shangshu dazhuan 尚書大傳. Compiled by Fu Sheng 伏勝 (2nd cent. BCE); annotated by Zheng Xuan 鄭玄 (127-200); and collated by Chen Shouqi 陳壽祺 (1771-1834). *SBCK*.

Shang Yongliang 尚永亮 and Deng Tielan 鄧鉄蘭. "'Ni Yezhong ji ba shou' de yonghuai xingzhi yu Xie Lingyun de jieshou xintai" 《擬鄴中集八首》的詠懷性質與謝靈運的接受心態. *Zhongguo yunwen xuekan* (2004:1): 35-38.

Shi ji 史記. Compiled by Sima Qian 司馬遷 (145-ca. 86 BCE). Beijing: Zhonghua shuju, 1959.

Shi pin jian zhu 詩品箋註. Annotated by Cao Xu 曹旭. Beijing: Renmin chubanshe, 2009.

Shisan jing zhushu 十三經註疏. Beijing: Zhonghua shuju, 1980. Photomechanically reduced reproduction of a woodblock edition by Ruan Yuan 阮元 (1764-1849).

Song shu 宋書. Compiled by Shen Yue 沈約 (441-513). Beijing: Zhonghua shuju, 1974.

Tang Zhangru 唐長孺. "Jiupin zhongzheng zhidu shishi" 九品中正制度試釋. In *Tang Zhangru wenchun.*

Tang Zhangru 唐長孺. "Shizu de xingcheng he shengjiang" 士族的形成和升降. In *Tang Zhangru wenchun.*

Tang Zhangru 唐長孺. *Tang Zhangru wencun* 唐長孺文存. Shanghai: Shanghai guji, 2006.

Wang Mei 王玫. *Jian'an wenxue jieshou shi lun* 建安文學接受史論. Shanghai: Shanghai guji chubanshe, 2005.

Wang Pengting 王鵬廷. *Jian'an qizi yanjiu* 建安七子研究. Beijing: Beijing daxue chubanshe, 2004.

Wang Wei 王巍. *Jian'an wenxue gailun* 建安文學概論. Shenyang: Liaoning jiaoyu chubanshe, 2000.

Wang Yunlu 王雲路. *Liuchao shige yuci yanjiu* 六朝詩歌語詞研究. Harbin: Heilongjiang jiaoyu chubanshe, 1999.

Wang Yunxi 王運熙 (1926-2014). "Cao Pi 'Dian lun Lun wen' de shidai jingshen" 曹丕《典論・論文》的時代精神. *Wenhui bao* (January 1962). Reprinted in *Zhongguo gudai wenlun guankui* 中國古代文論管窺. Shanghai: Shanghai guji, 2006.

Wang Yunxi 王運熙 "Liu Zhen pingzhuan" 劉楨評傳. In *Han Wei Liuchao Tang dai wenxue luncong (zengbu ben)* 漢魏六朝唐代文學論叢增補本. Shanghai: Fudan daxue chubanshe, 2002.

Wang Zhongluo 王仲犖. *Cao Cao* 曹操. Shanghai: Renmin chubanshe, 1956.

Watson, Burton, trans. *Records of the Grand Historian: Qin Dynasty*. New York: Columbia University Press, 1993.

Wei shu 魏書. Compiled by Wei Shou 魏收 (505-72) et al. Beijing: Zhonghua shuju, 1974.

Wen xuan 文選. Shanghai: Shanghai guji chubanshe, 1986.

Wilhelm, Hellmut (1905-1990). "The Scholar's Frustration: Notes on a Type of Fu." In *Chinese Thought and Institutions*, edited by John K. Fairbank. Chicago: Chicago University Press, 1973.

Wilhelm, Richard (1873-1930). *The I Ching; or, Book of Changes*. Translated by Cary F. Baynes. Princeton: Princeton University Press, 1967.

Williams, Nicolas Morrow. "Community and Individual at the Jian'an Court." In "The Brocade of Words: Imitation Poetry and Poetics in the Six Dynasties." Ph.D. diss., University of Washington, 2010.

Williams, Nicolas Morrow. *Imitations of the Self: Jiang Yan and Chinese Poetics*. Leiden: Brill, 2015.

Wu Fusheng. "Self-Foregrounding in the Panegyric Poetry of the Jian'an Era." In *Written at Imperial Command: Panegyric Poetry in Early Medieval China*. Albany: State University of New York Press, 2008.

Xia Chuancai 夏傳才, ed. *Cao Cao ji zhu* 曹操集注. Zhengzhou: Zhongzhou guji, 1986.

Yan Kejun 嚴可均 (1762-1843), comp. *Quan shanggu Sandai Qin Han Sanguo Liuchao wen* 全上古三代秦漢三國六朝文. Beijing: Zhonghua shuju, 1991.

Yiwen leiju 藝文類聚. Beijing: Zhonghua shuju, 1965.

Yu Shaochu 俞紹初. *Jian'an qizi ji* 建安七子集. Beijing: Zhonghua shuju, 2005.

Yu Ying-shih 余英時. *Shi yu Zhongguo wenhua* 士與中國文化. Shanghai: Shanghai renmin chubanshe, 1987.

Zhang Keli 張可禮. *Jian'an wenxue lungao* 建安文學論稿. Jinan: Shandong jiaoyu, 1986.

Zhao Jianjun 趙建軍. "Jian'an ershier nian de wenyi dui wenxue de yingxiang" 建安二十二年的瘟疫對文學的影響. *Yinshan xuekan* 20.1 (2007): 19-21.

Zheng Cibin 鄭滋斌. "Xie Lingyun 'Ni Wei taizi Yezhong ji shi" de xiezuo dongji" 謝靈運《擬魏太子鄴中集詩》的寫作動機. *Xinya yanjiusuo tongxun* 15 (2002): 7-16.

Zhu Xiaohai 朱曉海. "Du *Wenxuan* zhi 'Yu Zhaoge ling Wu Zhi shu' deng san pian shu hou" 讀《文選》之「與朝歌令吳質書」等三篇書後. *Guangxi shifan daxue xuebao (Zhexue shehui kexue ban)* 40.1 (2004): 70-75.

CHAPTER 5

Yu Xin's "Memory Palace": Writing Trauma and Violence in Early Medieval Chinese Aulic Poetry[*]

Xiaofei Tian

How does one remember a traumatic experience, write about it, and further-more, turn it into a work of literature? How does traumatic memory shape its literary representation, and how does its literary representation in turn shape one's memory? The study of trauma became prominent in the twen-tieth century with the rise of psychoanalysis and the outbreak of the world wars, especially after the Holocaust; but the causes of trauma—war, death, violence, displacement—had appeared throughout human history. In the case of a sixth-century aristocratic Chinese poet, these common questions about traumatic memories and their literary representation are more complicated and have a far-reaching impact in Chinese literary history.

The poet in question is Yu Xin 庾信 (513-581), one of the leading court poets in the Liang dynasty (502-557), the prosperous, sophisticated southern empire. In his mid-thirties he was caught up in the Hou Jing rebellion and the fall of the Liang; subsequently he was detained, and spent the rest of his life as an exile, in the courts of the non-Han northern dynasties. Acclaimed as a literary mas-ter in life, Yu Xin is considered by posterity the last great poet before the Tang. Most of his extant writings were written in the north. His is a poetry of trauma, loss, and mourning. One of the most intriguing questions is how a consum-mate court poet like Yu Xin writes pain and suffering in the elegant, restrained language of courtly poetry, a highly stylized form of writing with rigorous conventions.[1]

Focusing on several poems from Yu Xin's famous poetic series "Singing of My Cares" ("Yonghuai" 詠懷), this chapter argues that Yu Xin, finding the ex-isting poetic conventions no longer adequate to the writing of trauma and

---

[*]   This article is part of an ongoing project on early medieval Chinese courtly poetry tentatively entitled *Writing Empire, Writing Self in Early Medieval China*. I would like to thank the wonder-ful graduate students in my seminar of spring 2014 on "Trauma, Diaspora, and Nostalgia in the Sixth Century" for having made the class such a delight to teach, and for my fellow participants at the Medieval Workshop held at Rutgers University in April, 2016.

[1]   For a discussion of management of trauma through ritual, see Jack Chen's essay in this volume.

complex personal experience, invented a new poetic language and thus a new mode of autobiographical writing, and that he did so by constructing an intricate textual house of memory with the materials, resources, and technologies of southern court poetry.[2] Making explicit and implicit allusions to works of southern court poetry, Yu Xin reinvented the courtly style to represent pain and suffering. Prior to Yu Xin, a general knowledge of the broad outlines of the poet's life and historical background would usually be more than enough for a reader to grasp the import of a poem. In contrast, the new autographical mode of poetic writing requires an *intimate, detailed* knowledge of the poet's experiential *and* textual past to fully appreciate his poems.[3] This textual past certainly includes the more remote book tradition, i.e. canonical works in the bibliographical categories of "classics, histories, masters, and belletristic literature"; but more important is Yu Xin's frequent reference to the more recent past, that is, the literary milieu at the Liang court. This is the poet's *personal* textual past, not the textual past commonly shared by the elite: it is constituted of writings composed by the Liang princes Yu Xin served and by his fellow courtiers under specific circumstances, based on what Yu Xin as a privileged member of the court society knew about that highly literary court life. In this way the poet's experiential past and textual past are inseparable. The memory of his traumatic experience is thus closely intertwined with textual memories of the southern court.

This leads to a question: if an intimate knowledge of Yu Xin's southern past is, as this chapter argues, a prerequisite for understanding his poetry, then for whom was Yu Xin writing in the north? I suggest that he was writing for a specific audience: a diasporic community of fellow southern exiles who had

---

2 Yu Xin's series of twenty-seven poems is known today as "Ni Yonghuai" 擬詠懷 ("Emulating 'Singing of My Cares'"), evoking the well-known poetic series "Yonghuai" by Ruan Ji 阮籍 (210-263). However, one of the earliest sources, *Yiwen leiju* 藝文類聚 (completed in 624), cites the poems as simply "Yonghuai shi" 詠懷詩. *Yiwen leiju*, comp. Ouyang Xun 歐陽詢 et al. (Taipei: Wenguang chubanshe, 1974), 26.468.

3 This is a large, complex argument that needs to be expounded with a much longer exposition than this current piece of writing can provide. Whereas this chapter focuses more on the necessity to recognize the textual past to which the poet belongs, in my book manuscript I demonstrate that knowing certain details of the poet's personal past is crucial for understanding some of the "Yonghuai" poems. Regarding this latter point, the difference between Ruan Ji's "Yonghuai" poems and Yu Xin's is salient: scholars have tried to read Ruan's poems biographically but can only stop at unprovable speculation based on the premise that the poems were indeed written after the political events had happened (we do not know this); also, the events supposedly referred to in Ruan's poems were all larger events occurring in Ruan's day, not personal details.

shared the same life and textual memories. When the audience was gone, that intimate knowledge was gone as well. Over time Yu Xin became remembered mainly for the beautiful patterning of his poetry, as a master of perfectly crafted parallel couplets, but the deeper meanings beneath the patterning have grown obscure.

Below I will first briefly discuss and clarify the terminology used in the chapter. The second section discusses Yu Xin's peculiar move of transforming some of the conventional types and subgenres of southern courtly poetry to create a poetic language adequate to the articulation of personal trauma. The third and fourth sections focus on his construction of a "memory palace" out of his textual and experiential past. "Memory palace" normally refers to a mnemonic device that uses visualization to organize and store information in one's mind; here I borrow the term to describe Yu Xin's accessing of the southern textual past and his obsessive construction of a new house of memory during exile. This house of memory, built with the words and images of southern courtly poetry, is labyrinthine, harboring numerous nooks and crannies, secret passageways and hidden chambers.

"Aulic Poetry": Terminology and Usage

There is no exact Chinese equivalent of the English word "court," which can refer to the place where a sovereign resides, to a sovereign's retinue, or to the environs of a sovereign with his retinue. The term "court poetry" is often rendered as *gongting shige* 宮廷詩歌 in Chinese, but the term *gongting* 宮廷 more narrowly means "a sovereign's residence," with the architectural, fixed sense of the English word "palace." *Chaoting* 朝廷 is more flexible than *gongting* since it can refer to both the place where a sovereign holds state and the imperial governing body, but it evokes the political power of a sovereign and his government rather than the cultural power embodied by the sovereign, and *chaoting shige* does not exist in actual usage. The term *gongting shige* tends to reinforce a rather common perception of court poetry as being tied to a physical setting—the imperial or princely court—and as being largely composed on court occasions in the presence of the emperor or a prince.

Rather than being merely a physical place of assembly for the sovereign and his retinue, a court is a field of dynamic power relations, "a figuration of individual people."[4] It is an elite community of courtiers headed by an emperor or

---

4   Norbert Elias, *The Court Society* (New York: Pantheon Books, 1983), 141. Elias' work transformed European court studies, and even though later developments have revised and nuanced his

a royal prince, characterized by complex interactions between a sovereign and his retinue as well as amongst the courtiers themselves. It is important to note that a sovereign and his courtiers need each other in this field of literary production as much as in the political arena, and the latter are not puppets controlled by the former or vice versa. Court poetry is the product of this elite community, and is used as a category only when the court is the locus of cultural values, exerting a centripetal pull throughout the empire. If the court were nothing more than the seat of imperial power where a ruler holds state, then we would simply have "poetry composed at court" but not "court poetry." A good example of the former is the case of the Qing Emperor Qianlong (r. 1735-96), who had composed more than 40,000 poems through his long life and long reign; yet, despite his prolificacy, neither Emperor Qianlong nor his court was able to dictate literary tastes or cultural values, and the massive imperial poetic corpus had little impact on Qing poetry or Chinese literary culture in general. In contrast, in the southern empire, roughly from the second quarter of the fifth through the sixth century, all major writers were sovereigns, princes, and their courtiers, and the imperial and princely courts were the centers of cultural production. The emperors and princes participated in public poetic compositions alongside their courtiers on social occasions, a phenomenon that had not been a norm in earlier times; and, in addition to being practitioners, they were arbiters of tastes and values that profoundly influenced the contemporary cultural scene.[5] Indeed, this was a period when imperial families occupied a dominant position in the cultural life of society. In an effort to draw a distinction between the poetry of this period and the court literature of earlier or later times, to downplay its connection with physical setting and formal court occasions and yet to highlight its deep ties with the imperial family, I use "aulic poetry" rather than "court poetry" throughout this article.

In the Liang, Emperor Wu 武帝 (r. 502-549) and the princes of the Xiao 蕭 house—Tong 統 (501-531), Gang 綱 (503-551), and Yi 繹 (508-555)—were influential cultural figures. After Xiao Tong passed away, Xiao Gang was Crown Prince from 531 to 549. In Xiao Gang's circle poetry was being transformed, and the style espoused by the prince, himself a distinguished poet, was dubbed "Xu Yu Style" ("Xu Yu ti" 徐庾體) after his senior advisors Xu Chi 徐摛 (474-551) and Yu Jianwu 庾肩吾 (487-ca. 552). Yu Jianwu, who excelled at literary

---

argument, much of what he says in his seminal book remains inspiring, not only for the study of European courts of all historical periods but also for Chinese early medieval court studies.

5   See Xiaofei Tian, "Representing Kingship and Imagining Empire in Southern Dynasties Court Poetry," *T'oung Pao* 102.1-3 (2016): 3-6.

compositions, was Yu Xin's father. Xiao Gang's court clearly demonstrates the complex power dynamics in the literary field of the court: a potentate might be influenced by the older, accomplished literary courtiers, and his own taste in turn impacted contemporaries. Yu Xin, who had grown up in this milieu, internalized the aulic style espoused by his prince and his father, and it stayed with him for the rest of his life.

A persistent belief about aulic poetry is that it is largely constrained by imperial power and leaves little room for personal feelings or self-expression. Yet, the very notion of "personal feelings" is a product of our modern bourgeois society in which public/professional and private/personal are segregated. For a member of court society, the idea of a sharp distinction between professional and private, or work and leisure, would not have made sense; public and personal were inseparably tied to each other. Whereas aulic poetry demands decorum and restraint in line with unspoken rules of conduct governing a courtier in his social life, neither quality is synonymous with emotionlessness or impersonality. In the poetry of the late sixth-century southern diasporic community, emotional power is often intensified by formal decorum and restraint exercised by an author well-trained in the aulic style.

In the north, Yu Xin and others of the southern diaspora continued to write poetry with and to one another. Notable among the group were Wang Bao 王褒 (513-576), Xiao Hui 蕭撝 (515-573), Liu Fan 劉璠 (510-568), and Liu Zhen 劉臻 (527-598). They had belonged to the same elite circle in the south, and had experienced the same traumatic, life-shattering events. Now, their state and court destroyed, dislocated to a foreign land, they nevertheless continued doing what they had always done: namely, constructing a network amongst fellow courtiers through writing and reading, thus creating a shadow of their former court community. A couplet from Yu Xin "Yonghuai" No. 4, to which I will return in the last section of this article, directly alludes to this community and to the importance of audience and understanding: "Only those weeping at the end of the road / Understand the hardship of this path I travel" 惟彼窮途慟, 知余行路難. If the non-Han nobility of the northern dynasties spoke the Xianbei language amongst themselves, these members of the southern diaspora constituted the northerners' mirror image by constructing a community of their own, speaking a language only they themselves fully understood.

The Transformation of Types and Conventions

We will begin with "Yonghuai" No. 7, a relatively straightforward, though by no means simple, poem.[6]

榆關斷音信	The Elm Pass is severed from messages;[7]
漢使絕經過	Han envoys have stopped coming this way.
胡笳落淚曲	From Tartar pipes come melodies making tears fall;
4 羌笛斷腸歌	Tibetan flutes play songs that break the heart.
孀腰減束素	Widowed waist: a diminished reel of silk;[8]
別淚損橫波	Parting tears cut the sparkling ripples.
恨心終不歇	The bitterness in her heart shall never cease,
8 紅顏無復多	Yet the bloom of her face is no longer lush.
枯木期填海	With dead wood she expects to fill up the sea,
青山望斷河	And hopes to block the river with the green hill.

Ni Fan regards this female figure as a heroine in a generic "boudoir lament" and purely metaphorical, a line of interpretation that seems to be generally

---

6 The text used here is from Lu Qinli's 逯欽立 compilation, *Xian Qin Han Wei Jin nanbeichao shi* 先秦漢魏晉南北朝詩 (Beijing: Zhonghua shuju, 1995), 2368. All translations are the author's unless otherwise noted. For commentaries I have consulted the seventeenth-century commentator Ni Fan's 倪璠 *Yu Zishan jizhu* 庾子山集注 (Beijing: Zhonghua shuju, 1980; cited hereafter as *Jizhu*) and "Yü Hsin's 'Songs of Sorrow,'" an article that contains the translations, with notes and commentaries, of the entire poetic series. See William T. Graham, Jr. and James R. Hightower, "Yü Hsin's 'Songs of Sorrow,'" in *Harvard Journal of Asiatic Studies* 43.1 (June 1983): 5-55. With regard to the allusions in Yu Xin's poems, the point of departure is Ni Fan's annotations and Graham and Hightower's article, which references a number of premodern and modern annotations including Ni Fan's (see Hightower's note 3 on p. 6). Those not credited to the foregoing are the discovery of the author. Other modern annotations that have appeared since Graham and Hightower's article are also consulted, including: *Yu Xin xuanji* 庾信選集, annot. Shu Baozhang 舒寶章 (He'nan: Zhongzhou shuhuashe, 1983); *Xie Tiao, Yu Xin ji qita shiren shiwen xuanping* 謝朓庾信及其他詩人詩文選評, ed. and annot. Yang Ming 楊明 and Yang Tao 楊泰 (Shanghai: Shanghai guji chubanshe, 2002); and *Xie Tiao Yu Xin shixuan* 謝朓庾信詩選, annot. Du Xiaoqin 杜曉勤 (Beijing: Zhonghua shuju, 2006). However, there has been no new identification of allusions regarding the poems discussed in this chapter.

7 Ni Fan identifies the Elm Pass as "the pass of the Elms" constructed in the Qin. See *Jizhu*, 233. This is also known as Elm Grove Frontier 榆林塞 (modern Inner Mongolia). It functions as a general reference to northern frontiers.

8 A reel of silk is a common literary expression for a woman's slender waist. The line means that her waist is thinner than a reel of silk. *Shuang* also reads *xian* 纖 (slender).

adopted by modern annotators.[9] Yet for any sixth-century reader this poem would immediately recall a long tradition of verses on a Han woman forced to live in a barbarian land, most specifically Wang Zhaojun 王昭君, the Western Han palace lady married to the Xiongnu khan. Her story was featured in a Liang court song-and-dance performance[10] and was a popular poetic topic in the Southern Dynasties.[11] Yu Xin himself had composed two Wang Zhaojun poems. In the one entitled "Wang Zhaojun," he writes: "Her waistline measures no more than one foot, / Tears flow in a thousand streaks" 圍腰無一尺, 垂淚有千行.[12] These lines resemble the third couplet of the "Yonghuai" poem above, which likewise speaks of reduced waistline and of tears. Nevertheless, the latter exhibits a precious cleverness: "widowed waist" is a novel expression that understandably gave rise to a more conventional variant "slender waist";[13] *bielei* is tears shed at parting, but it literally means "departing tears," which reduce the "sparkling ripples," a kenning for a woman's eyes.

The poem contains other recognizable Wang Zhaojun motifs, such as the playing of music and the fading of her youthful beauty, caused by sorrow, natural aging, and the northern climate. In Yu Xin's other Wang Zhaojun poem,

---

9   Ni Fan comments on the fourth couplet: "[The poet] describes himself suffering from the bitter cold on the frontier, like in a boudoir lament" 自言關塞苦寒之狀若閨怨矣. *Jizhu*, 234. Hightower mentions Cai Yan 蔡琰 (fl. early 3rd century) (23); Yang Ming and Yang Tao find evocation of "the 'Wusun Princess,' Wang Zhaojun, and Cai Wenji [Cai Yan], and so forth" (*Xie Tiao, Yu Xin ji qita*, 98). Du Xiaoqin suggests that the poet is comparing himself to the Western Han emissary Zhang Qian 張騫 (d. 113 BCE) or the general Li Ling 李陵 (d. 74 BCE), even though he acknowledges that the fifth and sixth couplets "use boudoir lament as a metaphor for [the poet's] homesickness." See *Xie Tiao Yu Xin shixuan*, 178.

10   According to Zhijiang's 智匠 (fl. late 6th century) *Gujin yuelu* 古今樂錄, during the Liang Emperor Wu's Tianjian 天監 reign (502-519) the court musicians created a new Wang Zhaojun song-and-dance show based on the old Jin-Song musical. Cited in Guo Maoqian 郭茂倩 (fl. 11th century), comp., *Yuefu shiji* 樂府詩集 (Beijing: Zhonghua shuju, 1979), 29.425.

11   The poems, to the title "Wang Zhaojun" or "Mingjun ci" 明君辭 (or "Zhaojun yuan" 昭君怨), are conveniently collected together in Guo Maoqian's *Yuefu shiji*, 29.426-435. Notable poets include Bao Zhao 鮑照 (ca. 414-466), Shen Yue 沈約 (441-513), He Xun 何遜 (d. ca. 518), Xiao Gang, Xiao Ji 蕭紀 (508-553, Xiao Gang's younger brother), Shen Manyuan 沈滿願 (fl. 6th century, Shen Yue's grand-daughter), and others.

12   Lu Qinli, comp., *Xian Qin Han Wei*, 2348.

13   Shuang can also refer to a married woman living in solitude, as in Bao Zhao's "Emulating 'Hard Traveling'" ("Ni Xinglu nan" 擬行路難) No. 13: "Before coming here I heard that your wife / Lived in solitude, slept alone, and was widely known for her chastity" 來時聞君婦，閨中孀居獨宿有貞名. Lu Qinli, comp., *Xian Qin Han Wei*, 1277.

"Lyric of Zhaojun, Written to Imperial Command" ("Zhaojun ci yingzhao" 昭君辭應詔), he writes: "Petal after petal, red bloom falls from her face; / Tears in pairs flow forth from her eyes" 片片紅顏落, 雙雙淚眼生.[14] The reference to "red bloom of face" recalls line 8 of the above "Yonghuai" poem. Finally, like several other Southern Dynasties poems on the same topic, most notably by Bao Zhao and Shen Yue, both of Yu Xin's Zhaojun poems end with music-making,[15] which is evoked in the second couplet of the "Yonghuai" poem.

Yu Xin's poem in many ways constitutes a "matching poem" of the Wang Zhaojun poem by Shen Yue, the great master of Southern Dynasties aulic poetry. Shen's piece reads:[16]

	朝發披香殿	In the morning she set off from the Pixiang Palace;
	夕濟汾陰河	Toward evening she crossed the Fenyin River.
	於茲懷九折	Here her inside was twisted into nine bends;
4	自此斂雙蛾	From this point on she knitted her eyebrows.
	沾妝如湛露	Her make-up was soaked as if by heavy dews,
	繞臉狀流波	As tears flew down her cheeks like rippling waves.
	日見奔沙起	Every day she saw rolling sand rising in the wind;
8	稍覺轉蓬多	Gradually she felt the whirling tumbleweeds grow copious.
	胡風犯肌骨	The Tartar wind violates the flesh and bones,
	非直傷綺羅	Not just wounding her silks and gauze.
	銜涕試南望	With tears in her eyes, she looked toward the south—
12	關山鬱嵯峨	Mountains and passes towering in cluster.
	始作陽春曲	She first made the tune of sunny spring,
	終成苦寒歌	Which eventually turned into a song of bitter cold.
	惟有三五夜	Only on the night of the fifteenth
16	明月暫經過	Did the bright moon pass by for a short visit.

Remarkably, Yu Xin not only adopts the rhyme scheme of Shen's poem but also uses a number of identical rhyme words: *guo*, *ge*, *bo*, *duo*, and *he*, with two of them even appearing in the same positions. The moon's visit (*jingguo* in Shen l.16) is rewritten into the Han envoys' discontinuation of visit (*jingguo* in Yu l.2); "tune" (*qu*) and "song" (*ge*) in Shen's penultimate couplet are transformed

---

14   Ibid., 2348.

15   The first ends with: "The melody of parting is truly full of bitterness; / The sad strings must be tuned and tightened" 別曲真多恨, 哀絃須更張; the second ends with: "Just as she is playing the zither melody, / It mutates into the sound of the Tartar pipes" 方調琴上曲, 變入胡笳聲. On ending in music-making, see also p. 85 in this volume.

16   Lu Qinli, comp., *Xian Qin Han Wei*, 1614.

into foreign melodies (also *qu* and *ge*) in Yu's second couplet. Tumbleweed—
an image of a woman's disheveled hair—is "copious" (*duo*) in Shen (l.8) while
"red bloom" is no longer "lush" (*duo*) in Yu (1.8); "rippling waves" (*bo*) is a metaphor for tears in Shen (l.6) but becomes a kenning for eyes in Yu (l.6). Yu Xin is
paying homage to the earlier master by rewriting his poem and leaving clearly
discernible traces for his readers.

Yet, if most of Yu Xin's "Yonghuai" No. 7 reads like a "normal" variation of the
Zhaojun theme, its final couplet presents a shock. The first line is, as Ni Fan
notes, a reference to Jingwei 精衛,[17] a mythological female avenger who has no
place in a poem on the Han palace lady Wang Zhaojun. Notably, Yu Xin uses
the phrase *kumu*, "dead wood," to refer to the sticks with which Jingwei fills up
the sea. It is a phrase that does not appear in the source text but has a particular symbolic meaning for Yu Xin and other southern exiles, who regularly portrayed themselves as uprooted trees. Although Yu Xin's "*Fu* on the Dead Wood"
("Kushu fu" 枯樹賦) may be the most famous, Liu Zhen's poem "Dead Tree by
the River" ("Hebian kushu shi" 河邊枯樹詩) shows that it is a metaphor in
common circulation among members of the southern diaspora.[18]

No commentator has been able to convincingly identify the baffling "green
hill" in the last line of the poem.[19] I believe that it refers to a story about the
Western Han empress Dou 竇 (d. 135 BCE). Empress Dou's father had drowned
in a river while fishing. After the empress became Empress Dowager, she had
the river filled up and a huge grave mound built on top of it. The local people
called it "Dou's Green Hill" ("Doushi qingshan" 竇氏青山).[20]

---

17   Jingwei was a daughter of the Fiery Emperor. She drowned in the Eastern Sea and was
      transformed into a bird. To avenge herself, she carried sticks and pebbles with her beak to
      try to fill up the sea with them.

18   Lu Qinli, comp., *Xian Qin Han Wei*, 2656. Sun Wanshou 孫萬壽 (fl. late 6th century), a
      member of the eastern diaspora from the fallen state of the Northern Qi, also uses the
      figure of dead tree to describe his feeling of rootlessness after the Qi fell in a poem, "Dead
      Tree in the Courtyard" ("Tingqian kushu shi" 庭前枯樹詩). Lu Qinli, comp., *Xian Qin Han
      Wei*, 2641.

19   Ni Fan does not comment. Hightower tentatively identifies the "green hill" as Mount Hua
      that had originally blocked the course of the Yellow River, saying that if this is indeed the
      case, she is expressing "a vain hope that the past can be undone." He also cites modern
      scholar Tan Zhengbi 譚正璧, who takes the hill to be the mountains back home in the
      South, "in which case the hope is that they will protect the south from the Yellow River,
      representing the hostile forces of the North." But Hightower concedes that such an inter-
      pretation "is even more far-fetched." Graham and Hightower, 24.

20   Zhi Yu's 摯虞 (d. 311) commentary on *Sanfu juelu* 三輔決錄, cited in *Shiji* 史記 commen-
      tary. Sima Qian 司馬遷 (ca. 145 BCE-ca. 86 BCE), *Shiji* 史記 (Beijing: Zhonghua shuju,

Though both allusions are about vengeful women who were determined to fill up a large body of water, Jingwei is a common poetic image, whereas Empress Dou's green hill is rarely, if ever, alluded to in early medieval literature. It is unusual to pair a historical personage—an empress at that—with a mythical figure like Jingwei, but even more unusual to end a Wang Zhaojun poem with the evocation of two fierce, implacable heroines. This would have been quite shocking to Yu Xin's contemporary readers, who would recognize the conventional Zhaojun motif and the unconventional spin Yu Xin put on it.

The extraordinary ending in fact harks back to Xiao Gang's poem on Wang Zhaojun.[21] Unlike the other poems in the Zhaojun tradition, Xiao Gang's piece ends not with an aural image but with a visual motif, alluding to the story about a court painter deliberately misrepresenting Zhaojun's beauty in a portrait and thus leading to the Han emperor's neglect of her: "How unfair to be slandered by a skilled painter— / There is no way for her bitter feelings to get through" 妙工偏見詆, 無由情恨通. Yu Xin constructs his entire poem on a play with the word *tong* 通 (get through) by exploring the inability of getting through. His poem begins with news being cut off (*duan* 斷) and envoys no longer coming (*jue* 絕); even music, which as sound travels through space and reaches people easily, serves to break (the second *duan* in the poem) the heart. Ironically, in the last couplet the act of filling up (*tian* 填) and thus blocking (the third *duan* in the poem) the river only creates yet another kind of stoppage and obstruction. In Yu Xin's poem the only thing that never ceases or diminishes is "the bitterness in her heart" (*hen xin* 恨心), which evokes the "bitter feelings" (*qing hen* 情恨) in Xiao Gang's poem.

One could say that Yu Xin's poem is an elaboration on Xiao Gang's last line, or on Shen Yue's sixth couplet, which is about Zhaojun's southward gaze being obstructed by "mountains and passes towering in cluster." All this is reminiscent of the popular southern literary practice of *fude* 賦得 ("versifying on an assigned topic") on an earlier poetic line. The surprising evocation of two female avengers at the end is thus both based on, and subverts, the southern aulic tradition. Such a move is typical of Yu Xin's poetry written in the north, exemplifying an intimate textual memory shared by his fellow exiles.

The next example, "Yonghuai" No. 17, shows more clearly how Yu Xin destabilizes a reader's comfort with familiar poetic conventions by combining and twisting poetic subgenres; the outcome is all the more shocking exactly because its components are quite recognizable. This is Yu Xin's unique technology

---

1959), 49.1973. See also Li Daoyuan 酈道元, *Shuijing zhu jiaoshi* 水經注校釋 (Hangzhou: Hangzhou daxue chubanshe, 1999), 10.189.

21   The poem is entitled "Mingjun ci" 明君詞. Lu Qinli, comp., *Xian Qin Han Wei*, 1913.

in giving expression to traumatic experience, the articulation of which is an important step in the process of working through the past.

日晚荒城上	At dusk, on the desolate city wall:
蒼茫餘落暉	Vast and hazy, an endless sunset.
都護樓蘭返	The Protector comes back from Loulan;
4 將軍疏勒歸	The General returns from Shule.[22]
馬有風塵氣	Horses smell of wind and dust;
人多關塞衣	Men are all wearing frontier garments.
陣雲平不動	Battle-formation clouds hang flat, not moving;
8 秋蓬卷欲飛	Autumn tumbleweeds roll up, about to fly away.
聞道樓船戰	I hear talk of the campaign of warships,
今年不解圍	That the siege will not be lifted this year.

Regarding the first couplet, rather than succumbing to the sort of crude symbolism advocated by Tang and Song popular poetry manuals and taking the setting sun as "a symbol for the declining fortunes of a ruling house,"[23] one would do better to recall some of the most famous early medieval poems with similar openings. For instance, Pan Yue's 潘岳 (247-300) celebrated poem of homesickness, "Composed at Heyang County" ("Heyang xian zuo" 河陽縣作) No. 2, opens with, "At dusk, dark clouds rise; / I climb on the city wall, and gaze at the great River" 日夕陰雲起，登城望洪河.[24] Or Xie Lingyun's 謝靈運 (385-433) well-known poem, "Waiting for the Guest I Expected from the South Tower" ("Nanlou zhong wang suozhi ke" 南樓中望所遲客):[25]

杳杳日西頹	Darkly, the sun sets in the west;
漫漫長路迫	The endlessly long road presses on me.
登樓為誰思	Climbing the tower, for whom am I full of longing?
臨江遲來客	Looking upon the river, I eagerly await my guest....

Xie Tiao 謝朓 (464-499) and He Xun, both exerting a great influence on the sixth-century southern poets, also each have several poems about gazing into distance at dusk. In other words, Yu Xin's poem begins like any early medieval poem on climbing to a high place, gazing out into the distance, and yearning for home or for a loved one. However, the normalcy soon dissolves, and the reader's expectation is defeated.

---

22   Both Loulan and Shule are names of Central Asian countries.

23   Graham and Hightower, 40.

24   Lu Qinli, comp., *Xian Qin Han Wei*, 633.

25   Ibid., 1173. Like Pan Yue's poem, Xie's poem is also anthologized in the sixth-century literary anthology *Wen xuan* 文選 and must be familiar to a well-educated medieval reader.

In the earlier poems about climbing high and gazing into the distance, we always have a historical person—the poet—at a specific place and time, who describes the specific objects in his view. In contrast, Yu Xin's poem takes the reader in a different direction with the peculiar second couplet: "The Protector comes back from Loulan; / The General returns from Shule." The couplet is peculiar in a poem about climbing high. Such a couplet properly belongs to contemporary *yuefu* poetry, particularly to a subgenre of *yuefu* later known as "frontier poetry" (*biansai shi* 邊塞詩), which describes imaginary military campaigns and frontier life in northwestern China.

As is well known to any student of classical Chinese literature, beginning with Bao Zhao, frontier poetry took hold of the imagination of Southern Dynasties poets and was produced in great quantity. In those poems, place names from Central Asia and northwestern China abound to create an exotic atmosphere, and "Protector" and "General" form a customary pair in parallel couplets. Some examples include:

1. Wang Xun 王訓 (511-36) "Crossing Passes and Mountains" ("Du guan-shan" 度關山):

都護疲詔吏　　The Protector is tired of giving instructions to clerks;
將軍擅發兵　　The General arbitrarily dispatches troops.[26]

2. Dai Gao 戴暠 (fl. first half of the 6th century), "Crossing Passes and Mountains" ("Du guanshan" 度關山):

將軍一百戰　　The General has fought in one hundred battles;
都護五千兵　　The Protector commands five thousand troops.[27]

3. Liu Xiaowei 劉孝威 (d. 549), "Piebald Horse Gallops On" ("Congma qu" 驄馬驅):

且令都護知　　He wants to be known to the Protector,
願被將軍照　　And desires to be understood by the General.[28]

4. Yu Xin, "Coming out the North Gate of Ji" ("Chuzi Jibeimen xing" 出自 薊北門行):

將軍朝挑戰　　The general challenges the enemy in the morning;
都護夜巡營　　The Protector inspects the camps at night.[29]

26　Ibid., 1717.
27　Ibid., 2100.
28　Ibid., 1866.
29　Ibid., 2348.

The frequency with which the two official titles are paired in a sixth-century *yuefu*, in addition to the combination of the two exotic place names Loulan and Shule, would have strongly conditioned a contemporary reader to hear echoes of frontier *yuefu* poetry in Yu Xin's couplet, rather than to seek specific allusions behind them. Similarly, the third and fourth couplets of Yu Xin's poem—horses, warriors, battle-formation clouds and tumbleweeds—could also be easily taken as part of the general description of a frontier scene in *yuefu* poetry. But once again our expectation is thwarted, because the frontier *yuefu* tends to be upbeat and macho, and its protagonist is usually a warrior eager for victories and accomplishments; or he may be weary and homesick, but he would never climb high and gaze afar, because these were the traditional poetic gestures of a lyrical poet.

The worst breach of the frontier subgenre is the last couplet: "I hear talk of the campaign with warships, / That the siege will not be lifted this year." Something is terribly wrong with this couplet. Although it is not true that, as Hightower believes, "there is no place for warships 樓船 in the north,"[30] the mention of warships is indeed startling within the geographical setting established in the poem. It does not fit the imagery of cavalry returning from the desert kingdoms, and indeed the Southern Dynasties frontier poetry never mentions warships and navy—poetic convention dictates that a frontier poem only depict the northwest.[31] Notably, the naval battle is "heard" of by the poet, complementing what is seen by him from the city wall. Together with the action of "hearing," the temporal precision of "this year" instills a sense of historical specificity, and hence a sense of reality, into the poem and shatters the illusion of the anonymous generality of frontier *yuefu* carefully constructed in the second through fourth couplets. The poem is brought full circle from the opening couplet that evokes a particular historical voice. Its ending harks back

---

30   See Hightower, 40. However, the Northern Zhou's military campaign against the Northern Qi in 575 had, for instance, indeed deployed a large navy and many warships sailing from the Wei River onto the Yellow River. *Zhou shu* 周書 (Beijing: Zhonghua shuju, 1971), 6.93. I am not at all certain that this poem reflects "the poet's impressions when he first arrived in Chang'an, and the first couplet would refer to the decline of the Liang" (41). To me, it evokes the Northern Zhou's grim, relentless resolve to conquer its neighboring states and unify China, and its repeated military exercises and campaigns against the peoples of Central Asia, the Chen, and the Northern Qi. However, it is impossible to know for sure the date and circumstances of composition of this poem.

31   Southern frontier poetry is interested neither in the real frontier boundary between south and north China at the time nor in the southern or southwestern frontiers. See the discussion in Xiaofei Tian, *Beacon Fire and Shooting Star: The Literary Culture of the Liang (502-557)* (Cambridge, MA: Harvard Asia Center, 2007), 323-35.

to the motif of an individual lyric poet climbing high and gazing afar with longing for home or friend.

Aesthetically, the inconclusiveness of the naval battle is woven into a beautiful formal balance with the clouds hanging motionless over the horizon like battle formation. The stillness of the air, which implicitly causes the slow moving of the clouds, is also responsible for the temporary immobility of the autumn tumbleweed, which is a familiar poetic figure of a rootless traveler. The motionlessness is only temporary: the tumbleweed is "about to fly away," just as the poet will soon descend from the city wall—it is getting dark—and the siege will likewise end soon enough. The impending fall of a city, of a state, is momentarily suspended in a poem, whose ending points to a future beyond its own closure.

In this poem, the poet sets up expectation only to frustrate it. The poem becomes a meta-poetic text that brings together two different kinds of poetry: one kind of poetry involves a particular historical person's climbing high and gazing with longing into the distance—and that person is usually the poet himself; the other is about an imagined northwestern frontier, and the persona in that poetry is a type. Yu Xin is bending and changing poetic subgenres because existing poetic language and conventions are no longer adequate to articulate his individual experience.

Yu Xin's "Memory Palace"

As the Liang fell apart with the Hou Jing rebellion, Yu Xin suffered acutely, not the least because he had enjoyed an especially privileged position at the Liang court. Like his father, he was a favorite of the Crown Prince; his own talent and eloquence earned him accolades from the emperor and the princes, in the south and north alike. He was made the mayor of the capital city Jiankang (modern Nanjing) at the age of 35, and by all appearances had an illustrious career ahead of him. Then, when Hou Jing's rebel army approached Jiankang, Xiao Gang entrusted Yu Xin with the task of severing the Vermillion Bird Pontoon Bridge to the south of the Palace City. The soldiers under his command had just cut away one of the floats when Hou Jing's men loomed into full view. At the sight of their black iron masks, Yu Xin fell back, and his troops followed suit. According to another account, an arrow struck the gate pillar by which Yu Xin's horse was standing, and the sugarcane in his hand fell on the ground; at that moment he turned and fled in panic, and the defense collapsed. Hou Jing's men quickly reconnected the bridge and crossed the Qinhuai River. That was December 9, 548. The rest, as they say, was history.

Yu Xin, along with the royal family and many Liang courtiers, was trapped in the besieged city of Jiankang for five bloody months, bearing witness to acts of heroism and cowardice, violence, starvation, plague, and death. He himself lost both of his two sons and a young daughter. After Jiankang fell, he managed to get out and made his way to Jiangling (in modern Hubei), the provincial capital of Xiao Yi's prefecture. There he was reunited with his aging father, who died shortly afterward. In 553, Xiao Yi ascended the throne. Yu Xin was dispatched as emissary to the Western Wei court and was detained there. Meanwhile the Wei army attacked and captured Jiangling, sacked the city, and executed Xiao Yi, sealing the doom of the Liang. Numerous elites and commoners of Jiangling were taken as captives to the Wei capital Chang'an (modern Xi'an), and whatever was left of Yu Xin's immediate family was presumably among them. Later, while some southern courtiers were allowed to return to the south, Yu Xin was kept at the northern court because of his literary talent. He died there in 581.

While the word "trauma" has been used widely, even indiscriminately, in recent years, it is hard to regard Yu Xin's experience as anything less than traumatic. Everything he knew was stripped away from him, his state destroyed, his family members killed; he himself stared death in the face more than once. In Catherine Caruth's definition, "trauma describes an overwhelming experience of sudden, catastrophic events, in which the response to the event occurs in the often delayed, and uncontrolled repetitive occurrence of hallucinations and other intrusive phenomena."[32] Delay and repetition are the keywords in understanding traumatic memory. Rather than an event that simply happened in the past:

> ... a traumatic event cannot be localized in one specific time and place, because it keeps coming back to those who are traumatized. As many researchers working on trauma recognize, there is a belatedness, not only in the manifestation of the impact of the traumatic event, but in the very experience of the traumatic event itself. In many ways, trauma itself is a form of memory because it always exists only as memory.[33]

In other words, trauma has double temporalities, being both past and present, and in trauma writing memories are being both constantly recalled and constructed anew.

---

32   Catherine Caruth, *Unclaimed Experience: Trauma, Narrative, and History*, 11.

33   Xiaofei Tian, "Introduction," in Zhang Daye 張大野, *The World of a Tiny Insect* (Seattle: University of Washington Press, 2013), 16.

In Yu Xin's case, he deals with his traumatic experience by constantly invoking the textual past and literally recreating textual memories every time he recalls them in his own writings. As a writer, he is haunted by texts from the old south: they keep returning to him and reappearing in his poetry, mutated, fragmented, but recognizable to any reader sharing the same past. It is a particular form of traumatic memory: it is not so much working-through in the Freudian sense as being unable to get out of it, hopelessly trapped in a house of memory that is labyrinthian and nightmarish.

The following poem is No. 22 of "Yonghuai":[34]

日色臨平樂	The sun shines upon the Pingle Lodge;
風光滿上蘭	A breezy light fills Shanglan.[35]
南國美人去	The Fair One of the south is gone forever,
4 東家棗樹完	Though the eastern neighbor's date tree is saved.[36]
抱松傷別鶴	Embracing the pine, the separated crane grieves;
向鏡絕孤鸞	Facing a mirror, the widowed phoenix ends its life.
不言登隴首	Who would have thought that, climbing onto the Long Range,
8 唯得望長安	I only get to gaze at Chang'an![37]

The strangeness of this poem lies in the apparent disconnectedness of its two middle couplets from the opening and ending couplets. The middle couplets form a coherent unit of meaning in their depiction of separated spouses/lovers. Regarding the second couplet, one notes that although the object causing so much trouble and strife remains intact, the Fair One is not coming back as

---

34   Lu Qinli, comp., *Xian Qin Han Wei*, 2370.

35   Both Pingle and Shanglan were names of structures in the Western Han's imperial Shanglin Park at Chang'an. *Jizhu*, 245.

36   In the Eastern Han, Wang Ji's 王吉 (d. 48 BCE) wife fed him dates from his eastern neighbor's tree, and after he found out about the origin of the dates, he sent his wife away. His neighbor felt so bad that he decided to cut down the tree, and only desisted after Wang Ji relented and took his wife back. The locals made a song: "The eastern neighbor has a tree, / Wang Ji's wife goes away. / The dates are preserved in the eastern home, / The dismissed wife returns home." *Jizhu*, 245.

37   The last line, as Ni Fan observes, echoes Wang Can's famous couplet in his "Seven Sorrows" 七哀詩 No. 1: "To the south I climb onto the Ba Mound, / Turning back, I look toward Chang'an" 南登灞陵岸, 迴首望長安. Lu Qinli, comp., *Xian Qin Han Wei*, 365. For the penultimate line, the source text is Guo Zhongchan's 郭仲產 (d. 454) *Account of Qinzhou* (*Qinzhou ji* 秦州記), in which travelers from outside of the Qin region would climb onto the Long Range and gazes eastward at the Qin plains, filled with homesickness. Ni Fan cites this text to annotate the line from "Yonghuai" No. 3: "The man of Qin gazes from the Long Range" 秦人望隴頭. See *Jizhu*, 230.

Wang Ji's wife did. The Fair One of the South, clearly evoking the *Chu ci* tradition, is a figure both for the prince (i.e. Xiao Gang) and for the poet himself. The third couplet, with the pine representing a continuation, by the principle of association, of the date tree imagery, picks up the motif of lovers' separation and shows that one spouse has survived, bereaved. The lone phoenix that never sings for three years, upon seeing its reflection in a mirror, cries out and dies.[38] For the "separated crane" every commentator cites "The Tune of the Separated Cranes" ("Biehe cao" 別鶴操) and the related story of Muzi 牧子, who was forced to divorce his childless wife and played a sad melody to express his sorrow.[39] However, the juxtaposition of crane and pine compels us to seek an alternative source text, and in hunting down this source text we begin to enter a complicated web of texts.

The *ur*-text is from Wang Xinzhi 王歆之's (fl. early 5th century) *Account of Divine Realms* 神境記:

> There is a stone chamber to the south of Xingyang Commandery, and behind the chamber stands a solitary pine tree of a thousand feet tall. There is always a pair of cranes there, flying wing to wing in the morning and matching up their shadows at night. According to the local legend, a husband and wife once were recluses in that chamber, turning into a pair of cranes when they were hundreds of years old.[40]

In a poem entitled "Lamenting the Deceased on Behalf of Someone" ("Dairen shangwang" 代人傷往), Yu Xin conflates this legend with the famous story about the Green Field cranes:

青田松上一黃鶴	A single yellow crane on the pine at Green Field;
相思樹下兩鴛鴦	Two mandarin ducks under the Lovelorn Tree:
無事交渠更相失	Suddenly for no reason one loses the other;
不及從來莫作雙	Far better to have never been a pair at all.

The pathos of this quatrain certainly fits the "Yonghuai" poem under discussion, but we must mention two more texts that stand behind the quatrain. One is Xiao Yi's *Fu on Mandarin Ducks* ("Yuanyang fu" 鴛鴦賦), the topic of a group composition in which Xiao Gang, Yu Xin, and Xu Ling had notably all

---

38   *Jizhu*, 245.

39   Ibid.

40   *Yiwen leiju*, 90.1565, 88.1512. Ni Fan identifies this allusion in his "Summary Glossary," which is perhaps why Graham and Hightower missed it. See *Jizhu*, 251.

participated.[41] The *fu* contains the following lines: "The cranes of Green Field fly side by side night and day; the wild geese from South of the Sun have always returned in pair" 青田之鶴, 晝夜俱飛; 日南之鴈, 從來共歸.[42] This quotation shows that, although the original story about the Green Field cranes is about the parting of parents and child, the focus could be easily shifted to the two parent-birds as a couple. The other shadow text is Xiao Gang's poem, "Watching a Lone Goose Flying at Night" ("Yewang danfei yan" 夜望單飛雁), on which Yu Xin's quatrain is modeled:[43]

天霜河白夜星稀	In the frosty skies, the River gleams white, stars burning few;
一雁聲嘶何處歸	One wild goose cries hoarsely—where is home?
早知半路應相失	If it had known it would lose its companions midway,
不如從來本獨飛	Far better it would have been to always fly alone.

The second couplet of Yu's quatrain is a rewriting of Xiao Gang's second couplet, and Yu's quatrain provides that invisible link between Xiao Gang's quatrain and the "Yonghuai" poem. Perhaps to this maze of texts about bereaved birds one ought to add yet another, a couplet from Xiao Gang's poem entitled "On Someone's Abandoned Concubine" ("Yong ren qiqie" 詠人弃妾): "A lone swan stops its flight midway; / A widowed phoenix dies in front of the mirror" 獨鵠罷中路, 孤鸞死鏡前.[44]

The above analysis has demonstrated that the two middle couplets of "Yonghuai" No. 22 establish an intricate network of texts about painful separation of lovers/spouses, but we still need to account for their connection to the opening and concluding couplets. The beginning and ending couplets not only

---

41   Xu Ling was the talented son of the senior courtier Xu Chi, who along with Yu Xin's father sponsored the "Xu Yu Style."

42   Yan Kejun 嚴可均, comp., *Quan shanggu sandai Qin Han sanguo liuchao wen* 全上古三代秦漢三國六朝文 (Beijing: Zhonghua shuju, 1987), 3038. The "wild geese from Rinan" alludes to the story about a pair of wild geese always following the carriage of the magistrate of Rinan. *Yiwen leiju*, 91.1579.

43   Lu Qinli, comp., *Xian Qin Han Wei*, 1978. Yu Xin was familiar with Xiao Gang's poem, for he had in fact written a seven-syllable-line quatrain, "Watching a Lone Goose Flying on an Autumn Night" ("Qiuye wang danfei yan" 秋夜望單飛鴈); judging from the identical titles and their formal similarity, Yu Xin's quatrain was either composed on the same occasion as Xiao Gang composed his or as a *zhui he* 追和 ("writing a companion piece to an earlier poem") at a later time. Lu Qinli, comp., *Xian Qin Han Wei*, 2410.

44   Lu Qinli, comp., *Xian Qin Han Wei*, 1953.

form a coherent unit of meaning that frames the poem, but also are implicated in another web of texts on a related theme in the southern poetic repertoire.

In southern aulic poetry, Shanglan, like Pingle, is often used to refer to the capital Jiankang. Two particulars poems, one by Shen Yue and the other by Xiao Gang, constitute the subtext here. Shen Yue's poem is entitled "Climbing High and Viewing Spring" 登高望春:[45]

	登高眺京洛	Climbing high, I gaze afar at the capital Luoyang:
	街巷紛漠漠	Streets and alleys are numerous in a haze.
	廻首望長安	Turning back, I look toward Chang'an:
4	城闕鬱盤桓	Its walls and towers stretch endlessly.
	齊童躡朱履	Qi boys step in their crimson slippers;
	趙女揚翠翰	Zhao girls raise their kingfisher eyebrows.[46]
	春風搖雜樹	Spring wind stirs assorted trees:
8	葳蕤綠且丹	Their dense leaves and branches hang in greens and reds.
	寶瑟玫瑰柱	Bejeweled harp with rose-gem bridges;
	金羈瑇瑁鞍	Golden halters, saddles decorated with tortoise-shell.
	淹留宿下蔡	They linger and stay over at Xiacai;
12	置酒過上蘭	Then set out drinks when passing through Shanglan.
	日出照鈿黛	Up comes the sun, shining on jewelry and khol;
	風過動羅紈	A breeze passes, stirring her gossamer dress.
	解眉還復斂	Her eyebrows are relaxed, then knit together again—
16	方知巧笑難	Only now does one know "pretty smiles" are hard to come by.[47]
	佳期空靡靡	The happy reunion is far in sight;
	含睇未成歡	Gazing passionately, she fails to find joy.
	嘉客不可見	The fine visitor is not to be seen;
20	因君寄長歎	Through you she would like to send him her long sighs.

The third line of Shen Yue's poem transplants the third-century poet Wang Can's immortal line—"Turning back, I look toward Chang'an," but Shen's poem

---

[45] Ibid., 1633. I follow the *Yiwen leiju* version in positioning the "Up comes the sun" couplet as the seventh rather than the third couplet (*Yiwen leiju*, 28.504). Also see Richard B. Mather's translation of this poem in *The Age of Eternal Brilliance: Three Lyric Poets of the Yung-ming Era (483-493)* (Leiden: Brill, 2003), 1:143-45.

[46] Lu Ji writes that "her moth brows resemble kingfisher feathers" 蛾眉象翠翰 in his ballad "The Sun Comes Out from the Southeast" ("Richu dongnanyu xing" 日出東南隅行). Lu Qinli, comp., *Xian Qin Han Wei*, 652.

[47] "Pretty smile" or "artful smile" echoes a line in the *Shi jing* 詩經 poem "Shiren" 碩人: "So charming is her pretty smile" 巧笑倩兮. Mao #57.

is the opposite of Wang's, as Wang Can writes about the wretched poet going away from the devastated Han capital to the "barbarian" south and seeing a starving woman abandoning her baby on the way. Instead, Shen writes about a prosperous capital city.[48] In lines 11-12 Shanglan is paired with Xiacai, which is often associated with beautiful women;[49] then in ll. 13-20 the poet describes just such a beautiful woman, who seems to be part of a merry crowd on a spring outing but is filled with melancholy, longing for a "fine visitor . . . not to be seen."

In the poem by Xiao Gang that also brings up Shanglan, we again see the motif of a woman longing for her departed lover. The poem is entitled "On the Assigned Topic, 'In the Tavern'" ("Fude danglu" 賦得當壚):

	十五正團團	On the fifteenth, the moon being round,
	流光滿上蘭	Its rippling glow fills Shanglan.
	當壚設夜酒	In the tavern drinks are set out for the night,
4	宿客解金鞍	The guest staying over unties his golden saddle.
	迎來挾瑟易	It is easy to bring in the harp for a welcoming reception;
	送別但歌難	Seeing off the departed, she finds it hard to sing unaccompanied.
	欲知心恨急	Want to know how her heart is cut to the quick?
8	翻令衣帶寬	Just watch how it makes her sash hang looser.[50]

The second line of this poem reappears almost verbatim in Yu Xin's "Yonghuai" poem. But in Yu Xin's poem, the "Fair One of the South" is gone—both the "fine visitor" and the woman longing for him.

So in Shen Yue's and Xiao Gang's poems Shanglan appears connected with a lovelorn woman in the midst of "the good life of the capital city," and this proves to be the hidden link between the opening couplet of Yu Xin's poem and the middle couplets. The poet's viewing of the capital city from heights,

---

48   This motif also had had a long tradition by Shen Yue's time. One thinks of Lu Ji's "The Gentleman Longs for Someone" ("Junzi yousuosi xing" 君子有所思行 and Bao Zhao's "To 'Forming Bonds in the World of Young Men'" ("Dai jieke shaonianchang xing") 代結客少年場行) (Lu Qinli, comp., *Xian Qin Han Wei*, 662, 1267). The opening couplet of Shen's poem contains verbal echoes of Lu Ji's second couplet.

49   "With one charming smile she bewitched [the people of] Yangcheng and led [the people of] Xiacai astray." In *Fu on the Lecherous Master Dengtu* ("Dengtuzi haose fu" 登徒子好色賦), attributed to Song Yu 宋玉. Yan Kejun, comp., *Quan shanggu sandai*, 74.

50   That is, she is losing weight. I take some liberty with translating *xin hen ji* 心恨急, as *ji* 急 ("intense"; "tight") and *kuan* 寬 (relaxed; wide) form a pair of opposites and the poet is playing with the multiple meanings of the two terms.

invoked in Shen's poem quoting Wang Can, returns in full force in Yu Xin's ending couplet: "Who would have thought that, climbing onto the Long Range, / I only get to gaze at Chang'an!" 不言登隴首，唯得望長安. This may be glossed by a line from a poem by none other than Yu Xin's own father: "On the Long Range one is saddened gazing toward Qin" 隴頭悲望秦.[51] If a man of Qin climbs on the Long Range to look toward Chang'an to relieve his homesickness, or if a Wang Can looks yearningly toward his devastated capital one last time before going south, then with a great sense of bitter irony, Yu Xin, the one coming *from* the south, "*only* gets to look toward Chang'an." And his viewing of the real Chang'an reveals nothing but the textual city constructed by the southerner. The poem presents an intricate memory palace of words, filled with secret chambers and passageways that always lead the poet back to his lost south.

Specter and Shadow: Writing Trauma and Violence in the Aulic Style

This section will focus on No. 27, the last poem of the series. It is an elegy about the fall of Jiangling and the death of Xiao Yi, which marked the end of the Liang dynasty in reality, if not in name for a few more years. The poem's meaning can be construed at several levels. Its surface meaning is comprehensible to any premodern reader with a basic competence in the classical tradition; such a competence can be successfully restored for a modern reader by the supply of notes and glossaries. At a deeper level, however, this poem is a response to a more recent physical and textual event of the Liang court. As will be shown below, this poem is not only deeply embedded in the southern aulic tradition, but also evokes a specific occasion on which the two Liang princes—Xiao Gang and Xiao Yi—composed poetry together, and recreates a ghostly presence of the Liang court by making complex verbal allusions to that occasion.

被甲陽雲臺	Putting on the armor on Sunny Cloud Terrace:[52]
重雲久未開	Layered clouds, long unbroken.
雞鳴楚地盡	"Cocks Crow": all Chu's land has fallen;
鶴唳秦軍來	Cranes cried: the Qin army is here.[53]

---

51 Yu Jianwu, "Seeing Liu Zhilin Off at Xinlin" ("Xinlin song Liu Zhilin" 新林送劉之遴). Lu Qinli, comp., *Xian Qin Han Wei*, 1994.

52 Sunny Cloud Terrace is where the King of Chu had had an erotic dream about the Goddess of the Wu Mountain in "*Fu* on Gaotang" attributed to Song Yu. *Jizhu*, 249.

53 "Cocks Crow" is the name of the Chu song sung by the Han army as it surrounded the Chu troops, luring the Chu troops into thinking that the Han army had taken all of the Chu

羅梁猶下礌	Arrayed beams are still being cast down[54]
楊排久飛灰	Even as poplar shields have long turned into flying ashes.[55]
出門車軸折	The carriage axle breaks when he goes out the gate:
吾王不復回	Our prince will not come back.[56]

---

land and thus demoralizing them. See *Shi ji*, 7.333; *Jizhu*, 249. The Qin army refers to the army led by the Latter Qin ruler Fu Jian 符堅 (337-385), who was thoroughly defeated by the Eastern Jin army in the famous Battle of Fei River. To the panicked Qin soldiers in flight, even wind rustling and crane crying sounded like the Jin forces in pursuit. *Jin shu* 晉書 (Beijing: Zhonghua shuju, 1974), 114.2918. Here, however, Yu Xin gives an ironic twist to the allusion by saying that crying cranes to the defeated Liang troops suggests the advent of the Qin army, which is usually a stand-in for the Western Wei in Yu Xin's writings. *Jizhu*, 249.

54 This line evokes Pan Yue's well-known "Elegy for Lord Ma, Governor of Qian" 馬汧督誄. Yan Kejun, comp., *Quan shanggu sandai*, 1994. Ma Dun 馬敦 (d. 297) was a Western Jin official who engaged in a spirited defense of the besieged city against the Di barbarians. In the preface to the elegy, Pan Yue gives a vivid depiction of how the defenders cast down beams and rafters, tied with iron chains, to fend off the enemy forces and then pulled the beams and rafters back with the chains for reuse (於是乎發梁棟而用之, 罥 以鐵鑹機關, 既縱礌而又升焉). The elegy contains the line *di liang wei lei* 罥 梁为礌 (tying rafters to throw down at the enemies attacking the city). I wonder if *luo* 羅 may have been a mis-transcription of the less common word *di* 罥. In that case the line should be rendered as "Tied rafters are still being cast down [to thwart the attackers]."

55 For this line, Ni Fan cites the biography of Yang Xuan 楊琁 in *Hou Han shu* 後漢書 (Beijing: Zhonghua shuju, 1965), 38.1288: Yang Xuan filled leather bellows (*bainang* 排囊) with lime dust and then sprayed the dust on battlefield to blind the enemy troops. See *Jizhu*, 249. Ni Fan seems to have taken *yang* 楊 (poplar) as interchangeable with *yang* 揚, to raise. While this is not an impossible interpretation, I believe that *yang pai* here refers to shields made of poplar wood. Yu Xin was very familiar with *Zuo zhuan*, in which we see this statement: "[Yue Qi] presented Jianzi with sixty shields made of poplar wood" 獻楊楯六十於簡子. *Zuo zhuan zhushu* 左傳注疏, Ding 6, in Ruan Yuan 阮元, comp., *Shisanjing zhushu* 十三經注疏 (Taipei: Yiwen yinshuguan, 1955), 55.961. According to Hu Sanxing's 胡三省 (1230-1302) *Zizhi tongjian* 資治通鑑 commentary, "*Pai* [shield] 牌 was called *dun* 楯 in the ancient times. During the Jin and Song dynasties [i.e. fourth and fifth century], it was called *pangpai* 彭排 [sometimes written as 旁排]. In the south it was made of bamboo bound with leather for self-defense; the northerners used wood to make it. As *Zuo zhuan* states, 'Yue Qi brought on disaster with [his gift to Jianzi of] poplar shields.' Thus the use of wood had had a long tradition in the north." *Zizhi tongjian* (Beijing: Guji chubanshe, 1956), 222.7134. But in fact the usage of *pai* or *pangpai* continued into the Tang, with *pai* 牌 sometimes written as *pai* 排. See, for instance, *Zhou shu*, 29.504: "Xiong carried a shield himself" 雄身負排. *Yang pai* 楊排 in this line is basically poplar shields (*yang dun* 楊楯).

56 In the Western Han, the Prince of Linjiang 臨江 (d. 148) was summoned to court on criminal charges. When he was going out the northern city gate of Jiangling, the axle of his carriage broke, wrecking his carriage. Seeing that, the elders of Jiangling wept and said to

The opening couplet presents a striking incongruity with the literary tradition, which would constitute a shocking affront to the courtly decorum. In belletristic writings, Sunny Cloud Terrace is a site of erotic desire made famous by the "*Fu* on Gaotang" ("Gaotang fu" 高唐賦), in which the Chu king consummates his love with the goddess of the Wu Mountain in a romantic dream. Before departing, the goddess says to the king: "At dawn I shall be the passing cloud, at dusk the passing rain. Every day from dawn to dusk I will be right there beneath Sunny Terrace."[57] The image of Sunny Cloud Terrace or Sunny Terrace was popularized by the revival of the Han dynasty song "Wu Mountain Is High" ("Wushan gao" 巫山高) in the late fifth century. Its association with passionate love-longing is summed up in Jiang Yan's 江淹 (444-505) couplet: "Lovelorn at the foot of the Wu Mountain; / Sadly gazing at Sunny Cloud Terrace" 相思巫山渚, 悵望陽雲臺.[58] To connect Sunny Cloud Terrace with putting on the armor, as Yu Xin does, is positively shocking, and shock is an element that finds no place in aulic poetry.

To a Liang courtier, however, Sunny Cloud Terrace was far from being just a literary allusion: it was as much a physical site as a textual site. When Xiao Yi, the Prince of Xiangdong, served as governor of Jingzhou, he had constructed a large park known as the Xiangdong Park in the provincial capital Jiangling, and in the park he had a Sunny Cloud Tower built on an artificial hill.[59] During his term at Jingzhou, Xiao Yi became infatuated with a local girl named Li Tao'er 李桃兒. When upon finishing his term he went back to the capital to report for duty to the throne, he took her along with him. This, however, was an infringement on the law controlling the mobility of residents, and his brother Xiao Xu 蕭續 (506-547), who succeeded him as the Jingzhou governor, threatened to inform their emperor father. Xiao Gang tried to intervene and make peace between the brothers, but to no avail. Apprehensive of negative consequences, Xiao Yi was forced to send Li Tao'er back to Jiangling.[60] Subsequently Xiao Yi was appointed governor of Jiangzhou, where he composed a poem expressing his longing for Li Tao'er and referred to her as "the person on Sunny Terrace" ("Yangtai ren" 陽臺人). Several courtiers wrote poems in sympathetic

---

one another: "Our prince will not come back." The prince indeed committed suicide after he arrived at the capital. *Shi ji*, 59.2094. See *Jizhu*, 250.

57   Yan Kejun, comp., *Quan shanggu sandai*, 73.

58   Lu Qinli, comp., *Xian Qin Han Wei*, 1580.

59   "On the hill there was Sunny Cloud Tower, which was of a soaring height, and from which one could see everything near or far [or "which could be seen near or far"]" 山上有陽雲樓極高峻遠近皆見. *Zhugong gushi* 渚宮故事, cited in *Taiping yulan* 太平御覽 (Taipei: Shangwu yinshuguan, 1975 rpt.), 196.1075.

60   *Nan shi* 南史 (Beijing: Zhonghua shuju, 1975), 53.1321-22.

response to the prince, and all of the poems mention "Sunny Terrace."[61] This incident was widely known at the time.

In happier times, Xiao Yi had written a poem entitled "On the Willow Growing by the Eaves of Sunny Cloud Tower" ("Yong Yangyun lou yanliu" 詠陽雲樓簷柳):[62]

楊柳非花樹	The willow tree is not a flowering tree;
依樓自覺春	Yet as it leans against the tower, one feels the presence of spring.
枝邊通粉色	Between its branches gleams the color of powder;
4 葉裏映吹綸	Amidst its leaves shines forth the fluffy catkin-silk.[63]
帶日交簾影	Bathed in the sun, it intersects with the blind's shadow;
因吹掃席塵	Taking advantage of piping breeze, it sweeps the dust from the mat.[64]
拂簷應有意	Lightly brushing the eaves, it surely has feeling:
8 偏宜桃李人	In particular it is suited to the person of peach and plum.

Ostensibly a "poem on an object" (*yongwu shi* 詠物詩), this poem on willow is an unabashed love song praising Li Tao'er, whose name is embedded in the last line as "peach and apricot" (*tao li* 桃李). The "color of powder" and "fluffy catkin-silk" (i.e. the fabric of her dress) clearly point to a feminine presence. The third couplet, with the mention of hanging curtain and dusted mat, is rich in amorous suggestions about the inner chamber. The soft, supple willow tree "leaning against the tower" and conveying the message of spring is artfully blended with an erotically charged indoor scene, without violating the compositional mode of "poetry on object" in terms of strictly adhering to the topic at hand. The last line echoes the first, completing the poetic argument that, although the willow is not a flowering tree, it best complements the "person of peach and plum," the true flower of spring.

Xiao Gang understood his brother's sentiment perfectly. Below is his accompanying piece, which is the basis of Yu Xin's poem and deserves a detailed discussion.[65]

---

61 Xiao Yi's poem is entitled, "Ascending the Hundred Flowers Pavilion at Jiangzhou and Longing for Jing Chu" ("Deng Jiangzhou Baihua ting huai Jing Chu" 登江州百花亭懷荊楚). Lu Qinli, comp., *Xian Qin Han Wei*, 2048. The response poems were by Zhu Chao 朱超 and Yin Keng 陰鏗 (fl. 540s-560s). Ibid., 2094, 2451. I translate and discuss these poems in my book manuscript.

62 Ibid., 2053.

63 What I have translated loosely as "fluffy catkin-silk" (*chuilun* 吹綸) is a kind of airy and light fabric; it is also used to refer to willow catkins as in the phrase *chuilun xu* 吹綸絮.

64 *Chui* means the blowing of pan pipes, also referring to wind.

65 "Accompanying the Prince of Xiangdong's Poem on the Willow Growing by Sunny Cloud Tower" ("He Xiangdong wang Yangyun lou yanliu shi" 和湘東王陽雲樓簷柳詩). Lu Qinli, comp., *Xian Qin Han Wei*, 1959.

曖曖陽雲臺	Hazy and vague is Sunny Cloud Terrace,
春柳發新梅	Spring willow sprouts amidst new apricot blossoms.[66]
柳枝無極軟	Willow branches are infinitely soft;
4 春風隨意來	Spring wind comes as it will.
潭泛青帷閉	Rippling and heaving, green curtains are drawn;
玲瓏朱扇開	Light shimmering through traceries, vermillion doors swung open.
佳人有所望	The fair lady has someone she is expecting—
8 車聲非是雷	The sound of his carriage is not that of thunder.

Xiao Gang's poem is exemplary of an "accompanying poem" (*heshi* 和詩): not only does each couplet constitute a closely correlated variation on Xiao Yi's, his poem also illuminates details of the original poem that may have eluded a casual reader. The opening line mimics the duplicative binomes commonly found in second- and third-century "old poems." It is also an exquisite response to Xiao Yi because he calls our attention to the fact that Xiao Yi's poem is wittily evoking two couplets by the Xiao princes' favorite poet, Tao Yuanming 陶淵明 (365-427):

榆柳蔭後簷	Elms and willows shade the back eaves;
桃李羅堂前	Peach and plum are arrayed in front of the hall.
曖曖遠人村	Hazy and vague: the village afar;
依依墟里煙	Lingering: smoke from neighborhood hearths.[67]

Looking back to Xiao Yi's poem, we realize that its opening and closing lines contain many echoes of Tao's couplets: the willow brushing the eaves, the peach and plum, and the verbal transposition of the *yiyi* 依依 (lingering) of cooking smoke to the depiction of the willow branches (*yi lou* 依樓). Xiao Gang in his accompanying poem picks out the other binome in Tao's couplets, *aiai* 曖曖 (hazy and vague), as if to show Xiao Yi that he knows exactly what Xiao Yi

---

66 I have used "apricot" to render *mei* 梅 here rather than using the commonly accepted translation "plum" so as not to confuse it with *li* 李, also translated as plum. *Chun liu* 春柳 (spring willow) has a variant, *chun jiao* 春椒 (spring hilltop), though it is not attested to in *Yiwen leiju*, its earliest source (89.1533). Although this variant makes sense within the line by itself ("On spring hilltop apricot newly blossoms"), it does not make sense in the context of the poem, which is about willow, not plum (*mei*). In addition, the second couplet clearly develops the topic of "spring willow," with *liu* explicitly beginning the third line and *chun* the fourth, a common compositional technique in early medieval poetry.

67 From Tao Yuanming's famous poem, "Return to Dwell in the Gardens and Fields" ("Gui yuantian ju" 歸園田居) No. 1. Lu Qinli, comp., *Xian Qin Han Wei*, 991.

is doing. The binome is also particularly suitable to the new context, because Sunny Cloud Terrace, with the goddess lingering as the erotic "cloud and rain," is aptly enshrouded in mist.

The second line of Xiao Gang's poem succinctly underlines the keywords in Xiao Yi's first couplet: willow, spring, and the flowering tree ("apricot blossoms") that is brought up negatively by Xiao Yi (the "color of powder" in Xiao Yi's poem could be understood as a double reference to the lady and to the apricot blossoms present in the scene). The voluptuous second couplet closely follows Xiao Yi's: the first line depicts willow branches, whose suppleness (*ruan*) indicates new life and suggests a feminine sensuality; the second line about spring wind subtly rejoins the reference to *chuilun* (lit. blown yarn) in the corresponding line of Xiao Yi's poem.

Tantuo 潭沲 in the third couplet is an alliterative binome describes rippling water, here transferred to the undulating green curtains (in response to Xiao Yi's "blind"), a color evoking both the unfrozen spring pond and the willow tree; it is also a response to the "piping breeze" (*chui*) in Xiao Yi's fifth line. The sun in Xiao Yi's couplet reappears as the vermillion color of the doors with light shimmering through the traceries. The doors open up to receive the prince-lover while drawn curtains delineate an amorous private space, just as Xiao Yi's third couplet combines outdoor and indoor scenes.

Finally, just as Xiao Yi explicitly mentions "the person of peach and plum" in the last couplet, Xiao Gang brings up "the fair lady" (*jiaren* 佳人) expecting her lord. A witty line—"The sound of his carriage is not that of thunder"—concludes the poem, with its negation (*fei* 非) verbally echoing the same *fei* in Xiao Yi's opening line ("The willow tree is not a flowering tree"). Xiao Gang's line is a reversal of the couplet from the Western Han writer Sima Xiangru's 司馬相如 (ca. 179 BCE-117 BCE) "*Fu* on the Tall Gate" ("Changmen fu" 長門賦), which describes a neglected palace lady waiting for her lord in vain: "Thunder rumbled in the skies, / Its sound resembling that of my lord's carriage" 雷殷殷而響起兮, 聲象君之車音.[68] Xiao Gang turns the source text around and instead signals the happy meeting of the lovers.

One may point out here, at the risk of ruining the delicate touch in the poem, that in traditional cosmology thunder images the ruler or the heir apparent (Sima Xiangru's *fu* was believed to have been written on behalf of Han

---

68   Yan Kejun, comp., *Quan shanggu sandai*, 245. A fragment of the Western Jin poet Fu Xuan's 傅玄 (217-278) poem reads: "Thunder rumbles, moving my heart: / I listen to it attentively: it is not the sound of his carriage" 雷隱隱, 感妾心, 傾耳清聽非車音. Lu Qinli, comp., *Xian Qin Han Wei*, 575.

Emperor Wu's consort).[69] It is perhaps not so fanciful to detect an elusive tone just beneath the verbal surface here, which nevertheless forbids the reader to take it too seriously because it is meant exactly as a light touch: a breezy, brotherly reminder, perhaps imperceptible except to the subtle sensibilities of a Liang prince, of Xiao Yi's place as a *prince*.

If Xiao Gang's poem is a perfect response to Xiao Yi, then Yu Xin's poem is a response to Xiao Gang. Yu Xin uses the same rhyme as Xiao Gang does, and even uses three identical rhyme words: *tai* 臺, *lai* 來, and *kai* 開. While in later times writing an accompanying poem using the rhyme scheme of the original poem, a practice known as *heyun* 和韻, became extremely common, such a phenomenon does not exist in pre-Tang poetry as far as we know. Yu Xin's poem, which uses the same rhyme scheme and even identical rhyme words, is a rare prototype of such a practice.

His opening line reverberates with Xiao Gang's precisely: "Hazy and vague is Sunny Cloud Terrace" 曖曖陽雲臺→"Putting on the armor on Sunny Cloud Terrace" 被甲陽雲臺. The moisturizing cloud with erotic undertone is nevertheless transformed into the menacing "layered clouds, long unbroken" 重雲久未開, which reminds the reader of the "battle formation clouds" that "hang flat, not moving" in No. 17. There is no sunlight cracking open (*kai*) these clouds. The spring wind that comes (*lai* 來) as it will becomes the Qin army coming (*lai* 來) upon the Chu land; the Chu king himself is transformed from the dreamy monarch in "*Fu* on Gaotang" into the desperate army commander, Xiang Yu 項羽 (232-202 BCE), also known as the "Hegemon King of the Western Chu" ("Xi Chu bawang" 西楚霸王), surrounded and overwhelmed by enemy troops. The piping breeze is turned into "cranes' cries" (*heli* 鶴唳), a phrase that in the source text appears along with the sound of wind (*fengsheng* 風聲) as what strikes terror into the hearts of the fleeing soldiers.

Xiao Gang's third couplet, depicting lowered curtains and opened doors, are transformed into a violent scene of fierce battle in Yu Xin's third couplet: the city of Jiangling, in the heartland of Chu, tries in vain to close its gates against its powerful foe. The lover's entry, eagerly anticipated by the fair lady, mutates into that of a terrifying army. Finally, the rumbling sound of the prince's carriage finds its corresponding image as the ill-fated prince's carriage with the broken axle: the amorous prince's much awaited arrival is turned into the elders' lament, "Our prince will not come back."

Only when we keep the thunderous sound of the prince's carriage in mind do we understand Yu Xin's third couplet on the fierce battle, where his most

---

69   This is indicated by a preface in *Wen xuan* (Shanghai: Shanghai guji chubanshe, 1994),
      16.712.

significant transformation of Xiao Gang's poem is accomplished. A passage from the late Eastern Han warlord Yuan Shao's 袁紹 (154-202) biography in Fan Ye's 范曄 (398-445) *Hou Han shu* 後漢書, from which Yu Xin also quotes in "Yonghuai" No. 12, describes just such a battle:

紹為高櫓, 起土山, 射營中, [營中] 皆蒙楯而行, 操乃發石車擊紹樓, 皆破, 軍中呼曰霹靂車.[70]

Yuan Shao constructed high towers and made a dirt hill, from the top of which his men shot arrows into [Cao Cao's] camp. The soldiers in Cao's camp all covered themselves with shields. Cao then used catapult wagons to strike Shao's towers with rocks, and the towers all collapsed. The troops called those wagons "Thunderclap Wagons".

We can hear exactly how these verbal echoes reverberate in Yu Xin's poem: the imagery of rumbling thunder and the prince's carriage in Xiao Gang's poem, besides inspiring the "broken axle" couplet, evokes the "thunderclap wagon" and the bitter fight with hurled beams and raised shields. The willow tree, verdant and supple in the Liang princes' poems, metamorphoses into dead, and deathly, wood—timbers used for destruction and shields made of poplar, with *yang* echoing *yangliu*—and is ultimately reduced to ashes. In early medieval writings, the phrase "flying ashes" (*feihui* 飛灰) is primarily used to refer to the placing of reed ashes in tuning pipes to detect seasonal change, believed to be indicated by the ashes stirring and flying out from various tubes respectively corresponding to the various seasons. As such, the "flying ashes" in Yu Xin's poem is subversive of the "piping breeze" in Xiao Yi and the "spring wind" in Xiao Gang.

Yu Xin has written an "accompanying poem," albeit belated; the classical Chinese literary term for such a composition is *zhui he* 追和. By doing so, he reproduces the social occasion of the courtly group composition, as if he were still writing to princely command, even if he was an exile in the north and the prince in question had been long dead. He executed the courtier's craft with perfection, obeying the subtlest tone set by Xiao Gang in his last couplet: that is, by evoking Xiao Yi with an allusion to a Western Han prince, he seems to indicate that Xiao Yi was no more than a Liang prince, a pretender to the

---

70   *Hou Han shu*, 74.2400; also in the earlier *Sanguo zhi* 三國志 (Beijing: Zhonghua shuju, 1959), 6.199.

throne.[71] The allusion to the Western Han prince's broken axle hardly befits the dignity of imperial demise, which in medieval writings is regularly referred to as "Yellow Emperor's ascension at Cauldron Lake," "Shun's departure to Cangwu," and the like.

Everything is done just right, and yet everything is wrong. All the more glaringly wrong because Yu Xin is observing all the unspoken rules of writing an accompanying poem at imperial command. At the basic level, he responds to Xiao Gang's poem just as Xiao Gang responds to Xiao Yi's poem, echoing yet modifying the original text. However, unlike Xiao Gang's harmonious duet with Xiao Yi, Yu Xin's variation does violence to the content of the original poem and deliberately violates the decorum of courtly composition, embodying the brutality depicted in the poem. The effect of shock and disruption is precisely one of the ways in which Yu Xin manages to write intense traumatic experience in the stylized form of aulic poetry.

Conclusion

Yu Xin's "Yonghuai" No. 4, one couplet of which is quoted earlier in this chapter, is remarkable for its audacious breach of contemporary poetics and its aggressive demonstration of autobiographical contingency:

楚材稱晉用	Chu timbers fit Jin's purpose;[72]
秦臣即趙冠	The ministers of Qin don the Zhao king's hats.[73]
離宮延子產	To a detached palace Zichan was invited;[74]

---

71 Yu Xin's negative attitude toward Xiao Yi can be clearly seen in his poetic exposition, "The Lament for the South," in which he passes harsh judgment on Xiao Yi for refusing to save the capital from ruin and killing his brothers and nephews.

72 *Zuo zhuan*, Xiang 26, 37.635: "Although the materials were produced in Chu, Jin enjoyed the actual use of them'" 雖楚有材, 晉實用之. See *Jizhu*, 231. In this story, the "Chu material used by Jin" refers to Wu Ju 伍舉, a Chu native who fled from political trouble in Chu and was about to serve Jin, but longed to go home (and eventually did).

73 *Hou Han shu*, "Treatises" (*zhi*), 30.3668: "When Qin destroyed Zhao [in 222 BCE], they took the Zhao king's hats and bestowed them on favored ministers." See *Jizhu*, 231.

74 Zichan, the worthy minister of Zheng, was sent on a diplomatic mission to Jin, where he was put up in cramped guesthouse and not received in a timely manner by the Jin ruler. Zichan tore down the walls of the guesthouse to make room for his carriage and horses. When criticized by a Jin minister, he gave an eloquent speech on the inappropriate behavior of the Jin ruler; subsequently he was given respectful treatment becoming his dignity (*Zuo zhuan*, Xiang 31, 40.686-687). See *Jizhu*, 231. Hightower claims: "In none of this is the

羈旅接陳完	Chen Wan was received in exile.[75]
寓衛非所寓	Lodging in Wei—not a place for lodging;[76]
安齊獨未安	Settling in Qi—but not quite settled.[77]
雪泣悲去魯	Wiping away tears, one lamented departure from Lu;[78]
悽然憶相韓	Sorrowful, one remembered being a minister of Han.[79]
唯彼窮途慟	Only those weeping at the end of the road
知余行路難	Understand the hardship of this path I travel.[80]

term 'detached hall' 離宮 used, so it is not clear whether the allusion is to a reference to the initial shabby treatment or the lodgings provided subsequently" (18). However, Zichan said in his speech to the Jin minister: "Now the palace of Tongti extends many miles, and yet the feudal lords are put up in slaves' quarters." Du Yu 杜預 (222-285) comments on this remark: "The palace of Tongti was the Jin ruler's 'detached palace'" 銅鞮晉離宮. *Zuo zhuan*, 40.687. Thus it would seem that this line speaks of the favorable treatment that Yu Xin had received in the north.

75   *Zuo zhuan*, Zhuang 22, 9.162-163: "Chen Wan" refers to Wan, a noble lord of Chen, who sought refuge in Qi after a coup at Chen court. When he was offered a post of minister, he turned it down, saying, "I am a subject in exile....I would not presume to occupy a high position where I would be quickly slandered by my colleagues" 羈旅之臣…… 敢辱高位, 以速官謗. See *Jizhu*, 231.

76   According to the preface to the *Shijing* poem "Shiwei" 式微 (Mao #36), the Marquis of Li, after being driven out from his native land by the barbarian Di, lodged in Wei; he was well treated and felt at home there, and his ministers tried to persuade him to go home with the poem. See *Jizhu*, 250.

77   *Zuo zhuan*, Xi 23, 15.251: Duke Wen of Jin had wandered in exile for many years before returning to Jin and becoming its ruler. When he was in Qi, he was treated so well that he "settled" there happily (*anzhi* 安之). See *Jizhu*, 250.

78   Ni Fan cites *Mencius* that Confucius was reluctant and slow to depart upon leaving Lu, his native land. See *Jizhu*, 231. This allusion is used in Yang Xiong's 揚雄 (53 BCE-18 CE) "Fan Li sao" 反離騷 (*Han shu* 漢書 [Beijing: Zhonghua shuju, 1962], 87.3521), and Pan Yue's "*Fu on the Western Journey*" ("Xizheng fu" 西征賦) (*Wen xuan*, 10.442). However, in none of the earlier citations of the incident is Confucius said to have shed tears, only sighing and lingering. "Wiping away tears" (*xueqi* 雪泣) is usually associated with the general Wu Qi's 吳起 (440-381 BCE) departure from the state of Wei. When his attendant asked him why he wept, Wu Qi replied that he wept because he foresaw Wei's loss of land to Qin. Lü Buwei 呂不韋, *Lüshi chunqiu* 呂氏春秋 (Shanghai: Xuelin chubanshe, 1984), 20.1414. See *Jizhu*, 231. One may note that an explicit reference to Wu Qi is to appear in the next "Yonghuai" poem.

79   *Shiji*, 55.2033: Zhang Liang's 張良 (d. 186 BCE) grandfather and father had served as ministers to five generations of Han ruler. After Han fell to Qin, Zhang Liang was bent on revenge and sought someone to assassinate the First Emperor of Qin). See *Jizhu*, 231. One should note that Zhang Liang also appears in Yu Xin's "Yonghuai" No. 13.

80   *Jin shu*, 49.1361: Ruan Ji often went out in his carriage and randomly drove about, and would burst into tears when he came to the end of the road. See *Jizhu*, 232. "The Hardship

Think of the "Little Prefaces" in the Mao commentary on the *Shi jing*: a typical preface gives a terse statement about the general context and import of the poem, such as "a gentleman of the state of x laments the corruption of the times." There is no name attached, and we do not know anything about the said gentleman or his individual situation. Think of Tao Yuanming, the canonical poet best known for his autobiographical mode of poetic writing: all we need to know about his life in order to appreciate his poetry is that he resigned from office to become a recluse; in any case a typical Tao Yuanming poem itself provides all the information necessary for understanding the poem, and this is also the case with Xie Lingyun, the other major early medieval poet. Generally speaking, early medieval literature does not call for any strenuous attempt on the reader's part to know the details of a writer's life story in order to achieve a basic understanding of the content of a text, at least not at a literal level. This is, however, not true in Yu Xin's case: we could not even comprehend this poem's surface meaning if we did not already know who Yu Xin was and what he had gone through. The poem would have seemed to present a jumble of historical figures, whose connection with one another is tenuous at best and nonexistent at worst. This is *not* what a normal poem was supposed to look like in early medieval times.

Nor does this poem easily fit in with the contemporary poetic ideal. Beginning in the 480s, poets embraced a lucid, graceful style embodied by the poetry of Shen Yue, Xie Tiao, and He Xun, marking a drastic turn from the earlier "high court style" established by Yan Yanzhi 顏延之 (384-456) and Xie Lingyun. In Shen Yue's words, poetry should manifest "three kinds of easiness" (*san yi* 三易): "easy to understand the allusions; easy to know the meaning of words; and easy to read out aloud and recite" 易見事, 易識字, 易讀誦.[81] The use of allusions must not hinder a reader's understanding of a poem. The poetry critic Zhong Rong 鍾嶸 (ca. 468-518) goes even further in opposing the use of allusions at all in the writing of poetry.[82] Another distinguished writer, Xiao Zixian 蕭子顯 (489-537), speaks disapprovingly of the densely allusive style:

---

of Travel" ("Xinglu nan" 行路難) was an "old tune" refined and popularized by Yuan Song 袁崧 (aka Yuan Shansong 袁山松, d. 401). *Jin shu*, 83.2169.

81   Yan Zhitui 顏之推, *Yanshi jiaxun* 顏氏家訓 (Shanghai: Shanghai guji chubanshe, 1980), 253.

82   "As for singing of feelings and nature, why should the use of allusions be prized at all" 至於吟詠情性, 亦何貴於用事? Zhong Rong, *Shi pin jizhu* 詩品集注 (Shanghai: Shanghai guji chubanshe, 1994), 173.

次則緝事比類, 非對不發, 博物可嘉, 職成拘制。或全借古語, 用申今情,
崎嶇牽引, 直為偶說, 唯覩事例, 頓失清采。

Next we see a style that assembles allusions and brings together things of
the same category for comparison. The author does not write anything
without pairing up references. Although his broad knowledge is admirable, it eventually becomes a limitation. Sometimes one borrows the
words of the ancients in their entirety to express the feelings of a modern
person, which is like drawing a cart over a rugged road or a puppet talking. All that the reader sees are allusions and references, whereas the
lucid stylishness is altogether lost.[83]

"Yonghuai" No. 4 is a blatant violation of the prohibition against wanton use of
allusions, but Yu Xin's idiosyncrasy does not stop there. He employs a particular kind of allusion: rather than references to a phrase in an earlier text or to a
fictional figure such as those appearing in the parables of *Zhuangzi*, these are
mostly allusions to historical figures in early historiography. It must be noted
that referring to historical personages in a series of parallels is common in
early medieval poetry (or *fu*), but such references usually occur as only a small
part of a text, never taking up almost the entire poem; moreover, the personages alluded to in the other poems usually have an easily identifiable common
quality or identity (for example, noble-minded recluses refusing to serve in
government), which is clearly spelled out by the poet. It is uncommon to narrate one's own life story by enumerating historical persons whose identities
and characteristics are as diverse and incompatible as Wu Ju, Zichan, Chen
Wan, the Marquis of Li, Duke Wen of Jin, Confucius, and Zhang Liang, not to
mention the Zhao king (either King Wuling of Zhao, famous for his adoption of
Tartar-style jacket and hat, or his son King Huiwen of Zhao). Each of these
historical figures possesses one point of similarity to Yu Xin's own life, but none
provides the perfect parallel, and Yu Xin has to move rapidly through a succession of many historical figures to give a complete portrayal of his experience. If
a measure of solace for one's suffering could be sought by looking to historical
precedents, then it seems that the poet fails to find solace because he fails to
find any precedent for what he has gone through.

   This lack of perfect historical precedent can be said both for Yu Xin's experience and for the poetic conventions he worked with. Unlike the gradual unrav-
eling of the Han empire or even the collapse of the Western Jin due to civil
wars and then under the northern non-Han people's invasion, the fall of the

83   *Nan Qi shu* 南齊書 (Beijing: Zhonghua shuju, 1972), 52.908.

Liang was sudden, unexpected, and all the more traumatic for that reason. The Southern Dynasties aulic poetic tradition in which Yu Xin was most at home, beginning as it did with representing kingship and empire, offered no resources or technologies for Yu Xin to write about the failure of kingship and the fall of empire. And if he looked beyond that tradition, all he saw were poems so general and so unconcerned with historical particulars that they would have been of little use to him. The poet was confronted with the most difficult poetic topic he was ever assigned, and he grappled with it in a linguistic medium he found inadequate to the task at hand. He had to invent a new language in order to make sense of the senseless events happening to his state and to his own life.

"Yonghuai" No. 4 is both about the impossibility of articulating this traumatic experience and, with its deliberate awkwardness and thickness, embodies the very attempt the poet makes at articulation. The "ruggedness" (*qiqu* 崎嶇) of the poetic expression, being densely allusive and breaching the courtly decorum, becomes a perfect figure of the ruggedness of the symbolic road he travels on. Its last couplet directly addresses the problem of understanding: for Yu Xin, he was self-consciously writing a poetry of trauma and pain that he himself did not expect to be fully understood and appreciated by all readers.

Bibliography

Caruth, Catherine. *Unclaimed Experience: Trauma, Narrative, and History*. Baltimore: John Hopkins University Press, 1996.

Elias, Norbert. *The Court Society*. Translated by Edmund Jephcott. New York: Pantheon Books, 1983.

Graham Jr., William T. and James R. Hightower. "Yü Hsin's 'Songs of Sorrow.'" *Harvard Journal of Asiatic Studies* 43.1 (June 1983): 5-55.

Guo Maoqian 郭茂倩, comp. *Yuefu shiji* 樂府詩集. Beijing: Zhonghua shuju, 1979.

Han shu 漢書. Compiled by Ban Gu 班固. Beijing: Zhonghua shuju, 1962.

Hou Han shu 後漢書. Compiled by Fan Ye 范曄. Beijing: Zhonghua shuju, 1965.

Jin shu 晉書. Compiled by Fang Xuanling 房玄齡 et al. Beijing: Zhonghua shuju, 1974.

Li, Daoyuan 酈道元. *Shuijing zhu jiaoshi* 水經注校釋. Annotated by Chen Qiaoyi 陳橋驛. Hangzhou: Hangzhou daxue chubanshe, 1999.

Lu Qinli 逯欽立, comp. *Xian Qin Han Wei Jin nanbeichao shi* 先秦漢魏晉南北朝詩. Beijing: Zhonghua shuju, 1995.

Lü Buwei 呂不韋. *Lüshi chunqiu jiaoshi* 呂氏春秋校釋. Annotated by Chen Qiyou 陳奇猷. Shanghai: Xuelin chubanshe, 1984.

Mather, Richard B. *The Age of Eternal Brilliance: Three Lyric Poets of the Yung-ming Era (483-493)*. 2 vols. Leiden: Brill, 2003.

Nan Qi shu 南齊書. Compiled by Xiao Zixian 蕭子顯. Beijing: Zhonghua shuju, 1972.

Nan shi 南史. Compiled by Li Yanshou 李延壽. Beijing: Zhonghua shuju, 1975.

Sanguo zhi 三國志. Compiled by Chen Shou 陳壽. Beijing: Zhonghua shuju, 1959.

Shi ji 史記. Compiled by Sima Qian 司馬遷. Beijing: Zhonghua shuju, 1959.

Taiping yulan 太平御覽. Compiled by Li Fang 李昉 et al. Taipei: Shangwu yinshuguan, 1975 reprint.

Tian, Xiaofei. *Beacon Fire and Shooting Star: The Literary Culture of the Liang (502-557)*. Cambridge, MA: Harvard Asia Center, 2007.

Tian, Xiaofei. "Representing Kingship and Imagining Empire in Southern Dynasties Court Poetry." *T'oung Pao* 102-1-3 (2016): 1-56.

Xiao Tong 蕭統, comp. *Wen xuan* 文選. Shanghai: Shanghai guji chubanshe, 1994.

Xie Tiao 謝朓, Yu Xin 庾信 et al. *Xie Tiao, Yu Xin ji qita shiren shiwen xuanping* 謝朓庾信及其他詩人詩文選評, edited and annotated by Yang Ming 楊明 and Yang Tao 楊焘. Shanghai: Shanghai guji, 2002.

Xie Tiao 謝朓 and Yu Xin 庾信. *Xie Tiao Yu Xin shixuan* 謝朓庾信詩選. Edited and annotated by Du Xiaoqin 杜曉勤. Beijing: Zhonghua shuju, 2006.

Yan Kejun 嚴可均, comp. *Quan shanggu sandai Qin Han sanguo liuchao wen* 全上古三代秦漢三國六朝文. Beijing: Zhonghua shuju, 1987.

Yan Zhitui 顏之推. *Yanshi jiaxun jijie* 顏氏家訓集解. Annotated by Wang Liqi 王利器. Shanghai: Shanghai guji chubanshe, 1980.

Yiwen leiju 藝文類聚. Compiled by Ouyang Xun 歐陽詢 et al. Taipei: Wenguang chubanshe, 1974.

Yu Xin 庾信. *Yu Xin xuanji* 庾信選集. Edited and annotated by Shu Baozhang 舒寶章. He'nan: Zhongzhou shuhuashe, 1983.

Yu Xin 庾信. *Yu Zishan jizhu* 庾子山集注. Annotated by Ni Fan 倪璠. Beijing: Zhonghua shuju, 1980.

Zhang Daye 張大野. *The World of a Tiny Insect: A Memoir of the Taiping Rebellion and Its Aftermath*. Translated with a critical introduction by Xiaofei Tian. Seattle: University of Washington Press, 2013.

Zhong Rong 鍾嶸. *Shi pin jizhu* 詩品集注. Annotated by Cao Xu 曹旭. Shanghai: Shanghai guji chubanshe, 1994.

Zhou shu 周書. Compiled by Linghu Defen 令狐德棻 et al. Beijing: Zhonghua shuju, 1971.

Zizhi tongjian 資治通鑑. Compiled by Sima Guang 司馬光. Beijing: Guji chubanshe, 1956.

Zuo zhuan zhushu 左傳注疏. In Ruan Yuan 阮元, comp. *Shisanjing zhushu* 十三經注疏. Taipei: Yiwen yinshuguan, 1955.

CHAPTER 6

Structured Gaps: The *Qianzi wen* and Its Paratexts as Mnemotechnics

Christopher M.B. Nugent

Jan Assmann describes cultural memory as "that body of reusable texts, images, and rituals specific to each society in each epoch, whose 'cultivation' serves to stabilize and convey that society's self-image. Upon such collective knowledge... each group bases its awareness of unity and particularity."[1] Any "collective knowledge" depends on individuals' memories. It is not enough for what Herbert Grabes calls "valuable items from the past"[2] to be stored in written form; they must be present in the minds of writers, singers, and story tellers as sources of inspiration, allusion, and even objects of rejection, to maintain the kind of continuity Assmann's notion of cultural memory requires. For most of human history, individuals' memories have been the primary technology through which we have organized, preserved, and transmitted cultural knowledge. Even well into the age of print in both China and Europe, the ability to store a substantial volume of text in one's head was the mark of an educated person. Texts and memory have, as long as there have been texts, shared a complex relationship in which each has influenced the other's structures and content. While there is no indication that writers and scholars in medieval China developed the equivalent of medieval European *memoria*, defined by Mary Carruthers as "trained memory, educated and disciplined according to a well-developed pedagogy,"[3] works from the period demonstrate that their authors had a keen understanding of how to structure and use texts for mnemonic purposes as part of the process of literary training.

This essay examines textual evidence for some of the ways teachers and students used a popular "primer" from medieval China, the *Thousand Character Text* (*Qianzi wen* 千字文), as a mnemonic tool. Arguably one of the best-known works from medieval China, the *Qianzi wen* has seen its text reproduced

---

1   Jan Assmann, "Collective Memory and Cultural Identity," *New German Critique* 65 (1995): 132.

2   Herbert Grabes, "Cultural Memory and the Literary Canon," in *A Companion to Cultural Memory Studies*, ed. Astrid Erll and Ansgar Nünning (New York: Walter de Gruyter, 2010), 312.

3   Mary Carruthers, *The Book of Memory: A Study of Memory in Medieval Culture* (Cambridge, UK: Cambridge University Press, 1990), 7.

innumerable times by everyone from history's most famed calligraphers to contemporary school children begrudgingly copying out characters they will one day forget how to write (thanks to the ubiquity of digital devices that render such skills unnecessary). But the *Qianzi wen* is far more than a set of one thousand characters; it served important pedagogical functions in medieval China that have been obscured over the centuries. Finds in Dunhuang and Japan have recently provided new evidence of these functions and give intriguing indications of how teachers and learners actually used this work in the medieval period.

The text of the *Qianzi wen* itself, consisting of terse references to a much wider and deeper body of cultural knowledge, in some contexts functioned as a basic mnemonic structure in which a large volume of information is encoded into a small number of words. Users of the work in medieval China quickly realized this, creating a range of paratextual elements, including annotations and expansions of the original text, which took advantage of and augmented the utility of the original. In what follows I briefly describe the *Qianzi wen* itself and how it structures the information it presents. I then look in more detail at some of the paratexts that developed around it in the medieval period and which survive in manuscripts from the finds at Dunhuang. I argue that in terms of mnemonic structures and functions, we find here an unusual set of relationships: while the *Qianzi wen* text proper was clearly meant to be memorized, its true value was in serving as a series of mnemonic pegs on which to hang more important elements, namely the classical writings (ranging from poetry to historical anecdotes) and explanations found in the paratext (in the form of annotations). Additionally, new paratextual expansions were created that themselves aided in setting to memory not the text of the *Qianzi wen* itself, but the information to which its lines point and which is made explicit in the paratextual annotations. What these works show is an implicit but nonetheless sophisticated understanding of the workings of textual memory and the ways in which texts can be manipulated to increase their mnemonic utility.

The *Qianzi wen*

Scholars have long debated who composed the *Qianzi wen* and how they did so. Though definitive answers remain elusive, the general consensus is that at some point in the early sixth century, mostly likely between the years 507 and 510, Liang Emperor Wu (r. 502–549) gave one of his officials a set of one thousand characters collected from rubbings of the famous calligrapher Wang

Xizhi's 王羲之 (ca. 303–ca. 361) calligraphy.[4] The official, Zhou Xingsi 周興嗣 (d. 521), was tasked with composing a literary piece using these thousand characters, and only these thousand characters,[5] as described in an entry in the *Taiping Guangji* 太平廣記:

> [The emperor] ordered [his minister] Yin Tieshi to make rubbings of one thousand characters from the great Wang's writings without any repetitions. Each character was [put on] a slip of paper and they were all jumbled up without any specific order. Emperor Wu summoned Xingsi and said to him, "You have literary talent—set these to rhyme for me!" Xingsi compiled [the piece] over the course of a single evening and presented it. His hair had all turned white but he was richly rewarded.

> 令殷鐵石於大王書中。榻一千字不重者。每字片紙。雜碎無序。武帝召興嗣謂曰。卿有才思。為我韻之。興嗣一夕編綴進上。鬢髮皆白。而賞錫甚厚.[6]

---

4 No specific dates are given in earliest sources, but scholars generally agree that Zhou Xingsi likely composed the *Qianzi wen* between 507 and 521. Feng Chengjun 馮承鈞 argues for the more confined range of 507 to 510. See the discussion in Zhang Xinpeng 張新朋, *Dunhuang xieben* Kaimeng yaoxun *yanjiu* 敦煌寫本《開蒙要訓》研究 (Beijing: Zhongguo shehui kexue chubanshe, 2013), 125-26.

5 For Zhou Xingsi's biography see *Liang shu* 梁書, comp. Yao Cha 姚察 and Yao Silian 姚思廉 (Beijing: Zhonghua shuju, 1973), 49.697-98.

6 *Taiping guangji*, comp. Li Fang 李昉 et al. (Beijing: Zhonghua shuju, 1981), 207.1587. There are other accounts that attribute a work entitled *Qianzi wen* to Xiao Zifan 蕭子範, though without the connection to Emperor Wu (see, for example, *Nanshi* 南史, comp. Li Yanshou 李延壽, [Beijing: Zhonghua shuju, 1975], 42.1071). Zheng Qiao's 鄭樵 *Tongzhi* 通志 includes a *Qianzi wen* attributed to Xiao Ziyun 蕭子雲 and a "set to rhyme" version, *Ciyun Qianzi wen* 次韻千字文, attributed to Zhou Xingsi (see Zheng Qiao, *Tongzhi* [Taipei: Taiwan shangwu yinshuguan, 1987], 64.768a). Assuming the *Qianzi wen* attributed to Xiao Zifan is an entirely different work, it appears not to have survived. The first part of the Dunhuang manuscript Pelliot 2721 includes a work entitled "Miscellaneous excerpts: one scroll" 雜抄一卷. This consists of a long series of questions and answers about history, literature, culture (who were the five emperors, what is the third day of the third month, who compiled the *Wenxuan*, etc.). For the *Qianzi wen* it reads, "Composed by Zhong Yao, annotated by Li Xian, set to rhyme by Zhou Xingsi" 鐘繇撰李暹注周興嗣次韻 (with the first two attributions in smaller half-column characters and the attribution to Zhou in larger full-column ones). All Dunhuang copies of the *Qianzi wen* that included authorial information describe it as "set to rhyme" 次韻 by Zhou Xingsi. For a detailed discussion see Zhang Nali 張娜麗, "Dunhuang ben *Liuzi qianwen* chutan' xiyi—jian shu *Qianzi wen* zhuben wenti" 《敦煌本< 六字千文> 初探》析疑—— 兼述《千字文》注本問題, *Dunhuang yanjiu* 敦煌研究 69 (2001): 102-3. For our purposes in this discussion, the origin of the work is less important than the uses to which it would later be put.

The resulting work as it comes down to us today, both in received versions and in extant medieval manuscripts from Dunhuang, consists of one thousand non-repeating characters (though some versions repeat the character 潔) organized into rhyming couplets of four character lines.[7] Its effect on Zhou Xingsi's hair notwithstanding, the *Qianzi wen* is an impressive accomplishment of composition within a very strict set of limitations. Other early works that introduce basic vocabulary, such as the *Kaimeng yaoxun* 開蒙要訓 or the later *Baijia xing* 百家姓, include at least some repetition and consist primarily of lists of vocabulary. Zhou Xingsi arranged his assigned thousand characters not only into rhyming couplets, but also into phrases that are semantically meaningful and grammatically varied.

The *Qianzi wen* was immensely popular in its day and continued to be read and memorized in later periods as well. In his 746 presentation memorial for a Tang-period primer, the *Mengqiu* 蒙求, Li Liang 李良 gives a sense of the diffusion of the *Qianzi wen* in the centuries following its composition, writing, "In a recent era Zhou Xingsi composed the *Qianzi wen* and it has also spread through the realm" 近代周興嗣撰千字文。亦頒行天下.[8] We see concrete evidence of this spread in the manuscripts found at Dunhuang, which include over 140 separate documents that contain all or part of the *Qianzi wen* in some form (a number of which we will examine in detail below). As Li Pengfei notes, lines from the *Qianzi wen* were sufficiently well known in the Tang to be used as the basis of jokes and games in various anecdotes.[9] Indeed the work remained so popular in later periods that the characters in its text (in the *Qianzi wen* order) were used to classify and number documents, book collections, examination stalls, and even scrolls of the Buddhist Tripitaka.[10] For some fifteen hundred years, readers have found the work to have value and have continued to read, memorize, and reproduce it in a wide range of contexts down to the present day.

The earliest extant accounts give no explicit indication that either Emperor Wu or Zhou Xingsi originally intended the *Qianzi wen* to serve an educational purpose beyond preserving Wang Xizhi's model calligraphy. The content, however, implies that Zhou Xingsi was aiming to produce a pedagogically useful

---

7   The only exception to this pattern is the final couplet whose last five characters are all grammatical particles.

8   *Quan Tangwen* 全唐文 (Beijing: Zhonghua shuju, 1984), 19.10574.

9   See, for example, "Qianzi wen yu qi she" 千字文語乞社, *Taiping guangji*, 252.1957, and "Huan mu bi ren" 患目鼻人, *Taiping guangji*, 257.2007; and the discussion in Li Pengfei 李鵬飛, *Tangdai feixieshi xiaoshuo zhi leixing yanjiu* 唐代非寫實小說之類型研究 (Beijing: Beijing daxue chubanshe, 2004), 45.

10 Endymion Wilkinson, *Chinese History, A New Manual, 4th edition* (Cambridge, MA: Harvard University Asia Center, 2015), 601.

work, and the *Qianzi wen* has indeed long been categorized as a "primer" (*mengshu* 蒙書) or "children's book" (*ertong shu* 兒童書). Conveying a wide range of basic information about the human and natural world, it begins with the vastness of the universe ("Heaven and earth, dark and yellow; the universe, vast and desolate" 天地玄黃，宇宙洪荒) and moves next to smaller-scale meteorological patterns ("Clouds ascend and bring rain; dew congeals, becoming frost" 雲騰致雨，露結為霜). It gives moral guidance ("Women admire the chaste and pure; men emulate the talented and good" 女慕貞絜，男效才良) and articulates fundamental ideas of governance ("Good governance is rooted in agriculture" 治本於農) and law ("Execute and behead bandits and thieves; seize and capture rebels and deserters" 誅斬賊盜，捕獲叛亡). Early cultural heroes and their accomplishments are given their due ("First they made written characters; then they wore clothes. Giving up the throne and yielding the kingdom, [there were] the Holder of Yu [and he of] Tao and Tang" 始制文字，乃服衣裳。推位讓國。有虞陶唐). There are occasional close paraphrases of well-known sayings ("A foot of jade is not a treasure; an inch of shadow, this is contended for" 尺璧非寶，寸陰是競), but few if any exact quotes from classical texts, no doubt in part due to the limitations of vocabulary and rhyme.[11] Perhaps because of these limitations, the work does not have strictly maintained topical divisions by subject. Though there are frequently clusters of couplets on similar topics (and each couplet is thematically coherent internally), the organization appears more random than what one finds in the *Kaimeng yaoxun*, for example.

Within the larger category of primers, modern scholars have often described the *Qianzi wen* as a "character book" (*zishu* 字書) to be used to teach and learn how to read and write a basic set of characters. This description is fitting on a number of levels. Many of the Dunhuang documents containing parts of the work are clearly examples of writing practice. Both P. 3114 and S. 5657 have columns in which each character of the work is written again and again—a practice that will be familiar even to contemporary learners of the Chinese script.[12] As we can see in the account of the work's original compilation, the

---

11   The saying is first seen in the *Huainanzi* 淮南子 and reads: "The sagely person does not value a foot of jade, but considers important an inch of shadow" 聖人不貴尺之璧而重寸之陰. An "inch of shadow" refers to the movement of a sundial, with the saying thus indicating that the sagely value time more than they do jade. See Zhang Shuangdi 張雙棣, *Huainanzi jiaoshi* 淮南子校釋 (Beijing: Beijing daxue chubanshe, 2013), 1.13.

12   Manuscripts numbered with "P" were accessed electronically "gallica.bnf.fr" and those numbered with "S" manuscripts through "idp.bl.uk". P. 3114, like most copies of the *Qianzi wen* found at Dunhuang with the opening intact, begins with the title and a line crediting the work to Zhou Xingsi: "The Thousand Character Text, set to rhyme by Supernumerary

Qianzi wen has always had a close connection to calligraphic practice. The Dunhuang documents show this aspect as well: there are two fragmentary examples of the work with "seal script" (*zhuanshu* 篆書) characters written next to the regular *kaishu* 楷書 versions and four similar examples with "grass script" (*caoshu* 草書) including one, P. 3561, that can be dated to the mid-seventh century.[13] At the same time there is no reason to believe that Zhou Xingsi's intent was produce a work that would teach how to write characters in any kind of systematic fashion: there is no organization on the character level. That is, the work does not follow any kind of orthographically based progression, such as moving from simple characters to more complex ones. Indeed, it does not even include the characters for the numbers one, three, six, seven, and ten, or many other very simple characters. In spite of this lack of a systematic pedagogical structure, clearly learners did use the *Qianzi wen* as a convenient way to practice a set of characters that could function as the partial foundation of literate vocabulary.

The contrasts between the *Qianzi wen* and such vocabulary-based primers as the *Kaimeng yaoxun* are telling and it is thus worth giving a brief description of this latter work for comparative purposes. The *Kaimeng yaoxun* has been virtually unknown for a thousand years until it was re-discovered among the manuscripts from Dunhuang. The work does not show up in any official or unofficial bibliographies but appears, however, to have been very popular in its time, having circulated as far as Japan by the end of the Tang period. There are seventy-nine manuscripts from Dunhuang that contain part or all of the work, ranging from five full copies to twelve manuscripts that have various portions of it copied repeatedly for practice. The fullest version of the work that we have is 1400 characters long, divided up into 350 four-character lines grouped in couplets with the rhyme falling on every eighth character. Though some scholars previously believed it to be a poor knock-off of the *Qianzi wen*, Luo Changpei argues that, based on the rhymes used, the *Kaimeng yaoxun* was likely composed sometime between the Eastern Jin and the Qi-Liang periods.[14] Zhang Xinpeng claims that it was, in fact, probably composed prior to the composi-

---

Senior Recorder of Encyclicals Zhou Xingsi" 千字文勑員外散騎侍郎周興嗣次韻. In this case the scribe has copied those characters repeatedly as practice, in addition to those in the text proper.

13   The seal script examples are found in P. 4702 and P. 3658. The grass script examples are Дх. 8783, Дх. 8903, Дх. 5847, and P. 3561 (see IDP for links to some of the Russian-held manuscripts).

14   Luo Changpei 羅常培, *Tang Wudai xibei fangyin* 唐五代西北方音 (Beijing: Kexue chubanshe, 1961), 132.

tion of the *Qianzi wen*.[15] A few of the manuscripts we have from Dunhuang give the author as one Ma Renshou 馬仁壽, about whom nothing else is known.

The similarities between the *Qianzi wen* and the *Kaimeng yaoxun* are many. They appear to have been composed in the same historical period and share an almost identical surface structure (i.e. four-character lines organized into rhyming couplets). Both are meant to include a large set of vocabulary items: though the *Kaimeng yaoxun* does not avoid repetition to the extent that the *Qianzi wen* does, there are still very few repeats among its 1400 characters. Scholars have tended to categorize the *Kaimeng yaoxun* as a "popular" (*su* 俗) primer and the *Qianzi wen* as a work meant for higher social classes.[16] This assumption of very different audiences for the two works is, however, undermined by the evidence from Dunhuang. The manuscript copies of these works were produced in the same places by the same novice scribes and were probably used in similar ways.[17] Indeed there is at least one manuscript in which a copy of the *Qianzi wen* begins in the middle of a column directly following a partial manuscript copy of the *Kaimeng yaoxun*.[18] There is also significant overlap in content: 301 of the characters in the *Qianzi wen* appear in the *Kaimeng yaoxun* as well. It is most likely that both of these works had important roles to play in the educational process of the literary elite in the Dunhuang region (and elsewhere). They taught different types of knowledge, but both sets were important to anyone who was engaged with the full textual environment of the time. Reading and writing took place in a range of contexts, some of which would have required knowledge of figures in the historical past, such as that provided by the *Qianzi wen*, others of which required knowing how to write the characters for the names of everything from different fruits and vegetables to different medical conditions, as conveyed by the *Kaimeng yaoxun*.

There are important differences between these two works as well, some of which may explain why the *Qianzi wen* has enjoyed more long-term popularity and why it has made an appealing vehicle for paratextual additions. As noted above, the most obvious of these is that while the *Kaimeng yaoxun* arranges its

---

15   Zhang Xinpeng, *Dunhuang xieben* Kaimeng yaoxun *yanjiu*, 19.

16   Zhang Xinpeng (*Dunhuang xieben* Kaimeng yaoxun *yanjiu*, 162) goes as far as to suggest that the *Kaimeng yaoxun* is 40 percent longer than the *Qianzi wen* because the former is meant for farming families who would have had to cram their study into the brief months after the harvest but before the next planting, describing the work as focusing on the every-day vocabulary of lower class commoners (下層民眾日常生活用字為主).

17   For a related discussion see Imre Galambos, "Confucian education in a Buddhist environment: Medieval manuscripts and imprints of the *Mengqiu*," *Studies in Chinese Religions* 1 (2015): 269-88.

18   P. 4937.

content primarily in the form of lists, the *Qianzi wen* almost always does so in semantically meaningful phrases. We can see this on a basic level with such topics as agricultural products. The *Kaimeng yaoxun*'s extensive treatment of fruits and plants, for example, are organized into lists like the following: "Melon, peach, plum, crab-apple; jujube, apricot, pear, birchleaf pear. Scallion, garlic, chives, shallot; prickly-ash, fagara, ginger" 瓜桃李柰，棗杏梨棠。葱蒜韭薤，茱萸椒薑. The *Qianzi wen* instead has "Of fruits, plums and crab-apples are prized; of greens, mustard and ginger are esteemed" 果珍李柰，菜重芥薑. There are a few lines from the *Kaimeng yaoxun* that more closely resemble the kinds of phrases in the *Qianzi wen*, but these distinctions by and large hold true. The *Qianzi wen* is thus far more than a lengthy vocabulary list and this fact surely explains much of its enduring appeal to both students and teachers. Zhou Xingsi arranged these thousand characters such that they convey information, knowledge of which was ultimately as important as being able to write and recognize the characters themselves for anyone who hoped to function as a member of literate society.

On a deeper level, a fundamental difference between the *Qianzi wen* and such contemporaneous vocabulary-based primers as the *Kaimeng yaoxun* is that much of the information the *Qianzi wen* serves to convey is outside of the text proper. A comparison between these two modes of conveying information is revealing. The *Kaimeng yaoxun* encodes its information on the surface linguistic level. Put another way, essentially every line of the *Kaimeng yaoxun* is fully comprehensible without recourse to the textual, historical, and cultural world outside of the text of the *Kaimeng yaoxun* itself. Even sections that deal with more abstract ideas, such as notions of moral government, state basic truisms rather than alluding to specific figures and events in the historical past. A couplet like "Rulers and kings have the Way; their grace and favor is broad and extensive" 君王有道，恩惠弘廓 carries its information in the "dictionary" definition of the characters. If one learns the meanings of these characters, one has acquired the information the *Kaimeng yaoxun* seeks to convey through them. A similar couplet from the *Qianzi wen*, such as "Giving up the throne and yielding the kingdom, [there were] the Holder of Yu [and he of] Tao and Tang" 推位讓國，有虞陶唐, on the other hand, is not fully comprehensible through the basic meaning of these words alone. The notion of yielding the throne to a worthy successor indeed became a generalized moral-political ideal, but it was always tied to specific historical examples, knowledge of which would be necessary for this line to make sense. Other examples from the *Qianzi wen* are even less understandable without additional explanation. The couplet with lines 145 and 146—"Falsely, the road to destroy Guo; at Jiantu they met to forge a covenant" 假塗滅虢，踐土會盟—makes little sense without a fuller historical context explaining how a Duke of Jin 晉 obtained passage through the state of Yu 虞 under false pretenses to attack Guo and that there was a great meeting of the feudal lords at Jintu.

Not every line in the *Qianzi wen* is of the sort. Basic statements about the natural world, such as "The cold arrives and the heat departs; harvest in autumn and store in winter" 寒來暑往，秋收冬藏, do not differ meaningfully in either structure or content from similar lines in the *Kaimeng yaoxun*. Yet even many *Qianzi wen* lines that are understandable based on the meaning of the characters clearly point to another level of meaning involving historical accounts and figures. For example, "First they made written characters, and then they wore clothes" is not difficult to understand as a meaningful statement based simply on the words themselves. The particular process of cultural evolution indicated by these lines, however, requires more explanation for its full meaning to be realized. The *Kaimeng yaoxun*, on the other hand, includes writing only as part of a list of implements and forms "brush, inkstone, paper, ink; record, literary composition" 筆硯紙墨，記錄文章. There is no implied connection to a larger set of cultural issues and historical figures. The *Qianzi wen* does teach useful vocabulary, but it is almost always structured such that the lines and couplets function primary not simply as vocabulary items per se but as cues to call up additional information, be it literary or historical. As so many of its lines point to deeper layers of knowledge, it is much more information-dense (and efficient) than is the *Kaimeng yaoxun*: it encodes more information with less text.

This type of encoding is an important feature of many medieval European mnemonic techniques as well, and it is clear that Zhou Xingsi structured the *Qianzi wen* so that it would be easy to set to memory. Contemporary research on human memory has consistently held that that "working memory" is typically limited to a small number of units, "the magic number seven, plus or minus two" as George Miller wrote in his the seminal study on the topic.[19] At eight characters, each couplet of the *Qianzi wen* is a perfect fit. These couplets as individual units are, in the majority of cases, tied together with parallelism as well, as in the couplets on weather, fruit, seasons, and many others. Finally, couplets are joined with one another through the rhyme falling on the last character in each full couplet.[20] The key is to use these short chains of linguistic units to store larger amounts of information. Carruthers writes that "one of

---

19   George A. Miller, "The Magic Number Seven, Plus or Minus Two: Some Limits on Our Capacity for Processing Information," *Psychology Review* 63 (1956): 81-97

20   Similar structural features are at work in the most popular genres of medieval Chinese poetry as well. See Christopher M.B. Nugent, *Manifest in Words, Written on Paper:*

the fundamental principles for increasing mnemonic (recollective) efficiency is to organize single bits of information into informationally richer units by a process of substitution that compresses large amounts of material into single markers. In this way, while one is still limited by one's capacity to focus on no more than 8-9 units at a time, each unit can be made much richer."[21] The *Qianzi wen* is not a mnemonic technique per se: there is no indication that it was intended by Zhou Xingsi to serve as a multi-purpose mnemonic structure to which *any* content could be added in the manner of the European *loci* method (the best-known version of which is the "memory palace"). It is, however, structured in a similar way to efficiently encode a particular, but voluminous, array of knowledge: the aspects the literary and historical past deemed important by literate medieval Chinese society.

If much of the most important information "encoded" in the *Qianzi wen* is not actually contained in the text of that work itself, and students could hardly intuit it on their own simply by reading that text, then how did they learn it? The most obvious answer is that students would study the *Qianzi wen* with a teacher. It is easy to imagine how this process might work. A student would learn (i.e. memorize) the lines of the *Qianzi wen* and a teacher would explain them, giving the fuller literary and historical context to which the lines point. The *Qianzi wen* would, in this scenario, ultimately function as a memorized set of cues to call up the broader (and ultimately more important) knowledge conveyed by the teacher. Unfortunately, this speculation must remain as such: the historical sources provide no accounts of how the *Qianzi wen* was used in this sort of pedagogical context.

However, we do have documentary evidence that the particular manner in which the *Qianzi wen* conveys information made it an appealing base on which to add paratextual elements that served the same sort of functions that a teacher might; that is, providing the larger literary and historical context the *Qianzi wen* lines reference. It is to these annotations that we now turn.

Medieval Annotations to the *Qianzi wen*

It might seem surprising that a work categorized as a children's primer would be the subject of extensive annotations. Regardless of its popularity, the *Qianzi wen* is not a classic whose every line is deserving of careful commentary to

---

    Producing and Circulating Poetry in Tang Dynasty China (Cambridge, MA: Harvard University Asia Center, 2010), 117-25.

21   Carruthers, *The Book of Memory*, 84.

explain the full connotations of the wisdom it conveys. Yet bibliographic evidence indicates that people were writing and circulating annotations to the *Qianzi wen* very soon after its compilation. The *Nanshi* notes that the Record Keeper (*jishi* 記室) Cai Wei 蔡薳 was ordered to annotate the *Qianzi wen* attributed to Xiao Zifan.[22] Another passage in the *Nanshi* states that "At that time Liang Emperor Wu had the 'Thousand Word Poem' composed. [Shen] Zhong wrote annotations for it" 時梁武帝制千文詩，眾為之注解.[23] The *Suishu* attributes one set of annotations to the "Chancellor of the Directorate of Education Xiao Ziyun" 國子祭酒蕭子雲 and another to Hu Xiao 胡蕭.[24] Finally, a work simply entitled "Miscellaneous excerpts: one scroll" 雜抄一卷, found in Dunhuang manuscript P. 2721, describes the *Qianzi wen* as "Composed by Zhong Yao, annotated by Li Xian, set to rhyme by Zhou Xingsi" 鐘繇撰李暹注周興嗣次韻. Unfortunately, none of these sets of annotations are extant (with the possible exception of Li Xian's, as I will address below) and no other pre-Song commentaries have been known prior to the finds at Dunhuang.

These finds, however, include direct evidence for annotations of the *Qianzi wen* that are conclusively from medieval China, in the form of the two fragmentary manuscripts P. 3973 and S. 5471. The Pelliot manuscript is a large section of what was once a scroll. Measuring 27 cm in height and 52 cm in length, it contains *Qianzi wen* lines 23 (推位讓國) to 25 (弔民伐罪) and 43 (知過必改) to 59 (尺璧非寶). Lines 26 to 42 seem to be simply omitted, as there is no damage to the document where they would have appeared, though there is a full column left blank. The text of the *Qianzi wen* itself is written in larger characters with the annotations in double columns of smaller characters. The Stein manuscript is in booklet form with pages about 12 cm wide by 15 cm high. There are 34 full or partial page sides containing lines 14 (珠稱夜光) to line 50 (詩讚羔羊). The handwriting is messy and the formatting inconsistent. The *Qianzi wen* text proper is written in larger characters, but the annotations are sometimes in a single column and sometimes in double half-width columns.

Between these two manuscripts we thus have 45 lines of the *Qianzi wen* itself, of which 43 include annotations (with the annotations to the other two lines missing due to damage to the physical documents). In both texts the annotations follows each *Qianzi wen* line rather than after the couplet as a whole (with two exceptions). From what we can tell from the portions where there is overlap, the annotations in these two manuscripts are almost identical.

---

22   *Nanshi*, 42.1071. Though, as noted above, this is likely a different work from the *Qianzi wen* under discussion here.

23   *Nanshi*, 57.1414.

24   *Suishu* 隋書, comp. Wei Zheng 魏徵 et al. (Beijing: Zhonghua shuju, 1973), 32.942.

Variations primarily take the form of orthographic or phonetic differences, in-dicating that they likely share a similar origin. Because the documents are missing both the beginning and end of the *Qianzi wen* text, neither gives any indication of the author of the annotations.

There is another set of annotations that survived in Japan with a preface that attributes the annotations and the preface itself to the aforementioned Li Xian, who lived during the Eastern Wei 東魏 period (534–550).[25] Known as the Ueno manuscript 上野本, it is a handwritten copy found in 1972 in Japan with a date indicating that this particular manuscript was copied in 1278. Its head-ing includes the note that it has the "Li Xian annotations" 李暹注. This manu-script contains the full *Qianzi wen* text (all 250 lines) with annotations after every two-line couplet (rather than after every line, as in the Dunhuang ex-amples). The annotations are significantly shorter than those found in the Dunhuang manuscripts, though the two sets of annotations seem to be related: there is a fair amount of overlap both in content and in order of content. At the same time they are very different overall as if sharing a family relationship but one many generations removed. The Ueno annotations do give more of a sense of a single author and less of accretion over time, as we will see in a set of ex-amples below, and it is thus tempting to speculate that this makes it likely that the annotations in the Ueno manuscript are closer to the original Li Xian set. Any such claim must remain tentative.

The Ueno manuscript includes a preface attributed to Li Xian, in which he indicates he wrote the annotations at some point in the thirty-year period after 547 when he was unable to return to the capital Ye 鄴 and was stuck in the "Western Capital" (i.e. Chang'an 長安).[26] He portrays himself as someone who was not properly understood by his times—likening himself to Confucius, Qu Yuan, and others—and thus retired from the world of officialdom and wrote

25   The fullest study of the Ueno manuscript, including a full photo-reproduction and tran-scription, is found in Kuroda Akira 黒田彰, Gotō Akio 后藤昭雄, Tōno Haruyuki 東野之治, and Miki Masahiro 三木雅博, eds., *Ueno-bon Chū Senjimon chūkai* 上野本注千字文注解 (Ōsaka: Izumi Shoin, 1989). For further discussion of Li Xian, see 185-87. More recent studies include Tōno Haruyuki 東野之治, "Ri Sen no *Chū Senjimon ni tsuite*" 李暹の『注千字文』について, *Man'yōshū kenkyu* 万葉集研究, 13 (1985): 219-34; Wang Xiaoping 王曉平, "Shangye ben *Zhu qianziwen* yu Dunhuang ben *Zhu qianziwen*" 上野本《注千字文》與敦煌本《注千字文》, *Dunhuang Research* 敦煌研究, 103 (2007): 55-60; and Yang Haiwen 楊海文, "Riben cang Beichao Li Xian 'Zhu *Qianziwen* xu' liangzhong jiaod-ing" 日本藏北朝李暹" 注《千字文》序 " 兩種校訂, *Xixia yanjiu* 西夏研究 2 (2015): 28-32.

26   For a more detailed discussion of dating, see Yang Haiwen, "Riben cang Beichao Li Xian 'Zhu *Qianziwen* xu' liangzhong jiaoding," 29.

these annotations. The only indication he gives of his specific goals in annotat-
ing the *Qianzi wen* is that he "thought its literary patterning marvelous and was
resolved to transmit its lessons" 奇其文理志傳其訓.[27]

Though this preface to the purported Li Xian annotations tells us nothing
about his intentions in composing them, it is clear that the annotations in both
the Dunhuang texts and the Ueno manuscript perform a consistent set of functions: they explain the terms and historical figures in the *Qianzi wen* lines
themselves (when necessary) and provide additional information that most
often connects the lines to relevant passages from classical and other sources.
In terms of this latter function, in the 43 lines with at least partially intact annotations found in the Dunhuang documents, there are 44 quotations identified by the text itself, typically preceded by 云 or 曰. These quotations come
from 17 separate sources, ranging from such classics as the *Shi* 詩 to works no
longer extant, such as the "Rhapsody on the Heart" (*Xinfu* 心賦). The most frequently cited works are *Lunyu* 論語 (7), *Shi* (6), *Yi* 易 (5), *Shu* 書 (5), and *Liji* 禮
記 (4). We see both these functions of providing information and quotations at
work even in lines about such seemingly mundane topics as fruits and vegetables. *Qianzi wen* lines 15 and 16 and their annotations in S. 5471 and the Ueno
manuscript can serve to illustrate both the commonalities and the differences
among them:

15. Of fruits, plums and crab-apples are prized
菓珎李柰
An "Ode" says: "Among the hillocks grow the plum trees, there the men of
the Liu clan arise." The *Tales of the Age* says: "In High Road County in the
Kingdom of Yan, at Wang Feng's home there were fine plums as big as
geese. He was afraid that people would get hold of the pits so he bored
holes into their kernels and sold them damaged. Liangzhou produces
crab-apples. They are suitable for making preserves. Among fruits, the
fine ones are plums and crab-apples.
詩云。丘中有李。彼留子起。世說曰。燕國高道縣王豐家好李大如
鵝。恐人得種。鑽其核。破而賣之。涼州出柰。堪為脯。菓中美好者
李柰也.[28]

27   For transcription of the preface, see Kuroda, et al., *Ueno-bon Chū Senjimon chūkai*, 55.

28   For S. 5471 I have used the photographs of the manuscript included in Kuroda, et al., *Ueno-
bon Chū Senjimon chūkai*, 152-69. For P. 3973 I have used the images at "gallica.bfn.fr". For
both of these I have also benefited from the transcriptions by Zhang Nali, "Dunhuang ben
Zhu Qianzi wen zhujie" 敦煌本《注千字文》注解, *Dunhuang xue jikan* 敦煌學輯刊
(2002): 45-59, and Kuroda, et al., *Ueno-bon Chū Senjimon chūkai*, 172-80. For the Ueno

16. Of greens, mustard and ginger are esteemed
菜重芥薑

The Kingdom of Zhao produces mustard greens. They're fragrantly delicious and their seeds can be made into a sauce. The *Analects* says, "Minced
fish is the best thing with mustard sauce." It also says,[29] "He would not
clear away ginger when he ate, saying, 'These two things are both great.'"
趙國出芥。食之香美。子可為醬。論語曰。魚膾芥醬之屬。不云。不
徹薑食。曰此二物皆好也.

(Ueno)[30]

In High Road County in the Kingdom of Yan there are fine plums as big as
goose eggs. They ripen in the eighth month. At Wang Feng's home there
were fine plums. He was afraid that people would get hold of the pits so
he bored holes in their broken kernels and sold them. Liangzhou produces something called a "crab-apple." The whole realm knows their
name. They can be made into preserves. The "Rhapsody on the Shu
Capital" says, "White plums bear fruit in summer." The Kingdom of Zhao
produces great mustard greens. They're fragrantly delicious and you can
make a sauce out of their seeds. The *Analects* says, "Minced fish is the best
thing with mustard sauce." Shu produces fresh ginger. Linhai Commandery
produces dried ginger and galangal ginger. The *Analects* says, "He never
cleared away ginger when he ate."

燕國高道縣有好李。大如鵝卵。八月乃熟也。王豐家有好李。恐人得
種。鑽其破核而賣之也。梁州出曰椋。天下知名。可以為脯也。蜀都
賦曰。素李夏成矣。趙國出好芥菜。食之香吳（美）。其子可以為醬
焉。論語曰。魚膾芥醬之屬也。蜀地出生薑也。臨海郡出干薑高良薑
也。論語曰。不徹薑食.

Both the Dunhuang and Ueno annotations give basic information about the
subjects of the *Qianzi wen* lines. We learn where these fruits and vegetables
grow and different ways that they can be prepared and eaten. These entries
also give a good sense of the range of quoted sources, from classics such as the
Shi and *Lunyu* to the less canonical but popular and influential *Shishuo xinyu*

---

manuscript I have relied entirely on the photographs and transcriptions in Kuroda et al.,
Ueno-bon Chū Senjimon chūkai. The punctuation and translations are my own.

29   Reading 不 as 又, a consistent scribal error in this document.

30   As noted above, the Ueno manuscript has one set of annotations per couplet, rather than
following every line. This passage thus covers both 15 and 16.

世說新語 (referred to as 世說 "Tales of the Age" in the annotations). These are often quotations only in the broadest sense, and in most cases differ substantially from our received versions of these works. The quote from the *Shi* is from the last stanza of Mao #74: "Qiu zhong you ma" 丘中有麻 ("Among the Hillocks Grows the Hemp"). The received version reads, "Among the hillocks grow the plum trees, there are the men of the Liu clan" 丘中有李，彼留之子.[31] The received version of the quotation from *Shishuo xinyu* is much shorter, reading, "Wang Rong had fine plums which he sold. He was afraid that people would get hold of their pits and always bored holes in their kernels" 王戎有好李，賣之，恐人得其種，恆鑽其核.[32] The differences between the quotations from *Lunyu* and our received version of that text are even more substantial. The line, "He never cleared away ginger when he ate" 不徹薑食, is the only one of the three quoted that appears in the received main text of the *Lunyu*.[33] Nothing like the lines in the two sets of annotations about minced fish and mustard sauce appear the received text proper, with the closest approximation coming from the Ma Rong 馬融 commentary found in the *Lunyu jijie* 論語集釋. It reads, "With minced fish, if it was not [served with] mustard sauce, he would not eat it" 魚膾非芥醬不食.[34]

It is not surprising that for lines on more quotidian topics, such as fruits and vegetables, the annotations would include the kind of basic information we find here: where items are produced and how to prepare them. But it is telling that even in these cases the annotations tie the lines to important texts. The exact wording of the *Shishuo xinyu* passage is not itself as important as knowing the basic anecdote about Wang Rong's possessiveness with regard to his plums. Likewise, though mustard seeds and ginger are hardly crucial topics in the Confucian *Analects*, a memorized line from the *Qianzi wen* can provide a useful cue to recall at least a small part of classical text and one of its most important commentaries. The annotations to this couplet also give us a sense of the similarities and differences between the Dunhuang and Ueno texts. There is much common ground, in both general content and even specific wording. At the same time these are clearly different annotations, even if they likely share a distant ancestor.[35]

---

31   Ruan Yuan 阮元, ed., *Shisan jing zhushu fu jiaokanji* 十三經注疏附校勘記 (Nanchang fuxue kanben, 1815), 4.155-2.

32   Liu Yiqing 劉義慶, *Shishuo xinyu* 世說新語 (Taipei: Huazheng shuju, 1993), 874.

33   Which has 撤 for 徹.

34   Cheng Shude 程樹德, *Lunyu jishi* 論語集釋 (Beijing: Zhonghua shuju, 1990), 20.693.

35   Note also that here and elsewhere, as I will discuss in more detail below, the Ueno text seems to be more coherent: it describes the plums as being the size of goose *eggs* (鵝卵), rather than the size of actual geese.

In annotations for lines that deal with more abstract concepts, such as the nature of rulership, we find a similar mix of explanation of terms and connections drawn to historical and literary sources. Lines 35 and 36 are examples of *Qianzi wen* lines that are simple in linguistic terms but would require substantial explanation for students to grasp their deeper meaning in a fuller literary and historical context:

35 Their transformative influence reached the grasses and trees
化被草木

The graciousness of the House of Zhou was substantial. Their humaneness reached the grasses and trees. Thus, they were able to keep within the nine degrees of kin and thereby achieve fortune and favor. The *History of the Han* says, "Shen Feng had the courtesy name 'Penetrating Wisdom.' He was from Wu and when he served as governor of Lengling sweet dew fell through the five counties and there were seventy stalks of numinous fungi. Emperor Jing bestowed upon him one hundred measures of gold and added to that one hundred bolts [of silk]. Zhang Heng's "Capital Rhapsody" says, "His grace seeps down to the swarming insects; his might shakes the eight corners of the world."[36]

周家惠厚。仁及草木。故能內九族。以成福祿。漢書曰。沈豐字聖通。吳人也。作冷陵太守。甘露降五縣。芝草七十株。景帝賜黃金百溢。曾百疋張衡京都賦曰。澤浸混虫。振威八寓故也.

36 Their benefits reached the myriad regions.
賴及萬方

"Benefit" is "covered by." "Reach" is "to arrive at." The "myriad regions" are the "myriad kingdoms." In the time of King Wen, his [rule] reached to myriad domains and myriad regions. Of the common folk there were none who where not reached by his beneficent grace. Moreover, it is said that when Yu went to Mt. Tu, they brought jade and silk. The myriad domains were filial.

---

36   Translation from David R. Knechtges, trans., *Wen xuan or Selections of Refined Literature, Volume One: Rhapsodies on Metropolises and Capitals* (Princeton: Princeton University Press, 1992), 289.

賴者被也。及者至也。萬方万国也。文王之時。及万国万方。百姓無
不被恩及者。又雲禹察塗山。執玉帛者。万国孝也.[37]

The annotations for line 35 are almost fully made up of quotations from earlier sources, with those for 36 focusing on explanation. While it does not name a source, the first section of annotations for line 35 is excerpted entirely from the Zheng 鄭 commentary to *Shi* poem 246 "Wayside Reeds" (*xingwei* 行葦). That original reads, "The *loyalty* of the House of Zhou is substantial. Their humaneness reaches the grasses and trees. Thus, they are able to internally keep *harmony* among the nine degrees of kin *and externally respectfully served the elderly and cared for their noble and wise elders* thereby achieving fortune and favor *through this*" 周家思厚，仁及草木，故能內睦九族，外尊事黃耇養老乞言，以成福祿焉.[38] The numerous omissions from the original make the annotation passage read more awkwardly but also keep it more focused on the specific topic at hand. More importantly, the annotations tie the *Qianzi wen* line to a grammatically and thematically similar line in an important commentary to a classical text. The rest of the annotations to line 35 perform similar functions. Though the quotation from the *Han shu* does not appear in the received version of that work, a passage about Shen Feng with similar wording is found in his biography in the *Dongguan Han ji* 東觀漢記 and he is mentioned in connection with sweet dew and numinous fungi in a number of other sources.[39] Finally, the quotation from Zhang Heng's rhapsody, though actually from the "Eastern Metropolis Rhapsody" (*Dongjing fu* 東京賦), is exactly the same as our received version of that work found in the *Wenxuan*. In each of these cases the annotations provide not necessarily explanation of the meaning of the original line, but rather specific historical and literary examples that illustrate the theme of the line: moral achievement in the human world so great as to impact the realm of nature itself.

The annotations for line 36, while having a similar theme, focus more on explanation than quotation, showing the wide range of this sort of commentary. A number of the annotations from Dunhuang begin by defining terms, and we see this here as well.[40] The rest of the passage moves from the general

---

37   国 is the form used for 國 in the text. 雲 is clearly an error for 云.

38   Outlined characters in the Chinese and italicized words in the translation indicate parts that are left out of or are different in the annotations.

39   Wu Shuping 吳樹平, *Dongguan Hanji jiaozhu* 東觀漢記校注 (Beijing: Zhonghua shuju, 2008), 14.

40   Though it does seem surprising that the commentator would deem it necessary to define as basic word as *ji* 及, especially when its meaning in this line is its primary one, rather than a more obscure usage.

case of the benevolent and powerful rule of sage kings of the past to a more specific historical incident with the mention of Yu's famous gathering of the realm's rulers at Mt. Tu. This passage shows up in a number of early sources, from the *Zuo zhuan* to the *Huainanzi*, with 執玉帛者万国 as a set wording (though the mention of filiality [*xiao* 孝] is absent in these other sources). We thus see that though this annotation concentrates more on explanation, it still manages to include an important quote from an earlier source, even if unattributed, thus grounding the generalities of the original *Qianzi wen* line in historical and textual specifics.

The annotations in the Ueno manuscript are shorter. For the full couplet they read:

> The myriad regions are the myriad domains. When rulers have the Way, their gracious transformative influence has a broad reach. Their beneficence reaches the grasses and trees. Flowers and leaves blossom. "Benefit" means "profit." When there is a ruler with humaneness and moral power, profit reaches the myriad kingdoms. In the past when the Yellow Emperor ruled the realm, his standards covered ten thousand *li* and he obtained ten thousand hundred-*li* domains.

> 萬方者，萬国也。君王有道，惠化廣被，澤及草木，花葉敷榮也。賴，利也。有君仁德，利及万国也。昔黃帝之王天下。規方萬里。得百里之国者萬也.

The differences between this passage and the Dunhuang annotations are quite substantial, both in content and style, with the only real overlap being the definition of the "myriad regions." There are also no direct quotations here, acknowledged or not. The passage seems to holds together better than do the Dunhuang ones, moving from definitions and general ideas about what the lines say about rulership to a single historical (or at least mytho-historical) example. At the same time, by failing to connect the *Qianzi wen* lines to earlier text, the Ueno annotations miss the opportunity to use the mnemonic cue possibilities that are exploited in the Dunhuang annotations.

The final set of annotations I will examine both shows the value of this sort of additional material for the learner and also highlights the often haphazard nature of how the annotations use earlier sources, especially in the case of the Dunhuang passages. The annotations for line 21 are relatively straightforward:

21 First they created writing.

始制文字

"The *Changes* says, "In the time of earliest antiquity, they cut marks on wood and knotted cords of thirty feet and two inches. The sages of later generations replaced these with inscriptions. The emperor's astrologer Cang Jie saw bird prints and created written characters. After this, written characters increasingly flourished and thus things were recorded.""

易曰。上古之時。刻木結繩。三丈二寸。而後世人聖易之以書契。皇帝史官倉頡見鳥跡而造文字。自斯之後。文字漸興。故記之也.

This is a loose paraphrase of a portion of the "Appended Phrases" (*Xici* 繫辭) to the *Yi*. The closest passage in the received *Yi* reads: "In earliest antiquity, they governed with knotted strings. In later ages the sages replaced these with writing. The hundred officials could thereby be regulated, and the myriad people examined"   上古結繩而治，後世聖人易之以書契，百官以治，萬民以察.[41] But as we have seen with other examples, exact quotation is not as important as conveying a basic narrative. The stages in the process of developing writing—moving from marks on wood and knots to written characters inspired by the footprints of birds—were well-known and appear in a range of sources from the *Yi* to the *Shuowen jiezi* 說文解字 and even the preface to the *Wenxuan*.

The Dunhuang annotations for the second line in the couplet continue on this same topic of the creation of writing, in spite of the line itself being about the transition to wearing clothes:

22 乃服衣裳

Then they wore clothes

Before the time of Fuxi the world of men was simple. They lacked writing and only cut marks on wood and knotted cords in order to record their days. When came the days of Fuxi ruling the realm, people were wicked and false, thus he formulated teachings and used them to bring order to [the people]. The ten words were the eight hexagrams and "ebb" and "flow."[42] The *Changes* says: "In antiquity when Fu Xi [ruled] the realm he first devised the eight hexagrams and from this it is said that writing was first created." The *Changes* says, "In antiquity[43] they brought order through knotted cords. Later ages from these writing created and replaced

41   *Yijing* 易經, "Xici xia" 繫辭下, in Ruan Yuan 阮元, ed., *Shisan jing zhushu fu jiaokanji, Zhouyi jianyi* 十三經注疏附校勘記 (Nanchang fuxue kanben, 1815), 8.165-2.
42   Reading 息 for 自.
43   Reading 者 for 孝.

sages and kings." The *Changes* says: "It with inscriptions in order to wear clothes.[44] In the beginning it was the emperor Shun."[45] The *Changes* says: "The Yellow Emperor, Yao, and Shun let their clothes hang in order to begin the realm. They probably took this from the *qian* and *kun* hexagrams." This is explained in the "Appended Explanations."

自伏羲以前。人代淳朴。無其文字。唯剠木結繩以記其日。至伏羲氏王天下。人奸偽。故計教而用治之。十言謂八卦与消自。易曰古孝伏羲氏之天下。始畫八卦。由此言文籍之字始制。易曰。古者結繩而治。後世由此文籍制。易聖王。易曰。之以書契。以服衣裳。始皇帝舜七。易曰。黃皇帝堯舜垂衣裳以始天下。蓋取諸乾坤。繫辭詳之矣.

There is much that is odd in this passage. The language is awkward and though the reader can guess at the likely meaning, some parts are barely coherent, even when clear mistakes in the characters are taken into account (I have noted these in the footnotes). Some parts seem similar to the annotations for the couplet's first line, and the passage does eventually turn to the topic of clothing at the end. Still, the overall sense one gets is a lack of coherence.

When we compare this passage with the Ueno annotations on this couplet, however, it becomes possible to at least meaningfully speculate about what might be going on. I will first give a translation of the Ueno annotation and then give the original text paired with the original of the Dunhuang passage ("U" indicating Ueno and "D" Dunhuang, with outlined characters indicating points of difference).

Before the time of Fuxi the people were simple. Their writing was only cut marks on wood and knotted strings for recording matters. When Fuxi ruled the realm, the people were wicked and false. Thus he established the teaching of the ten words and used it to bring order to [the people]. The ten words were the eight hexagrams and "ebb" and "flow." The *Changes* says: "In antiquity when Fuxi ruled the realm he first made the eight hexagrams and from these writing was first created." The *Changes* says: "In remote antiquity they ruled through knotting cords. In later ages sages used these to make inscriptions. Then they wore clothes. In the beginning it was under the Yellow Emperor, Yao, and Shun." The *Changes* says: "The Yellow Emperor, Emperor Yao, and Emperor Shun

---

44   I have intentionally translated this into ungrammatical English. This passage is likely a result of repeated copying errors and conflation of other passages and I have tried to convey that in the translation.

45   Reading 也 for 七.

let their robes hang and thereby brought order. They probably took this from the *Qian* and *Kun* hexagrams." This is explained in the "Appended Explanations."

(U) 自伏羲氏以前人民淳□□其文字也唯剋木結繩以記其事也
(D) 自伏羲□以前人代淳朴無其文字□唯剋木結繩以記其日

(U) □伏羲氏王天下人民姦偽
(D) 至伏羲氏王天下人□奸偽

(U) 故設廿言之教而用治之
(D) 故□□計教而用治之

(U) 十言者謂八卦与消息也。
(D) 十言□謂八卦与消自□。

(U) 易曰古者伏羲氏王天下始作八卦由此□文□字始制也。
(D) 易曰古孝伏羲氏之天下始畫八卦由此言文籍之字始制□。

(U) 易曰上古結繩而治後世□□□聖人□□以為書契乃服衣裳也。
(D) 易曰古者結繩而治後世由此文籍制易聖王易曰之以□書契以服
    衣裳□。

(U) 始黃帝堯舜也易曰黃□帝堯帝舜帝垂衣服以治 蓋取諸乾坤繫辭詳
    也。
(D) 始皇帝□舜乜易曰黃皇帝堯□舜□垂衣裳以始天下蓋取諸乾坤繫
    辭詳之矣。

While our evidence here is limited, it points to two sets of annotations that are unquestionably related. Indeed, in many cases in which we have annotations from both the Dunhuang documents and from the Ueno manuscript, the former appears to be an expansion of the latter. The Ueno annotations are always shorter and much more tightly written. The sentences are coherent and the quotations often closer to the received versions.

Lines 21 and 22 provide a particularly interesting example in that the elaboration and expansion in the annotations to them appears so sloppily done. Very little new information is added (unlike what we saw with lines 35 and 36 above, in which the Dunhuang annotations add a number of new quotations from classical and other sources), but rather the changes are on the level of added characters. In some cases these added characters result in grammatically erroneous and even incomprehensible statements, such as 後世由此文籍制。易聖王。易曰。之以書契。以服衣裳。始皇帝舜七. In this case 由此文籍制 appears to be an accidentally repeated phrase due to an eye skip from its previous appearance interspersed into the middle of the paraphrase of the line from the *Yi* that appears in the annotation to line 21: 後世人聖易之以書契. Because he misread this 易, a verb meaning "replace," as a reference to the *Yi*, the copyist added the quotation introducing particle 曰 directly after it. This puts 之, the grammatically appropriate object pronoun originally referring to tying knots in cords, into a nonsensical quasi-subject position. It is, of course, impossible to know at what point in the long process of transmission this error may have occurred. Unfortunately, the annotations in P. 3973 do not begin until line 23, just following these, thus prohibiting comparison. While the Ueno manuscript was likely produced at least four hundred years after S. 5471, we know nothing about the history of transmission of either work. It is quite possible that the Ueno text is much closer to an earlier set of annotations, perhaps those by Li Xian, that were the ultimate origin of the much altered Dunhuang versions.

The early bibliographic citations indicate that there were different sets of annotations to the *Qianzi wen* circulating before and during the Tang. The different but related annotations found in the Dunhuang documents and the Ueno manuscript both provide evidentiary support for this and give a sense of what different annotations might have looked like. Most importantly, we get a sense of how the *Qianzi wen* was actually used as a base text to which writers added substantially longer paratextual elements. If we assume that the annotations in the Ueno manuscript represent an earlier stratum, as is likely, we further see how these paratextual elements were in flux. In many cases the Dunhuang annotations appear to use the older annotations for a full couplet as the basis for annotations for a single line. For the other line in a couplet they might use a single sentence or two (or none) but add substantial new material. This is the case for lines 21 and 22 and we see it elsewhere as well. Compare, for example, the annotations for the couplet made of up lines 27 and 28: "Sitting in court and inquiring about the Way; with hanging robes and folded hands they pacified and regulated" 坐朝問道，垂拱平章:

(U) 昔堯舜帝有天下舉十六族任以為政並得其人故端坐朝堂垂拱無為問至治之道　。

(D) 昔堯舜帝有天下舉十六族任以為政並得其人故端坐朝堂垂拱無為問主治道之事。

> In the past when Emperors Yao and Shun possessed the realm, they promoted to office the sixteen worthy ones and entrusted them with governing, obtaining all of them. Thus they sat upright at court and let hang their garments without taking action. They would ask the ruler about the way of orderly government.

As we can see, the Dunhuang annotations are almost identical until the last few characters. However, the Dunhuang text then adds "one explanation says" 一解云, and continues with additional text twice the length of the Ueno passage, consisting primarily of a story about a Han emperor and his ministers discussing the *Laozi*. For line 28, the Dunhuang annotations begin with quotation from the *Shu* that also makes up the second half of the Ueno annotations for the couplet and describes Yao's fine qualities as a ruler. The annotations are almost identical, though the Dunhuang passage adds a few phrases.

The Dunhuang annotations in particular provide strong indications that they both functioned in a way similar to how a teacher would—by defining difficult or important terms, giving historical and literary context, and connecting the basic text to the classical canon—and quite possibly grew out of that sort of pedagogical practice. They give a sense of being teachers' notes, accumulated over time, and in this case likely building on a base of something more terse, such as the purported Li Xian commentary found in the Ueno manuscript. Those annotations themselves would require additional explanation to be useful to students at an early stage of their education. Indeed there are indications that the Dunhuang annotations contain material that is not only different from that in the Ueno manuscript but also clearly later, as they include what scholars have identified as Tang period vernacularisms and cite works that that were themselves composed in the Tang.[46] This would also explain some aspects of the seeming sloppiness of the Dunhuang annotations, as quotations there are, in many cases, paraphrases rather than exact quotations. Even if the earlier cited texts were well known, the author(s) of the annotations may well have considered paraphrases sufficient for the purpose at hand. Carruthers describes something similar in textual citation practices in medieval Europe, warning us not to misinterpret the "inaccuracy" in medieval quotations as either sloppiness or poor memory. She notes that "many writers gave paraphrases of texts, even when the manuscripts containing the complete text were available to them.... They are quoting from memory 'sententialiter,' according to the matter or *res* [gist], rather than word-for-word."[47] In the case of

---

46   See Zhang Nali, "Dunhuang ben *Zhu Qianzi wen* zhujie," 47-48.
47   Carruthers, *The Book of Memory*, 87.

the Dunhuang annotations, the two works that tend to be quoted most "accurately" (using the admittedly problematic standard of our received versions of the texts) are the *Shi* and *Lunyu*. These were works that nearly every educated man would have, at some point, memorized to some extent. Yet even in these cases, the Dunhuang commentaries will conflate the main texts with commentary passages (especially in the case of *Lunyu*) and omit phrases. With quotations of historical works such as the *Zuo zhuan* or the *Han shu* the tendency towards paraphrase is even more pronounced. So long as we think of these annotations in terms of their broader pedagogical function, such practices are understandable.

Annotations and commentaries to classical works such as the *Shi* or *Lunyu* are meant to help the reader better read and understand those classical texts themselves. The annotations to the *Qianzi wen* are doing something quite different: they use the *Qianzi wen* base as a way to help readers learn and remember parts of *other* works, be they classical or historical, that are more important than the *Qianzi wen* itself. The *Qianzi wen* can function this way both because of what it does include and, crucially, what it does not. The lines of the *Qianzi wen* can function as mnemonic pegs precisely because of their incompleteness. Rather than tell the whole story, they give critical pieces in a form—parallel rhyming couplets—that make them easy to set to memory. Moreover, these pieces are small enough that they allow for flexibility in the fuller story that is ultimately told. The degree of flexibility might vary depending on the line or couplet, but it is always there. This incompleteness is, to use a contemporary phrase, a feature, not a bug. By constantly pointing to a larger literary, historical, and cultural context, the *Qianzi wen* invited commentary in a way other surviving primer-type works did not. The explanations themselves connected to additional explanation and appear to have resulted in an ongoing accretion of new quotations and explanations. These added considerably to the informational value of the base text and put in the hands of learners a large amount of important information specifically tied to an easy-to-remember structure of cues to call it to mind.

Liuzi qianwen

Two partial manuscripts discovered at Dunhuang provide additional support for the notion that teachers and students often took the *Qianzi wen* as a frame on which to build new pedagogical structures meant to teach knowledge beyond what is contained in the *Qianzi wen* itself. These manuscripts include parts of a work that takes each line of the original *Qianzi wen* and adds two additional characters. Entitled *Liuzi qianwen* 六字千文 in one case and *Xinhe liuzi qianwen* 新合六字千文 in another, the work appears in no extant bibliographies and was unknown to scholars until discovered among the finds at Dunhuang. Unfortunately, due to damage to the manuscripts, neither of the two copies discovered at Dunhuang is complete.[48] The version entitled *Liuzi qianwen* (for simplicity's sake, this is the title I will use to refer to the work) appears in S. 5467, a booklet 10.5 cm wide by 15 cm high. It includes, in addition to some unrelated Buddhist writings, only a small portion of the work: 22 total lines, of which 5 lines are a fragmented preface and the rest are the text proper. In all there are only 133 characters. Our other source, S. 5961, is much fuller. It is in the form of a scroll, 27 cm high by 137 cm long. The text of what is here called the *Xinhe liuzi qianwen* is complete at the beginning but cut off at the end, with line 199 being the last. In addition, 25 lines are missing completely because a portion was removed from the manuscript and 21 other lines are partially missing. In all this leaves 159 lines in which both of the added characters are present, or about 64 percent of what would have presumably been the full text.

The origins of the work remain obscure. S. 5467 begins with the title *Xinhe liuzi qianwen* followed by a brief preface, the first two lines of which read, "Zhong Zhu compiled the *Qianzi wen*. It is particularly intended for the instruction of young boys" 鍾銖撰集千字文，唯擬教訓童男. Tai Huili erroneously concludes from this that Zhong Zhu, who is otherwise unattested, is the author of this work.[49] It seem clear, however, that the preface is crediting Zhong Zhu with the compilation of the original *Qianzi wen*, not the later work. Recall that both the preface to the Ueno text and entry in the Dunhuang "Zachao" from P. 2721 credit one Zhong Yao 鐘繇 with "composing" (*zhuan* 撰) the *Qianzi wen* (with Zhou Xingsi setting it to rhyme and Li Xian writing the annotations). It is possible that the Zhong Zhu of the preface is an error for this Zhong Yao. Moreover the rest of the preface, all in six-character lines, is a severe truncation of the preface found in the Ueno text. It tells a very brief story

---

48   Scholarship on the *Liuzi qianwen* is very limited. The only writings I have found in any language are Tai Huili's 邰惠莉 "Dunhuang ben *Liuzi qianwen* chutan" 敦煌本《六字千文》初探, *Dunhuang yanjiu* 敦煌研究 (1997): 148-54; and Zhang Nali's response, "Dunhuang ben *Liuzi qianwen* chutan' xiyi——jian shu *Qianzi wen* zhuben wenti" 《敦煌本< 六字千文> 初探》析疑—— 兼述《千字文》注本問題, *Dunhuang yanjiu* 敦煌研究 69 (2001): 100-105 and its continuation, "'Dunhuang ben *Liuzi qianwen* chutan' xiyi (xu) ——jian shu *Qianzi wen* zhuben wenti" 《敦煌本< 六字千文> 初探》析疑（續）—— 兼述《千字文》注本問題, *Dunhuang yanjiu* 敦煌研究 71 (2002): 93-96.

49   Tai Huili, "Dunhuang ben *Liuzi qianwen* chutan," 153. For a discussion of other errors Tai makes in his reading of the preface, see Zhang Nali, "Dunhuang ben *Liuzi qianwen* chutan' xiyi," 100-101.

of the creation of the *Qianzi wen* but says nothing about the *Liuzi qianwen* itself. Tai speculates that the author was a local figure from the Dunhuang region with a high level of education.[50] This seems reasonable but can be no more than speculation without additional evidence.

Tai Huili further argues that the *Liuzi qianwen* adds nothing to the *Qianzi wen* in aesthetic terms, but does provide a text that is more concrete and easier for younger learners to understand.[51] Both these points are supported by a closer examination of the text, which often integrates new and useful information that clarifies the references in the original *Qianzi wen* line. At the same time, the lack of consistency in the ways the new characters are integrated into the existing *Qianzi wen* lines can detract from the appealing simplicity and order of the original. Placement of the new characters can seem haphazard, though certain patterns do emerge. The most pronounced of these is that the additional characters in a given line are typically added in adjacent positions rather than separated by characters in the original *Qianzi wen* text. We see basic examples of this in lines 5 and 6. The original lines read, "The cold comes and the heat departs; harvest in fall and store in winter" 寒來暑往，秋收冬藏. To the beginning of line 5 the *Liuzi qianwen* adds "the four seasons" (*sishi* 四時), and to the beginning of line 6, "the five grains" (*wugu* 五穀). Contiguous additions of this sort appear in 141 of the 159 lines (89 percent) for which both additional characters are present and legible.

In most of the few examples in which the additional characters are separated, at least one of the characters serves a grammatical function, often one already implied in the original, rather than adding new information. The original text of line eleven, for example, reads "Gold comes from the Li River" 金生麗水. The additions in the *Liuzi qianwen* line (in outlined characters here)—黃金生於麗水—result in no change in meaning, but simply use a binome for gold (*huangjin* 黃金) and make explicit an implied locative preposition (*yu* 於). The most common position for characters added as contiguous pairs is at the front of the original line (as in lines 5 and 6). This occurs 91 times (over half the lines), while there are only 6 instances of pairs added the end of a line (and only 2 examples in which this occurs in the second line of a couplet, no doubt owing to the added difficulty of conforming to the pre-existing *Qianzi wen* rhyme scheme). These patterns notwithstanding, the overall impression is of a less carefully composed new text, richer in information but less appealing in literary aesthetic terms and less consistent in structure.

---

50   Tai Huili, "Dunhuang ben *Liuzi qianwen* chutan," 154.

51   Ibid., 153.

In terms of the content, the most common functions of the added words are grammatical elaboration and providing additional, and sometimes more specific, information. The former tends to involve adding verbs, prepositions, particles, or other words that do not add to the meaning of the original lines of the *Qianzi wen* text in any significant way. This is what we see with the additions of 黃 and 於 to line eleven, and something similar occurs in the couplet made up of lines 57 and 58. The *Liuzi qianwen* lines read 受禍因其惡積，享福實緣善慶. Without the additions, the *Qianzi wen* lines would translate as "Misfortune follows from accumulated wickedness; good fortune results from goodness being favored." The differences in the *Liuzi qianwen* versions are minor: "*Suffering* misfortune follows from *one's* accumulated wickedness; *enjoying* good fortune *in fact* results from goodness being favored." These changes add grammatical elaboration or clarification but do little else.

Additions that bring new information to the original line are more varied and, potentially, provide more insight into the pedagogical goals of the *Liuzi qianwen*. The most common category of this kind of addition is names, be they historical or mythological.[52] We see a basic example of this in the couplet made up of lines 23 and 24. The *Qianzi wen* reads, "Giving up the throne and yielding the kingdom, there were the Holder of Yu and he of Tao and Tang" 推位讓國，有虞陶唐. The *Liuzi qianwen* version uses grammatical elaboration in one line and additional information in the other, reading, "*If discussing* giving up and yielding the throne, there were the Holder of Yu—*Yao and Shun*—and he of Tao and Tang" 若論推讓國，有虞堯舜陶唐.[53] The key addition here is in line 24: while literate adults would surely know that the original *Qianzi wen* line referred to Yao and Shun, with the former having been the Lord of both Tao and Tang and the latter having held the territory of Yu, this may not have been obvious to younger or less educated learners. Adding the better-known appellations "Yao and Shun" clarifies the reference of the line. Note that these additions do not appear in parallel positions in the couplet. We have 65 full couplets of the *Liuzi qianwen* in which the full lines, including the additional characters, are present. In 34 of these couplets the added characters in the *Liuzi qianwen* are in parallel positions (though not necessarily parallel in other ways, such as grammatically or conceptually), indicating that the author preferred to place the new characters in parallel positions when possible. In the case of this particular couplet the grammar of the original *Qianzi wen* lines, in addition to an apparent desire to maintain the original rhyme scheme,

---

52   Zhang Nali counts thirty-four examples. See "Dunhuang ben *Liuzi qianwen* chutan' xiyi," 103.

53   The *Liuzi qianwen* omits 位 from the original *Qianzi wen* line, presumably in error.

would make doing so quite difficult (resulting in the awkwardness of line 24). Thus while the versions of these lines in the *Liuzi qianwen* would not necessarily be easier to set to memory, they would provide the learner with more information.

The couplet made up of lines 21 and 22, discussed in detail in our earlier examination of the annotations, functions in a similar manner but with full parallelism and additional information provided in both lines. The *Liuzi qianwen* lines are: 伏羲始制文字，黃帝乃服衣裳 ("*Fuxi*, first they created writing; *Yellow Emperor*, then they wore clothes"). Whereas the addition of "Yao and Shun" simply provided more common names of historical figures already mentioned in the original *Qianzi wen*, in this case the *Liuzi qianwen* does something more: it explicitly credits these stages in the evolution of human society specific historical figures. Of course the Dunhuang and Ueno annotations do something quite similar, only with substantially more additional text.[54] Place names, though less common than names and titles of historical and mythological figures, are another important category of *Liuzi qianwen* additions that provide new information. Lines 15 and 16 read as follows: 燕國菓珍李柰，蜀郡菜重芥薑 ("*Kingdom of Yan*, of fruits, plums and crab-apples are prized; *Shu Commandery*, of greens, mustard and ginger are esteemed"). Recall that Wang Feng's plums, of which he was most possessive, grew at his home in the Kingdom of Yan. Shu, in turn, is cited by the Ueno commentary as place that produces fresh ginger.

New information can also be of the conceptual sort, clarifying general statements whose more specific meanings might be unclear to learners. We have seen how lines 35 and 36 tell of the extensive reach of the "transformative influence" and "benefits" of sage rulers reaching to the myriad domains and even the grasses and trees. The *Liuzi qian wen* expands these lines to make the mechanisms of this influence more explicit: 仁慈化被草木，恩德賴及萬方 (*With humaneness and kindness*, their transformative influence reached the grasses and trees; *with beneficent moral power* their benefits reached the myriad regions"). Again, this more explicit articulation of the specific virtues performing these far-reaching transformative acts might not add much new information for educated older readers, but for other learners this elaboration could serve a pedagogical function left unfulfilled by the original *Qianzi wen* lines.

The questions of the function and origin of the additional characters are related. It seems clear that the *Liuzi qianwen* as a stand-alone text would be more difficult to set to memory than the *Qianzi wen* itself. The additional

---

54   We will return to this commonality, which appears not to be coincidental, below.

characters disrupt the parallelism and the rhythm of the original and add a
third again as much text to remember. There was also no apparent attempt to
maintain the non-repetition found in the original, as many of the added characters not only appear in the *Qianzi wen* itself, they are often repeated multiple
times in the additions found in the *Liuzi qianwen*. However, I would argue that
the *Liuzi qianwen* was not intended to be used as a stand-alone text. That is, it
instead assumes that the reader would already know the full text of the *Qianzi
wen* and indeed have set that text to memory. We know that it was common
practice in the period for students to memorize texts aurally by hearing them
recited by a teacher. They also memorized written texts without fully understanding the content of what they were memorizing. For a student who had
already memorized the *Qianzi wen*, learning the additions found in the *Liuzi
qianwen* would be much less burdensome. Moreover, there was a practice of
adding additional words to *Qianzi wen* lines in other contexts. The *Taiping
guangji* story cited above has people doing just that as part of a game. Indeed
one of the lines from that story: 當須務茲稼穡 (*One must* focus on this: sow-
ing and reaping") is identical to line 164 of the *Liuzi qianwen*.[55] While this appears to be more coincidence than evidence of wider knowledge of the *Liuzi
qianwen*—there are no other shared lines—it shows that the *Liuzi qianwen* is
not the only example of manipulating *Qianzi wen* lines in this way. A student
who had memorized the *Qianzi wen* lines but did not fully understand their
references would likely find the additions in the *Liuzi* to be helpful, especially
if accompanied by instruction from a teacher.

Tōno Haruyuki has noted that "As a result of the additions, the content of
the *Qianzi wen* is made more concrete and made to have a kind of independent, simple *leishu*-like quality."[56] This is an important insight. As do certain
kinds of *leishu*, the *Qianzi wen* functions as a synecdochal mnemonic: it contains parts that point to and help one bring to mind a greater whole. Taking
this a step further, I believe that the point of the *Liuzi qianwen* is *not* to help
students remember the *Qianzi wen*, but rather to use the *Qianzi wen* as scaf-
folding to remember other parts of the whole (i.e. the knowledge conveyed by
the annotations) to which the additional characters point. The *Liuzi qianwen* is
thus a paratext pointing to another paratext, namely content of the annotations to the *Qianzi wen* that were circulating at the time, and using the *Qianzi
wen* text proper as a facilitator. The student who had previously memorized the

55   *Taiping guangji*, 252.1957. This is noted by also by Tai Huili, "Dunhuang ben *Liuzi qianwen*
      chutan," 153.

56   Tōno Haruyuki 東野之治, "Ri Sen no *Chū Senjimon ni tsuite*" 李暹の『注千字文』に
      ついて, *Man'yōshū kenkyu* 万葉研究 13 (1985): 424.

Qianzi wen would then have to simply learn two new characters for each line, which would provide easier access to the larger body of knowledge.

Analyzing the source of the additional characters in the *Liuzi qianwen* provides support for this theory. It is true that in some cases it is likely these additions were simply thought up by the author to expand a given line to six characters. This is almost certainly the case for additions that function simply as grammatical elaboration or clarification. As we have seen, these add little or nothing to the meaning of the original line and do not point to a wider body of knowledge. For other categories, such as names, places, and other types of specific new information, however, there is a clear link between the additions and the kinds of annotations found in the Dunhuang and Ueno texts. This connection was first noted by Zhang Nali, who has done a preliminary examination of commonalities between the *Liuzi qianwen* additions and the Ueno annotations. Her conclusion is that a "major part either directly or indirectly appear in the annotated version."[57] Though she gives a number of instances of this connection, she does not provide any comprehensive numbers and bases her work almost solely on the Ueno manuscript.

The Dunhuang *Qianzi wen* annotations, though they cover fewer lines of that text, are more copious and involve more direct citations of classical and other sources (even if these are rarely exact). To more carefully assess Zhang's claim, I have thus examined the 43 lines from the *Liuzi qianwen* that are both fully intact and correspond to *Qianzi wen* lines that appear in the Dunhuang annotated versions (both S. 5471 and P. 3971) to look for connections between the additional words and the annotations in either these Dunhuang materials or in the Ueno manuscript. To count as a connection, the additional words must either actually appear in the annotations or very clearly make reference to material in the annotations (for example, giving a different name for a historical figure who appear in the annotations). Of these 43 lines, in 18 cases the added words are clearly traceable to both the Dunhuang and Ueno annotations. In 12 of the lines there is a clear connection to the Dunhuang annotations but not the Ueno ones. In 5 instances there is a connection to the Ueno annotations but not those found in Dunhuang. This adds up to 35 out of 43 lines (81 percent) in which the added characters are closely tied to the annotations we have. Of the 8 lines in which the added words do not seem to be connected to the annotations, 5 are examples of grammatical elaboration/clarification. This means that there are only 3 instances out of 38 in which in which the added words provide some sort of new information but that information is *not* reflected in the annotations. This evidence not only shows that

---

57   Zhang Nali, "'Dunhuang ben *Liuzi qianwen* chutan' xiyi," 103.

Zhang Nali's observation is solid, it implies that the more different sets of annotations we have, the more connections between them and the *Liuzi qianwen*
additions we are likely to find.

The couplet with lines 33 and 34 is a good example of the connections between the *Liuzi qianwen*'s additional characters and the annotations found in
the Dunhuang and Ueno manuscripts. The original *Qianzi wen* lines read: "The
singing phoenix is in the tree; the white colt grazes in the clearing" 鳴鳳在樹，
白駒食場. The *Liuzi qianwen* versions read, "The singing phoenix—*the parasol
tree*—is in the tree; *a worthy man*, the white colt grazes in the clearing" 鳴鳳
梧桐在樹，賢人白駒食場. The Dunhuang annotations for the first line open
with a quotation from the *Shi*: "The phoenix sings, on that high ridge. The parasol tree grows, on that sunny slope" 鳳凰鳴矣，于彼高岡。梧桐生矣，于彼
朝陽.[58] Following this is an (unattributed) line from the Zheng Xuan commentary to the poem that further connects the phoenix to the parasol tree: "The
phoenix will perch only in the parasol tree and eat only bamboo seeds" 鳳凰非
梧桐不栖，非竹實不食. There is no mention of the parasol tree in the Ueno
annotations, but these do show a connection with the added characters in the
second line of the couplet, with the statement, "There was a worthy man who
rode a white colt, coming in the morning" 有賢人乘白駒來朝也.[59] This is followed (in both sets of annotations) by a quotation from the *Shi* poem that is
the locus classicus of the "white colt" reference.[60] In each of these cases the
additional words in the *Liuzi qianwen* provide new information to the reader—
the association between the phoenix and the parasol tree and between worthy
men and white colts—that is found in the annotations as well. The annotations, of course, are fuller, and explicitly quote the corresponding poems from
the *Shi* from which these allusions ultimately derive. Both the *Liuzi qianwen*
and the annotations thus tie the *Qianzi wen* lines to the broader literary and
historical tradition, with the much shorter *Liuzi qianwen* additions functioning
as mnemonic cues connecting not to the *Qianzi wen* itself but rather to the
annotations.

We see something very similar in the *Liuzi qianwen* additions to *Qianzi wen*
lines whose annotations we examined earlier. Lines 15 and 16—"*Kingdom of
Yan*, of fruits, plums and crab-apples are prized; *Shu Commandery*, of greens,
mustard and ginger are esteemed" 燕國菓珍李柰，蜀郡菜重芥薑—add place

---

58   Mao #252. The quotation matches the received version of the poem perfectly, as is often
        the case in *Shi* quotations in the annotations.

59   The Dunhuang annotations have the same phrase but with the near synonym *sheng* 聖 in
        place of 賢.

60   Mao #186.

names to the original *Qianzi wen* text that are brought up in the annotations as well. This is especially meaningful in the case of line 15, for which the addition of "Kingdom of Yan" specifically ties the line to the story of Wang Feng's large and beloved plums from the *Shishuo xinyu* quoted in both the Dunhuang and Ueno commentaries. The addition of "Shu Commandery" does not involve as extensive a set of associations, but does mirror the Ueno commentary's quotation of the "Rhapsody on the Shu Capital" and its note that fresh ginger is grown in the region. Likewise, the figures Fuxi and the Yellow Emperor, added by the *Liuzi qianwen* to the beginnings of the *Qianzi wen* lines about creating writing and beginning to wear clothes, both figure prominently in the annotations to these lines in the Dunhuang and Ueno manuscripts. Finally, of the virtues articulated by the *Liuzi qianwen* at the beginnings of lines 35 and 36—*"With humaneness and kindness*, their transformative influence reached the grasses and trees; *with beneficent moral power* their benefits reached the myriad regions" 仁慈化被草木，恩德賴及萬方—all but 慈 appear in the annotations. In all of these cases we cannot definitively show that these additional words came from these specific annotations, as we know nothing about the author of the *Liuzi qianwen* or his compositional process. Moreover, it is possible that the *Liuzi qianwen* additions did not come directly from *any* annotations but rather from the same general body of knowledge and earlier texts from which the annotations draw. However, it is clear that, at the very least, the additional characters and the annotations are related in both content and function: the annotations explain and contextualize the *Qianzi wen* lines through and within a larger literary and historical context and the added characters provide cues to help the learner recall key parts of this context.

Conclusion

The *Qianzi wen* has proven to be an astoundingly stable and successful work. It has been set to memory by generation after generation for some fifteen hundred years, and the versions of its text we find in documents from Dunhuang are essentially the same as the received version that came through the later print culture. Its versatility—from a medium for calligraphy practice to an introduction to important elements of the literary and historical past—is part of what has allowed the work to maintain its popularity through periods that have had very different educational goals and demands. By considering the *Qianzi wen* in terms of its mnemonic utility, we not only get a sense of how it was used in the period closest to its creation, we also gain insights into how individuals in that period learned and remembered the elements of their literary and historical past that together constitute Assmann's notion of cultural memory.

One could argue that the annotations to the *Qianzi wen* found in the Dunhuang and Ueno manuscripts and the *Liuzi qianwen* were not themselves successful works. These annotations fell out of circulation and the *Liuzi qianwen* never even made it into any known bibliographies. At the same time, they help us understand some of the ways people interacted with and used a much more successful work. The annotations demonstrate a recognition that the *Qianzi wen* required explanation and that this was, in mnemonic terms, one of its strengths. As Carruthers notes, "While the storage capacity of memory is virtually limitless, the amount of information that can be focused upon and comprehended at one time is definitely limited."[61] The *Qianzi wen*'s short and memorable lines stay within that limit of comprehensibility while making reference to a much vaster body of knowledge. The annotations supply some of that knowledge, typically in short quotations and explanations that themselves often stay within an eight- to ten-word limit. They expand the informational value of the base text while keeping the scope within the bounds what would be reasonable and meaningful for a young student to learn. The *Liuzi qianwen* in turn attempts to connect that content even more directly to the original *Qianzi wen* lines. It uses memorized mnemonic cues to direct the learner to additional cues that connect to the wider body of knowledge. This complicated, even ungainly, relationship between text and paratexts is, we might surmise, one of the reasons it appears not to have circulated widely either in time or in space. Rather than make the task of remembering more efficient, it made it more cumbersome.

Yet considered together in their success and failures, these three works provide us with a fuller and more complex picture of the early stages of an individual's literary training in medieval period than what we can observe through the received tradition alone. They show that in spite of the apparent lack of treatises on mnemonic techniques, scholars and teachers understood the workings of textual memory and how to exploit those workings through textual structures and additions in ways that allowed individuals to learn and remember the key parts of their cultural inheritance. Even if some of these attempts were ultimately pedagogical dead-ends, they show the dynamism and fluidity of the medieval Chinese relationship with its cultural inheritance and the ways that inheritance could be put to use.

---

61   Carruthers, *The Book of Memory*, 84.

Bibliography

Assmann, Jan. "Collective Memory and Cultural Identity." Translated by John Czaplicka. *New German Critique* 65 (1995): 125-33.

Carruthers, Mary. *The Book of Memory: A Study of Memory in Medieval Culture.* Cambridge, UK: Cambridge University Press, 1990.

Cheng Shude 程樹德. *Lunyu jishi* 論語集釋. Beijing: Zhonghua shuju, 1990.

Erll, Astrid, and Ansgar Nünning, eds. *A Companion to Cultural Memory Studies.* New York: Walter de Gruyter, 2010.

Galambos, Imre. "Confucian Education in a Buddhist Environment: Medieval Manuscripts and Imprints of the *Mengqiu*." *Studies in Chinese Religions* 1 (2015): 269-88.

Grabes, Herbert. "Cultural Memory and the Literary Canon." In *A Companion to Cultural Memory Studies*, edited by Astrid Erll and Ansgar Nünning, 311-19.

Knechtges, David R., trans. *Wen xuan or Selections of Refined Literature, Volume One: Rhapsodies on Metropolises and Capitals.* Princeton: Princeton University Press, 1992.

Kuroda Akira 黑田彰, Gotō Akio 后藤昭雄, Tōno Haruyuki 東野之治, and Miki Masahiro 三木雅博, eds. *Ueno-bon Chū Senjimon chūkai* 上野本注千字文注解. Ōsaka: Izumi Shoin, 1989.

Li Chuo 李綽. *Shangshu gushi* 尚書故實. Taipei: Taiwan shangwu yinshuguan, 1983.

Li Pengfei 李鵬飛. *Tangdai feixieshi xiaoshuo zhi leixing yanjiu* 唐代非寫實小說之類型研究. Beijing: Beijing daxue chubanshe, 2004.

Liang shu 梁書. Compiled by Yao Cha 姚察 and Yao Silian 姚思廉. Beijing: Zhonghua shuju, 1973.

Liu Yiqing 劉義慶. *Shishuo xinyu* 世說新語. Taipei: Huazheng shuju, 1993.

Luo Changpie 羅常培. *Tang Wudai xibei fangyin* 唐五代西北方音. Beijing: Kexue chubanshe, 1961.

Miller, George A. "The Magic Number Seven, Plus or Minus Two: Some Limits on Our Capacity for Processing Information." *Psychology Review* 63 (1956): 81-97.

Nanshi 南史. Compiled by Li Yanshou 李延壽. Beijing: Zhonghua shuju, 1975.

Nugent, Christopher M.B. *Manifest in Words, Written on Paper: Producing and Circulating Poetry in Tang Dynasty China.* Cambridge, MA: Harvard University Asia Center, 2010.

Quan Tangwen 全唐文. Beijing: Zhonghua shuju, 1984.

Ruan Yuan 阮元, ed. *Shisan jing zhushu fu jiaokanji, Zhouyi jianyi* 十三經注疏附校勘記. Nanchang fuxue kanben, 1815.

Suishu 隋書. Compiled by Wei Zheng 魏徵 et al. Beijing: Zhonghua shuju, 1973.

Tai Huili 邰惠莉. "Dunhuang ben *Liuzi qianwen* chutan" 敦煌本《六字千文》初探. *Dunhuang yanjiu* 敦煌研究 (1997): 148-54.

Taiping guangji 太平廣記. Compiled by Li Fang 李昉 et al. 10 vols. Beijing: Zhonghua shuju, 1981.

Tōno Haruyuki 東野之治. Ri Sen no *Chū Senjimon ni tsuite* 李暹の『注千字文』につい
  て. *Man'yōshū kenkyu* 万葉研究 13 (1985): 219-34.

Tōno Haruyuki 東野之治. "Kunmōsho" 訓蒙書. In *Kōza Tonkō* 講座敦煌5: *Tonkō Kanbun
  bunken* 敦煌漢文文献, edited by Ikeda On 池田温, 401-38. Tōkyō: Daitō Shuppansha,
  1992.

Wang Xiaoping 王曉平. "Shangye ben *Zhu qianziwen* yu Dunhuang ben *Zhu qianziwen*"
  上野本《注千字文》與敦煌本《注千字文》. *Dunhuang yanjiu* 敦煌研究, 103 (2007):
  55-60.

Wilkinson, Endymion. *Chinese History, A New Manual, 4th edition*. Cambridge, MA:
  Harvard University Asia Center, 2015.

Wu Shuping 吳樹平. *Dongguan Hanji jiaozhu* 東觀漢記校注. Beijing: Zhonghua shuju,
  2008.

Yang Haiwen 楊海文. "Riben cang Beichao Li Xian 'Zhu *Qianziwen* xu' liangzhong jiaoding" 日本藏北朝李暹"注《千字文》序"兩種校訂. *Xixia yanjiu* 西夏研究 2 (2015):
  28-32.

Zhang Nali 張娜麗. "'Dunhuang ben *Liuzi qianwen* chutan' xiyi——jian shu *Qianzi wen*
  zhuben wenti" 《敦煌本〈六字千文〉初探》析疑—— 兼述《千字文》注本問題.
  Dunhuang yanjiu 敦煌研究 69 (2001): 100-105.

Zhang Nali 張娜麗. "'Dunhuang ben *Liuzi qianwen* chutan' xiyi (xu)——jian shu *Qianzi
  wen* zhuben wenti" 《敦煌本〈六字千文〉初探》析疑（續）—— 兼述《千字文》
  注本問題. *Dunhuang yanjiu* 敦煌研究 71 (2002): 93-96.

Zhang Nali 張娜麗. "Dunhuang ben *Zhu Qianzi wen* zhujie" 敦煌本《注千字文》注解.
  Dunhuang xue jikan 敦煌學輯刊 (2002): 45-59.

Zhang Shuangdi 張雙棣. *Huainanzi jiaoshi* 淮南子校釋. Beijing: Beijing daxue chubanshe, 2013.

Zhang Xinpeng 張新朋. *Dunhuang xieben* Kaimeng yaoxun *yanjiu* 敦煌寫本《開蒙要
  訓》研究. Beijing: Zhongguo shehui kexue chubanshe, 2013.

Zheng Qiao 鄭樵. *Tongzhi* 通志. Taipei: Taiwan shangwu yinshuguan, 1987.

CHAPTER 7

Genre and the Construction of Memory: A Case Study of Quan Deyu's 權德輿 (759-818) Funerary Writings for Zhang Jian 張薦 (744-804)

Alexei Kamran Ditter

> Recollection ... is not simply a repetition but rather a rebirth of the past; it implies a creative and constructive process. It is not enough to pick up isolated data of our past experience; we must really re-collect them, we must organize and synthesize them, and assemble them into a focus of thought. It is this kind of recollection which gives us the characteristic human shape of memory.
>
> ERNST CASSIRER, *An Essay on Man*

In recent years, the field of memory studies has moved away from perceptions of memory as static—what is "contained" within a particular form—to instead explore memory formation as a dynamic process encompassing "the mental, material, and social structures within which experience is embedded, constructed, interpreted, and passed on."[1] Genre is one such structure that has been explored. Genre within memory studies however has often been understood rather simplistically, as "conventionalized formats" used to "encode events and experiences" within written texts that allow competent readers to anticipate the kinds and patterns of information they might encounter.[2] Within genre studies, however, genres are understood somewhat differently. As with memory studies, genre studies in recent years has focused increasingly on understanding genres as processes rather than products. No longer viewing genres simply as "containers" for content or "schemes" for organizing compositions or classifying writings, genres are instead conceived of as "forms of cultural knowledge that conceptually frame and mediate how we understand and typically act within various situations" and "as both organizing *and* generating kinds of texts and social actions, in complex, dynamic relation to one another."[3]

---

1   Astrid Erll, *Memory in Culture*, trans. Sara B. Young (New York: Palgrave Macmillan, 2011), 112.

2   Ibid., 147, 148.

3   Anis S. Bawarshi and Mary Jo Reiff, *Genre: An Introduction to History, Theory, Research, and Pedagogy* (West Lafayette, IN: Parlor Press, 2010), 4.

© KONINKLIJKE BRILL NV, LEIDEN, 2018 | DOI 10.1163/9789004368637_009

Genres understood in this manner are more than just "conventionalized formats." They influence multiple aspects of a discursive act, defining (and defined by) the unique circumstances of a specific situation, the actors and audiences involved, and the objectives, both socially recognized and private, that the speakers of the genre may attempt to realize through their particular instantiation of a genre. In that they mediate how texts are composed, interpreted, and circulated, genres play a key role in influencing how memory is constructed and transmitted. Simply stated, genres shape memory.

In what follows, I explore the thesis that genres shape memory through a limited investigation of two genres used during the mid-Tang to commemorate the dead, the "offering" (*jiwen* 祭文, alternatively translated as "sacrificial prayer") and the "entombed epitaph" (*muzhiming* 墓誌銘, alternatively translated as "tomb epitaph inscription" or "grave memoir").[4] Both genres were produced in response to death, provided accounts of the lives of their subjects, and typically identified not only for whom they were written but also who authored them and when they were used or performed.

In this study, moreover, I restrict my investigation of these two genres to two compositions ideally suited for exploring how genre might shape memory, the "Offering for the Late Minister of Works Zhang" 祭故張工部文[5] and the "Entombed Epitaph and Preface for His Excellency Zhang, Late Grand Master of the Palace, Acting Attendant Gentleman of the Ministry of Works of the Department of State Affairs, concurrently appointed Censor-in-chief and Senior Compiler in the Historiography Institute, Supreme Pillar of State, Awarded the Scarlet and Gold Fish [Tally] Bag and Serving as Imperial Envoy to Offer Condolences to the Turfan, Posthumously Appointed Minister of Rites of the Tang" 唐故中大夫守尚書工部侍郎兼御史大夫史館修撰上柱國賜紫金魚袋充吊贈吐蕃使贈禮部尚書張公墓誌銘並序 (hereafter abbreviated as "Entombed Epitaph for His Excellency Zhang")[6]. Both these texts were written by the same author—the eminent mid-Tang literary patron and official Quan Deyu 權德輿 (759-818)—, treat the same subject—Quan's close friend and colleague Zhang Jian 張薦 (744-804)—, and were produced around the same

---

4 In addition to entombed epitaphs and offerings, other genres used since the early medieval period (ca. 200-600) entirely or in part to commemorate the dead included "stele inscription" (*bei* 碑), "dirge" (*lei* 誄), "condolence" (*diao* 弔), and "lament" (*aici* 哀辭), as well as "poetry" (*shi* 詩), "rhapsody" (*fu* 賦), and even "preface" (*xu* 序). In addition to these, many other genres were used during the Tang as well to record the lives and experiences of individuals, including "biography" (*zhuan* 傳) and "accounts of conduct" (*xing zhuang* 行狀).

5 *Quan Deyu shi wen ji* 權德輿詩文集 (hereafter abbreviated QDYSWJ), ed. Guo Guangwei 郭廣偉 (Shanghai: Shanghai guji, 2009), 49.775-77.

6 QDYSWJ, 22.337-39.

time—the introductory portion of Quan's offering states it was performed on August 2, 805, while his entombed epitaph records that Zhang was buried on August 4, 805. Controlling for these variables—authorship, subject, and time of composition—makes it easier to recognize how the distinct conventions of the entombed epitaph and offering helped shape the construction of Zhang's memory within these two compositions.

In the first part of this study, I identify literary, social, and material conventions that distinguish these two genres and, where appropriate, identify within Quan's two compositions where we see these conventions in play. In the second part, I closely examine these two compositions' respective treatment of an identical topic—Zhang's career as an official and diplomat—in order to further clarify how genres influence the construction of memory in terms of diction, choice of content, and narrative sequence.

Conventions of Memory Making in Entombed Epitaphs and Offerings

As discussed above, within contemporary theory, genres are not simply "types of texts." They are rather "typified rhetorical actions based in recurrent situations,"[7] highly structured and conventionalized communicative events that respond to specific exigences and which are constrained in terms of participant roles, objectives, and lexical-grammatical resources. While both entombed epitaphs and offerings in the mid-Tang responded to the same exigence,[8] namely the death, real or anticipated, of their subjects, they differed in terms of a number of other distinguishing conventions: who was socially permitted to employ the genre, the kinds of information they were supposed to communicate, the audiences they nominally addressed, and the conventional objectives they should realize.

Authorship and Identity

Genres are restricted in terms of their speaking subjects, meaning that only individuals socially recognized as being permitted to "speak" the genre could legitimately produce them. In making use of genres, then, authors to some

---

7   Carolyn R. Miller, "Genre as Social Action," *Quarterly Journal of Speech* 70 (1984), 159.

8   As defined by Anis Bawarshi, exigence represents "a learned recognition of significance that informs why and how we... respond in and to various situations." See Bawarshi, *Genre and the Invention of the Writer: Reconsidering the Place of Invention in Composition* (Logan: Utah State University Press, 2003), 41.

degree needed to craft their identities within their texts to conform to those permitted speaking positions. In this sense, genres shape memory on one level by delimiting and defining how relationships between authors of these compositions and their subjects might be represented.

For entombed epitaphs, the appropriate speaking subject was an individual who could narrate and evaluate the life of the deceased with authority and, to a greater or lesser degree, objectivity. In many cases, that appropriate speaking subject was a close male relative of the deceased. When not written by close family members however, authors seem to have required the explicit or tacit approval of someone sanctioned to delegate the responsibility of the composition of the entombed epitaph to another. Furthermore, especially in cases where compositions were written by individuals completely outside of the deceased's extended family, they often included explanations for why they had been chosen to write it as well.[9]

In the "Entombed Epitaph for His Excellency Zhang," we see Quan providing just such an explanation:

> I, Deyu, time and again served together [with Zhang] in the Offices of the Hanlin Academy and the inner court. Because there were indeed many days in which I indulged in pleasures with their honored father [when he and I] lived in the neighborhood of the benevolent and applied ourselves to righteousness,[10] [Zhang's son,] weeping tears, presented [me with] his deceased father's writings and requested that I [have them] made presentable and inscribed.

> 以德輿再同玉堂金華之署，承先子之歡，里仁服義，為日固久，泣狀遺懿，以表識為請.[11]

In this passage, Quan not only explicitly recounts his being asked to write the entombed epitaph by Zhang's son, but also explains why he was chosen to

---

9   For a general discussion of the practice of commissioning *muzhiming* during the latter half of the Tang dynasty, see Alexei Ditter, "The Commerce of Commemoration: Commissioned *Muzhiming* in the Mid- to Late-Tang," *Tang Studies* 32 (2014), 21-46.

10 "Neighborhood of the benevolent" 里仁 alludes to *Analects* 論語 4/1: "Of neighborhoods, benevolence is the most beautiful" 里仁為美. "Applied ourselves to righteousness" alludes to the second line of the "Summons of the Soul" 招魂 in the *Chuci* 楚辭: "My body was imbued with unfailing righteousness" 身服義而未沫. See D.C. Lau, *The Analects*, 2nd ed. (Hong Kong: Chinese University Press, 1992), 28; David Hawkes, *The Songs of the South: An Ancient Chinese Anthology of Poems by Qu Yuan and Other Poets* (Harmondsworth and New York: Penguin Books, 1985), 223; Hong Xingzu 洪興組, *Chuci bu zhu* 楚辭補注 (Taipei: Tiangong shuju, 2000), 9.197.

11 *QDYSWJ*, 22.339.

write it in the first place, namely because of his decades-long professional and personal relationship with Zhang Jian.

The appropriate speaking subject of an offering was also restricted, albeit in a manner distinctly different from entombed epitaphs. Offerings might be composed by anyone for whom the death of the subject represented (or was represented to be) a heartfelt personal loss. In this sense, they could be composed by family members, friends, acquaintances or colleagues of the deceased, or even by individuals who might only know the subject of the offering through the historical record, their transmitted written legacy, or some other physical trace. Similarly, composing an offering for a subject required no special invitation. Instead, offerings were often represented as seemingly unprompted and visceral responses to an individual's loss or absence.

In his "Offering for the Late Minister of Works Zhang," we see that Quan, in sharp contrast to the vague, generalized description found in the entombed epitaph, offers specific details about many aspects of his friendship with Zhang Jian. Whereas in the entombed epitaph, Quan flatly stated that he and Zhang had "indulged in pleasure" 承歡 together, in the offering their shared activities are enumerated individually—"drinking together, singing poems, / [Engaging in] candid discussions and skillfully telling humorous tales" 觴酒歌詩，清言善謔.[12] When stating the duration and frequency of their get-togethers, in the entombed epitaph Quan straightforwardly declares that there were "indeed many days" 為日固久; in his offering, however, he touchingly writes that "there were no days we were apart, throughout the year we made merry" 靡日而間，彌年以歡.[13] Finally, Quan's response to Zhang's death differs dramatically between these two texts. Within the entombed epitaph, Quan responds philosophically to Zhang's death, proclaiming in the prose portion of the entombed epitaph that "the way of the gentleman has a beginning and an end" 君子之道，有初有終 and in the elegy (*ming* 銘) portion that "all things that live will inevitably transform" 有生必化.[14] Within the offering, Quan's responds emotionally, describing his poignant realization that he will never again be able to enjoy the company of his dear friend and his heartfelt promise to always remember him:

一瞬之間，	In the space of the blink of an eye,
奄成今古。	Suddenly [these things] become the present and past.
以此哀思，	Given these mournful recollections—
如何可忘？	How can you be forgotten?[15]

---

12   Ibid., 49.776.
13   Ibid.
14   Ibid., 22.338, 339.
15   Ibid., 49.776.

As these examples illustrate, the manner in which an author might represent his relationship with the deceased subject seems to have been to some degree contingent upon the genre being used. In the entombed epitaph, Quan's friendship with Zhang is muted, with equal emphasis given to their status as professional colleagues. In the offering, Quan's friendship with Zhang is emphasized, with the inclusion of specific details—their time together, their shared activities, and Quan's heartfelt sense of loss—further underscoring its depth and sincerity of feeling.

Sources, Schemata, and Production Process

In addition to distinctions in their respective appropriate speaking subjects, entombed epitaphs and offerings differed in terms of the sources upon which they might draw in constructing the memory of their subjects. Writers of entombed epitaphs, in addition to their own personal memories of the deceased, seemed to rely as well upon a diverse range of oral and written sources. These might include accounts narrated by friends or family, "family histories" (*jia zhuan* 家傳) and "genealogical records" (*pudie* 譜諜 or *shipu* 氏譜), "accounts of conduct" (*xingzhuang* 形狀), and the collected writings (*wenji* 文集) of the deceased. In the case of Quan's entombed epitaph for Zhang, for example, Quan explicitly mentions two sources, his own recollections of Zhang and the corpus of Zhang's writings presented to him by Zhang's son. Offerings by contrast were mostly, although not always, grounded in the personal experiences of the author with the subject.[16] In this regard, Quan's offering is quite conventional, drawing exclusively upon his personal memories of Zhang.

Entombed epitaphs and offerings also differed in their "schemata," the kinds of information they conventionally used to construct their respective memories of the deceased. As defined by Nicolas Pethes and Jens Ruchatz, schemata consist:

> ... of slots and conditions governing what can occupy these slots (and thus, what can, according to the schema, be comprehended, perceived, remembered, or anticipated). Schemata thereby have an economical function for memory, as now not all the details have to be remembered; instead just the particular slots of the particular schema currently activated have to be concretely filled... [in this way] schemata make it

---

16   In instances in which offerings were written to subjects long dead, they were grounded in their author's experiences with the subject as they imagined them to be.

possible for various pieces of information to be *meaningfully* related to one another and organized.[17]

Despite sharing certain informational slots—their description of their subject's career, for example, and of the author's relationship with the subject—, even a cursory examination of entombed epitaphs and offerings reveals several differences. Entombed epitaphs conventionally included their subject's taboo name (*hui* 諱), byname (*zi* 字), family name and choronym, the date and circumstances of their death, their age when they died, the family name and choronym of spouses and the names of children, as well as the date, place, and circumstances of burial.[18] They moreover listed, if any, the titles and positions held by subjects over the course of their careers as well as positions held by predeceased ancestors, either at time of death or granted posthumously.[19] Offerings by contrast conventionally included the date offerings were performed, the name of their performer, an explicit identification of sacrifice, and the conventional closing phrase "I reverently [present this offering] for you to consume" (*shang xiang* 尚饗). In all of these regards, Quan's entombed epitaph and offering for Zhang were again both entirely conventional.

Finally, entombed epitaphs and offerings were distinct in terms of how "final" versions of texts were produced. To begin with, in composing entombed epitaphs, authors needed to accommodate not only the various sources upon which they drew but also the desired representation of the deceased as communicated by friends or family and the social and political realities of the immediate and broader context within which the text of the entombed epitaph was written, displayed, and circulated.[20] Furthermore, prior to the inscription

---

17   *Gedächtnis ind Erinnerung: Ein interdisziplinäres Lexikon*, ed. Nicolas Pethes and Jens Ruchatz (Reinbek: Rowohlt, 2001), 520; translation from Erll, *Memory in Culture*, 83.

18   Scholars have long been aware of entombed epitaph's conventional use of these information slots. See for example Wang Xing 王行 (14th c.), *Selected Examples of Tomb Inscriptions* 墓銘舉例, in *Shike shiliao xinbian* 石刻史料新編, 3rd series (Taipei: Xin wenfeng, 1986), 40:65.

19   Note that for subjects who never held office, entombed epitaphs might focus instead on other aspects of their lives, such as their religious practices.

20   One way in which authors and families might mediate between the desired representation of the deceased and the immediate circumstances surrounding the composition of the entombed epitaph is demonstrated by the "Entombed Epitaph for Li Rao" 李饒墓誌銘. This text described the tumultuous details of the career of the husband of its deceased subject, Xue Dan 薛丹, narrating details that were earlier too politically sensitive for Xue Dan to include within his own self-authored entombed epitaph. See Lu Yang 陸揚, "Cong xinchu muzhi zailun jiu shiji chu Jian'nan Xichuan Liu Pi shijian ji qi xiangguan wenti" 從

of the text on the epitaph stone, family authorities would review the manuscript draft for factual or clerical errors as well as filling in any missing information.[21] In this regard, the "final" version of the entombed epitaph might be understood, to a limited extent, as the outcome of a collaborative production process.[22] Offerings, by contrast, from inception through composition were far more clearly the work of an individual author. Even in those rare cases when others were involved in the production process—as in Quan's offering for Zhang Jian, the content of which Quan "orally dictated" (*kou zhan* 口占) from his sickbed—the work nonetheless fundamentally represents itself as personal and individual, the outcome of the singular efforts of its author.[23]

As the above demonstrates, entombed epitaphs and offerings could differ dramatically in terms of their respective conventional sources, schemata, and production processes. Their authors drew upon, or at least discursively represented themselves as drawing upon, different sources of information during composition. They were moreover delimited in the informational "slots" they conventionally had available for use. Finally, these genres differed in the

---

新出墓誌再論九世紀初劍南西川劉闢事件及其相關問題, *Tang Yanjiu* 唐研究 17 (2011), 331-56.

21 For discussion of the degree to which families may have edited entombed epitaphs between initial composition and final engraving, see David McMullen, "Boats Moored and Unmoored: Reflections on the Dunhuang Manuscripts of Gao Shi's Verse," *Harvard Journal of Asiatic Studies* 73.1 (June 2013), 110-20.

22 Other ways in which entombed epitaphs might be understood of as collaborative, in addition to the above reasons, include works that are literally the work of multiple authors, as for example when one author is responsible for producing the prose portion of the entombed epitaph and the other the eulogy, or when a single entombed epitaph includes two separate eulogies written by different people. See Hu Kexian et al., *Kaogu faxian yu Tangdai wenxue yanjiu* 考古發現與唐代文學研究 (Hangzhou: Zhejiang daxue chubanshe, 2014), 48-9; Lu Yang 陸揚, "Shangguan wan'er he ta de zhizuozhe" 上官婉兒和她的製作者, in *Qingliu wenhua yu Tang diguo* 清流文化與唐帝國 (Beijing: Beijing daxue chubanshe, 2015), 264-82. On the collaborative aspect of text production, see also Robert Ashmore's essay in this volume.

23 I should note that I make this claim somewhat tentatively. I am thinking in particular of texts that were "ghost-written," as for example the "Sacrificial Prayer for Supernumerary Mu [Yuzhi 與直], Written on Behalf of Attendant Censor Cui [Su 愬]" 為崔侍御祭穆員外文 that was authored by Han Yu. Although the text must have been to some degree collaborative—it expresses the personal memories and feelings of Cui Su 崔愬 towards Mu Yuzhi 穆與直, memories that Cui likely communicated to Han Yu who then incorporated them into his text—it nonetheless still represents itself as the unique speaking voice of the subject's close friend addressing him in the first person. See *Han Yu wenji hui jiao jianzhu* 韓愈文集彙校箋注, ed. and annot. Liu Zhenlun 劉真倫 and Yue Zhen 岳珍 (Beijing: Zhonghua shuju, 2010), 12.1304-14.

degree to which their authors needed to accommodate others' agendas or rely upon collaboration during the production process. All of these factors further influenced how the memory of an individual might be constructed when using these genres.[24]

Audiences and Objectives

The audiences of entombed epitaphs and offerings overlapped to large extent, although there were a few significant differences. These differences were in large part related to material distinctions between the two genres. Entombed epitaphs existed in both manuscript (paper) and inscribed (stone) form. In manuscript form, they could address a broad and diverse audience, which included the immediate family and friends of the deceased as well a broader contemporary reading public who might acquire a copy of the entombed epitaph from family or friends of the deceased, the author, or other parties. Manuscripts of entombed epitaphs also addressed slightly later audiences: copies of entombed epitaphs were, at least in some cases, preserved within family archives. Authors of entombed epitaphs moreover typically kept copies for inclusion within their own collected works. As enduring stone objects located within tombs, entombed epitaphs also were understood as speaking to audiences who might encounter these tombs in the far distant future.[25]

The audience of the offering seems to have been more limited. Nominally addressed to the deceased, it would be "overheard" during its performance by other mourners present at the funeral where it was read out loud and then burned.[26] As with manuscript copies of the entombed epitaph however, offer-

---

24 Note that, as I will discuss in detail below, even when entombed epitaphs and offerings relied upon the same sources—as for example Quan's personal recollections of Zhang—or "filled" an identical informational slot—as for example Quan's description of Zhang's career—we find the ways in which that information might be framed or presented within these genres could differ dramatically.

25 The issue of how entombed epitaphs might speak to future readers is discussed in Shi Jie, "'My Tomb Will Be Opened in Eight Hundred Years': A New Way of Seeing the Afterlife in Six Dynasties China," *Harvard Journal of Asiatic Studies* 72.2 (2012): 217-57. Note that during the early medieval period, entombed epitaphs as objects also likely addressed denizens of the underworld. See Timothy B. Davis, *Entombed Epigraphy and Commemorative Culture in Early Medieval China* (Leiden and Boston: Brill, 2015), in particular, 138-41.

26 The earliest extant description of the performance of an offering is found in Sima Guang's 司馬光 (1019-86) *Sima shi shuyi* 司馬氏書儀, in which he describes the etiquette followed when a guest arrived to make a "condolence visit": "When a condoler entered, the mourners wailed; the condoler expressed his sympathy in formal language, then would move to the soul seat where he would make an offering of tea or wine and present an elegy (literally "sacrificial text"), which might be burnt after being read." See Patricia

ings could circulate among a broader audience—possibly a closed group of those who knew the author or the deceased or who were interested in the work of a particular author—or be preserved within the collected works of their author.[27]

"Objective" refers to the socially recognized communicative purposes of a genre. For the entombed epitaph, conventional objectives included the need to create an enduring record of the life of the deceased (*ji ren* 記人) and a durable marker for identifying the tomb occupant in perpetuity (*ji mu* 記墓).[28] These objectives were often, but not always, stated within the text of the entombed epitaph, albeit with greater or lesser degrees of explicitness. In his entombed epitaph for Zhang, Quan wrote that he had "highlighted what was significant and omitted what was insignificant [about Zhang's life] in order to eulogize him at the door of his tomb" 舉其大而略其細，銘諸墓門.[29] His text not only identifies its objective to construct the memory of Zhang's life and to locate that record within Zhang's tomb, but also points towards the selective manner in which that memory was constructed and his criteria for the content he included.

The objectives of the offering, by contrast, were primarily to communicate to the deceased—and to others who might otherwise "overhear" the text—an intimate sense of the loss and grief felt by an author in response to the death of the subject of his or her composition.[30] In his offering for Zhang we thus find

---

Ebrey, *Confucianism and Family Rituals in Imperial China: A Social History of Writing about Rites* (Princeton: Princeton University Press, 1991), 85, citing *Sima shi shuyi*, 9.55-57.

27   At least in the case of Quan Deyu, we know that his commemorative compositions did indeed circulate outside of their nominal communicative context. In a letter written earlier by Quan Deyu to Zhang Jian, Quan wrote about a string of recent deaths in his family. He stated that copies of the offerings he had written for his daughter-in-law, his father-in-law Cui Zao 崔造 (737-87), and for another son-in-law, as well as a copy of the entombed epitaph he had written for his own daughter were "appended at the end of this letter" 附於書末. See *QDYSWJ*, 2:630-31. Zhang's response to Quan's letter in turn expressed his praise for Quan's funerary compositions and shared some of his own memories of Cui Zao. See ibid., 2:631-33.

28   Let me note that I am not claiming that entombed epitaphs did not have other conventional objectives as well. Many scholars have catalogued how during their initial inception as a genre in the third and fourth centuries entombed epitaphs served to identify the tomb occupant to the afterworld and protect the sacred space of the tomb from hostile spirits. Entombed epitaphs continued to fulfill at least some of these functions during the Tang as well. See Davis, *Entombed Epigraphy*, 92-151.

29   *QDYSWJ*, 22.339.

30   I should note that I do not claim that offerings were unique in this regard. The writing of commemorative genres like dirges and laments seem to have similarly been motivated by

Quan identifying a very personal reason for writing his composition, namely so that he might "lodge heartfelt feelings in this composition" 寄懷斯文.[31]

As the discussion above demonstrates, genre could significantly impact how the memory of a subject might be constructed on several levels.[32] Choices regarding whether an author might speak from the position of family, friend, or colleague, whether the content of the composition was presented as personal memory or the conscientious reconstruction of a life based on multiple sources, and what kinds of information about the subject might be judged significant or irrelevant were all governed, at least in part, by the conventions of the genre used. Considerations of the audiences to whom compositions might speak and the objectives that they were intended to accomplish were similarly influenced by genre. Genre can thus be understood as playing a significant role in shaping how memory of individuals might be constructed.

Construction of Memory in an Entombed Epitaph and Offering

Closer examination of how Quan's entombed epitaph and offering structured and narrated an identical topic—Zhang's professional career—illustrates more specifically how genre could shape memory. I focus below in particular on three issues: how Quan's entombed epitaph and offering "emplotted" discrete episodes and information in constructing their respective narratives of Zhang's career, the degree to which those respective narratives differed in tone and rhetoric, and what broader significances these texts attributed to Zhang's life and career.

Emplotment

By emplotment, I refer to how the different bits and pieces of information that conventionally make up these genres are arranged to form their respective narratives. In this sense emplotment can be understood as closely tied to schemata: whereas schemata delimited the kinds of information, the "slots,"

---

the loss and grief felt by the author over the death of their subject. In some entombed epitaphs as well, in particular those produced by husbands for deceased wives, we see similar descriptions of the grief felt by an author over the death of the subject. In the case of those entombed epitaphs however, it seems that expressions of grief commonly are used to explain why *that* particular author had written the text rather than as the reason the text had been written in the first place.

31   *QDYSWJ*, 49.776.

32   On creating the posthumous image of a literary figure, see also pp. 97ff. and 255ff. in this volume.

conventionally included in a particular genre, emplotment can be understood as the ways in which those pieces of information might be sequenced within a composition in constructing the memory of the deceased.

Emplotment in Quan's entombed epitaph and offering for Zhang are very different. In the entombed epitaph, descriptions relating to Zhang's career recur across several parts of the text. Zhang's office and duties are first briefly mentioned in the opening section of the entombed epitaph as part of the description of what office he held and the duties he was discharging when he died. Following a brief narration of the career accomplishments of his great-grandfather, grandfather, and father, and Zhang's own early academic achievements—which included excelling at writing poetry by age seven, mastery of the works of the Grand Historian by age ten, and a commanding reputation by age twenty—, Quan then provides a succinct and chronological overview of Zhang's entire career, from his first recommendation for office through the appointment he held at time of death.[33] The majority of this section consists of listing the official appointments Zhang held during his lifetime but it also briefly mentions his having been "maligned by powerful sycophants" 為權幸者 所侵. The section immediately following this one in turn describes and assesses Zhang's performance as a historian, as a ritual specialist, and as an imperial envoy.[34] After a brief discussion of his personal character, Quan then again discusses Zhang's career, describing this time the cordial nature of his relationships with colleagues and some of his specific professional accomplishments.[35] Finally, more than half of the elegy that concludes the entombed epitaph lauds Zhang in terms of his performance in his various offices.[36] The narration of Zhang's career in the offering by contrast occurs in one large 36-line section of the text and is treated chronologically. It first discusses his service as a historian and as a ritual specialist, then describes his unfortunate encounter with "ruinous slander" (chanshuo 讒鑠), finally returning to recount his performance as an imperial envoy.[37] Despite the fact that both entombed epitaph and offering devote roughly one half of their respective narratives to information about Zhang's career—54% and 47% respectively—, the narrative sequence they follow in so doing differs dramatically. Whereas the entombed

---

33   This section totals 175 characters or approximately 18% of the entombed epitaph.

34   This section consists of 186 characters or approximately 19% of the total text.

35   This section totals 86 characters or 9% of the entire text combined.

36   This consists of 65 characters or approximately 7% of the entire text. In total, 512 characters or roughly 54% of the entombed epitaph treats Zhang's career.

37   These sections are 37 characters, 29 characters, 51 characters, and 54 characters in length respectively. In total, 171 characters or roughly 47% of the entire offering treat Zhang's career.

epitaph circles repeatedly back through Zhang's career—first listing his various titles, then listing his performance in different positions, and then providing specific examples of his accomplishments—, the offering treats it only once, narrating his career in a more or less chronological manner.

Quan's entombed epitaph and offering also differ in terms of the amount of space they use to narrate discrete episodes within Zhang's career. The most notable difference is Quan's description of Zhang's encounter with slander in his two texts. The incident in question, as recorded in the *Xin Tang shu* 新唐書, involved Zhang having submitted a memorial criticizing Pei Yanling 裴延齡 (728-96), a detested favorite in the court of Dezong 德宗 (r. 779-805). Pei slandered Zhang to the emperor, claiming that remonstrance officials were the ones responsible for critiquing shortcomings at court and not historians. Pei not only had Zhang removed from his position as a historian but also, when the opportunity presented itself, had him sent away from the capital, first to the Uighur empire and then, after Zhang's return, to the Turfan. It was while serving in his duties as an envoy to the Turfan that he died.[38]

In the entombed epitaph this episode is treated concisely in only six characters, "maligned by a powerful sycophant" 為權幸者所侵, and offered only as an explanation for why he was moved from his position as a Grand Master of Remonstrance of the Left (*zuo jianyi daifu* 左諫議大夫) to the position of Vice Director of the Palace Library (*bishu shaojian* 秘書少監).[39] In the offering, however, this incident was given much more narrative space, almost as much as used to describe Zhang's service as a historian or as a ritual specialist. Quan wrote:

終然違難，	Throughout your whole career you avoided difficulties,
皎潔貞厲，	Remaining pure and unsullied, holding steadfastly to the proper course.
狺狺權幸，	The yipping yaps of the powerful and favored—
惡厥中立，	Despised for your standing firm without bias.
一罹讒鑠，	From a single encounter with ruinous slander,
遂去清近，	You were then expelled from pure offices close to the emperor.
秘丘十年，	Sent far away for ten years,
不得自是。	[But] never becoming "one who considers himself right."[40]

---

38 See *Xin Tang shu* 新唐書, comp. Ouyang Xiu 歐陽修 and Song Qi 宋祁 (Beijing: Zhonghua shuju, 1975), 161.4981-82.

39 *QDYSWJ*, 336.

40 *QDYSWJ*, 776.

The different emphases placed on this episode in these two texts change the "plot" of Zhang's narrative. In the entombed epitaph, the "flattening" of this episode through concision and omission of any detail reduces its overall significance in the story of Zhang's career; it becomes simply information explaining his reappointment from one office to another. In the offering, by contrast, the "sharpening" of the details of this episode—the exaggerated contrast between a "pure and unsullied" protagonist "standing firm without bias" who is "subsequently expelled from pure offices"—presents the story of his career as analogous to those of righteous but wronged officials.[41] This example thus illustrates how accounts in different genres might relate similar episodes yet, through differences in the ways they are emplotted and the details they include, significantly alter the representation and perception of those episodes.

Tone and Rhetoric

In addition to their emplotment, Quan's entombed epitaph and offering also differed in terms of the tone and rhetoric they used to evaluate Zhang's performance in office and describe the significance of his achievements. In the entombed epitaph, Zhang's career and accomplishments are described by Quan in a relatively objective and precise manner: he mentions specific dates, titles, texts mastered, duties performed in an exemplary manner, and accomplishments or writings for which Zhang was especially renowned. In the offering by contrast Quan's descriptions are more subjective and non-specific; as in the earlier discussed example of Zhang's encounter with slander, there is no mention of dates, of parties involved, of specific actions or responses taken, nor is any attempt made to substantiate claims made or suggest that they were public knowledge.

---

41   In his "Narrative Psychology and Historical Consciousness," Donald Polkinghorne argues that when episodes are assembled into narratives, they often follow plots adapted from a culturally-available repertoire of stories. Narratives moreover "in contrast to life as lived, usually concerns a single major plot, incorporating only the subplots and events that contribute to that plot and selecting out all irrelevant happenings. In configuring a story of a life episode, narratives often omit details and condense parts ('flattening'), elaborate and exaggerate other parts ('sharpening'), and make parts more compact and consistent ('rationalization') to produce a coherent and understandable explanation." See Polkinghorne, "Narrative Psychology and Historical Consciousness: Relationships and Perspectives," in *Narration, Identity, and Historical Consciousness*, ed. Jürgen Straub (New York: Berghahn Books, 2005), 9.

This difference in terms of nominally more objective or subjective presentations of a subject's life is most clearly seen in how Quan offers evaluations of Zhang's performance in office during his career. In the entombed epitaph, evaluations of Zhang's performance as, respectively, a historian, a ritual specialist, and an imperial envoy are presented as reported speech. In serving as a historian, Quan wrote that Zhang "elucidated the praiseworthy and the censure deserving" 修明襃貶, such that "those who were aficionados of the ancient past proclaimed that the gentleman was judiciously concise yet forthright" 好古者謂君辨裁而直. Zhang's ability to resolve points of argument in the application of confusing ritual codes was such that "those who understood ritual proclaimed that he had an extensive understanding [of ritual] and possessed a sharp intellect" 知禮者謂之閎達而敏. Finally, Zhang's death in office while serving as an imperial envoy led "those who sighed with sorrow to proclaim the gentleman had spared no effort and was loyal" 感慨者謂君盡瘁而忠.[42] These opinions, Quan's entombed epitaph implies, are not Quan's; rather, they are proclamations made about Zhang by those qualified to render judgment upon him and merely quoted by Quan.

By contrast, in the concluding lines of sections that similarly describe Zhang's service as historian, ritual specialist, and imperial envoy in Quan's offering, the evaluation of Zhang's career is presented quite differently: "Can it not be said that you were a fine writer?" 可不謂文乎; "Can it not be said that you were erudite?" 可不謂學乎; "Can it not be said that you served your lord loyally?" 可不謂事君之忠乎.[43] Posed as a series of rhetorical questions, Quan's evaluations are both more subjective and open-ended, inviting a broader audience to confirm the truth of their implicit claims about Zhang.

As these examples illustrate, while both Quan's entombed epitaph and offering praise more or less the same aspects of Zhang's performance in his various offices—his classically concise writing, his broad erudition and fine mind, and his loyalty and service until death—they take dramatically different tones in presenting their evaluations, more objective in the entombed epitaph—dutifully recording the judgments of others— and more subjective in the offering—implicit claims phrased as rhetorical questions posed by the author to his audience.

Broader Significance of a Life

The differences in both entombed epitaph and offering in the way in which the narrative is emplotted and the tone and rhetoric used in narrating their

---

42   *QDYSWJ*, 338.

43   *QDYSWJ*, 776.

subject's life are intimately connected to the broader construction of the significance of that life.

In his entombed epitaph, Quan portrays Zhang as someone whose life was meaningful in terms of its broader social and historical contexts. He was descended from a prestigious lineage of accomplished men. He was a successful official who "altogether passed through ten positions, of which eight were ranked" 凡歷十官，而八在列 and who had "in addition three times held concurrent appointments, twice held concurrent temporary appointments, and once was given posthumous honors" 其他三帖職，二承攝，一追命. Finally, he was a man of "exceptional worth" 長者 who "quietly stored up knowledge in the mind" 默識,[44] whose ritual decisions were "considered to be [in accord with] the true meaning of the ancients and made into precedents" 稱典義而為故事,[45] and whose writings "had on their own become a recognizably unique style" 自成一家之言.[46]

In the offering, by contrast, Quan described Zhang as someone whose life was exemplary, significant in its realization of those ideals—fine writing, erudition, correctness, and loyalty—to which literati aspire both personally and professionally. In its opening lines, Quan's offering first relates these ideals to professional success and personal steadfastness:

士君子之所以暢其業者，文也、學也；	Those which enable scholar-gentlemen to flourish in their endeavors are fine writing and erudition.
士君子之所以植其本者，正也、忠也。	Those which enable scholar-gentlemen to firmly plant their roots are correctness and loyalty.[47]

---

44   In the entombed epitaph, the references to Zhang as both a "man of exceptional worth" and someone "who quietly stored up knowledge in the mind" are allusions. The first is a description of the local official Chen Ying in the "Basic Annals of Xiang Yu" 項羽本紀 in the *Records of the Historian* 史記: "Chen Ying had formerly been secretary to the district magistrate of Dongyang. He was unfailingly honest and circumspect in all his duties in the district and was known as a man of exceptional worth" 陳嬰者，故東陽令史，居縣中，素信謹，稱爲長者. See Burton Watson, *Records of the Grand Historian*, rev. ed. (Hong Kong and New York: Columbia University Press, 1993), 19. The latter alludes to the *Analects* 7/2: "The Master said, 'Quietly to store up knowledge in my mind, to learn without flagging, to teach without growing weary. For me there is nothing to these things.'" 子曰：默而識之，學而不厭，誨人不倦，何有於我哉. See Lau, *The Analects*, 57.

45   *QDYSWJ*, 338.

46   Ibid., 339.

47   Ibid., 776.

The subsequent narration of Zhang's career in the offering is in turn subordinated to this larger frame, with each discrete episode respectively exemplifying one of these ideals: his work as a historian exemplified fine writing; his work as a ritual specialist exemplified good scholarship; in being slandered he demonstrated correctness; and in his service as an imperial envoy he demonstrated loyalty. The offering also in part frames Zhang's life in terms of the close friendship he shared with Quan as well as the personal loss and grief that Quan felt at Zhang's death: the unfairness of his early demise, his reminiscence of good times shared, the sorrow he felt as "tears and mucus fall like rain" 涕洟如雨, and the realization that they will be "from this day forever parted" 今日永訣.[48]

The differences identified here between Quan's entombed epitaph and offering in how he emplotted his account of Zhang's career (recurring across several parts of the text versus narrated in a single chronological segment), the tone and rhetoric he used to frame his narration of discrete episodes (objective and specific versus subjective and non-specific), and the ways in which he shaped those respective narratives to serve broader arguments about the significance of Zhang's life (as historically and socially significant versus as exemplary of literati ideals) offer a concrete example of how writers adapted their compositions to serve the specific commemorative objectives of the genres they used. Quan's structuring of Zhang's career in his entombed epitaph corresponds with that genre's objective to produce an encomiastic yet trustworthy account of a life. Quan thus imbricates in detail and on multiple levels Zhang's successful performance in office and his many specific accomplishments in a way that, despite its strong praise, nonetheless comes across as objective and reliable. The offering on the other hand aimed to express an individual's sorrow over the death of its subject. Quan thus clearly communicates in his offering the personal grief and loss Zhang's passing engendered among those who knew him best. In addition, by arguing for the broader significance and worth of Zhang's life as exemplifying shared literati ideals as well, he demonstrates one way in which the mid-Tang offering might be adapted to serve a broader rhetorical purpose.[49]

---

48   Ibid., 776.

49   As Anna Shields has argued, "In the hands of the strongest mid-Tang writers, funerary texts did not merely praise or commemorate; they made claims about the meaning of a deceased person's life and served as platforms from which to advocate deeply-held beliefs, such as the importance of antiquity to the present or the need for fidelity in hardship." See Shields, "Words for the Dead and the Living: Innovations in the Mid-Tang "Prayer Text" (*Jiwen* 祭文)," *T'ang Studies* 25 (2007), 112.

Conclusion

As this examination of these two compositions by Quan Deyu has illustrated, entombed epitaphs and offering could differ dramatically in how they constructed the memories of their subjects. They could include different kinds of information about the deceased or, in places where they used the same kinds of information, emplot or frame it in narratively distinct ways. Finally, they could present different views on how their subjects' lives should be understood and why they were significant, as well as use their respective arguments to serve different commemorative objectives.

These differences stem, at least in part, from the conventions of their respective genres. Genre delimited who might appropriately speak about the dead and how, the kinds of information that authors might use to construct the memory of the deceased, the degree to which the author was responsible for acknowledging or engaging with other accounts or people in how they constructed their memories of their subjects, the arguments that conventionally might be made about a person's life, and the objectives that a text might be used to realize. In this regard, I would argue that the examination of these two compositions by Quan Deyu offers strong support for the broader thesis that genre plays a significant role in shaping the construction of memory.

I would add in conclusion two further methodological implications of this study of genre and memory. The first is that an author's choice to use a particular genre to commemorate a deceased individual represents in practice a choice regarding how the memory of the deceased would be constructed. Responding to the exigence of death with an entombed epitaph or an offering, a poem or a lament, meant deciding what kinds of information would be used to construct the memory of the subject, how that information would be presented and framed, what audiences would be addressed, and the objectives that the composition would be used to realize. In that sense, as latter-day readers of these texts, we need to be cognizant of how the genres we examine were practiced at the time when they were composed when we use them as sources for understanding the lives and events they record.

The second implication of this study is that in these compositions, in addition to subjects, genres shaped the construction of the memory of others as well, not least of all the author. As discussed earlier, an author's use of any genre necessitated that they assume the identity and voice appropriate for that genre. In the case of entombed epitaphs—in particular those like the one discussed above by Quan, written for an individual who had served in office—this involved describing and offering evaluations of the life of the deceased with a voice that was credible and could be trusted by contemporary and later readers. In the offering, by contrast, it involved speaking in the voice of someone whose sincere grief and sorrow were easily apparent to sympathetic contemporary and later readers. Recognizing how the conventions of these genres necessitated their being produced by "appropriate" speakers means questioning whether authors wrote in the voices they did because they *were* objective authorities or their subjects' friend, or because they needed to *represent* themselves as such in order to produce that genre. The former assumes identity as authentic whereas the latter recognizes it as constructed. As contemporary readers, we need always to be aware of this distinction as we rely upon these sources to make our arguments about the past.

Bibliography

Bawarshi, Anis S. and Mary Jo Reiff. *Genre: An Introduction to History, Theory, Research, and Pedagogy.* West Lafayette, IN: Parlor Press, 2010.

Bawarshi, Anis S. *Genre and the Invention of the Writer: Reconsidering the Place of Invention in Composition.* Logan: Utah State University Press, 2003.

Chuci bu zhu 楚辭補注. Compiled by Hong Xingzu 洪興組. Taipei: Tiangong shuju, 2000.

Davis, Timothy B. *Entombed Epigraphy and Commemorative Culture in Early Medieval China.* Leiden and Boston: Brill, 2015.

Ditter, Alexei. "The Commerce of Commemoration: Commissioned *Muzhiming* in the Mid- to Late-Tang." *Tang Studies* 32 (2014): 21-46.

Ebrey, Patricia. *Confucianism and Family Rituals in Imperial China: A Social History of Writing about Rites.* Princeton: Princeton University Press, 1991.

Erll, Astrid. *Memory in Culture.* Translated by Sara B. Young. New York: Palgrave Macmillan, 2011.

Han Yu wenji hui jiao jianzhu 韓愈文集彙校箋注. Edited and annotated by Liu Zhenlun 劉真倫 and Yue Zhen 岳珍. 7 vols. Beijing: Zhonghua shuju, 2010.

Hawkes, David. The *Songs of the South: An Ancient Chinese Anthology of Poems by Qu Yuan and Other Poets.* Harmondsworth and New York: Penguin Books, 1985.

Hu Kexian 胡可先, Meng Guodong 孟國棟, and Wu Xiahong 武曉紅. *Kaogu faxian yu Tangdai wenxue yanjiu* 考古發現與唐代文學研究. Hangzhou: Zhejiang daxue chubanshe, 2014.

Lau, D.C., trans. *The Analects.* 2nd ed. Hong Kong: Chinese University Press, 1992.

Lu Yang 陸揚. "Cong xinchu muzhi zailun jiu shiji chu Jian'nan Xichuan Liu Pi shijian ji qi xiangguan wenti" 從新出墓誌再論九世紀初劍南西川劉闢事件及其相關問題. *Tang Yanjiu* 唐研究, 17 (2011): 331-56.

Lu Yang, "Shangguan wan'er he ta de zhizuozhe" 上官婉兒和她的製作者. In *Qingliu wenhua yu Tang diguo* 清流文化與唐帝國. Beijing: Beijing daxue chubanshe, 2015.

McMullen, David. "Boats Moored and Unmoored: Reflections on the Dunhuang Manuscripts of Gao Shi's Verse." *Harvard Journal of Asiatic Studies* 73.1 (June 2013): 83-145.

Miller, Carolyn R. "Genre as Social Action." *Quarterly Journal of Speech* 70 (1984): 151-67.

Pethes, Nicolas and Jens Ruchatz, eds. *Gedächtnis ind Erinnerung: Ein interdisziplinäres Lexikon*. Reinbek: Rowohlt, 2001.

Polkinghorne, Donald. "Narrative Psychology and Historical Consciousness: Relationships and Perspectives." In *Narration, Identity, and Historical Consciousness*, edited by Jürgen Straub, 3-22. New York: Berghahn Books, 2005.

Quan Deyu shi wen ji 權德輿詩文集. Edited by Guo Guangwei 郭廣偉. 2 vols. Shanghai: Shanghai guji, 2009.

Shields, Anna. "Words for the Dead and the Living: Innovations in the Mid-Tang "Prayer Text" (*Jiwen* 祭文)." *T'ang Studies* 25 (2007): 111-45.

Shi Jie. "'My Tomb Will Be Opened in Eight Hundred Years': A New Way of Seeing the Afterlife in Six Dynasties China." *Harvard Journal of Asiatic Studies* 72.2 (2012): 217-57.

Wang Xing 王行. *Selected Examples of Tomb Inscriptions* 墓銘舉例. In *Shike shiliao xinbian* 石刻史料新編. 3rd series. 40 vols. Taipei: Xin wenfeng, 1986.

Watson, Burton. *Records of the Grand Historian*. Rev. ed. 2 vols. Hong Kong and New York: Columbia University Press, 1993.

Xin Tang shu 新唐書. Compiled by Ouyang Xiu 歐陽修 and Song Qi 宋祁. 20 vols. Beijing: Zhonghua shuju, 1975.

CHAPTER 8

Figments of Memory: "Xu Yunfeng" and the Invention of a Historical Moment

Sarah M. Allen

The value of the historical anecdote for remembering and understanding the past was a common trope in late medieval Chinese historiography.[1] Collecting anecdotes, and their use by historians, was justified by the notion that anecdotes preserve crucial information that might otherwise be lost. The historian and historiographer Liu Zhiji 劉知幾 included anecdotes in the category of "miscellaneous narrations" 雜述 that he deemed crucial to the historical enterprise, writing in his *Shitong* 史通 (early eighth century) that, "The responsibility of state historians is to record deeds and words, [but] what they see and hear is incomplete, and there are bound to be omissions. Thus gentlemen with an interest in the unusual fill in what they have missed…. These are what are called anecdotes" 國史之任，記事記言，視聽不該，必有遺逸，於是好奇之士，補其所亡…. 此之謂逸事者也.[2] Recorders of anecdotes justified their work in similar terms. In 834, for example, the statesman Li Deyu 李德裕 (787-850) presented a brief collection of anecdotes about the Tang dynasty emperor Xuanzong 玄宗 (r. 712-756) to Xuanzong's great-great-great-great-great grandson, the emperor Wenzong 文宗 (r. 827-840), with the explanation that "I fear that [this information] will be lost to transmission… and have carefully recorded it below to guard against the history officials' omissions" 懼失其傳… 謹

---

1   I have elsewhere discussed some of the same material under the broader rubrics "tale" and "story," but I use "anecdote" here to emphasize the purported historicity of the subset of materials with which I am concerned in this essay. Anecdotes may be transmitted orally or in writing. In this chapter I focus on written anecdotes, but assume that many of them had lives as oral anecdotes as well. For a discussion of the definition and scope of the English term "anecdote," see Lionel Gossman, "Anecdote and History," *History and Theory* 42.2 (May 2003): 143-68, especially 147-150. In Chinese, *yishi* 軼事 and *yishi* 逸事 have both been used to characterize this material, as in the following quotations from *Shitong* 史通.

2   Liu Zhiji, *Shitong tongshi* 史通通釋, ed. Pu Qilong 浦起龍 (Taipei: Yiwen yinshuguan, 1978), 10.248. Later in the same section he clarifies his conception further, writing, "Anecdotes are all what the former historians have missed and later people have recorded, seeking it [i.e., the added material] in alternative narratives, to increase the number of facts" 逸事者，皆前史所遺，後人所記，求諸異說，為益實多 (10.249).

錄如左，以備史官之闕云。[3] Such comments frame anecdotes and anecdote collections as a space for remembering past events that is explicitly contrasted with formal channels for the preservation of historical information, namely the History produced and reified by the state Historiographical Office 史館。[4]

Yet the very aspects that make anecdotes so important for preserving historical knowledge also render them suspect. The anecdote's capacity to supplement other historical accounts means conversely that the information they convey can never be fully verified. At best, an anecdote may represent an eyewitness's report on a personal experience, with all the attendant danger of misremembering inherent in human memory; at worst, it may be a fabrication. Most historical anecdotes probably lie somewhere in between, built upon a kernel of information with some historical truth whose precise dimensions are impossible to determine. Indeed, an anecdote's influence on our ideas about the past depends more upon its ability to persuade us of its plausibility—a capacity aided by the anecdote's narrative form—than on its actual historical accuracy. As James Fentress and Chris Wickham have observed, "a story is... a way of sequencing a set of images, through logical and semantic connections, into a shape which is, itself, easy to retain in memory.... The fact that we assimilate stories so readily, accepting them as representations of reality (even when we know that they are fictions), renders their function as containers of memories all but imperceptible."[5] The result is that though we recognize the genre's inherent potential unreliability, we may simultaneously buy easily into a given anecdote's claims, caught up by its narrative and the glimpse of events it provides. Thus Liu Zhiji concludes his discussion of the usefulness of anecdotes and other miscellaneous narratives with a reminder that historians must also

---

3   Tao Min 陶敏 et al., eds., *Quan Tang Wudai biji* 全唐五代筆記 (Xi'an: Sanqin chubanshe, 2012), 2:1006. Li Deyu's collection is most commonly known today under the title *Ci Liushi jiuwen* 次柳氏舊聞.

4   The Tang Historiographical Office was established in 629 at the direction of the second emperor, Taizong 太宗 (r. 626-49). See Denis Twitchett, *The Writing of Official History Under the T'ang* (Cambridge: Cambridge University Press, 1992), 13.

5   James Fentress and Chris Wickham, *Social Memory* (Oxford and Cambridge: Blackwell, 1992), 50-51. Ann Rigney makes a similar point in her work on the ways that the much larger-scale narratives of historical events found in historical novels shape readers' understanding of history, writing, "Stories 'stick.' They help make particular events memorable by figuring the past in a structured way that engages the sympathies of the reader or viewer" ("The Dynamics of Remembrance: Texts Between Monumentality and Morphing," in Astrid Erll and Ansgar Nünning, eds., *A Companion to Cultural Memory Studies* [Berlin and New York: Walter De Gruyter, 2010], 347; see also her "Portable Monuments: Literature, Cultural Memory, and the Case of Jeanie Deans," *Poetics Today* 25.2 [Summer 2004], especially 369, 371 and 381).

exercise discretion in using such materials, warning that, "The scholar is broad in his information: it's a matter of selecting from within it [i.e., that larger store of information], and that's all" 學者博聞，蓋在擇之而已.[6]

Anecdotes thus occupied an amorphous ground between the historical and the literary, defined on one hand by their claim to preserve crucial information that might otherwise be lost, and on the other by the possibility for the production of new "facts" that might appear reliable. These qualities are captured in Joel Fineman's comment—made in reference to Elizabethan England, but equally applicable to Tang dynasty China—that the anecdote "is the literary form... that uniquely refers to the real." Fineman's description of the anecdote as both "literary" and "directly pointed towards or rooted in the real" reflects both the claim that anecdotes make to represent events that really happened, and their generic capacity to privilege a good story, vividly conjured, over a strict adherence to confirmable facts.[7]

The anecdote's power to shape understanding of the past is nowhere clearer than in the accumulation of anecdotal material, over the course of the ninth century, about the reign of the Tang emperor Xuanzong 玄宗 (r. 712-756). Xuanzong's early years on the throne were conventionally regarded as model for good governance, but his reign came to an ignominious end due to the rebellion of his general An Lushan 安祿山 in 755. This story of descent from strength into tragedy—popularly blamed on his infatuation with his Prized Consort Yang 楊貴妃—made the emperor and his era objects of continual fascination in the decades and centuries after his death. Hundreds of poems, anecdotes, and longer accounts survive from the latter half of the Tang, both about Xuanzong himself and about the act of remembering his era.[8] And as

---

6   Liu Zhiji, *Shitong tongshi*, 10.251.

7   Fineman, "The History of the Anecdote: Fiction and Fiction," in H. Aram Veeser, ed., *The New Historicism* (New York and London: Routledge, 1989), 56, 57. Fineman suggests further that the anecdote's ability to produce that "reality effect" is tied to its limited scope and the fact that anecdotes are short narratives, not subsumed into a larger narrative or explanatory framework: "The anecdote produces the effect of the real, the occurrence of contingency, by establishing an event as an event within and yet without the framing context of historical successivity, i.e., it does so only in so far as its narration both comprises and refracts the narration it reports" (61).

8   Some of the most prominent anecdote collections giving significant attention to Xuanzong's reign include Li Zhao's 李肇 *Guoshi bu* 國史補, Li Su's 劉肅 *Da Tang xinyu* 大唐新語, Li Deyu's *Ci Liushi jiuwen*, Zheng Chuhui's 鄭處誨 *Minghuang zalu* 明皇雜錄, Zheng Qi's 鄭棨 *Kai-Tian chuanxin ji* 開天傳信記, and Wang Renyu's 王仁裕 *Kaiyuan Tianbao yishi* 開元天寶遺事. See Manling Luo's discussion of the latter four collections in "Remembering Kaiyuan and Tianbao: The Construction of Mosaic Memory in Medieval Historical Miscellanies,"

Paul W. Kroll has pointed out, rather than reaching a peak within the lifetimes of those who had lived through those events, the production of such works increased as the emperor's reign grew more distant.[9] Mid-eighth century writers such as Du Fu 杜甫 (712-770) or Wei Yingwu 韋應物 (ca. 737-ca. 792) who had lived through the end of Xuanzong's years on the throne could draw upon their own memories, but the evocative depictions found in the works of later writers such as Bai Juyi 白居易, born after Xuanzong's death, must have been built from "memories" learned through hearing and reading stories from others. That poems and narratives illuminating some detail of Xuanzong's story were still accumulating so long after the emperor's own life had ended indicates both the continuing allure of the period and the continuing production of new information to be collected. These in turn became fodder for how Xuanzong's era was remembered in later centuries.

One such "memory" whose impact on how Xuanzong's era is remembered and envisioned persists to this day is a scene of a group of child musicians performing for the emperor and his Prized Consort on her birthday. The perceived aptness of the young musicians as a representative symbol of Xuanzong's era can be seen in the fact that they are included in the account of Xuanzong's famous "Pear Garden" 梨園 musical troupe in the treatise on "Ritual and Music" 禮樂 in the Xin Tang shu 新唐書, where the group is described as follows:

> The Pear Garden Dharma division additionally established a junior division of thirty-odd musicians. When the emperor traveled to Mount Li, on Prized Consort Yang's birthday, he ordered the junior division to perform in Changsheng Hall, so they played a new tune which did not yet have a name. It happened that lychees were presented from the south, and so [the tune] was named "Fragrance of Lychees."

T'oung Pao 97 (2011): 263-300. Xuanzong's glories and follies were also a favorite topic in poetry of the ninth century. Paul W. Kroll counts over a hundred shi 詩 and fu 賦 on Xuanzong's reign and its destruction that survive from the late eighth century through the dynasty's end (in 907), and "nearly two dozen" anecdote collections that focus on the period ("Nostalgia and History in Mid-Ninth-Century Verse: Cheng Yü's Poem on 'The Chin-yang Gate,'" T'oung Pao 89 [2003], 288 and 290). For a brief discussion of how later ninth-century poetry treated the era, see Stephen Owen, The Late Tang: Chinese Poetry of the Mid-Ninth Century (Cambridge, MA: Harvard University Asia Center, 2006), 221-25. For a recent anthology of poems about the period, see Jin Jicang 靳極蒼, Changhen ge ji tong ticai shi xiangjie 長恨歌及同題材詩詳解 (Taiyuan: Shanxi guji chubanshe, 2002).

9   Kroll, "Nostalgia and History in Mid-Ninth-Century Verse," 299.

梨園法部，更置小部音聲三十餘人。帝幸驪山，楊貴妃生日，命小部
張樂長生殿，因奏新曲，未有名，會南方進荔枝，因名曰荔枝香.[10]

This passage is itself an anecdote in miniature, and yields valuable information about the membership, duties, and repertoire of one of the chief musical establishments of Xuanzong's court. The preservation of these details in the *Xin Tang shu*—through which they have come to the attention of historians—seems fortuitous, since they are attested in only a single surviving Tang anecdote, and all subsequent references derive either from that Tang text or the *Xin Tang shu*. That is, just as Liu Zhiji had advised, and Li Deyu hoped for his own anecdotes, information from an anecdote has been used to fill out the historical record.[11]

However, this scene of youthful musicians performing for the emperor and consort on her birthday almost certainly never occurred. Instead it appears to have been the invention of a late-ninth century writer, Yuan Jiao 袁郊. Yuan Jiao's collection *Ganze yao* 甘澤謠 was evidently the Song historians' source for the anecdote from which the passage quoted above derives, and is the lone extant Tang source today. In the original anecdote (of which the section borrowed by *Xin Tang shu* is only a short section), the scene is framed as a memory recounted by a survivor from Xuanzong's reign, one of the young musicians who was a member of the group. In that context, traces of the scene's invented-ness are left in conspicuous view for attentive readers to notice—in itself a feature that marks Yuan Jiao's collection as more "literary" than many others from the same period. But once unmoored from that context, Yuan Jiao's fabricated "facts" could take on a life of their own as new details in the larger picture of the past.

In this essay I will explore why this image was so compelling to later audiences, despite its evident spuriousness. The story of its construction and afterlife reveals Yuan Jiao's innovations as a writer of anecdotes, while also underscoring the power a striking anecdote can have to shape subsequent generations' memories of a past they lived too late to experience firsthand.

---

10   Ouyang Xiu 歐陽修 et al., *Xin Tang shu* (Beijing: Zhonghua shuju, 1975), 22.476. The "Dharma division" 法部 specialized in Central Asian-influenced music.

11   As for which historians' supposed omissions are being rectified here, the "junior troupe" is not referenced in the *Jiu Tang shu* 舊唐書 monograph on music: Denis Twitchett has shown that the monograph on music was based largely on the National History 國史 begun by Wei Shu 韋述 and others during the Kaiyuan period and further edited by Liu Fang 柳芳 and Yu Xiulie 于休烈 in the 750s and 760s ("A Note on the 'Monograph on Music' in *Chiu T'ang shu*," *Asia Major*, 3rd series, 1 [1990], especially 54-58 and 62).

Ganze yao and "Xu Yunfeng"

"Xu Yunfeng" 許雲封, the source of the scene of Xuanzong's youthful musicians, is the last of the eight (or nine) stories to comprise the brief late ninth century collection *Ganze yao*, assembled by Yuan Jiao in the 860s.[12] The events recounted in the collection span roughly 170 years, with the tale first taking place in the early sixth century, just before the founding of the Tang dynasty, and the last in the post-An Lushan rebellion period.[13] This range in itself is striking, especially in such a short collection, since typically a given collection will cluster multiple entries around a given temporal span. The dating of the various entries positions the collection as a whole as a reflection upon a substantial swath of Tang history—somewhat more than the first half of the dynasty, though Yuan Jiao could not have known that as he was writing. The impression that the collection is structured so as to provide a survey of early and mid-Tang history is heightened by the temporal settings of individual items at key moments in the dynasty's past, such as its founding, the reign of Empress Wu, the An Lushan Rebellion, and the post-rebellion period conflicts between central and regional governments.[14] In keeping with the nature of the historical anecdote collection as a genre, the stories touch on the larger histori-

---

12   The Song bibliographer Chen Zhensun 陳振孫 describes *Ganze yao* as containing nine
      entries and having a preface dated 868 in his *Zhizhai shulu jieti* 直齋書錄解題 (Shang-
      hai: Shanghai guiji chubanshe, 2015; 11.320). *Taiping guangji* 太平廣記 cites *Ganze yao* as
      the source for eight items. The collection is found in several Ming and Qing collectanea
      (including *Jindai mishu* 津逮秘書, 40.1a-24b; *Tang Song congshu* 唐宋叢書, 14.1a-21a;
      and Tao Zongyi's 陶宗儀 [*Chongbian*] *Shuofu* [重編] 說郛, 115.1a-21a). These latter edi-
      tions add "Nie Yinniang" 聶隱娘 (linked to another late ninth century collection, Pei
      Xing's 裴鉶 *Chuanqi* 傳奇, in some other sources) to the eight found in *Taiping guangji*
      to make up the total of nine tales; but some scholars, including Li Jianguo 李劍國, believe
      the attribution to be inaccurate. The various texts are very similar, but not identical, and
      it is possible that the collectanea texts may all have been at least partly reconstructed
      from *Taiping guangji*. See Li Jianguo, *Tang Wudai zhiguai chuanqi xulu* 唐五代志怪傳奇
      敘錄 (Tianjin: Nankai daxue chubanshe, 1998), 2:799-801. I have relied primarily on the
      text in *Congshu jicheng, chubian* 叢書集成初編, 2699 (Changsha: Shangwu yinshuguan,
      1939).

13   If "Nie Yinniang" belongs in *Ganze yao*, it would be the tale with the latest temporal set-
      ting, extending into the Kaicheng 開成 period (837-841). If "Nie Yinniang" is excluded,
      then the final story, chronologically (as well as in the present ordering of the collection) is
      "Xu Yunfeng," set in the late 780s.

14   Li Jun 李軍 has suggested that Yuan Jiao's family background and professional appoint-
      ments would have given him deep familiarity with history, even though he does not
      appear to have held a government position as a historian himself ("*Ganze yao* yu shiguan

cal context indirectly, giving us glimpses of peripheral people and occurrences that shed light on more momentous events.[15]

Though the larger arc of historical reflection found in *Ganze yao* is worth exploring in its own right, I will focus here on "Xu Yunfeng" because the "after-life" of the information within it brings into particularly sharp relief the question of how anecdotes influence our knowledge of the past. The "new information" in "Xu Yunfeng"—which I suspect to have been invented whole cloth by Yuan Jiao—succeeds because it closely resembles images of Xuanzong's era already present in contemporaneous social memory.[16] The intricate interweaving of the familiar and the new in "Xu Yunfeng" shows how easily historical knowledge can be manipulated, foregrounding the anecdote's capacity for not just preserving but also creating information.

---

wenhua guanxi lunlüe" 《甘澤謠》與史官文化關係論略, *The Northern Forum* 北方論叢, No. 230 [2011, No. 6], 99).

15   *Ganze yao*'s entries are longer than those in many—but not all—anecdote collections, and in modern Chinese literary historical terminology they are typically categorized as *chuanqi* 傳奇 ("transmitting the marvelous") rather than *biji* 筆記 or *biji xiaoshuo* 筆記小說, terms often used for shorter collections of historical anecdotes. But as the following discussion shows, *Ganze yao* is very much engaged in the same enterprise of recording stories about the past; the modern terms are anachronistic and do not reflect a contemporaneous sense of generic difference.

16   By "social memory" I mean the generalized, if amorphous and shifting, understanding of the past common within a social group. The wealth of recent work in the field of "memory studies" has resulted in a corresponding wealth of terminology used to differentiate types of memory, several of which (including "cultural memory") are potentially applicable to the case I am describing here. I have chosen to use "social memory" because it appears to be often used to refer to specifically to the formation of knowledge about large-scale historical events of public importance. Thus Geoffrey Cubitt defines social memory as "the process (or processes) through which a knowledge or awareness of past events or conditions is developed and sustained within human societies, and through which, therefore, individuals within those societies are given the sense of a past that extends beyond what they themselves personally remember" (Cubitt, *History and Memory* [Manchester and New York: Manchester University Press, 2007], 14-15); he gives a more detailed discussion in chapter 5, "Social Memory and the Collective Past" (especially 199-214). See also Fentress and Wickham's discussion in *Social Memory*, especially chapter 2, "The Ordering and Transmission of Social Memory." Rigney opts to use "cultural memory" to refer to closely related phenomena (Rigney, "Portable Monuments," 365). In the Tang case the "social group" was comprised at a minimum by the educated, literate, potentially office-holding men who also formed the social elite, and who told and recorded the anecdotes in question. It is likely that at least some of the social memories I discuss here were shared beyond that group, but our evidence is limited by the absence of much in the way of written records.

"Xu Yunfeng" recounts a meeting between the poet and official Wei Yingwu and a flute-player, the Xu Yunfeng of the title, at the beginning of the Zhenyuan 貞元 reign (785-805).[17] Xu Yunfeng tells Wei Yingwu that he learned to play the flute from his maternal grandfather, Li Mo 李謩, and recounts two incidents from his childhood during the emperor Xuanzong's Tianbao reign period. In the first, Xu Yunfeng receives his name from no less a literary luminary than the poet Li Bai 李白 (701-762). The second provides the scene of the group of young musicians, as Yunfeng recalls how he had played for the emperor Xuanzong and Prized Consort Yang in the summer of 755, just a few months before An Lushan rebelled. At the end of the tale Xu Yunfeng plays—and breaks—a flute that Wei Yingwu has in his possession, one that Wei Yingwu says came from Li Mo himself. In effect, "Xu Yunfeng" conjoins three separate anecdotes under the umbrella of Xu Yunfeng's meeting with Wei Yingwu, two of which are re-counted as personal experiences by Xu Yunfeng. The third takes place in the present interaction between the two men, but it too references the past in rec-reating a story told elsewhere about Xu Yunfeng's grandfather Li Mo (though this is not acknowledged in "Xu Yunfeng").

Xu Yunfeng himself does not appear elsewhere in the contemporaneous his-torical or anecdotal record. But his experiences are made plausible by the fa-miliar figures and scenes that populate the different segments of the narrative: Wei Yingwu, himself known for poems that look back at Xuanzong's Tianbao reign; Li Bai; Xuanzong and Consort Yang; even the flutist Li Mo. This in turn invites us to read "Xu Yunfeng" for its insights into these better-known histori-cal actors. Xu Yunfeng's first memory, of Li Bai, does not appear to have at-tracted the interest that the young musicians did: though the segment is included in full in a section devoted to "other records" 外記 about the poet in Wang Qi's 王琦 *Li Taibai quanji* 李太白全集, the poem Li Bai composes in the course of "Xu Yunfeng" is not integrated into Li Bai's other works within his collection.[18] Nor does Xu Yunfeng appear to have ever gained the retrospective renown of the flutist whose grandson he is said to have been. The Pear Garden junior division, however, lives on. Dissecting how each of these three incidents are constructed within the framework of ninth century social memory of

17   Wei Yingwu's birth has been dated to both ca. 733 and 737, and his death to ca. 792 or shortly after. See Tao Min 陶敏 and Wang Yousheng 王友盛, *Wei Yingwu ji jiaozhu* 韋應物集校注 (Shanghai: Shanghai guji chubanshe, 1998), 1 and 668; and Sun Wang 孫望, *Wei Yingwu shiji xinian jiaojian* 韋應物詩集繫年校箋 (Beijing: Zhonghua shuju, 2002), 1.

18   *Li Taibai quanji* (Beijing: Zhonghua shuju, 1977), 3:36.1619-1620. The poem, with a sum-mary of the alleged context of its composition, is also found in *Quan Tang shi* 全唐詩, but is relegated to a section gathering poems on "libel and riddles" 謗謎 rather than being found among Li Bai's other poems (Beijing: Zhonghua shuju, 1960; 25:877.9938-39).

Xuanzong's reign, and how a brief section of the longer narrative came to transcend its initial context, reveals both the sophistication of "Xu Yunfeng" as (quasi-) historical anecdote, and how a particular incident can become embedded in the stories people remember about a past they did not experience firsthand.

Xu Yunfeng's Memories

I turn first to the two stories about his own childhood that Xu Yunfeng recounts to Wei Yingwu. These segments, in which Xu Yunfeng narrates his memories, invest Xu Yunfeng with the authority of an eye-witness to Xuanzong's reign. Both provide vivid glimpses of ostensible events that conform with common depictions of figures and events from that period and so become plausible.[19]

The first incident, Yunfeng's naming by Li Bai at his grandfather Li Mo's request, is set at the very beginning of the Tianbao reign, when both Li Bai and Li Mo were traveling in Xuanzong's imperial entourage. Yunfeng describes the scene in detail:

> When the reign was changed to Tianbao, and I was just a month old, the imperial carriage stopped at Rencheng upon [the emperor's] return from performing sacrifices at the eastern [sacred peak, Mount Tai].[20] My grandfather heard I had just been born. He was delighted to see me, and carried me to see Academician Li Bai and asked him to give me a name. At the time, His Honor Li was sitting in a tavern, loudly ordering ale. The barkeeper Mr. Helan was over ninety years old, and invited Li to take his drinking upstairs. My grandfather presented him with ale, playing his flute loud and clear, and His Honor Li wielded his brush and drunkenly wrote on my chest:
>> Beneath the tree: who is that man?
>> he doesn't talk: the true me is fine.
>> If our talk lasts till midday,
>> in the mist thanking Chenbao.[21]

---

19   See Cubitt's discussion of how the use of "a familiar narrative mould" makes narratives plausible to their audience (*History and Memory*, 149; cf. also 161-65).

20   Rencheng was between Chang'an and Mount Tai. Xu Yunfeng had previously identified it as his native place.

21   My translation here is tentative: 陳寶 is the name of a minor god, but could also mean "arrayed treasures." Given Li Bai's explanation of the meaning of the line (see below), I

My grandfather protested, "I'd originally asked you to select a name, but now I don't understand a word of what you've written!"

His Honor Li said, "The name's right there within them. 'The man beneath the tree' 樹下人 is 'tree' 木 plus 'son' 子, which makes the character Li 李. 'Doesn't talk' 不語 is 'don't' 莫 plus 'speak' 言, which makes the character Mo 蕒. 'Fine' 好 is made up of 'daughter' 女 plus 'son' 子, and a daughter's son is a grandson through one's daughter. 'Talk lasting till midday' 語及日中 is 'speaking' 言 plus 'midday' 午, which makes the character Xu 許. 'In the mist thanking Chenbao' 煙霏謝陳寶 is 'clouds emerging during the sacrifice': that's 'cloudy' 雲 (yun) plus 'sacrifice' 封 (feng). Thus: 'Li Mo's grandson through his daughter: Xu Yunfeng.'"

Afterward I was duly given this name.

天寶改元。初生一月時。東封回駕。次至任城。外祖聞某初生。相見甚喜。乃抱詣李白學士。乞撰令名。李公方坐旗亭。高聲命酒。當壚賀蘭氏年且九十餘。邀李置飲於樓上。外祖高籛送酒。李公握筈醉書某胸前。樹下彼何人。不語真吾好。語若及日中。煙霏謝陳寶。外祖辭曰。本於李氏乞名。今不解所書之語。李公曰。此即名在其間也。樹下人是木子。木子李字也。不語是莫言。莫言譓也。好是女子。女子外孫也。語及日中。是言午。言午是許也。煙霏謝陳寶。是雲出封中。乃是雲封也。即李譓外生孫許雲封也。後遂名之.[22]

The vision of the poet at work occupies center stage. The scene is novel (the story is not found elsewhere), but also familiar in the pose in which it casts Li Bai as, in Du Fu's words, an "immortal in his cups" 酒中仙 who composes better drunk than sober.[23] The narrative arc parallels that of another story popular in the ninth century in which a drunken Li Bai is said to have received an unexpected summons from the emperor, but managed to rise to the occasion and dash off a perfect set of poems.[24] In "Xu Yunfeng" the stakes are lowered con-

---

have chosen to take the two characters as the former. In Li Fang 李昉 et al., comps., *Taiping guangji* (Beijing: Zhonghua shuju, 1961; 204.1554), *Li Taibai quanji* (36.1620), and *Quan Tang shi* (25:877.9938-39), 陳 is replaced by 成.

22   *Ganze yao*, 12.

23   Du Fu is ostensibly quoting Li Bai himself here. See "Song of Eight Immortals Drinking" 飲中八仙歌, in Du Fu, *Du shi xiangzhu* 杜詩詳注 (Taipei: Liren shuju, 1980), 1.83; and *The Poetry of Du Fu* (Boston and Berlin: Walter de Gruyter, 2016), 1:1.54-57.

24   The *Guoshi bu* version is fuller than most other versions but still short enough to quote in full:

      "When Li Bai was in the Hanlin Academy, he frequently drank to his heart's content. Xuanzong ordered him to compose some lyrics, but he was so drunk he couldn't stand.

siderably, but the tensions are the same: the poet's drunkenness and the seemingly nonsensical poem he produces initially suggest that he will fail in Li Mo's commission, until his explanation reveals that once again he has succeeded masterfully despite his inebriated state. With its vivid visual and aural details (the aged barkeeper, Li Mo's flute playing, Li Bai scribbling on the baby boy's chest), Xu Yunfeng's description of the circumstances of his naming confirms the image of the poet found in other sources. The critical reader might note that Yunfeng himself could not possibly recall this scene himself, as by his own account he was still an infant: if we are to take his account at face value, it must be a secondary memory of what others had told him about how he had been named. But the scene itself remains plausible within the context of contemporaneous representations of the poet.

The flutist Li Mo, while less prominent than Li Bai, is also found in lore about Xuanzong's reign in the ninth century. "Xu Yunfeng" tells us that Li Mo was a specialist in "Dharma tunes" 法曲 and a member of Xuanzong's famed Pear Garden troupe. Though he is not identified in precisely these terms elsewhere, Li Mo appears in multiple sources as an eighth century flutist of legendary skill. Two stories are told about him in the ninth century material that survives today. The first, found in poems by Yuan Zhen 元稹 and Zhang Hu 張祜, relates that Li Mo (not a Pear Garden performer in this scenario) overheard Xuanzong playing a new tune, memorized it on the spot, and later performed it himself in a bar.[25] In prose anecdotes, Li Mo is associated with a second

---

[Someone] splashed water on him, and then Li Bai was able to move a bit. With a wave of his brush he dashed off ten-odd pieces, his text needing not a jot of correction. 李白在翰林。多沈飲。玄宗令撰樂辭，醉不可待，以水沃之，白稍能動，索筆一揮數十章，文不加點 (Quan Tang Wudai biji, 1:802)."

The story is also found in Wang Dingbao's 王定保 Tang zhiyan 唐摭言 (Quan Tang Wudai biji, 4:2905), Meng Qi's 孟棨 Benshi shi 本事詩 (Quan Tang Wudai biji, 3:2385-86), and Wang Renyu's Kaiyuan Tianbao yishi (Quan Tang Wudai biji, 4:3174), as well as in Wei Hao's 魏顥 preface to Li Bai's collection (in Li Taibai quanji, 31.1449)—evidently written while Li Bai himself was still alive—and Li Bai's biographies in the Jiu Tang shu 舊唐書 (Liu Xu 劉昫 et al., Jiu Tang shu [Beijing: Zhonghua shuju, 1975], 190B.5053) and Xin Tang shu, 202.5763). Collectively these different accounts provide an array of slightly different details as to where Li Bai had been drinking, how exactly he managed to rally to his task, and what poems he produced.

25 See Yuan Zhen's "Song of Lianchang Palace" 連昌宮詞 and Zhang Hu's quatrain "Li Mo's Flute" 李謨笛. Both poems locate the incident in Luoyang, though Yuan Zhen's note to his poem identifies Li Mo as a "Chang'an youth" 長安少年. The notes also add the detail that Xuanzong himself overheard Li Mo playing and had him summoned to the palace the next day (for the poems, see Quan Tang shi, 12:419.4612-13 and 15:511.5839). The scene is expanded and transformed in Hong Sheng's 洪昇 eighteenth-century drama Changsheng

motif, in which his own flute shatters upon being played by or in accompaniment to a superior musician (a motif that, as noted above, is echoed in "Xu Yunfeng"). Li Mo's social status, connection to Xuanzong, and even his name—given as Li Mo 李謩 (or 謨), Li Mou 李牟, or Li Zimou 李子牟—all differ from source to source, as he is described variously as a performer at Xuanzong's court, a prince's son, or simply a consummate flutist.[26] "Xu Yunfeng's" account of Li Mo adds another layer to this palimpsest of shifting identifications, but is consistent with the other portrayals of him as the leading flutist of his day. In fact it is Li Mo's distinctive artistry that brings Wei Yingwu and Xu Yunfeng together and sets the stage for the recitation of memories that ensues: Wei Yingwu hears Xu Yunfeng playing and recognizes traces of Li Mo's style. Xu Yunfeng's first story thus adds further evidence to the repertoire of Li Bai's drunken antics (and a new poem) and clarifies Li Mo's identity by placing him in the Pear Garden troupe, as well as offering a glimpse of the extravagance of Xuanzong's imperial processions, with musicians and poets in tow.

----

      dian 長生殿, where the melody Li Mo overhears is none other than "Rainbow Skirts and Feather Coats" 霓裳羽衣曲. There the music is said to have been written by Prized Consort Yang (after a dreamed trip to the moon, where she hears it played) rather than Xuanzong, and Li Mo overhears the Pear Garden troupe rehearsing it (Hong Sheng, *Changsheng dian* [Beijing: Renmin wenxue chubanshe, 1958], scene 14: 71-77).

26   A *Guoshi bu* anecdote calls him (under the name Li Mou 李牟) simply "the best flute-player in the world" 吹笛天下第一 (*Quan Tang Wudai biji*, 1:847). In an account from Lu Zhao's 盧肇 *Yishi* 逸史, Li Mo is said to be a member of the Training Quarters 教坊, the other musical establishment at Xuanzong's court (*Taiping guangji*, 204.1553-54). One of two shorter anecdotes from Duan Anjie's 段安節 *Yuefu zalu* 樂府雜錄 (which postdates *Ganze yao*) also makes Li Mo a court performer, though it does not make explicit which troupe he belongs to (*Quan Tang Wudai biji*, 3.2473). In Xue Yongruo's 薛用弱 *Jiyi ji* 集異記, in contrast, he is identified as Li Zimou 李子牟, the seventh son of the Prince of Cai (*Taiping guangji*, 82.526). The Prince of Cai was Li Xian 李憲 (679-742; originally named Li Chengqi 李成器), Xuanzong's eldest brother; Li Xian was granted—but declined—the title of Prince of Cai in 705 and was himself said to be a skilled flute (笛) player (*Jiu Tang shu*, 95.3009; *Xin Tang shu*, 81.3596; Sima Guang, 司馬光, *Zizhi tongjian* 資治通鑑 [Beijing: Zhonghua shuju, 1956], 211.6701). That both "Li Mo" and "Li [Zi]mou" referenced the same figure is clear from the similarity in the stories told about each; see also the discussion in Li Jianguo, *Tang Wudai zhiguai chuanqi xulu*, 1:167-68. The pronunciations of the two characters do not appear to have been identical in the Tang, as they are not in modern Mandarin (Kroll gives "mjuw" for 牟 and "mu" for 謩; Paul W. Kroll, *Student's Dictionary of Classical and Medieval Chinese* [Leiden and Boston: Brill, 2015], 312 and 314). For convenience I will continue to use "Mo" here as this is how he is named in "Xu Yunfeng."

The second incident recounted by Xu Yunfeng shifts attention to Xuanzong's own doings, as seen through Yunfeng's eyes. Yunfeng reports that he had moved to Chang'an as a teenager after being orphaned, where his grandfather took him in and taught him to play the flute. This led to Yunfeng's own moment of glory playing for Xuanzong and Consort Yang. Yunfeng describes the circumstances under which the performance occurred:

> It came about that the Pear Garden Dharma Division established a junior division of musicians—altogether some thirty people, all under the age of fifteen *sui*. One day in the sixth month of the fourteenth year of the Tianbao reign period—at the time the imperial carriage was staying at Mount Li, and it was the Prized Consort's birthday—the emperor ordered the junior division musicians to play at Changsheng Hall, so we performed a new tune that didn't yet have a name.[27] It happened that lychees were presented from Nanhai, so the tune was named "Fragrance of Lychees." Everyone cheered, the sound stirring the mountains and valleys.
>
> That year An Lushan rebelled, and the imperial carriage returned to the capital. Afterwards we all met with chaos, and I wandered in Nanhai for nearly forty years.

值梨園法部。置小部音聲。凡三十餘人。皆十五以下。天寶十四載六
月日。時驪山趾蹕。是貴妃誕辰。上命小部音聲樂長生殿。仍奏新曲
未有名。會南海進荔枝。因以曲名荔枝香。左右歡呼。聲動山谷。
是年安祿山叛。車駕還京。自後俱逢離亂。漂流南海。近四十載。[28]

Like the first, this scene weaves together familiar lore about Xuanzong's reign. The Pear Garden troupe, also mentioned earlier in the tale in identifying Li Mo, was one of two musical institutions attached to Xuanzong's court. Established in the early years of Xuanzong's reign, the troupe figures in ninth century and later texts as a symbol of imperial pleasures once enjoyed and then irrevocably lost.[29] An anecdote in *Minghuang zalu*, for example, describes how during

---

27   The sixth month of Tianbao 14 was July 14 to August 11, 755 in the Gregorian calendar (see Liangqiannian Zhong-Xi li zhuanhuan 兩千年中西曆轉換 [Academia Sinica Computing Center 中央研究院計算中心, found at <http://sinocal.sinica.edu.tw/>], accessed March 23, 2017).

28   *Ganze yao*, 13.

29   Wang Pu 王溥, *Tang huiyao* 唐會要 (Beijing: Zhonghua shuju, 1955; 34.629), *Xin Tang shu* (22.476) and *Zizhi tongjian* (211.6694) date the founding of the Pear Garden troupe to 714 (Kaiyuan 2), as does *Minghuang zalu* (*Quan Tang Wudai biji*, 2:1031). For a detailed

the Tianbao reign, Xuanzong "ordered several hundred palace women to serve as Pear Garden Pupils, and they all lived in the Yichun north court.... When An Lushan came from Fanyang for an audience, he also presented several hundred pipes of white jade. [The pipes] were all distributed among the Pear Garden [players], and from this point [the troupe's] sound was practically not of this world" 上命宮女子數百人爲梨園弟子，皆居宜春北院。... 安祿山自范陽入觀，亦獻白玉簫管數百事，皆陳於梨園，自是音響殆不類人間。[30] In "Xu Yunfeng," the date of the junior troupe's performance—the sixth month of Tianbao 14, or mid-July to mid-August of 755—immediately brings to mind the events of the following fall, when An Lushan's rebellion brought about the end of Xuanzong's reign and the death of the Precious Consort whose birthday is being celebrated here. The location of the "junior division" performance at Mount Li in itself evokes the indulgence associated with the later years of Xuanzong's reign: Du Fu famously contrasts the extravagance enjoyed by courtiers accompanying Xuanzong to Mount Li with the privation suffered by ordinary people in "Going from the Capital to Fengxian County, Singing My Feelings (five hundred words)" 自京赴奉先縣詠懷五百字, and Zheng Yu's 鄭嵎 long mid-ninth century poem "Jinyang Gate" 津陽門 describes the luxuries of Xuanzong's Mount Li establishment in even greater detail.[31] Consort Yang's love of lychees, and the cost at which they were rushed to the capital region,

---

exploration of the surviving evidence on the origins and structure of the Pear Garden troupe, see Kishibe Shigeo 岸邊成雄, *Tōdai ongaku no rekishiteki kenkyū: gakusei hen* 唐代音樂の歷史的研究：樂制篇 (Tokyo: Tokyo University Press, 1960), 1:449-90, as well Zuo Hanlin's 左漢林 recent articles.

30   *Quan Tang Wudai biji*, 2:1035. Again Du Fu's poetry provides early references to the troupe; see "Writing My Feelings in Kui on an Autumn Day, Respectfully Sent to Director Zheng and Li, Adviser to the Heir Apparent: One Hundred Couplets" 秋日夔府詠懷奉寄鄭監李賓客一百韻 (*Du shi xiangzhu*, 19.1699-25; *Poetry of Du Fu*, 5:19.192-217 [the relevant line is on 19.1701 and 5:19.196-97]); and "On Seeing a Student of Mistress Gongsun Dance the 'Sword Dance'" 觀公孫大娘弟子舞劍器行 (*Du shi xiangzhu*, 20.1815-18; *Poetry of Du Fu*, 5:20.332-37). Bai Juyi is but one of many later poets to describe troupe members in "Encountering an Old Musician from the Tianbao Era in Jiangnan" 江南遇天寶樂叟 and "Pear Garden Pupil" 梨園弟子; see the brief discussion below (*Bai Juyi ji jianjiao* 白居易集箋校, ed. Zhu Jincheng 朱金城 [Shanghai: Shanghai guji chubanshe, 1988], 2:12.632-34 and 3:19.1300).

31   *Du shi xiangzhu*, 4.264-75; *Poetry of Du Fu*, 1:4.208-17. "Jinyang Gate" describes Zheng Yu's purported encounter with a former palace guard who had served Xuanzong, and consists mostly of the guard's recitation of his memories of that time (*Quan Tang shi*, 17:567.6561-66). Kroll translates and annotates Zheng Yu's entire poem in "Nostalgia and History in Mid-Ninth-Century Verse."

was also the stuff of legend.[32] Especially à propos here is the first of Du Mu's 杜牧 (803-52) quatrains "On Passing Huaqing Palace" 過華清宮, which describes Consort Yang awaiting a delivery of lychees there.[33] Yuan Jiao's tale combines these potent and evidently well-known motifs in the memorable image of the young musicians performing for the emperor and his consort, and adds further details: the existence of the "junior division" of the Pear Garden troupe, the summer concert at Changsheng Hall 長生殿, and that among the music to come from Xuanzong's court was a piece known as "Fragrance of Lychees" 荔枝香.

Xu Yunfeng's status as a junior Pear Garden flutist further links his present meeting with Wei Yingwu to the popular topos of the encounter with a lesser member of Xuanzong's entourage, found in both poems and anecdotes from the eighth and ninth centuries. Such encounters stage opportunities for expressing sorrow about the changes wrought in the aftermath of the An Lushan rebellion and/or for the transmission of information about doings at court in years past. Many feature musicians who once performed for Xuanzong, again calling to mind the vision of a pleasure-filled past that contrasts sharply with the musician's circumstances in the present. Du Fu again provides an early example in his quatrain "Meeting Li Guinian in Jiangnan" 江南逢李龜年, in which the poet runs into the once-prominent musician in the rebellion's aftermath.[34] The poet recalls pre-rebellion encounters with the musician and comments on the Jiangnan scenery, leaving the contrast between past and present an unstated but looming presence in the poem. Du Fu's image of the former imperial musician fallen on less fortunate times is fleshed out in the same anecdote from *Minghuang zalu* quoted above, which ends by recounting that after the rebellion, Li Guinian "wandered destitute in Jiangnan. Whenever he encountered lovely scenes in fine weather, he would always sing a few songs for people. Guests hearing him would all cover their faces and weep, putting aside their wine" 流落江南，每遇良辰勝景，常爲人歌數闋，座客聞之，莫不掩泣罷酒.[35] Bai Juyi's "Encountering an Old Musician from the Tianbao Era in Jiangnan" narrates a similar story about an unnamed pipa player in the Pear

---

32   See Du Fu's "Twelve Poems Dispelling Glumness" 解悶十二首 (*Du shi xiangzhu*, 17.1511-19; *Poetry of Du Fu*, 4:17.368-75). *Guoshi bu* notes the superiority of Nanhai lychees and the need for prompt delivery (*Quan Tang Wudai biji*, 1:805). An anecdote tentatively linked to *Kaiyuan Tianbao yishi* claims that both men and horses died in the rush to deliver the lychees, causing resentment among the people (*Quan Tang Wudai biji*, 4:3178).

33   *Quan Tang shi*, 16:521.5954.

34   *Du shi xiangzhu*, 23.2060-61; *Poetry of Du Fu*, 6:23.192-93.

35   *Quan Tang Wudai biji*, 2:1035-36. The *Taiping guangji* text of the anecdote appends Du Fu's poem (*Taiping guangji*, 204.1549).

Garden troupe. Like Xu Yunfeng, the old man had played "Dharma tunes" and accompanied the emperor to the hot springs on Mount Li in years past, only to fall into a life of drifting in the south after the rebellion.[36]

"Xu Yunfeng'" echoes Chen Hong(zu)'s 陳鴻(祖) prose account "The Old Man of the Eastern Wall" 東城老父傳, a longer account, particularly closely.[37] Like Xu Yunfeng, the titular "old man" Jia Chang 賈昌 owes his service to Xuanzong to an older family member, his father.[38] Both stories locate important plotpoints during expeditions undertaken by Xuanzong to perform sacrifices at the eastern sacred mountain Mount Tai, though in "Eastern Wall" this is the death of Jia Chang's father, whereas "Xu Yunfeng" replaces death with birth when Li Mo's journey brings him the opportunity to see his newborn grandson for the first time. Moreover, both Jia Chang and Xu Yunfeng are said to have been born with one of Xuanzong's major reign periods, Jia Chang at the very beginning of the Kaiyuan era (conventionally the most successful period of Xuanzong's rule) and Xu Yunfeng in the first year of the Tianbao reign (the period of his decline).[39] Jia Chang is even said to be married to a daughter of a member of the Pear Garden troupe. "Xu Yunfeng" adds an extra layer of distance from Yunfeng's story, identifying Wei Yingwu as his interlocutor but not as the recorder his story (arguably necessary for a story written over a century after Xuanzong's own death), but it mimics the framework of "Eastern Wall" in which an encounter with a survivor is used as a structural device allowing for eye-witness accounts of the era.

All of these figures are relicts of a happier past, and they are portrayed as still belonging more to that past than to the present. Their interest to the poet or anecdotist lies in their link to and memories of the Kaiyuan or Tianbao eras rather than to their experiences since. Xu Yunfeng's accounts of his childhood

---

36   *Bai Juyi ji jianjiao*, 2:12.632-34; see also Bai's "Pear Garden Pupil," describing an elderly performer who cries at the memory of imperial favor received in the past (3:19.1300).

37   See *Taiping guangji*, 485.3992-95, as well as Robert Joe Cutter's translation and analysis in his "History and 'The Old Man of the Eastern Wall,'" *Journal of the American Oriental Society* 106 (1986): 503-528. For discussion of the uncertainty of the name of the recorder of "Old Man of the Eastern Wall," see Li Jianguo, *Tang Wudai zhiguai chuanqi xulu*, 1:345-46; and Cutter, 503-4. Zheng Yu's "Jinyang Gate" and Yuan Zhen's "Song of Lianchang Palace" adopt a similar narrative framework in ostensibly describing encounters with men who had formerly served Xuanzong in some capacity. As Kroll notes, Zheng Yu's informant would have had to be at least 110 when the encounter occurred ("Nostalgia and History in Mid-Ninth-Century Verse," 293).

38   Jia Chang is not a musician, however, but rather Xuanzong's gamecock trainer.

39   Cutter notes that Jia Chang was "born with the [Kaiyuan] reign" between December 22, 713 (the first day of the Kaiyuan reign) and January 20, 714 (Cutter, 508 n. 37).

encounters with both poet and emperor likewise offer glimpses of a different, and fabled, age. It is his past—embodied in the flute-playing that so strongly echoes his grandfather's—that brings him to Wei Yingwu's attention, and causes the poet to "sigh for a long time" 嗟嘆久之 even before he has ascertained who Xu Yunfeng is.[40] That Yunfeng tells Wei Yingwu nothing of what has happened to him in the years since the outbreak of the rebellion (beyond the brief reference to "wandering in Nanhai for close to forty years") suggests that like these other performers, Xu Yunfeng's life remains centered in his past.

My claim is not that Yuan Jiao methodically assembled Xu Yunfeng's story out of the particular items I have referenced here—it is impossible to know at this remove what of these or other oral or written sources he may have encountered—but that he used topoi prominent in contemporaneous social memory of Xuanzong's reign to create scenes that both accord with and expand upon prevalent understandings of that era. The aggregation of other sources leave little question that the images of a drunken Li Bai and of Xuanzong enjoying musical performances and other pleasures in the company of Consort Yang were familiar fare in the mid-ninth century—as indeed they still are today— and that a meeting with a survivor from Xuanzong's day was a favored device to create a platform for reflecting upon that age.[41] "Xu Yunfeng" offers further evidence for both of these points in the form of another drunken poem from Li Bai and another scene of Xuanzong's untimely enjoyment of music, in two incidents that bracket the ill-fated Tianbao reign period. Except for his use of the first-person pronoun "I" 某 and the reference to "my grandfather" 外祖 in his first anecdote, neither of the scenes Xu Yunfeng describes would be out of place as individual items within a collection of anecdotes about Xuanzong's reign.

For all the vividness, and aptness, of the scenes Yuan Jiao sketches, however, it is quite likely that none of the events in Xu Yunfeng's stories actually occurred as described. Xu Yunfeng himself is not attested, beyond the *Ganze yao* tale, until the mid-tenth century, when the Southern Tang poet and official Li Zhong 李中 invokes his name in a quatrain entitled "The Fluteplayer" 吹笛兒.[42]

---

40 *Ganze yao*, 12.

41 To this we might add that the poem embedded in the first incident, not preserved elsewhere, also links it to innumerable anecdotes from the ninth century purporting to give the back-story to particular poems, found in Meng Qi's *Benshi shi* and Fan Shu's 范攄 *Yunxi youyi* 雲谿友議, but also within other collections not exclusively devoted to explaining poems.

42 The second couplet of Li Zhong's poem reads, "Seeing you playing a tune before your goblet/makes me recall Xu Yunfeng once more" 見爾樽前吹一曲，令人重憶許雲封; a note explains "Yunfeng was a skilled flute-player in the Kaiyuan reign period" 雲封開元

The reference is sparse enough that it could easily derive from the tale. I have found no other mentions of Li Bai having accompanied Xuanzong on any journey further than Mount Li during his brief stint as a member of the emperor's court, nor does a story about his naming of a baby in a riddling poem appear in any surviving text that does not derive directly from "Xu Yunfeng."[43] Perhaps more surprisingly given its standing in later texts, the "junior division" of the Pear Garden troupe is also not referenced in other surviving earlier or contemporaneous sources. And we know just enough about Wei Yingwu's career to know that he did not hold the posts "Xu Yunfeng" credits him with.[44]

Individually, such discrepancies are not surprising: anecdotes are not well-researched history, and a given anecdote is as likely to report "facts" contradicted elsewhere—whether in other anecdotes, the state histories, or other materials—as not. Nor does the absence of corroboration prove decisively that these events did *not* occur or (more to the point) that they were not rumored to have occurred. But the amount of otherwise unsupported information is unusual for the corpus as a whole.

We can say with even more confidence that neither incident, whatever its basis or lack thereof, occurred in the time and place where Xu Yunfeng sets them. Each, as we have seen, is tied to Xuanzong's own presence in its respective locale: the sacrificial expedition to Mount Tai provides Li Mo with the opportunity to ask Li Bai to name his grandson, and the birthday celebration for Consort Yang at Mount Li occasions the junior troupe's performance. But

---

善笛者 (*Quan Tang shi*, 21:749.8537). The Southern Song *leishu Hailu suishi* 海錄碎事, compiled by Ye Tinggui 葉廷珪, cites the couplet but reads "meeting" 逢 instead of "seeing" in the first line (Beijing: Zhonghua shuju, 2002; 16.789). Yuan Jiao of course places Xu Yunfeng in the Tianbao era, but this discrepancy tells us only that Li Zhong, writing a century or so later, associated Xu with Xuanzong's earlier reign, and does not in itself preclude Yuan Jiao's fabrication of Xu and his stories.

43   Neither the biographical information in *Li Taibai quanji* (see the yearly chronology appended to the collection in *juan* 35, especially 35.1584-90) nor the more diverse lore preserved in *Li Bai ziliao huibian: Tang Song zhi bu* 李白資料彙編：唐宋之部 (ed. Jin Taosheng 金濤聲 and Zhu Wencai 朱文彩; Beijing: Zhonghua shuju, 2007) include incidents in this mode.

44   In the tale, Wei Yingwu is said to meet Xu Yunfeng while en route from the capital, where he had held the post of Gentleman Attendant in the Orchid Pavilion (that is, the Palace Library), to a new post as prefect of Hezhou 和州. The historical Wei Yingwu did get transferred from a capital post to a provincial post as a prefect in 788—arguably within the scope of the "early Zhenyuan" date for the alleged meeting with Xu Yunfeng—but a different capital post (Bureau Director of the Left Office of the Department of State Affairs) and prefecture (Suzhou 蘇州). See Tao Min and Wang Yousheng, *Wei Yingwu ji jiaozhu*, 666-67.

Xuanzong's own movements as emperor are recorded in some detail in his Basic Annals 本紀 in the *Jiu Tang shu*, and we can check "Xu Yunfeng's" claims about when the emperor was where against that record. Neither is supported by the ample evidence.[45]

On one hand, these discrepancies remind us anew that anecdotes, and literary representation, are not reliable sources of historical information. They offer impressionistic truths rather than historically verifiable ones, and while historically-minded readers may take issue with their inaccuracies, such quibbles are arguably beside the point. On the other hand, however, the aggregation within one account of the degree of unsupported and mis-information that we find in "Xu Yunfeng" is unusual. It suggests that Yuan Jiao may have invented much of "Xu Yunfeng" (rather than elaborating on kernels of

---

45 "Xu Yunfeng" dates Xuanzong's sacrifices at Mount Tai to the change in the reign name (to Tianbao) in 742. But Xuanzong's only sacrifice at Mount Tai was made much earlier, in 725, in the thirteenth year of the Kaiyuan reign (*Jiu Tang shu*, 23.891-904; *Xin Tang shu*, 14.352-53)—a date that *is* accurately reflected in "The Old Man of the Eastern Wall." Nor do the Basic Annals record a trip to Mount Li in the sixth month of Tianbao 14, though other visits to his Huaqing Palace on the mountain are noted—including from November 14-December 30, 755 (i.e., Tianbao 14), during which period An Lushan began his revolt (*Jiu Tang shu*, 9.230). Instead Xuanzong's trips to Mount Li were typically made in winter, to take advantage of the hot springs there. The only recorded visit to Mount Li that did not occur between the tenth and first months (roughly November through January or February) was in the fourth month of Tianbao 8 (April 22–May 20, 749; *Jiu Tang shu*, 9. 223). At the same time, the notion that Xuanzong traveled to Mount Li during the summer appears to have been prevalent during the ninth century. I noted above that Du Mu's quatrain "On Passing Huaqing Palace" describes Prized Consort Yang anticipating a delivery of lychees on Mount Li; as Fan Zhengmin 范正敏 noted in the early twelfth century, this puts the consort on the mountain during the summer months, when lychees ripened. Likewise in Bai Juyi's "Song of Endless Sorrow" 長恨歌, Consort Yang recalls the vows of eternal devotion she and the emperor exchanged, in Changsheng Hall on Mount Li, on the seventh day of the seventh month (which fell in high summer, between July 29 and August 24, for all the years of the Tianbao reign period). In placing Xuanzong on Mount Li in the sixth month, "Xu Yunfeng" thus both hints at its historical unreliability and repeats current lore. See Fan Zhengmin (sometimes given as Chen Zhengmin 陳正敏), *Dunzhai xianlan* 遯齋閒覽, in Tao Zongyi, [*Chongbian*] *Shuofu*, 1646); digitized by the Harvard College Library/Harvard-Yenching Library and found at <https://iiif.lib.harvard.edu/manifests/view/drs:42849611$1i , 27.2a-2b>; and Li Fang 李昉 et al., comps., *Wenyuan yinghua* 文苑英華 (Taipei: Dahua shuju, 1985), 346.812, as well as *Bai Juyi ji jianjiao*, 2:12.661. For the dating of the seventh day of the seventh month in Tianbao, see Liangqiannian Zhong-Xi li zhuanhuan, accessed March 23, 2017. An anecdote in Wang Renyu's *Kaiyuan Tianbao yishi* also locates the couple at Huaqing Palace on the seventh of the seventh month (in this case describing it as a yearly affair; *Quan Tang Wudai biji*, 4:3166-67).

inherited information as I have argued elsewhere was more common), and that he may have deliberately included pointers hinting that Xu Yunfeng's stories might be suspect, as a knowing wink to astute readers.[46]

The Shattered Flute

I turn now to the third incident contained beneath the narrative umbrella of "Xu Yunfeng." Rather than recounting (purported) past events, this third segment unfolds in the present of Wei Yingwu's encounter with Xu Yunfeng. And in contrast to Xu Yunfeng's two recollections, which echo existing lore but do not appear to build from any single event, this third incident is more pointed in its appropriation of a particular incident whose frequent appearance in the anecdotal record suggests that it was well-known in the mid- and late ninth century. This is the story about Li Mo mentioned above, in which the flutist's instrument is shattered upon encountering a superior musician. The story survives today in no less than five separate versions from the ninth century, the earliest dating to the 820s (in *Guoshi bu* and *Jiyi ji*), and the latest to the last decades of the ninth century (two separate versions preserved in Duan Anjie's 段安節 *Yuefu zalu* 樂府雜錄).[47] In one version, in *Yuefu zalu*, the flute splits when Xuanzong orders Li Mo to play with a renowned singer, as a result of the singer's skill.[48] The four others (including the second from *Yuefu zalu*) feature a mysterious stranger who borrows Li Mo's flute and destroys it after playing it only briefly, proving him to be a musician of unearthly skill far surpassing Li Mo's own.[49]

The details of the story vary from source to source: I noted above that Li Mo's identity and even his name vary, as do the dating and location of the events. The *Yishi* version, for example, dates Li Mo to the Kaiyuan period and

---

46   Though I do not have space in this chapter to examine the seven or eight other *Ganze yao* accounts, it is worth noting that they also exhibit a combination of unique "facts" built upon inherited information similar to what we find in "Xu Yunfeng," further supporting the notion that Yuan Jiao was deliberately playing with his readers' expectations in crafting pseudo-historical anecdotes.

47   Li Jianguo and Li Yifei 李一飛, the editor for *Guoshi bu* in the *Quan Tang Wudai biji*, both suggest that the story ultimately derives (directly or indirectly) from an account written by Li Zhou 李舟 (739-87), who is said in the *Guoshi bu* anecdote to have given Li Mo his flute and to have made a record of the encounter with the strange old man (Li Jianguo, 1:167-68; the *Guoshi bu* reference is in *Quan Tang Wudai biji*, 1:847).

48   *Yuefu zalu*, in *Quan Tang Wudai biji*, 3:2473.

49   Ibid., 3:2480.

places the incident in Yuezhou 越州, whereas the second *Yuefu zalu* anecdote dates it to the post-rebellion period, while also giving the location as Yuezhou; *Jiyi ji* does not give a date for the events, but situates them in Jiangling 江陵.[50] In all four the implication is that the flute-playing stranger is not of this world, made explicit in the *Guoshi bu* version, which concludes with the comment that witnesses "suspected that he might be a dragon" 疑其蛟龍也.[51] These anecdotes display the variation typical of their kind: the similarities in narrative that allows us to call them versions of "the same" story, the discrepancies in dating and location and names that speak to the fluidity of a story transmitted and embellished as hearsay, and the occasional detail that can be confirmed through other sources, lending the narrative an aura of reliability that may or may not reflect some actual historical basis for the events at hand. The overlap and differences among them suggest both that the story circulated widely in the ninth century, and that the particular details remained unstable.

In "Xu Yunfeng," this scene of the flute being split by the skilled player is re-enacted with Wei Yingwu providing the flute and Xu Yunfeng assuming the role of the superlative player whose playing destroys Li Mo's flute. The scene is close enough to the story of Li Mo's flute being shattered by the mysterious stranger to be unmistakably referential, but it alters the narrative in ways that change its significance and its message about Li Mo. After hearing Xu Yunfeng's two stories of his past, Wei Yingwu reveals that he too can claim an indirect connection to Li Mo: his wetnurse's son (now dead) had studied the flute with Li Mo, and Wei has in his possession the student's flute, which Li Mo himself had given the young man. Xu Yunfeng examines the flute and tells Wei Yingwu that it cannot be one that his grandfather would have played himself, because the bamboo was cut out of season.[52] The result is a flute with limitations that would not be detected by the ordinary player; but, "If [the flute] were to meet a consummate musician," he tells Wei Yingwu, "it would be sure to shatter. This is how I know that it was not one that was played by my grandfather" 遇至音必破。所以知非外祖所吹者.[53] Wei Yingwu invites Xu Yunfeng to put the flute to the test, and indeed the flute breaks, showing that Yunfeng himself is just such a consummate musician:

---

50 *Yishi's* "Li Mo" and *Jiyi ji's* "Li Zimou" are both found in *Taiping guangji*, in 204.1553-54 and 82.526, respectively. For the second *Yuefu zalu* anecdote, see *Quan Tang Wudai biji*, 3:2480.

51 *Quan Tang Wudai biji*, 1:847.

52 At this juncture Xu Yunfeng gives a lengthy disquisition on the selection of bamboo for flutes.

53 *Ganze yao*, 13.

Yunfeng then raised up the flute, and played the "Six Prefectures" tune. Before he had finished a single stanza, hwack! it split down the middle.

Wei sighed in astonishment for a long time. Subsequently he recommended Yunfeng for the Music Office.

雲封乃奉篴吹六州遍。一疊未盡。騞然中裂。韋公驚歎久之。遂禮雲封於曲部.[54]

Though there is no hint in "Xu Yunfeng" itself that this moment is an echo of existing stories about Li Mo, the allusion is unmistakable. It is still "Li Mo's flute," transferred to Wei Yingwu's possession through his wetnurse's son, that is shattered, while Xu Yunfeng plays the role of the mysterious stranger. But with the shift of the identity of the flutist, the incident of the shattering flute gains new meaning. Within the narrative space of "Xu Yunfeng" itself, the split flute demonstrates Xu Yunfeng's own skill and the truth of his claim to be Li Mo's heir. Read in reference to the stories about Li Mo, however, the *Ganze yao* tale responds to, and reverses, their lesson. Though Li Mo himself appears in the tale only in Xu Yunfeng's and Wei Yingwu's memories, Xu's pronouncement that Wei Yingwu's flute could never have been played by his grandfather asserts that Li Mo *was* a superior player, who would have cracked the flute had he played it—in contrast to the other anecdotes, which show his playing trumped by the other musician. The event that proves Li Mo's imperfection in the earlier tales is transformed into yet another example of the mythic splendor of Xuanzong's age, when Xuanzong's flute-players were out of this world. But only the reader who knows the more common versions of the shattered-flute story will recognize its significance here.

It is this unmistakable but unacknowledged manipulation of an existing story that inclines me to think that Yuan Jiao's "mistakes" regarding the timing of Xuanzong's expeditions to Mount Tai and the Mount Li hot springs may also be knowing winks to an alert reader, rather than unintended slips. But the reader needs to recognize these clues—the subtle variations on current stories, the historical errors, the shattering flute—to understand the joke that signals Yuan Jiao's technique. The uninitiated reader will read the three anecdotes contained within the tale at face value.[55] As time passed and Tang gossip passed out of living social memory, readers in the know were increasingly

---

54   Ibid. Here following Li Jun's suggestion that 禮 means "to recommend"; Li Jun, Ganze yao *pingzhu* 《甘澤謠》評注 (Beijing: Zhongguo shehui kexueyuan chubanshe, 2013), 116.

55   Meaning not that such a reader will necessarily assume the tale's information is true, but that they will assume that it is supposed to be taken as true.

scarce, allowing the events recounted to be treated simply as information relating to Xuanzong's reign.

The Surprising Afterlife of the "Junior Division"

Xu Yunfeng's description of the Pear Garden junior division caught the attention of many later readers who recorded the incident anew, many of them seemingly taking it at face value. In the centuries since *Ganze yao* first entered circulation, Yuan Jiao's description of the young players and their performance of "Fragrance of Lychees" has been quoted or referenced by poets, informal historians, musicologists, and playwrights, as well, as we have seen, by the Song dynasty government historians who compiled the *Xin Tang shu*. A brief sampling of the range of usages, in rough chronological order:

- Yue Shi 樂史 (930-1007) includes the junior division's Mount Li performance in his "Unofficial Biography of Yang Taizhen" 楊太真外傳 as the final happy event of Yang's lifetime, followed immediately by the outbreak of the An Lushan rebellion.[56]
- Li Shangjiao 李上交 quotes much of Xu Yunfeng's description, including the account of origins of the name "Fragrance of Lychees," in a section of notes on Tang tune titles in his *Jinshi huiyuan* 近事會元 (preface dated to 1056), a compilation of miscellaneous information from the Tang and Five Dynasties periods contemporaneous with *Xin Tang shu*.[57]

---

56 The "Unofficial Biography" strings together incidents involving Prized Consort Yang gathered from many different sources, relying heavily on *Minghuang zalu*, *Guoshi bu*, and other anecdote collections as well as the *Jiu Tang shu*. For Yue Shi's dates, see Li Jianguo, *Songdai chuanqi ji* 宋代傳奇集 (Beijing: Zhonghua shuju, 2001), 13; Li Jianguo discusses Yue Shi's use of sources in *Songdai zhiguai chuanqi xulu* 宋代志怪傳奇敘錄 (Tianjin: Nankai daxue chubanshe, 1997), 28-29.

57 This date suggests that the collection was completed just four years before *Xin Tang shu* was presented to the throne. Li Shangjiao cites "*Ganze yao* from the Tang" 唐甘澤謠 as his source. In addition to other minor textual discrepancies, his text drops a "ten" 十 and dates the event to the fourth year of the Tianbao reign rather than the fourteenth (*Jinshi huiyuan*, ed. Yu Yunguo 虞雲國 and Wu Aifen 吳愛芬, *juan* 4, in *Quan Song biji* 全宋筆記, ed. Zhu Yi'an 朱易安 and Fu Xuancong 傅璇琮, 1st series [Zhengzhou: Daxiang chubanshe, 2003], 4:176).

- The eleventh century calligrapher Cai Xiang 蔡襄 (1012-1067) recalls the scene in a quatrain entitled "The Pear Garden Junior Division" 梨園小部.[58]
- Twelfth century fact-checkers reference it in discussions of the veracity of claims about Xuanzong's reign made in various literary works, and in particular the question of whether or not the emperor would have been at Mount Li during the summer months.[59]
- The two great post-Tang accounts of government institutions, Zheng Qiao's 鄭樵 (1104-62) *Tongzhi* 通志 (compiled 1149) and Ma Duanlin's 馬端臨 (1254-1323) *Wenxian tongkao* 文獻通考 (presented in 1319), both reproduce the *Xin Tang shu* description of the junior division verbatim.[60]
- The scene's continued currency in later centuries as a topic of literary reference is suggested by the inclusion of abbreviated snippets from the scene as examples of the originary usage of terms such as "fragrance of lychees" 荔枝香 or "junior division musicians" 小部音樂 in several general-purpose *leishu* from the eleventh century on.[61]

---

58   The poem was included in Cai Xiang's collection *Ruiming ji* 瑞明集 (see Fu Xuancong 傅璇琮 et al., *Quan Song shi* 全宋詩 [Beijing: Beijing daxue chubanshe, 1992], 7:391.4814). The explanatory preface that sets the scene for the quatrain differs from the *Xin Tang shu* description only in the omission of a single character, suggesting that Cai Xiang may have drawn his inspiration from the history.

59   See the discussions of the veracity of Du Mu's description of Consort Yang awaiting lychees at Huaqing Palace in his first quatrain "On Passing Huaqing Palace" and of details found in Bai Juyi's "Changhen ge" in for example Cheng Dachang's 程大昌 *Kaogu pian* 攷古編, in *Xuejin taoyuan* 學津討原 (Shanghai: Hanfenlou, 1922), 8.1a-b.

60   Zheng Qiao, *Tongzhi* (Beijing: Xinhua shuju, 1987), 49.635; Ma Duanlin, *Wenxian tongkao* (Beijing: Xinhua shuju, 1986), 142.1256. Wang Yinglin's 王應麟 (1223-1296) compendium of historical documents, the *Yuhai* 玉海, includes it as well (though Wang cites as his source *Zizhi tongjian*, in which the scene does not appear; see *Yuhai* [Taipei: Dahua shuju, 1977], 106.23a).

61   To give a few representative examples: *Hailu suishi* includes items for both "junior division musicians" and "fragrance of lychees" (16.779 and 16.799; it also includes a citation for "Xu Yunfeng," though the reference is to the poem by the tenth-century writer Li Zhong; see note 42 above). *Bai Kong liu tie* 白孔六帖 also has a "fragrance of lychees" entry, and explicitly cites *Ganze yao* (Bai Juyi and Kong Chuan 孔傳, *Tang Song Bai Kong liu tie* 唐宋白孔六帖 [1465-1620; digitized by the Harvard College Library/Harvard-Yenching Library and found at <https://iiif.lib.harvard.edu/manifests/view/drs:54153830$1i>], 61.7b-8a). *Gujin hebi shilei beiyao* 古今合璧事類備要 gives brief snippets of the story under "presenting a new tune: its name" 進新曲名 (for which it cites Yue Shi's "Unofficial Biography") and "lychee: the name of a tune" 荔枝名曲 (Xie Weixin 謝維新, *Gujin hebi shilei beiyao* [Xia Xiang 夏相, printer, 1552-56; digitized by the Harvard College Library/Harvard-Yenching Library and found at <http://listview.lib.harvard.edu/lists/drs-54165381>], *bieji* 別集, 40.1b and *waiji* 外集, 11.10a). Centuries later, *Peiwen yunfu* 佩文韻府 cites the

– One of the most telling cases is a solitary reference to "the Pear Garden junior division" 梨園小部 in Hong Sheng's 洪昇 seventeenth century drama *Changsheng dian* 長生殿, in which it is not Xuanzong but An Lushan who looks forward to their performance as one of the spoils of his conquest of the capital: stripped of all of its original context, the term remains tied to Xuanzong's story.[62]

– Finally, the passage has also repeatedly been quoted as evidence regarding aspects of Tang musical practices. The earliest examples I have found are twelfth century comments on origins of the tune title "Fragrance of Lychees," but the practice continues to this day in scholarly speculations on the nature of the Pear Garden Dharma division's junior contingent in studies published within the past decade.[63]

Most of these works cite either *Xin Tang shu* or *Ganze yao* itself as the source of their information. Some of them—the fact-checkers, the music historians, the document collectors—treat the existence of the junior division and the origins of "Fragrance of Lychees" as historical facts. *Xin Tang shu*'s appropriation of "Xu Yunfeng's" description—and the history's status as a product of the Song Historiography Office, and the state-sanctioned summation of the Tang— brought Yuan Jiao's scene of youthful musicians entertaining the emperor into

---

Xin Tang shu under "fragrance of lychees," "junior division" 小部, and "new tune" 新曲 (Zhang Yushu 張玉書 et al., comps. [Shanghai: Shanghai guji chubanshe, 1983], 2:37 *xia*.1711-3 and 3:91.3508-1).

62 Hong Sheng, *Changsheng dian*, scene 28: 148.

63 In the twelfth century, both Wang Zhuo 王灼 in his *Biji manzhi* 碧鷄慢志 and Wu Zeng 吳曾 in his *Nenggai zhai manlu* 能改齋漫錄 cite the *Xin Tang shu* passage in discussing "Fragrance of Lychees" (Wang Zhuo, *Biji manzhi*, in *Tang Song congshu*, vol. 16 [Jingde tang, 1465-1620; digitized by the Harvard College Library/Harvard-Yenching Library and found at <http://nrs.harvard.edu/urn-3:FHCL:23477511>], 28a-b; Wu Zeng, *Nenggai zhai manlu*, in *Congshu jicheng, chubian* 叢書集成，初編, 289 [Shanghai: Shangwu yinshu-guan, 1939], 3.61). The Ming scholar Han Banqi's 韓邦奇 *Yuanluo zhiyue* 苑洛志樂 also appears to have been influential in bringing the passage to the attention of later music historians. More recently, Qiu Qiongsun's 丘瓊蓀 *Yanyue tanwei* 燕樂探微 references the passage (Shanghai: Shanghai guji chubanshe, 1989; 85, 97); while the Japanese scholar Kishibe Shigeo cites *Ganze yao* in his discussion of the Pear Garden troupe in *Tōdai ongaku no rekishiteki kenkyū: gakusei hen* (1:469). Among contemporary scholars, Zuo Hanlin adduces the *Xin Tang shu* passage to discuss the junior division and Dharma tunes in several recent articles; he includes Xu Yunfeng (as well as Li Mo and Li Guinian) on a list of Pear Garden pupils in "Guanyu Tangdai Liyuan de jige wenti kaolun" 關於唐代梨園的幾個問題考論 (*Dongfang luntan* 東方論壇, 2007, No. 2), but does not cite a source (p. 91).

mainstream history and gave the junior division's performance an authority and a breadth of reach that *Ganze yao* itself could not have. The imprimatur of "official" history might at first glance appear to serve as a welcome independent confirmation of the junior troupe's existence, but the near identity of the wording of the *Xin Tang shu* passage to "Xu Yunfeng" indicates that, directly or indirectly, the latter was the historians' source. In the more literary works, the historical authenticity of the reference to the junior division matters far less than the flavor evoked by the image of Xuanzong's youthful musicians performing for the emperor and his beloved on the eve of the rebellion.

We do not of course have concrete evidence that the Pear Garden junior division did *not* exist. Seeking further evidence in other Tang sources, Kishibe Shigeo 岸邊成雄 has identified a number of additional references to young musicians, and suggests that they may refer to the same or a similar group under different names.[64] But the fact that virtually all subsequent descriptions of the junior division per se show close similarity in wording to "Xu Yunfeng" (as we see in the *Xin Tang shu* passage quoted above) indicates that "Xu Yunfeng" is their source. Yuan Jiao's technique in "Xu Yunfeng," in which figures and motifs from established lore are pointedly manipulated (found elsewhere in *Ganze yao* as well), suggests that these details of the junior division's performance and perhaps the junior division itself are also his personal embellishments.[65]

What is striking, however, is that though some of these many scholars and compilers list *Ganze yao* as the source for their information, none of them mentions Xu Yunfeng himself. Most pare the incident down further and omit the details about the formation of the junior division within the Dharma division and the ages of the musicians. But in these truncated forms, Yuan Jiao's scene of youthful musicians, which all evidence suggests was invented over a century after it allegedly occurred, continued to shape later generations'

---

64   See Kishibe's discussion in *Tōdai ongaku no rekishiteki kenkyū: gakusei hen*, 1:469-71.

65   The many references to Xuanzong's interest in music in sources such as *Minghuang zalu* also make it surprising that the junior division would not have been mentioned there, had it existed. In fact the only evidence that points, weakly, towards the possibility that Yuan Jiao was drawing on a prior source is a citation of *Minghuang rilu* 明皇日錄—presumably an error for *Minghuang zalu*—as the source for a description of the Mount Li birthday celebration in one edition of the Song *leishu Hailu suishi* (16.779). The *Hailu suishi* text, under the heading "junior division musicians" 小部音樂, follows that in the "Unofficial Biography," and it is clear from other sections of the "Unofficial Biography" that Yue Shi relied heavily on *Minghuang zalu* in constructing his narrative. However, the citation of *Minghuang rilu* is found in only one edition of *Hailu suishi*, and it is more likely that it is in fact a misattribution of a quotation from the "Unofficial Biography" (see *Quan Tang Wudai biji*, 2:1042).

understanding, and imagining, of Xuanzong's reign for centuries thereafter. Its impact on our knowledge of the broader course of Tang history, or even of the particulars of Xuanzong's reign, is limited: as we saw above, in general outline it reaffirms images already found elsewhere. But its weight is magnified when the topic is Tang music, for which the sources are much more limited; and the care with which scholars such as Zuo Hanlin 左漢林 have parsed Yuan Jiao's brief description speaks to the value with which such slight snippets of data are invested in the attempt to reconstruct a detailed picture of any aspect of such a distant age. The incident has come unmoored from its original context as the musician Xu Yunfeng's personal experience, and has become simply a set of useful or interesting facts about Xuanzong's reign.

Why did the junior troupe catch the attention of later readers and writers to a degree that Yuan Jiao's new story about Li Bai, or Xu Yunfeng's association the story of shattered flute, did not? Surely it is in part due simply to serendipity. But "Xu Yunfeng's" memory of Li Bai also pales in comparison to the stories of the poet's antics at court, while the tale's version of the shattering flute stands out only in its clever referentiality: there is little to make these two incidents eclipse the stories on which they build. The scene of junior division's performance, however, combines familiar references (music, the Prized Consort, lychees, Mount Li) with novel information and striking imagery, helping to feed the continuing hunger for information about Xuanzong and the decline of his reign.

The intricate web centered on "Xu Yunfeng" of, on one hand, the thematic and narrative borrowings that went into creating Yuan Jiao's tale, and on the other, the quotations, references, and citations (of both *Ganze yao* and the *Xin Tang shu*) that derive from it, is an illuminating example of how later generations' "memories" of past events are contingent upon both the information available and on contemporaneous understanding of what is right for the period. In its own time "Xu Yunfeng" represented a seemingly deliberate destabilization of common tropes concerning Xuanzong's reign and an experiment with the possibilities of the genre of the historical anecdote. Its use of familiar lore—Li Mo's shattered flute especially—as objects of reference suggest that Yuan Jiao saw that material as sources of literary inspiration rather than information to be assessed for its historical value. Both the manipulation and the referentiality found in "Xu Yunfeng" mark the text as a site of play and experimentation, which recasts the anecdote, and the anecdote collection, as a literary rather than a primarily historical genre. But the inventiveness implicit in this conception of the genre resulted in a striking new image that proved to have far greater influence than the full tale itself.

Bibliography

Bai Juyi 白居易. *Bai Juyi ji jianjiao* 白居易集箋校. Shanghai: Shanghai guji chubanshe, 1988.

Bai Juyi 白居易 and Kong Chuan 孔傳, comps. *Tang Song Bai Kong liu tie* 唐宋白孔六帖. 1465-1620; digitized by the Harvard College Library/Harvard-Yenching Library and found at <https://iiif.lib.harvard.edu/manifests/view/drs:54153830$1i>.

Chen Zhensun 陳振孫. *Zhizhai shulu jieti* 直齋書錄解題. Shanghai: Shanghai guji chubanshe, 2015.

Cheng Dachang 程大昌. *Kaogu pian* 攷古編. *Xuejin taoyuan* 學津討原. Shanghai: Hanfenlou, 1922.

Cubitt, Geoffrey. *History and Memory*. Manchester and New York: Manchester University Press, 2007.

Cutter, Robert Joe. "History and 'The Old Man of the Eastern Wall.'" *Journal of the American Oriental Society* 106 (1986): 503-528.

Du Fu 杜甫. *Du shi xiangzhu* 杜詩詳注. With commentary by Qiu Zhao'ao 仇兆鰲. Taipei: Liren shuju, 1980.

Du Fu. *The Poetry of Du Fu* 杜甫詩. Translated and edited by Stephen Owen. Boston and Berlin: Walter de Gruyter, 2016.

Fan Zhengmin 范正敏. *Dunzhai xianlan* 遯齋閒覽. In Tao Zongyi 陶宗儀, [*Chongbian*] *Shuofu* [重編] 說郛. 1646; digitized by the Harvard College Library/Harvard-Yenching Library and found at <https://iiif.lib.harvard.edu/manifests/view/drs:42849611$1i>.

Fentress, James, and Chris Wickham. *Social Memory*. Oxford and Cambridge: Blackwell Publishers, 1992.

Fineman, Joel. "The History of the Anecdote: Fiction and Fiction." In *The New Historicism*, edited by H. Aram Veeser, 49-76. New York and London: Routledge, 1989.

Fu Xuancong 傅璇琮 et al., comps. *Quan Song shi* 全宋詩. Beijing: Beijing daxue chubanshe, 1992.

Gossman, Lionel. "Anecdote and History." *History and Theory* 42.2 (May 2003): 143-68.

Hong Sheng 洪昇. *Changsheng dian* 長生殿. Beijing: Renmin wenxue chubanshe, 1958.

Jin Jicang 靳極蒼. *Changhen ge ji tong ticai shi xiangjie* 長恨歌及同題材詩詳解. Taiyuan: Shanxi guji chubanshe, 2002.

Jin Taosheng 金濤聲 and Zhu Wencai 朱文彩. *Li Bai ziliao huibian: Tang Song zhi bu* 李白資料彙編：唐宋之部. Beijing: Zhonghua shuju, 2007.

Kishibe Shigeo 岸邊成雄. *Tōdai ongaku no rekishiteki kenkyū: gakusei hen* 唐代音樂の歷史的研究：樂制篇. Tokyo: Tokyo University Press, 1960.

Kroll, Paul W. "Nostalgia and History in Mid-Ninth Century Verse: Cheng Yü's Poem on 'The Chin-yang Gate'." *T'oung Pao* 89 (2003): 286-366.

Kroll, Paul W. *Student's Dictionary of Classical and Medieval Chinese*. Leiden and Boston: Brill, 2015.

Li Bai 李白. *Li Taibai quanji* 李太白全集. With commentary by Wang Qi 王琦. Beijing: Zhonghua shuju, 1977.

Li Fang 李昉 et al., comps. *Taiping guangji* 太平廣記. Beijing: Zhonghua shuju, 1961.

Li Fang 李昉 et al., comps. *Wenyuan yinghua* 文苑英華. Taipei: Dahua shuju, 1985.

Li Jianguo 李劍國. *Songdai chuanqi ji* 宋代傳奇集. Beijing: Zhonghua shuju, 2001.

Li Jianguo 李劍國. *Songdai zhiguai chuanqi xulu* 宋代志怪傳奇敘錄. Tianjin: Nankai daxue chubanshe, 1997.

Li Jianguo 李劍國. *Tang Wudai zhiguai chuanqi xulu* 唐五代志怪傳奇敘錄. Tianjin: Nankai daxue chubanshe, 1998.

Li Jun 李軍. Ganze yao *pingzhu* 《甘澤謠》評注. Beijing: Zhongguo shehui kexueyuan chubanshe, 2013.

Li Jun 李軍. "*Ganze yao* yu shiguan wenhua guanxi lunlüe" 《甘澤謠》與史官文化關係論略. *The Northern Forum* 北方論叢, No. 230 (2011, No. 6): 99-102.

Li Shangjiao 李上交. *Jinshi huiyuan* 近事會元. Edited by Yu Yunguo 虞雲國 and Wu Aifen 吳愛芬. *Quan Song biji* 全宋筆記, 1st series, 4:133-193. Zhengzhou: Daxiang chubanshe, 2003.

Liu Xu 劉昫 et al. *Jiu Tang shu* 舊唐書. Beijing: Zhonghua shuju, 1975.

Liu Zhiji 劉知幾. *Shitong tongshi* 史通通釋. Edited by Pu Qilong 浦起龍. Taipei: Yiwen yinshuguan, 1978.

Luo, Manling. "Remembering Kaiyuan and Tianbao: The Construction of Mosaic Memory in Medieval Historical Miscellanies." *T'oung Pao* 97 (2011): 263-300.

Ma Duanlin 馬端臨. *Wenxian tongkao* 文獻通考. Beijing: Xinhua shuju, 1986.

Ouyang Xiu 歐陽修 et al. *Xin Tang shu* 新唐書. Beijing: Zhonghua shuju, 1975.

Owen, Stephen. *The Late Tang: Chinese Poetry of the Mid-Ninth Century*. Cambridge: Harvard University Asia Center, 2006.

Qiu Qiongsun 丘瓊蓀. *Yanyue tanwei* 燕樂探微. Shanghai: Shanghai guiji chubanshe, 1989.

Quan Tang shi 全唐詩. Beijing: Zhonghua shuju, 1960.

Rigney, Ann. "The Dynamics of Remembrance: Texts Between Monumentality and Morphing." In *A Companion to Cultural Memory Studies*, edited by Astrid Erll and Ansgar Nünning, 345-53. Berlin and New York: Walter De Gruyter, 2010.

Rigney, Ann. "Portable Monuments: Literature, Cultural Memory, and the Case of Jeanie Deans." *Poetics Today* 25 (2004): 361-96.

Sima Guang 司馬光. *Zizhi tongjian* 資治通鑑. Beijing: Zhonghua shuju, 1956.

Sun Wang 孫望. *Wei Yingwu shiji xinian jiaojian* 韋應物詩集繫年校箋. Beijing: Zhonghua shuju, 2002.

Tao Min 陶敏 and Wang Yousheng 王友盛. *Wei Yingwu ji jiaozhu* 韋應物集校注. Shanghai: Shanghai guji chubanshe, 1998.

Tao Zongyi 陶宗儀. [*Chongbian*] *Shuofu* [重編] 說郛. 1646; digitized by the Harvard College Library/Harvard-Yenching Library and found at <https://iiif.lib.harvard.edu/manifests/view/drs:42849611$1i>.

Twitchett, Denis. *The Writing of Official History under the T'ang*. Cambridge: Cambridge University Press, 1992.

Twitchett, Denis. "A Note on the 'Monograph on Music' in *Chiu T'ang shu*." *Asia Major*, 3rd series, 1 (1990): 51-62.

Wang Pu 王溥. *Tang huiyao* 唐會要. Beijing: Zhonghua shuju, 1955.

Wang Yinglin 王應麟. *Yuhai* 玉海. Taipei: Dahua shuju, 1977.

Wang Zhuo 王灼. *Biji manzhi* 碧鷄慢志. *Tang Song congshu*, vol. 16. Jingde tang, 1465-1620; digitized by the Harvard College Library/Harvard-Yenching Library and found at <http://nrs.harvard.edu/urn-3:FHCL:23477511>.

Wu Zeng 吳曾. *Nenggai zhai manlu* 能改齋漫錄. *Congshu jicheng, chubian* 叢書集成，初編, 289-91. Shanghai: Shangwu yinshuguan, 1939.

Xie Weixin 謝維新. *Gujin hebi shilei beiyao* 古今合璧事類備要. Xia Xiang 夏相, printer, 1552-56; digitized by the Harvard College Library/Harvard-Yenching Library and found at <http://listview.lib.harvard.edu/lists/drs-54165381>.

Ye Tinggui 葉廷珪. *Hailu suishi* 海錄碎事. Beijing: Zhonghua shuju, 2002.

Yuan Jiao 袁郊. *Ganze yao* 甘澤謠. *Congshu jicheng, chubian* 叢書集成初編, 2699. Changsha: Shangwu yinshuguan, 1939.

Zhang Yushu 張玉書 et al., comps. *Peiwen yunfu* 佩文韻府. Shanghai: Shanghai guji chubanshe, 1983.

Zheng Qiao 鄭樵. *Tongzhi* 通志. Beijing: Xinhua shuju, 1987.

Zuo Hanlin 左漢林. "Guanyu Tangdai Liyuan de jige wenti kaolun" 關於唐代梨園的幾個問題考論. *Dongfang luntan* 東方論壇 (2007, No. 2): 91-94.

Zuo Hanlin 左漢林. "Tangdai Liyuan dizi de chansheng yu yange kaoshu" 唐代梨園弟子的產生與沿革考述. *Journal of Qinghai Normal University* (*Philosophy and Social Sciences*) 青海師範大學學報（哲學社會科學版）, No. 105 (2004, No. 4): 61-64.

Zuo Hanlin 左漢林. "Tangdai Liyuan faqu xingzhi kaolun" 唐代梨園法曲性質考論. *Journal of the Central Conservatory of Music* 中央音樂學院學報 (2007, No. 3): 47-55.

CHAPTER 9

The Mastering Voice: Text and Aurality in the Ninth-century Mediascape

Robert Ashmore

Introduction: The Social Construction of Voice in Tang Writing

How a text captures or creates a voice seems most properly to belong to the realm of poetics, and particularly to the texts we call poems. The formation of a poet's idiom, the play of register, dialect, verbal tics or sonic signatures, as well as disruptions of verbal convention or violations of register that solicit the reader's attention to the voice not of a class or era, but of a lone consciousness appealing to a sympathetic ear—all these concerns are central to our practice whenever we try to understand a poet's work. Poetry, moreover, is perhaps of all the traditional literary genres the one that makes the most peremptory demand to be read aloud; it is a kind of text that demands that we "allow it to speak."

In the larger sense of the term as employed by anthropologists, however, poetics is an inquiry into more general questions of how the members of a cultural group engage in a wide range of meaning-making activities, which may include social behaviors beyond the sphere of verbal communication per se. Particularly when our critical inquiry into text and voice has a historical or cross-cultural dimension, a broader inquiry into cultural practices relating to text and voice, and to historically specific conventions whereby texts have been deemed to function as an encoding medium for voice, justify an expanded perspective that looks for poetics (and even perhaps a brand of lyricism) in places where we might not have thought to look for it.[1]

---

[1] Another way of stating the broad perspective of this essay is as an examination of how texts worked in ninth-century China as a technology geared toward specifically *aural* production or reproduction. In this regard one might refer to the recent work by the classicist Shane Butler, for example, which attempts to reactivate our sense of how written texts served in classical antiquity as a literally "phonographic" medium. See Butler, *The Ancient Phonograph* (New York: Zone Books, 2015). Jesper Svenbro's study of text as a technology of voice in *Phrasikleia: Anthropologie de la Lecture en Grèce Ancienne* (Paris: Editions La Découverte, 1988) remains unparalleled.

© KONINKLIJKE BRILL NV, LEIDEN, 2018 | DOI 10.1163/9789004368637_011

In the case of medieval China, and particularly in the ritual, textual, and administrative culture that takes definitive shape in the mid- to late-Tang dynasty, we are faced with provocative anomalies when we expand our investigation of the relation between texts and the authentic voices they enact beyond poetry in the narrow sense: in short, the weightiest instances in which figures of political or ritual authority speak "in their own persons" are routinely underwritten by texts composed by someone else. In fact, it can be stated as a general tendency that the weightier the utterance, the more likely it is to have been scripted by a proxy writer who crafts the text to which the "proper" speaker then simply provides the voice. Not only was this stagecraft of the authoritative voice not euphemized or glossed over by Tang writers, it was celebrated. The successful collaboration between a drafter and the ruler or high official in whose voice the drafter's script was to be formally "bodied forth" generated prestige for both—the latter gaining from the elegance, erudition, and expressive power of the spoken text, and the former gaining not only material compensation in the form of salary or official preferment, but also social capital from this interweaving of the proxy text into the utterance of a socially prominent person on a weighty occasion. Such an association, moreover, could then be perpetuated through the circulation of the script in literary collections under the proxy's name, in which the identities of prominent clients would typically be preserved as a point of pride.[2] Mastery of the demanding art of drafting proxy texts was held in the highest social and cultural esteem, and the ideal of the *ci chen* 詞臣, or "rhetorical minister," who possessed such attainments, was a model of governmental service linked to the highest and most elite postings at court and in the regional administrations.[3]

---

2   The vast bulk of our evidence derives from Northern Song imperial compendia such as the *Wenyuan yinghua* 文苑英華 and *Cefu yuangui* 策府元龜, so we are working at one or more removes when attempting to make inferences about the editorial practices of Tang manuscripts. Whereas certain context-specific information such as dates, given names, burial sites (in the case of funerary genres) and so forth is typically elided when proxy texts are compiled into literary collections, the general impression is that the identities of clients for proxy writings are omitted only where their social status is not particularly elevated. This is also the general practice in the Dunhuang manuscripts of collections of administrative writing, such as the *Gantang ji* 甘棠集. See Zhao Heping 趙和平, *Dunhuang biao zhuang qian qi shuyi yanjiu* 敦煌表狀箋啓書儀研究 (Nanjing: Jiangsu guji chubanshe, 1997) and *Dunhuang ben Gantang ji yanjiu* 敦煌本甘棠集研究 (Taipei: Xin wenfeng chuban gongsi, 2000).

3   On the general narrative regarding the rise and characteristics of the "literary minister" in the Tang, I follow the overview presented by Lu Yang 陸揚, in, for example, his "Tangdai de qingliu wenhua—yige xianxiang de gaishu" 唐代的清流文化——一個現象的概述.

The central and emblematic instance of the function of proxy texts in the Tang textual world was the collaborative construction of the voice of the emperor himself, and of the emperor's ministers in dialogue with him—exchanges conceived of as analogous to the emotionally charged and often rhetorically figured utterances that the *Classic of Documents* 尚書 tradition terms "heightened speech" (*yang yan* 颺言).[4] The collaborative effort of the emperor and his literary officials in drafting edicts is both the emblematic instance of the creation of voice through a performing body and a proxy script, and also, for the ministerial elite, the most prestigious venue for the expression of literary talent. In fact, as Tang elites were well aware, this regime of representation was itself a core dimension of the political and ritual work of empire itself. To "elaborate the bands of silk" (*yan si lun* 演絲綸)—that is, to write proxy texts through which a synthesized imperial voice could be efficaciously transmitted—was an undertaking held in the very highest esteem.[5]

These underlying guidelines and assumptions of Tang administrative textual culture are familiar commonplace for institutional historians.[6] What this essay proposes is to attempt to think through possible implications for a historicist account of the field of literary writing in medieval China that would center not on the sorts of writing and self-expression suggested by modern notions of the literary (e.g. poetic genres and narrative prose), but rather on the literary habitat of the "rhetorical minister." The typical training grounds for the ninth-century "rhetorical minister" were the clerical staffs of metropolitan and regional officials, particularly the secretarial staffs of regional governors. This is the world in which particularly elegant or moving proxy texts were eagerly copied and transmitted by an avid audience of readers and aspiring imitators, and where collections such as the *Gantang ji* 甘棠集 of Liu Ye 劉鄴 or the *Jishi beiyao* 記室備要 of Yu Zhiyan 郁知言, comprising proxy texts written in just

---

4 The phrase derives from the "Yi Ji" 益稷 chapter of the *Shang shu*, where it describes the loud and impassioned tone of voice in which Shun's minister Gao Yao responds to a lyric utterance by Shun. See *Shang shu zheng yi* 尚書正義, 5.32C.

5 Sun Mei 孫梅 (1739-1790), an important late imperial critic and theorist of the "four-six" genres, cites, and in essence assents to, the proposal by the Tang scholar Liu Zhiji 劉知幾 (661-721) that these formal administrative texts representing dialogue between (notionally) sage rulers and their advisors ought to be conceived of as continuing the institution of "recording speech" (i.e. of sage rulers) in the *Classic of Documents*. See Sun's *Siliu cong hua* 四六叢話 (Beijing: Zhonghua shuju, 2010), 131.

6 Thus in such scholarship the phrase *wang yan* 王言 is often used simply as a designation for the various sorts of legal and policy documents emanating from the court, as for example in the useful study by Nakamura Hiroichi 中村裕一 of the genres and functions of such texts, *Zui Tō ōgen no kenkyū* 隋唐王言の研究 (Tōkyō: Kyuko shoin, 2003).

such postings, had an eager and ready-made market.[7] It was the world moreover in which it was not the poetic collections through which modern accounts
have typically retold the story of Tang literature, but rather compilations such
as Li Deyu's 李德裕 (787-850) *Huichang yipin ji* 會昌一品集—assembling together the edicts that Li had drafted during the reign of, and in the voice of,
Emperor Wuzong 武宗 (r. 840-846)—that would have been viewed as the
crowning realization of literary culture.

   This essay will focus on a particularly intriguing pair of figures, Linghu Chu
令狐楚 (766-837) and Li Shangyin 李商隱 (813-ca. 858). Linghu Chu, who first
gained fame while serving as a drafter of proxy texts in the regional administration at Taiyuan, and who later rose to the most preeminent posts both at court
and in the provinces, is in many ways a prime exemplar of the "rhetorical minister." Linghu Chu transmitted to his protégé Li Shangyin the compositional
techniques of the so-called "study of documents and memorials" (*zhangzou
zhi xue* 章奏之學)—that is, the skill of composing official communications in
the "modern" or "four-six" style. Li Shangyin's own career, however, to his lasting regret, was to become emblematic instead of another typical career track
for scholar-official elites in the ninth century; that is, he spent the greater part
of his official service as part of the secretarial service of a series of regional
governors and military commanders.

Linghu Chu and the Ideal of the "Rhetorician Minister"

The account of Linghu Chu's early career in his *Jiu Tang shu* 舊唐書 biography
is in many ways an idealized representation of the "rhetorician minister."[8]
A *jinshi* graduate of 791, his early career followed the path that was to become
typical for ninth-century rhetorician ministers: as a young man of elite parent-
age, whose literary reputation was established from an early age, he had re-
fused or declined to stay long in a series of secretarial posts in other regions in
order to perform his filial obligations to his father, who was stationed at
Taiyuan. Subsequently Linghu Chu held posts in the secretarial staffs of a series of regional governors at Taiyuan. The following passage begins during the

---

7   These two texts survive in Dunhuang manuscripts (see the two works of Zhao Heping cited
    in note 32 above). As the following discussion will show, this was also the market that prompt-
    ed the issuing of the two *Fannan siliu* 樊南四六 anthologies of Li Shangyin's proxy texts.

8   *Jiu Tang shu*, 172.4459-65. His biography in the *Xin Tang shu* (166.5098-101) is shorter, and seems
    more reserved in its overall assessment of his role in the period. It reproduces the passage
    from the *Jiu Tang shu* biography cited here, however, with only minimal variations.

time Linghu Chu was in the service of the last of these, named Zheng Dan 鄭
儋 (741-801):

a) Chu was a rare and exquisite talent. Dezong 德宗 (r. 779-805) was fond
of literary culture—when the memorials from Taiyuan came in, he could
discern which had been drafted by Chu, and was quite complimentary in
his assessments of them. b) Zheng Dan suddenly died in his provincial
post, not having had time to make arrangements as to his successor.
There was tumult through the garrison, and things were about to reach a
crisis point. In the middle of the night a dozen-some-odd mounted soldiers, weapons in hand, compelled Chu to go to the command post. There
all the commanders surrounded him, and ordered him to draft [Zheng
Dan's] deathbed memorial. Chu, amidst those naked blades, grasped the
brush and was done straightaway. When it was read aloud and promul-
gated to the three armies, there were none who did not shed tears—and
thereupon the sentiments among the troops were pacified. From this
point Chu's reputation grew all the more imposing. c) On meeting with
the loss of his father, he was renowned for exemplary filial piety. When
the term of mourning ended, he was summoned into service as Omis-
sioner of the Right, a commission that was then amended to Erudite of
the Court of State Sacrifices and Vice-Director of the Ministry of Ritual.
He left these posts during the mourning period for his mother. When the
mourning period was completed, he was summoned into service as Vice-
Director in the Ministry of Justice, and then promoted to Director of the
Bureau of Operations in the Ministry of War, Participant in Drafting of
Proclamations.

a) 楚才思俊麗，德宗好文，每太原奏至，能辨楚之所為，頗稱之。b)
鄭儋在鎮暴卒，不及處分後事，軍中喧譁，將有急變。中夜十數騎持
刃迫楚至軍門，諸將環之，令草遺表。楚在白刃之中，搦管即成，讀
示三軍，無不感泣，軍情乃安。自是聲名益重。c) 丁父憂，以孝聞。
免喪，徵拜右拾遺，改太常博士、禮部員外郎。母憂去官。服闋，以
刑部員外郎徵，轉職方員外郎、知制誥。9

This narrative falls into three distinct sections, marked a, b, and c above for
convenience. Each section centers in one way or another on Linghu Chu's skill
in the crafting of authoritative voices through proxy writing. The relation to
imperial authority in particular is central throughout: an implicit but crucial

9 *Jiu Tang shu*, 172.4459-60.

narrative of his rise to imperial favor begins with the account of how Dezong was able to detect Linghu Chu's distinctive style in proxy texts drafted in the voice of Zheng Dan, and reaches its culmination with the final official title mentioned in this passage, "Participant in Drafting of Declarations," which he attains under Dezong's grandson Xianzong 憲宗 (r. 805-820): this title marks the point from which Linghu Chu, at this point over forty-five years old, and having completed the mourning periods for both parents, first applied his literary skills to crafting the voice of the emperor himself.

The central moment in this thumbnail sketch of Linghu Chu's rise is clearly the anecdote appearing in section (b) in the above passage. Succession crises in regional military governorships were the emblematic form of political crisis for the early to mid-ninth century Tang empire. The breakdown of imperial control over the designation of successors to these posts was the salient indication of the decline in imperial sway, and it was by reasserting control over these successions that emperors such as Dezong and Xianzong in particular sought to restore the dynasty to its former glory. From the court's perspective—that is, from the perspective assumed as normative for the culture of writing itself during this period—such moments were conceived of in terms of a stark confrontation between civilization and barbaric violence, specifically, as key tests of the scope and power of the sage-emperor's *sheng jiao* 聲教, or "teaching via the voice." What Linghu Chu was able to "make audible" that night before the assembled commanders at the Taiyuan garrison was Zheng Dan's declaration of loyalty and devoted service to the very moment of death.[10] The military officers who as it were overhear this deathbed speech from a loyal minister to his emperor are direct witnesses to the speech's fictionality, yet they are moved to tears, and recalled to their sense of the duty they in turn owe to their commander and his memory. However we imagine the relation between this anecdote and the actual events of a crisis in the succession of com-

---

10   The deathbed memorial was a subgenre of its own in Tang administrative writings. The political sensitivity of such moments, as reflected in this anecdote from Linghu Chu's biography, meant that the drafting of such documents would be entrusted only to the most skilled and trusted staff members. The key administrative task in such texts was naturally to announce and assert continuity and unbroken imperial control of the command itself. It was also expected that, whether they happened to be sketched out or drafted in advance of the signatory's death, or drafted entirely after the fact by secretarial staff members, as in cases of sudden death such as Zheng Dan's, these texts would give voice to the abiding feelings and concerns of a loyal servant of the emperor. Again, regardless of the actual timing of their composition, such documents characteristically present themselves as speaking from the very last moments of life.

mand at Taiyuan, it is vital to note that what the anecdote praises in Linghu Chu is not the canny management of an administrative dilemma, or the resolution of a political conflict—his success in defusing a potential garrison revolt is not represented as a matter of judiciously allocating posts so as to avoid discontent. Rather, Linghu Chu's drafting of the deathbed memorial succeeds above all in the emotional power it exerts over its hearers. At the risk of belaboring the point, it is also important to note that this emotional power is not one that these military men feel emanating from Linghu Chu himself, but rather from their deceased commander. Linghu Chu's literary talent is the specific and all-important one of making the voice of authority audible, on behalf of a principal in whose person that authority formally resides. Such an anecdote thus takes on a nearly mythic order of significance, both for the ideology of empire as Tang elites conceived it, and for the unique power of the "rhetorical minister."

Li Shangyin: *Guwen* and the Silent Text

For posterity, Li Shangyin was to become Linghu Chu's most renowned protégé. In fact, although Linghu Chu, as we shall see, did speak of being remembered through Li Shangyin, he cannot have anticipated the degree to which this would be the case in later ages, when, through the application of different standards of literary value, Li Shangyin was to become the major figure, and Linghu Chu the footnote. But Linghu Chu did seem to recognize and appreciate not simply Li Shangyin's character, personality, or general talent, but his specific gift that made him likely to be a powerful drafter of proxy texts. It was under Linghu Chu's personal tutelage that Li Shangyin was to become the preeminent writer of "four-six" texts for the entire tradition.[11]

In a passage from a letter to a friend in which he recounts his early years as a young scholar seeking patronage at the capital, Li Shangyin offers an unusually detailed reflection on the varieties of ninth-century writing and reading practice:

> Often those close to me would say, "You ought to submit your writings to so-and-so—so-and-so could serve as a bulwark and refuge for you..." And so I'd rush off and submit them. When they took out my writings, there would be those who set them aside, lacking the time to read them. And again there would be those who looked over them silently, lacking the

---

11 See, for example, the assessment by Sun Mei in *Siliu conghua*, 662-63.

time to read them aloud. And again there would be those who would
begin reading them aloud, but who would come upon words they missed
or sentences they misconstrued, and who thus did not see the original
meaning. So, embarrassed to ask, unable to understand on their own,
they would leave it at that, silently, no longer an occasion for sighing.
Thus after Taihe 7 (833), though I still participated in the exams, apart
from ritual correspondence relating to weddings and funerals, or official
correspondence, inscriptions, or memorials to the throne commissioned
by others, I wrote no more compositions. And since I didn't even compose, how much the less could I imitate others in "circulating scrolls"? At
that time Rectifier of Omissions Linghu[12] was alone my most generous
friend; each year he would copy out old works of mine to submit to the
Examination Office.

比有相親者曰：子之書宜貢於某氏，某氏可以為子之依歸矣。即走往
貢之，出其書，乃復有置之而不暇讀者；又有默而視之，不暇朗讀
者；又有始朗讀而中有失字壞句，不見本義者。進不敢問，退不能
解，默默已已，不復咨歎。故自太和七年後，雖尚應舉，除吉凶書，
及人憑倩作牋啟銘表之外，不復作文。文尚不復作，況復能學人行卷
耶。時獨令狐補闕最相厚，歲歲為寫出舊文納貢院。[13]

By Li Shangyin's own account, the "compositions" he refers to here were works
of classicist scholarship he had written under the inspiration of the *Liu shuo* 六
說 of Liu Zhiji's son Liu Xun 劉迅 (?–ca. 760).[14] Li Shangyin describes himself as

---

12   Linghu Tao 令狐綯, son of Linghu Chu.

13   "Yu Tao jinshi shu" 與陶進士書, in *Li Shangyin wen biannian jiao zhu* 李商隱文編年校
     注 (hereafter WBN), ed. Liu Xuekai and Yu Shucheng, 1:434. "Circulating scrolls" (*xingjuan*
     行卷) refers to the common practice for examination candidates to circulate sample dos-
     siers of their works to influential persons in advance of the examinations to build a repu-
     tation; what Linghu Tao is said to have done on Li Shangyin's behalf is the mandatory
     submission of works to the Examination Office ahead of the examinations proper. For an
     overview of these practices, see Fu Xuancong 傅璇琮, *Tangdai keju yu wenxue* 唐代科舉
     與文學 (Xi'an: Shaanxi renmin chubanshe, 1986), 247-86.

14   A work expounding on the informing principles of the classics and bringing them "up to
     date" for the Tang. Liu Xun was the fourth son of Liu Zhiji. As noted below, we have no way
     of knowing exactly which texts Li Shangyin submitted to these figures, but his general
     characterization of the project calls to mind as well Li Shangyin's own description of an
     uncle who was an influential early teacher: "he grew ever more conversant with the 'Five
     Classics,' composing separate exegeses on each, in which he set aside chapter and verse
     exegesis to provide a synthetic account of their overall import" 益通《五經》，咸著別
     疏，遺略章句，總會指歸. See Li Shangyin's "Dossier Requesting Minister Lu to

producing these texts from his deep engagement with the Classics, "writing out with my hand and intoning in my mouth" 手書口詠. Understanding of a text is here equated with full and immersive oral declamation (and thus aural realization) by the reader, whereas various degrees of faulty or inadequate realization are equated with skimming, silent reading, or, finally, mere non-reading.

In his own writing and in historical accounts of his career, Li Shangyin is described as having first become well-versed in "ancient-style writing" (*guwen* 古文), and later learning to write in the parallel style of formal ritual and administrative texts only as a result of his service as a secretary under Cui Rong 崔戎 (780-835) and Linghu Chu. We cannot be sure whether the few surviving *guwen* works by Li Shangyin might have been included in the submissions to potential patrons described in this letter, but the starkness of the opposition Li Shangyin posits here between "writing compositions" (*zuo wen* 作文) on the one hand and "mere" ritual correspondence or commissioned secretarial proxy texts on the other makes it clear that the samples of his own work were one sort of *guwen* or another.

Two points emerge as worthy of note here: first, though Li Shangyin came to be known during his own lifetime and through the early Northern Song primarily as a master of formal administrative and ritual genres in the so-called "modern style," he remained ambivalent about this aspect of his reputation, and never missed an opportunity to stipulate that at some level his primary affinity was with classical studies and with *guwen* writing. Second, while the densely allusive and tonally regulated antithetical style of the formal "modern" genres may seem dauntingly opaque to us today, it is *guwen* writing that is consistently represented in this period as difficult to render aurally. Such difficulty is in fact almost an ideological requirement for *guwen* writing, particularly as practiced by Han Yu and his successors, since the claim of almost material "hardness" is what links such writing to the ancient sources to which it claims to cleave more closely than "modern" styles. As Han Yu says of his own compositions in his essay "An Apologia for Promoting Study" (*Jin xue jie* 進學解), such writing is "[like] the 'Decrees' of Zhou, or the '*Pan geng*' of Yin—twisted and tooth-bending" 周誥殷盤, 佶屈聱牙.[15] By the same token, it is the "modern"

Compose a Burial Inscription for the Former Gentleman in Retirement Li [*redacted*] of Guzang" 請盧尚書撰故處士姑臧李某誌文狀, *WBN* 2:780.

15   *Quan Tang wen,* 558.5646b. This resistance to easy entry into the realm of orality is analogous to the reclusive scholar's resistance to easy entry into converse with worldly powers: compare the striking parallel example of Li Shangyin's uncle, who is said to have mastered several ancient types of calligraphy, but to have insisted on corresponding with contemporaries only through dictated letters; when a stele inscribed with his calligraphy attracted an unseemly crowd of people wanting to copy its style, he had it placed among a temple

forms that form the currency in which power and social status in the ninth-century world find their textual—and oral—expression.

Li Shangyin eventually did compile two collections of proxy texts during his lifetime, which he titled simply—using a toponym for an area he once dwelt in as a student, along with the characteristic metrical pattern in formal modern-style writing—"Fannan Four-six" 樊南四六 and "Fannan Four-six B" 樊南四六乙.[16] His prefaces to these collections, composed in elegant but perhaps deliberately informal (and non-parallel) prose style, are fascinating documents of Li Shangyin's deep and fraught relation with the modern forms. Here we will focus on the first:

> I, Master Fannan, at the age of sixteen, was able to compose a "Discourse on Talent" and a "Discourse on the Sage," finding a reputation as a *guwen* writer among the various authorities. Later I found favor, one after the other, with Minister of Yun and Governor of Hua;[17] when I was a retainer in their households, they commanded me to edit memorials and records, and only then did I become conversant in the modern style. Later more-over I twice served as an officer in the Palace Library, where I browsed with abandon among the collections of ancient authors, and found myself giddy with delight time and again among the works of Ren Fang 任昉 (460-508), Fan Yun 范雲 (513-581), Xu Ling 徐陵 (507-583), and Yu Xin 庾信 (513-581). When someone requested a piece from me, some-times I'd come upon a nice antithesis or a well-fitting allusion, a sonorous effect or a natural image, mournful and lofty, floating and powerful, such as is able to move people. I lived ten years at the capital, cold and emaci-ated; someone characterized me as follows: Han's prose, Du's poetry, and Pengyang's memorials and declarations—someone among the freezing masses at Fannan knows these. My younger brother Shengpu[18] is exclu-sively skilled at *guwen* writing; during the Huichang period he was in the top one or two in the *jinshi* examination. He always takes me to task

---

collection of ancient inscriptions where it could remain "hidden." See the "Dossier" regarding this uncle, cited above in note 14.

16   The *Fannan si liu* collections do not survive as intact works; extant collections of Li Shangyin's works in non-poetic genres are assemblages of works included in the *Wenyuan yinghua* and *Tang wencui*. A supplementary collection was produced by adding works collected in the *Yongle dadian*.

17   Linghu Chu and Cui Rong.

18   *Zi* of Li Xisou 李羲叟. He passed the *jinshi* examination in 847 (see *Deng ke ji kao* 登科記考, 22.809).

about my modern style writing, but I have not been able to quit.[19] In Dazhong 1 (847), I was drafted to go through the mountains to serve as a head secretary, and there too I composed a lot of these. In the winter as I travelled to the Southern Commandery,[20] while on board the boat I suddenly decided to assemble everything of this sort I had: some fire-scorched, some ink-smeared, about half were lost. Thereupon I trimmed my brush by Mount Heng, and rinsed my inkstone in the Xiang River, and, arranging them according to type, came up with four hundred thirty-three pieces, which I arranged into twenty scrolls, titling the collection *Four-Sixes of Fannan*. The term "four-six" is a name whose derivation is like those of [the games] *liubo*, *gewu*, *sishu*, and *liujia*—it's nothing worth feeling smug about. On the twelfth day of the tenth month, night, by moonlight, I have written this preface.[21]

樊南生十六能著才論、聖論，以古文出諸公間。後聯為鄆相國，華太守所憐，居門下時，敕定奏記，始通今體。後又兩為祕省房中官，恣展古集，往往咽噱于任、范、徐、庾之間。有請作文，或時得好對切事，聲勢物景，哀上浮壯，能感動人。十年京師寒且餓，人或目曰：韓文、杜詩、彭陽章檄，樊南窮凍人或知之。仲弟聖僕特善古文，居會昌中進士為第一二，常以今體規我，而未焉能休。大中元年，被奏入嶺當表記，所為亦多。冬如南郡，舟中忽復括其所藏，火燹墨汙，半有墜落。因削筆衡山，洗硯湘江，以類相等色，得四百三十三件，作二十卷，喚曰樊南四六。四六之名，六博、格五、四數、六甲之取也，未足矜。十月十二日夜月明序。

Li Shangyin describes the two opposed pulls between his early allegiance to *guwen* writing and what he describes almost as an occupational hazard of his secretarial duties whereby he became conversant in the modern style—the latter tendency bolstered by what he describes almost as a guilty pleasure he derives from the sumptuous parallel works of the Southern Dynasties masters that served as the foundational models for the modern style. There is a hint of pride, however, in his observation that his productions in this mode have often

---

19 It is thus possibly ironic then that Li Shangyin in fact composed a "modern style" letter in Li Xisou's name to Wei Fu 魏扶 (?–850), the official under whose auspices Xisou passed the 847 *jinshi* examination. The implication would seem to be that notwithstanding his principled objection to the modern style, when it came to actual issues of power and patronage, Li Xisou understood what the occasion required, and had the sense to seek out a qualified proxy.

20 Jingzhou.

21 "Preface to Fannan Collection A" 樊南甲集序 (*WBN*, 4:1713).

been found able to stir the readers' emotions. The list of skills Li Shangyin claims to have become known for is a strikingly disparate one, and this disparity again reveals the conflicting pulls, and conflicting sorts of writing, that shaped his character as a literary man. The poetry of Du Fu and prose of Han Yu are canonical references that fit squarely in the *guwen* mold: Han Yu had been an energetic advocate of Du Fu's poetry, whose reputation was just beginning to form around the first decades of the ninth century. Du Fu himself had lived out his life in obscurity, and his work never gained currency in cosmopolitan fashion of his age. Han Yu, though himself a major figure of the politics and literary culture of his age, was not only the preeminent practitioner of *guwen*, but the preeminent shaper of an ideology of *guwen* that cast it as an oppositional sort of writing practice, at odds with secular fashion and power. By contrast, the toponym "Pengyang" in the final item in Li Shangyin's list, "Pengyang's memorials and declarations," designates Linghu Chu, not only a literary model but also a tutor in the modern style, and the figure who at the outset of Li Shangyin's career had presented the best promise of career and literary success.

Li Shangyin's proxy text collections date from 847 and 853, and thus from a stage of his career when it had become clear that his succession to Linghu Chu's mastery of *zhangzou* writing was not to be paralleled in a comparable official career. It is thus difficult to determine how much of the diffidence he expresses here about the form stems from a conflicting allegiance to *guwen* ideas, how much from personal frustration, and how much from conventional self-deprecation of the preface writer. But the bifurcation between the relative obscurity of his status and the widespread appetite for the products of his skills as a drafter was palpable. As he noted in the preface to the second collection, his works, while not efficacious in securing his own social prominence, had been the means through which reputations of some of the most powerful figures in the age were enhanced or cemented:

> In this year was the funeral for Commander in Chief Niu,[22] and throughout the world there were commemorative sacrifices held in the hundreds. On a later day the Governor told me: "When our Commander in Chief passed away, there was the tomb inscription of Du of the Bureau of Merit Titles[23] and your sacrificial script—it is through these two things his memory will not decay."[24]

---

22   Niu Sengru 牛僧孺 (779-848).

23   Du Mu 杜牧 (803-852).

24   "Preface to Fannan Collection B," 樊南乙集序 (*WBN,* 5:2176).

是歲，葬牛太尉，天下設祭者百數。他日尹言：吾太尉之薨，有杜司勳之誌，與子之奠文，二事為不朽。

Composing the Voice: Linghu Chu's Testaments

Another reputation that Li Shangyin was instrumental in shaping was that of his patron and tutor Linghu Chu.[25] On the occasion of the latter's death, Li Shangyin composed several texts, including a sacrificial script and a tomb inscription, as well as a deathbed memorial to Emperor Wenzong 文宗 (r. 827-840)—this latter a proxy text drafted in Linghu Chu's voice. Linghu Chu's career was not free of controversy—having risen at last to prime ministerial rank in 819 (by then in his mid-fifties), he was banished, and was lucky to escape with his life in the following year, when, after Xianzong's death, it came to light that while Linghu Chu was supervising construction at the imperial tomb precinct, members of his household staff had embezzled project payroll funds.[26] His close connection with figures such as Huangfu Bo 皇甫鎛 (?–820) and Li Fengji 李逢吉 (758-835), moreover, along with his resistance to Pei Du's 裴度 (765-839) hard-line military approach to long-lasting rebellions in Caizhou and Huaixi rendered him suspect in many contemporaries' eyes; and with the consolidation of opinion in the Northern Song in favor of Li Deyu and his partisans as "gentlemen" and of his rivals as therefore "petty persons," it was impossible for Linghu Chu to escape some degree of negative assessment. The *Xin Tang shu* 新唐書 deems Linghu Chu to have proved "jade on the exterior but common stone inside" in a time of national crisis.[27] But in an historiographical tradition heavily weighted towards the interests and ideology of scholar-official elites, Linghu Chu is credited with a basic loyalty to his class and profession, particularly in the aftermath of the "Sweet Dew Incident" of late 835, when he did his utmost, through tact and rhetorical skill as well as

---

25   On creating the posthumous image of a literary figure, see also pp. 97ff. and 203ff. in this volume.

26   *Jiu Tang shu*, 172.4460-61. The implication of the *Jiu Tang shu* account is that Linghu Chu was supervising construction at Xianzong's tomb, but the *Xin Tang shu* account specifies that the work was at Jingling, the tomb precinct of Dezong, who had died in 805. See *Xin Tang shu*, 166.5099.

27   This assessment is applied equally to the two other figures whose biographies are grouped together with Linghu Chu's, Jia Dan and Du You. See *Xin Tang shu*, 166.5104.

through bold and forthright conduct, to try to mitigate the worst excesses of the wholesale purge of court officials by the eunuch faction at court.[28]

Whatever the overall assessment of Linghu Chu's political career, however, his image as the embodiment of a particularly ninth-century ideal of the "rhetorical minister" remains undisturbed. Just as it delineated his rise to prominence through the anecdote of his handling of Zheng Dan's deathbed memorial, the *Jiu Tang shu* biography draws the curtain on Linghu Chu's career with another case of exemplary production of such a text (again, for convenience of discussion, sections are marked with lower-case letters):[29]

(a) Three days before his death, he was still at ease, chanting verses. When his illness grew dire, his sons offered medicines, but he did not swallow any of these, saying instead, "As for one's term of long or short life, this is fixed by destiny—what need is there for this stuff?" The day before he died, he summoned his Retainer Li Shangyin and said, "My bodily spirits are exhausted, and my sensibility and mind are all gone. Yet the things I feel concerned about have not ended, and I wish to force myself to vent my thoughts in the hearing of heaven. But I fear my phrases may be disordered and faulty—you must help me finish it." Whereupon he took up a brush and himself wrote: (b) *Your subject ever considers his fortune, in receiving profound grace from the state,* (c) *through grandfather and father, who all received fine titles and gifts, and through younger brothers and sons, who are ranked together among the officers. To follow my ancestors, having kept waist and neck intact; to leave behind this body so as to go to serve my late Emperor—anyone failing to feel satisfied in a moment such as this would indeed be exceedingly stupid.* (d) *Yet as I go off forever to the gates of the springs below, and take leave once and for all of the cloud-wrapped dais, I lay out once more a "remonstrance of the corpse," and persist in submitting these words of a blind man. Though I am unable to wail and cry out, how should I dare forget what is earnest and bright? Now your Majesty is at the full flourishing of years, and the world and seas around are clear as a mirror. This is the initiating point for the practice of*

---

28   For an overview of the sequence of events and implications of the "Sweet Dew Incident," see for example Denis Twitchett and John K. Fairbank, eds., *The Cambridge History of China, Volume 3: Sui and Tang China, 589–906, Part I* (Cambridge: Cambridge University Press, 1979), 654–59.

29   As noted above, the *Xin Tang shu* biography seems overall somewhat more critical of Linghu Chu, but it nonetheless reproduces the *Jiu Tang shu* "deathbed memorial" scene, along with the previous one involving Zheng Dan, more or less intact (though eliding the actual text of Linghu's draft).

transformative teachings, just the moment from which order and justice return. However, since summer and spring of last year, those demoted and banished have been exceedingly many, and those submitted to execution and slaughter not few. I yearn for a general application of vast generative power; for some diminution of August severity. Let those who have passed away be purified in clouds and thunder, and those who survive be moistened with rain and dew, so that the five grains might reach propitious ripeness and the millions of folk be at peace and well. Accept your minister's bitter words from near the end, so as to bring comfort to your minister's lonely soul in its perpetual dormancy..." (e) When he had finished writing, he said to his sons Xu and Tao, "I was of no use to others when alive; do not request a posthumous title. On the day of burial, do not invite musicians; use only a single white-draped hearse, and as for the rest use no further ornament. In drafting the inscription and account relate only the affairs of the lineage, and as for the drafter do not seek out someone of high station." (f) On the evening of his passing, a large meteor fell above his bedchamber, its light illuminating the courtyard. Chu, seated formally, took leave of his family, and died when he had finished speaking. His heirs dutifully followed his bequeathed instructions.

a）未終前三日，猶吟詠自若。疾甚，諸子進藥，未嘗入口，曰：「修短之期，分以定矣，何須此物？」前一日，召從事李商隱曰：「吾氣魄已殫，情思俱盡，然所懷未已，強欲自寫聞天，恐辭語乖舛，子當助我成之。」即秉筆自書曰：b)　　臣永惟際會，受國深恩。c)　　以祖以父，皆蒙褒贈；有弟有子，并列班行。全腰領以從先人，委體魄而事先帝，此不自達，誠為甚愚。d)　但以永去泉扃，長辭雲陛，更陳尸諫，猶進瞽言。雖號叫而不能，豈誠明之敢忘？今陛下春秋鼎盛，寰海鏡清，是修教化之初，當復理平之始。然自前年夏秋已來，貶謫者至多，誅戮者不少，望普加鴻造，稍霽皇威。歿者昭洗以雲雷，存者霑濡以雨露，使五穀嘉熟，兆人安康。納臣將盡之苦言，慰臣永蟄之幽魄。」e)　　書訖，謂其子緒、絢曰：「吾生無益於人，勿請諡號。葬日，勿請鼓吹，唯以布車一乘，餘勿加飾。銘誌但志宗門，秉筆者無擇高位。」f)　當歿之夕，有大星隕於寢室之上，其光燭廷。楚端坐與家人告訣，言已而終。嗣子奉行遺旨。[30]

The "rhetorical minister" faces death with the equanimity of the well-read scholar; his formidable rhetorical gifts and force of will allow him to compose a written text for his deathbed address to the emperor, and his judgment of

---

30   *Jiu Tang shu*, 4464-65.

talent and character allow him to choose the proper person—regardless of formal status—to complete the written text of this address so as to express all he has in mind to say; he passes from life with no lapse in decorum, and his dying wishes are carried out faithfully with no commotion or dissent. Regardless of any controversies surrounding Linghu Chu's reputation, this account of his passing accords him a high degree of dignity, and even a sort of heroism—it is notable that in the longest section of this draft memorial (the section marked [d] above), Linghu Chu reverts, in one final effort at remonstrance, to his concerns about the excesses of the executions and suppression of court officials in the "Sweet Dew" purge.

The notion that a virtual speech directed to the emperor in the form of a proxy text represented the authentic voice and feelings of the signatory was no doubt in much of the administrative routine of empire no more than a polite fiction. The above account of Linghu Chu's death seems to go out of its way, however, to convey the sense that in this instance the secretary, chosen not for his status but for his talent and his closeness to the principal, was serving as a sort of amanuensis in extremis—that is, he was simply being called on to fill in what the principal had in mind to say but was prevented from saying by the onset of physical dissolution.[31]

Linghu Chu's complete deathbed memorial as completed by Li Shangyin is preserved in the *Wenyuan yinghua* 文苑英華,[32] affording us a rare opportunity to compare preliminary and final versions of such a text. The length of the final version makes it unwieldy to cite in full, but reference to a few passages will indicate the general approach taken by Li Shangyin. Perhaps unsurprisingly, Linghu Chu's draft as transcribed in the *Jiu Tang shu* is reproduced with minimal variation. Li Shangyin added a few elements required by convention that the first draft did not include: between the sections marked (b) and (c) above, Li Shangyin inserts a long section, roughly half the length of the completed memorial, of what amounts to an extended official autobiography, in the required formal and euphuistic style. In addition, as required both by convention and by administrative necessity, Li Shangyin adds a short section near the end describing the assignments of provisional official posts to be put into effect after Linghu Chu's death and pending the assignment of a successor.

---

31   The drafter selected for the burial inscription, predictably, was also Li Shangyin. This text itself does not survive, but Li Shangyin wrote a poem on completing it: "Stirred by Feelings on Completing the Inscription Text for the Duke of Pengyang" 撰彭陽公誌文畢有感 (*Quan Tang shi*, 541.6222).

32   *Wenyuan yinghua*, 626.06b.

Beyond these substantive additions to make the memorial structurally and administratively complete, Li Shangyin attends throughout to what, without detracting from the real solemnity of the text or the occasion, might be termed the "staging" of Linghu Chu's address to Wenzong. Compare sections (b) and (c) of Linghu Chu's draft, for example, with the way Li Shangyin, while deriving his basic material from the draft, enhances the solemnity, dramatic vividness and emotional tension of the address, above all heightening the sense of a voice that speaks from the edge of dissolution:

> Thus speaks your minister [Chu]:[33] Your subject has heard from the bywords of deep thinkers, that they take life as a sojourn in wayfarer's lodge; and from the legated instructions of the ancients, how they called the dead "people who have gone home." If one meets a good end, what fear is there in transformation? *Your subject ever considers his fortune*, in meeting with a flourishing age of peace. Yet before I have manifested any merit worth casting in bell or cauldron, this substance of mine, fleeting as wind or dew, first dissolves away. Though there is no fleeing from the grand allotment, still, this is a betrayal of Your Majesty's pure court. Yet now I present a speech even as the gossamer is held before my mouth;[34] facing my coffin, I hold out yet a while against death. In the bright sun I have no further share; yet how long is the dark night! Tears mingled with blood drip from my face, as my eyesight along with my soul breaks off.

> 臣某言：臣聞達士格言，以生為逆旅；古者垂訓，謂死為歸人。苟得其終，何怛于化。**臣永惟際會**，獲遇昇平。鐘鼎之勳莫彰；風露之姿先盡。雖無逃大數，亦有負清朝。今則舉纊陳詞，對棺忍死；白日無分，玄夜何長。淚兼血垂，目與魂斷。

In other passages, Li Shangyin's completed version of the deathbed memorial incorporates directly into Linghu Chu's speech events from his final days and

---

33 Certain sensitive words or information (e.g. given personal names, places and dates of burial) or purely formulaic phrases (conventional expressions of self-deprecation or congratulation in letters) appearing either in correspondence or in burial inscriptions are typically redacted in the versions of these texts that circulate in literary collections. Here "so-and-so" (*mou* 某) is a transparent redaction at a point where the original text would have had Linghu Chu referring to himself by his own given name.

34 A procedure described in ritual texts for determining the moment when a moribund person had died: a fine silk cloth was placed over the person's mouth; when the cloth failed to stir this indicated the cessation of breath and thus life.

hours that figure in the scene-setting narrative of the *Jiu Tang shu* account.[35]
The admonishment to his sons about avoiding ostentation in his funeral observances (appearing in section [e] of the *Jiu Tang shu* version cited above), for
example, appears as part of Linghu Chu's report to the emperor regarding his
final arrangements. While the astronomical anomaly of the shooting star reported in the *Jiu Tang shu* biography might ordinarily be the sort of thing we
would assume was simply a later embellishment, the memorial as completed
by Li Shangyin shows that if it was an embellishment, it was one that had
emerged more or less from the moment of Linghu Chu's death:

> At the coming of this night of the twelfth, a servant reported to your min-
> ister: "A great star has fallen to earth, precisely aligned with the main hall,
> piercing the whole courtyard with light." Your minister thereupon sat
> upright to await the hour, speaking properly without any deviation. Your
> minister's years have grown full; your minister's honors are indeed suffi-
> cient. *Through grandfather and father...*

> 至十二日夜，有僕夫告臣云：大星隕地，雅當正室，洞照一庭。臣即
> 端坐俟時，正辭無撓。臣之年亦極矣，臣之榮亦足矣。以祖以父…

At this point Li Shangyin's text reverts to Linghu Chu's draft (the long final section marked [d] in the above *Jiu Tang shu* citation) through to the end. There
follows the added section related to administrative assignments—placing the
procedural substance of such texts immediately before the closing seems to
have been a fairly fixed matter of protocol, perhaps to allow for quick reference
when administrative consultation rather than fully immersive reading was
called for. One might equally read this, however, as the expression of a devoted
minister whose meticulous attention to his duties persists even into the final
moments of life. Li Shangyin adds a final closing section which melds the conventional gestures of ministerial awe and trembling at the moment of submitting an utterance to imperial audition with a return to the insistently reiterated
idea that these are the speaker's final words. As noted above, the closing topoi
of abject awe and the ritualized closing phrases that are part of the memorial
as a genre gain particular poignancy in these circumstances:

---

35   Here for convenience we speak in terms of the *Jiu Tang shu* biography as a provisionally
     viable account of the actual events on which Li Shangyin drew in crafting his final version
     of the Linghu Chu memorial. In terms of actual documentary evidence, of course, the
     sequence was reversed—it is quite likely that Li Shangyin's completed memorial itself
     would have been a source for the *Jiu Tang shu* account of Linghu Chu's death.

Though your minister's mind is settled and clear, my breath has already grown unsteady and short. As my words grow more they become more urgent; as my cry grows pressing it turns ever more mournful. When they climb the house to call thrice—shall I come? I rush headlong into the ravine and depart, never again to return. My earnest sincerity and my straightforwardness in the way, in the end these are to be buried and engulfed in this borderland; it is mere rotting bones and desiccated frame that will return emptily to my former land. Turning my head to gaze back at this splendid age, I am overcome by the extremity of yearning and attachment in this final leave-taking. I reverently submit this memorial as a substitute for speech to Your Majesty's hearing. Your minister [Chu], with heartfelt wails and heartfelt sobs, bows his head to the ground.

臣心雖澄定，氣已危促。辭多逾切，鳴急更哀。升屋而三號豈來，赴壑而一去無返。忠誠直道，竟埋没于外藩；腐骨枯骸，空歸全于故國。迴望昭代，無任攀戀永訣之至。謹奉表代辭以聞。臣某誠號誠咽頓首頓首。[36]

As with the account of his rise to power, so in the rendering of his final speech, Linghu Chu, whatever his shortcomings, is remembered as a figure who fully embodied the ideal of the "rhetorical minister." This meant not only drafting the voice of imperial authority, but also playing his own role in dialogue with that authority. Throughout, as we have seen, the crafting of the authentic voice is a collaborative effort.[37]

The Disembodied Voice

Li Shangyin was renowned as a writer of compositions for funerary occasions from very early on, and apart from administrative texts produced during his various tenures in secretarial positions in regional governorships, the largest proportion of his surviving non-poetic works is comprised of commissioned burial inscriptions and sacrificial scripts. In these, we most typically see him deploying the skills of his trade in transposing the circumstances of each decedent into the orotund and richly textured tapestry of the "modern style," the language of elite authority and commemoration—the sort of language that prompts its audiences to savor and recite for themselves. The proxy sacrificial

---

36   "Testamentary Memorial on Behalf of the Duke of Pengyang" 代彭陽公遺表 (*WBN*, 1:141).

37   On the collaborative aspect of text production, see also p. 200 in this volume.

script for Niu Sengru that Li Shangyin mentions in the preface to his second collection of proxy texts would have been written as an address to Niu Sengru's departed spirit in the voice of a prominent sponsor, to be recited at a public sacrifice as part of a flurry of public mourning rituals in the wake of Niu's death in 848. As we saw in that instance, these public recitations, along with the circulation in manuscript form of the scripts, were a powerful medium for shaping and perpetuating the memories of eminent figures of the age.

In this regard the sacrificial script that Li Shangyin composed in his own voice for a sacrifice to Linghu Chu is remarkable. In addressing the departed spirit of the man who initiated him into the "modern style," Li Shangyin adopts a very spare and economical version of that style: the regular tetrasyllabic versification and rhyme pattern is highly reminiscent of the lyrical closing sections of burial inscriptions—that is, the section specifically designated *ming* 銘 in the *muzhiming*.[38] Many lines reflect a general sense of antithetical balance, but there is almost no allusion. What is still more fascinating is the dimension of voice: whereas the sacrificial script is ritually and generically defined as a ritual address to the departed spirit, here Li Shangyin, both writer and reciter in this instance, in addressing the man who gave him the power to construct voice, seems to succumb to a vertiginous unclarity about who is speaking and who is addressed, who remains and who departs.

> In the year *wuwu* (55=838), in the month beginning with a *dingwei* (44) day and ending with an *yihai* (2) day,[39] your disciple Li Shangyin of Yuxi bows his head to the ground, making offerings to former prime minister, bestowed with the office of Minister of Works, Duke of Pengyang:

---

38   On the basic nature and structure of the *muzhiming*, see the exposition in Timothy Davis, *Entombed Epigraphy and Commemorative Culture in Early Medieval China* (Leiden: Brill, 2015), 4-33. In the main rhymed portion of this sacrificial script, after an opening group composed of a rhymed couplet aa and a quatrain rhyming bbxb (together marked as section [i] below), there follow nine quatrains rhyming xcxc, xdxd, etc.

39   *Wuwu* (55), *dingwei* (44) and *yihai* (2) are terms in the ancient sixty-member "stems and branches" (*gan zhi* 干支) counting cycle (with their positions noted by the Arabic numerals in parentheses) by which dates are often recorded in traditional texts. Inscriptions specify months both by an ordinal number (e.g. "in the sixth month") and by giving the "stems and branches" dates for the first and last days of the month in question. Here we have what are represented as first and last days, but no explicit mention of which month of the year this was. Feng Hao identifies the sixth month as the one thus indicated; there are however problems with at least one of the sources for this identification, and the date itself as written cannot be correct.

(i) Alas! In former dream I was wafting dust, following your carriage wheels; now I dream of that mountain slope, where I send you off with grief-stricken song. In antiquity there was the custom of following in death; now there is not—what can one do?

(ii) In the years at Tianping, amid the scimitars and halberds, there by the general's drinking cup, was one person clad in white.

(iii) Ten years have passed in a daze; and the cicada has completed its shell-shedding change. When others praised me you were fond of them; when others slandered me you cursed them.

(iv) You are as high as heaven; I am as lowly as earth. Shedding and molting like a snake; changing like the weather.

(v) I was assigned duties in the capital, as you were ill at Liangshan. Traversing cliffs and flying over bridges, a thousand *li* of mountain roads.

(vi) We drafted a memorial to the Son of Heaven; we carved phrases in the gate of your tomb. Your earnest entreaties as you approached the end—"*...through you I shall endure.*"

(vii) From this departure of yours, a ban forbids timely return. The phoenix perches upon the plain: new and old, the ministerial robes.

(viii) Your road now is that of the springs below; your terrace, the one where all is night. Those who have departed in the past—it is fitting that they should persist there.

(ix) For sageliness there is Confucius, for probity, Bo Yi. Amidst the floating souls and submerged spirits, may you, sir, commune with them!

(x) That former mountain towers loftily; a Jade Stream flows through its midst. On returning from sending you off, I shall endure a life of brush and tumbleweed. Alas!

戊午歲丁未朔乙亥晦，弟子玉谿李商隱叩頭哭奠故相國贈司空彭陽公：嗚呼，(i) 昔夢飛塵，從公車輪；今夢山阿，送公哀歌。古有從死，今無柰何。(ii) 天平之年，大刀長戟，將軍樽旁，一人衣白。(iii) 十年忽然，蜩宣甲化。人譽公憐，人譖公罵。(iv) 公高如天，愚卑如地。脫蟬如蛇，如氣之易。(v) 愚調京下，公病梁山，絕崖飛梁，山行一千。(vi) 草奏天子，鐫辭墓門，臨絕丁寧，託爾而存。(vii) 公此去耶，禁不時歸。鳳棲原上，新舊袞衣。(viii) 有泉者路，有夜者臺。昔之去者，宜其在哉。(ix) 聖有夫子，廉有伯夷。浮魂沉魄，公其與之。(x) 故山巖巖，玉谿在中。送公而歸，一世蒿蓬。嗚呼。40

---

40   "Text for an Offering to His Honor Linghu, Minister of the State" 奠相國令狐公文 (*WBN*, 210).

The entirety of Li Shangyin's connection with Linghu Chu is conveyed in a tele-scoped manner. We see (in section [ii]) the young Li Shangyin as the "one fig-ure clad in white" beside Linghu Chu—that is, the one young talent so favored as to be given an informal role in Linghu's regional administration, despite his not having earned office-holding status by passing the examinations. Further down (section [v]) we see telegraphic reference to Li Shangyin's hurried jour-ney from his post at Chang'an to Xingyuan, the site of Linghu Chu's final post-ing as a governor, to attend his patron in his final illness.

The references to dream in the first two couplets of the verse section pre-pare the ground for a pervasive sense of unreality or indeterminacy as to time, place, or person, even as the relevant facts of Linghu Chu's death are adum-brated. Dream, like death, is understood as a wandering of the spirit; what may seem a hyperbolic wish to be able to follow the ancient custom of being en-tombed along with one's deceased lord is of a piece with the idea that this be-reavement involves the destruction of Li Shangyin's own identity, brought home in the closing remark that his existence after this moment will be that of a mere rootless drifting tumbleweed.

The references to the transformations of the cicada that emerges from its husk and the snake that sheds its skin suggest a doubling or conflation of two seemingly quite distinct transformations, namely, Li Shangyin's transforma-tion from a precocious youth to a full-fledged member of the office-holding elite and Linghu Chu's transformation in death (we may recall that it was only in the year before Linghu Chu's death that Li Shangyin had passed the *jinshi* examination, through the machinations of Linghu Chu and his son Linghu Tao). The merging of their voices and persons was most concretely enacted in their collaboration in crafting Linghu Chu's deathbed memorial, and the ac-tual composition of deathbed and funerary texts is the focus of section (vi). The ability to dispense with personal pronouns in literary Chinese is especially welcome here, since between the "drafting" (of the deathbed memorial) and the "carving" (of the funerary inscription) here there intervenes the death of Linghu Chu himself, but what emerges through the indeterminacy of pronoun in the two lines is the dreamlike unclarity—as we pass from the text begun by Linghu Chu and completed by Li Shangyin as his amanuensis, to the text drafted by Li Shangyin alone at the posthumous behest of Linghu Chu—as to what agent is doing the action and what speaker is speaking the words.

The culminating point of this dynamic in the script centers on the personal pronoun that does appear in the following line, "through you I shall endure..." In the midst of a sacrificial address by Li Shangyin to Linghu Chu's spirit, this abrupt appearance of a second-person pronoun that Li Shangyin could never have addressed to Linghu Chu requires that this line be understood as a quote from Linghu Chu's actual spoken deathbed leave-taking of Li Shangyin. Such a recollection of the final words heard from a dying man is naturally fraught with pathos. In this instance, the breakdown or infinite regress created in the relation between speaker and addressee by the recitation of these particular words by Li Shangyin himself in this ritual context carries particular force. It was Linghu Chu who gave Li Shangyin the skill to craft utterances that would be respected and remembered, and who entrusted to his disciple the task of composing his final formal utterance even as he composed himself for death. Li Shangyin's sacrificial script is a powerful expression of bereavement as the loss of oneself along with the other. Perhaps as well it is an indication of the ways in which close attention to the textual and aural dimensions of a distinctively ninth-century conception of the power of writing as proxy speech might continue to speak to us today.

Bibliography

Butler, Shane. *The Ancient Phonograph*. New York: Zone Books, 2015.

Davis, Timothy B. *Entombed Epigraphy and Commemorative Culture in Early Medieval China*. Leiden and Boston: Brill, 2015.

Fu Xuancong 傅璇琮. *Tangdai keju yu wenxue* 唐代科舉與文學. Xi'an: Shaanxi renmin chubanshe, 1986.

Jiu Tang shu 舊唐書. Compiled by Liu Xu 劉昫 et al. 16 vols. Beijing: Zhonghua shuju, 1975.

Li Shangyin wen biannian jiao zhu 李商隱文編年校注. Edited by Liu Xuekai 劉學鍇 and Yu Shucheng 余恕誠. 5 vols. Beijing: Zhonghua shuju, 2002.

Lu Yang 陸揚. "Tangdai de qingliu wenhua—yige xianxiang de gaishu" 唐代的清流文化——一個現象的概述, in idem, *Qingliu wenhua yu Tang diguo*, 213-63.

Lu Yang 陸揚. *Qingliu wenhua yu Tang diguo* 清流文化與唐帝國. Beijing: Beijing daxue chubanshe, 2016.

Nakamura Hiroichi 中村裕一. *Zui Tō ōgen no kenkyū* 隋唐王言の研究. Tōkyō: Kyuko shoin, 2003.

Quan Tang shi 全唐詩. 25 vols. Beijing: Zhonghua shuju, 1960.

Quan Tang wen 全唐文. Compiled by Dong Gao 董誥 et al. 11 vols. Beijing: Zhonghua shuju, 1983.

Shang shu zheng yi 尚書正義. In *Shisan jing zhu shu*.

Shisan jing zhu shu 十三經注疏. 2 vols. Beijing: Zhonghua shuju, 1980.

Sun Mei 孫梅. *Siliu cong hua* 四六叢話. Beijing: Zhonghua shuju, 2010.

Svenbro, Jesper. *Phrasikleia: Anthropologie de la Lecture en Grèce Ancienne*. Paris: Éditions La Découverte, 1988.

Twitchett, Denis, and John K. Fairbank, eds. *The Cambridge History of China, Volume 3: Sui and Tang China, 589-906, Part I*. Cambridge: Cambridge University Press, 1979.

Wenyuan yinghua 文苑英華. Compiled by Li Fang 李昉 et al. 6 vols. Beijing: Zhonghua shuju, 1966.

Xin Tang shu 新唐書. Compiled by Ouyang Xiu 歐陽修 and Song Qi 宋祁. 20 vols. Beijing: Zhonghua shuju, 1975.

Xu Song 徐松. *Deng ke ji kao* 登科記考. 3 vols. Beijing: Zhonghua shuju, 1984.

Zhao Heping 趙和平. *Dunhuang biao zhuang qian qi shuyi yanjiu* 敦煌表狀箋啓書儀研究. Nanjing: Jiangsu guji chubanshe, 1997.

Zhao Heping 趙和平. *Dunhuang ben* Gantang ji *yanjiu* 敦煌本甘棠集研究 (Taipei: Xin wenfeng chuban gongsi, 2000).

Index

Printed in the United States
By Bookmasters